Sexuality

FOUCAULT'S EARLY LECTURES AND MANUSCRIPTS

FOUCAULT'S EARLY LECTURES AND MANUSCRIPTS

ENGLISH SERIES EDITOR: BERNARD E. HARCOURT
GENERAL EDITOR: FRANÇOIS EWALD

The philosopher and social critic Michel Foucault began lecturing in the early 1950s on key topics that later gave rise to his major publications, including *The Order of Things*, *Discipline and Punish*, and *The History of Sexuality*. These early lectures and related manuscripts explore central themes ranging from sexuality, existentialism, and phenomenology to anthropology and philosophical discourse, in conversation with key interlocutors including Nietzsche, Husserl, Descartes, and Binswanger. Delivered at universities around the world—from Tunis and São Paulo to Montreal, Buffalo, Paris, Lille, and Clermont-Ferrand—these early lectures and manuscripts shed a whole new light on Foucault's lifelong critical project. Collected in this official edition, these works are presented here for the first time in English.

MICHEL FOUCAULT

Sexuality

THE 1964 CLERMONT-FERRAND & 1969 VINCENNES LECTURES

Edited by **CLAUDE-OLIVIER DORON**

General Editor:
FRANÇOIS EWALD

English Series Editor:
BERNARD E. HARCOURT

Translated by **GRAHAM BURCHELL**

Foreword by **BERNARD E. HARCOURT**

Columbia University Press   *New York*

Columbia University Press
Publishers Since 1893
New York   Chichester, West Sussex
cup.columbia.edu

First published in French as
La Sexualité
Cours donné à l'université de Clermont-Ferrand (1964)
suivi de
Le Discours de la sexualité
Cours donné a l'université de Vincennes (1969)
© 2018 Seuil/Gallimard

Library of Congress Cataloging-in-Publication Data
Names: Foucault, Michel, 1926-1984, author. |
Burchell, Graham, translator.
Title: Sexuality : the 1964 Clermont-Ferrand and 1969
Vincennes lectures /
Michel Foucault ; foreword by Bernard E. Harcourt ; translated by
Graham Burchell.
Other titles: Sexualité. English
Description: New York City : Columbia University Press, 2021. |
Includes index.
Identifiers: LCCN 2020057788 (print) | LCCN 2020057789 (ebook) |
ISBN 9780231195065 (hardback) | ISBN 9780231195072 (trade
paperback) | ISBN 9780231551168 (ebook)
Subjects: LCSH: Sex—Social aspects. | Sex (Psychology) |
Sex customs—History. | Sex—Philosophy.
Classification: LCC HQ12 .F68713 2021 (print) | LCC HQ12
(ebook) | DDC 306.7—dc23
LC record available at https://lccn.loc.gov/2020057788
LC ebook record available at https://lccn.loc.gov/2020057789

Columbia University Press books are printed on permanent and
durable acid-free paper.
Printed in the United States of America

Cover design: Chang Jae Lee

CONTENTS

PART II:
The Discourse of Sexuality:
Lectures at the University of Vincennes (1969)

COURSE CONTEXT
by Claude-Olivier Doron

The Discourse of Sexuality: Lectures at the University of
Vincennes (1969)   323

A PREFACE TO
PHILOSOPHICAL PRAXIS

BERNARD E. HARCOURT

The practice of philosophy is not linear. It is more of an irruption. And it defies any conventional notion of progress. Although we like to imagine that a philosophical advance represents enduring progress from more rudimentary times, more often it overcomes an obstacle in the moment. It confronts a new problem. It finds a new way out.

Philosophical methods evolve, but that does not mean that earlier approaches are wrong or no longer operative. Nor does it mean that those earlier approaches gave birth to better ones. They addressed a different time. They faced a different conjuncture. They resolved a discrete problem. They served a special purpose. And often, they unveiled one illusion only to expose another.

Indeed, a philosophical praxis from an earlier time may be just as performative today, perhaps even more so. It depends on the situation it confronts. We may need it just as badly, or even more than we did at an earlier time. The exigencies of a new crisis may demand a return—though even that is never simply a repetition.

To believe otherwise would be to buy into a speculative philosophy of history that has no purchase today. We have long been warned not to believe in origin stories, but instead to see in them a will to know and a will to power.

*

The two sets of lectures on sexuality in this volume—the first from 1964, the second from 1969—address two very different political moments, separated by the upheaval of the student revolution of May 1968. Both of those moments, moreover, differ greatly from the political situation in 1976, when Michel Foucault published the first volume of *The History of Sexuality*, or in 1984, when he published volumes 2 and 3 and made final revisions to volume 4. Those earlier moments differ even more radically from our political times today—even putting aside the digital revolution that gave birth to our expository society and the myriad ways it intersects with sexual regulation and prohibitions. The term "transgender"—in its current connotation, using the notion of "gender" rather than "transsexual"—would not even have been entirely comprehensible at those earlier times. As Jack Halberstam remarks, "only a few decades ago, transsexuals in Europe and the United States did not feel that there was a language to describe who they were or what they needed."[1]

The first set of lectures—Foucault's 1964 lectures on "Sexuality" delivered at the University of Clermont-Ferrand—were delivered at a time marked by a resurgence of a soft humanism surrounding sexuality following the publication of Simone de Beauvoir's influential book *The Second Sex* (1949) and the rise of second-wave feminism. This was a humanism that sought to place sexuality within the ethical framework of loving, equal, respectful relations between men and women; but in the process of ethicizing and equalizing heterosexual relations, it further entrenched homosexuality and other "perversions" into officially diagnosed mental disorders, as in the *Diagnostic and Statistical Manual of Mental Disorders*, first published in 1952, in which

homosexuality was listed as a sociopathic personality disturbance. The new humanism of sexuality went hand in hand with
a demonization of alternative forms of sexuality—of anything
that did not fit comfortably in a film like *A Man and a Woman*
(released at around the same time, in 1966).[2]

In the face of this mounting sexual humanism, Foucault
turned to the writings of Georges Bataille and, before him, the
Marquis de Sade to highlight the experiences of sexuality that
were excluded from the dominant ethical conception of sexuality and human nature. Foucault deployed the notions of exclusion, limits, and transgression in 1964 in order to more precisely
delineate the character of contemporary Western culture. The
spaces of transgression identified precisely the limits of social
acceptance—what could not be allowed to be seen or heard in
Western society. Foucault shone a light on "perversions" precisely to reveal how Western culture idiosyncratically developed
its own unique troubled consciousness of sexuality: how it alone
had developed a "science" of sexuality on the basis of those very
behaviors; how that science of sexuality had given birth to the
social sciences and, at their head, psychoanalysis; how psychoanalysis had begun, thanks to Freud, to reintegrate those "perversions" into more ordinary conceptions of sexuality; in sum,
how Western culture had transformed sexuality into an object of
scientific knowledge in order to regulate it. Foucault held a mirror up to contemporary Western society to expose the cunning,
hidden devices it used to judge and regulate human behavior—
and at what cost.

Five years later, in 1969, in the wake of massive student
uprisings, of a more hegemonic Marxist (and Maoist and post-
Marxist) discourse, and of movements for supposed sexual liberation, the political landscape was radically different. The
moment was now marked by Herbert Marcuse's unique blend of

Freudo-Marxism, in *Eros and Civilization*, and that of Wilhelm Reich. Foucault's philosophical engagement would take new shape. Now at the brand-new university campus just outside Paris—"experimental" was in the official name of the new campus, opened just months after May 1968: "*le Centre universitaire expérimental de Vincennes*"[3]—Foucault faced not only a different political conjuncture and different political struggles, but also an entirely different audience: surrounded by hundreds of Parisian students who had just lived through a revolution, Foucault confronted an intellectual milieu that was thoroughly imbued with Marxist, Maoist, and Althusserian theories of ideology and of the reproduction of power, and Marcusian notions of sexual emancipation. His own earlier proximity and distantiation from Marxism—he had been a member of the French Communist Party during his time at the École Normale Supérieure (1950–1952)—would be tested, even as he himself began to embrace a more *marxisant* language.

In the second set of lectures—"The Discourse of Sexuality," delivered at Vincennes in 1969—Foucault deployed a Marxian framework to motivate his own new unique philosophical method, as applied once again to the domain of sexuality. Foucault developed an analysis of the discourse of sexuality, focusing on the literary, philosophical, scientific, medical, and juridical texts and practices that made sexuality their object—a method we would come to call "discourse analysis." He built common ground with his audience on the basis of a structural analysis of economic forces, tracing the emergence of capitalism from "primitive accumulation" to the "need for labor for the reserve army of capitalism" and discussing "forces of production," "ideology," and "ideological effects."[4] These are all Foucault's words, or rather Marx's—clear catchwords from the hegemonic Marxist discourse that permeated the times—none of them used ironically by Foucault.

No, instead, Foucault plies this Marxian framework to develop his own unique philosophical approach: an analysis of discourse intended to show how sexuality was transformed through complex and pervasive social practices into an explicit focus of literary, scientific, and juridical discourse in modern times. Foucault demonstrates how deeply and seamlessly judgment is woven into the fabric of culture, in domains we would never have imagined: how, in realms apparently so distant from the public sphere of politics—our private bedrooms and closets—cultural norms are woven into our daily lived experience and shape our deepest subjective reality; how they pervade our consciousness and experience of life; how they shape our very epistemology—the way we see and understand the world, distinguish between science and opinion, make claims to truth; and how much work and social practice it takes to make these cultural ways of being natural and invisible throughout our lived experience.

Foucault extends his new archaeological method to the domain of sexuality and, in the process, displaces the traditional notion of ideology in order to underscore both the amount and the pervasiveness of the social practices necessary to achieve the invisibility of cultural norms, and to expose how the latter undergird, even more invisibly, our deepest judgments of morality and truth. In the place of Marxian notions of ideology, of false consciousness, of Althusserian theories of ideological effects, Foucault excavates the layers of discourse that limit our ability even to judge truth or falsity. As Foucault would emphasize a year later, on December 2, 1970, in his inaugural lecture at the Collège de France: "before [a proposition] can be pronounced true or false it must be, as Monsieur Canguilhem might say, 'within the true.'"[5] Critiques of ideology that merely invert the base and the superstructure do not adequately take account of the deeper epistemological structures of discourse that would allow someone even to articulate a legible claim to truth, one that could be heard by their contemporaries.

This entails for Foucault a fundamental reorientation from theory to critical praxis. What we tend to call, too easily, "ideology" is not merely ideational or superstructural; it is not merely in our heads, nor for that matter in our subconscious. It is, rather, the product of persistent and deeply penetrating social practices that shape the way we understand ourselves and the world around us, how we judge and comport ourselves in every facet of our existence, and how we can utter and understand judgments of truth and falsity. The domain of discourse is not in an ideational realm only. It is shaped by extensive and pervasive social practices. And changes over time—the diachronic dimension—are the result of changing social practices. Thus, what human agents must work on, in order to transform society, is not just ideas or theories, but praxis. Foucault formulated this even more crisply a few years later in his lectures on *The Punitive Society*, where he notes: "The conclusion to be drawn from this is that morality does not exist in people's heads; it is inscribed in power relations and only the modification of these power relations can bring about the modification of morality."[6]

Sexuality, again, is the space where this is most hidden from sight, but at the same time most operative. Note that Foucault is teaching philosophy at Vincennes in 1969, no longer psychology, as he was at Clermont-Ferrand (1960–1966) and Lille before that (1952–1955), where sexuality formed part of the ordinary curriculum of general psychology. Foucault turns sexuality—as he had madness and death—into prime soil for philosophical investigation.

As the times change, so do the philosophical concepts. The struggles Foucault faced in 1964—regarding the resurgence of a humanist heterosexuality coupled with the science of homosexual perversion—differed from the political struggles he would face in 1969, during a more hegemonic period of Marxist ideology critique, or for that matter in 1976, a time of even greater dominance of the repressive hypothesis. Earlier notions of transgression, limits, or exclusion were less operative, necessary, or useful in 1969.

Foucault's philosophical method evolves as the political context changes. Lecturing several years later at the Collège de France, Foucault openly critiques the notions of exclusion and transgression he had used so fruitfully in 1964. "For a given period they were critical reversers in the sphere of juridical, political, and moral representation," Foucault states in his lectures on *The Punitive Society* on January 3, 1973. They "made it possible to circumvent notions like abnormality, fault, and law" and to understand Western culture through the metaphor of limits and boundaries. But new circumstances and new problems call for new methods of analysis, to pursue "new dimensions in which it is no longer a question of law, the rule, the representation, but of power rather than the law, of knowledge rather than representation." Those earlier philosophical approaches "were important historically"; but different times call for different philosophical praxis.[7]

Here is where we must remind ourselves to eschew the naïve idea of philosophical progress or linearity. The philosophical texts in this volume are political interventions. They are punctual, of the moment—a new theoretical method to address a new political conjuncture. They are philosophical acts.[8] They constitute a form of praxis.

In the end, philosophical praxis is a political intervention. It addresses political problems. It constitutes a political engagement. This is especially true for a philosopher and social critic like Foucault, who so adamantly believed, with Nietzsche, that knowledge can never be divorced from relations of power in society—and that we must do everything we can to liquidate, in every aspect of our theorizing and praxis, the naïve belief that knowledge is only true when it is detached from power.[9]

*

With this publication of Foucault's early lectures on sexuality from the 1960s—never before published in the original French nor in English—we now have access to some of his earliest thinking on the topic of sexuality. The year 1964 was by no means the first time Foucault wrote or lectured on sexuality. His "Preface to Transgression," published in 1963 and written in tribute to Georges Bataille, could well serve as a preface to the 1964 lectures, and Foucault had been reflecting and lecturing on sexuality as part of his general instruction in psychology at Clermont-Ferrand and Lille before that. Even earlier, for his master class during his *agrégation* examination in philosophy in 1951, Foucault was assigned, by lot, the topic of "sexuality," a new topic that had been proposed for the first time by Georges Canguilhem.[10] But these are the first preserved lectures on sexuality, and with them, we finally begin to see one bookend of a lifelong project on the subject.

The publication comes at an especially interesting time: the other bookend, the fourth and final volume of *The History of Sexuality, Les Aveux de la chair* (Confessions of the flesh), has finally been published as well. The manuscript of the fourth volume had been corrected by Foucault, but set aside, and was published posthumously in French in 2018 and is being published in English contemporaneously with these early lectures.[11] And even though we are mostly familiar with the broad strokes of the historical analysis of *The History of Sexuality*, the fourth volume performs important new work that had been heretofore missing.

The various times of publication of the earlier volumes of *The History of Sexuality* are, again, important. The first volume,

The Will to Know, was published in 1976 and it announced, on the back cover, a set of five more volumes to appear: *La chair et le corps* (The flesh and the body); *La croisade des enfants* (The children's crusade); *La femme, la mère et l'hysterique* (The woman, the mother, and the hysteric); *Les pervers* (The perverts); and *Populations et races* (Populations and races).[12] Foucault changed course, though, and published instead a second volume called *The Use of Pleasures* and a third volume titled *The Care of the Self* in 1984, only a month before his untimely death.[13] He explained the change of course in a short chapter titled "Modifications" in the introduction to the second volume—one of his most brilliant clarificatory texts. I could not recommend it more highly.

Those two moments—1976 and 1984—were, importantly, different political times, especially for Foucault and in terms of his own political engagements. The first, 1976, followed on the heels of his deep engagement with prison abolition as part of the Prisons Information Group and the publication in 1975 of the monograph that grew out of those political engagements, *Discipline and Punish: The Birth of the Prison*, in which Foucault set forth a model of disciplinary power; but it was a peculiar time, at the cusp of a new political formation, specifically French neoliberalism, with the new presidency of Valéry Giscard d'Estaing, who assumed power in 1974. The year 1976 is precisely when Foucault began to revise his theory of power from discipline to the biopolitical, and the study of the modern regulation of sexuality was at the very heart of that reimagination. The second year, 1984, came at a different time: in the late seventies, Foucault addressed neoliberal governmentality head-on in his lectures at the Collège de France, which then inspired him to trace a genealogy of the modern desiring subject back through history to the Christian fathers, the Roman period, and the ancient Greek thinkers.

The multivolume history metamorphized, from 1976 to 1984, into a history of the shaping of contemporary desire.[14] It evolved into the project of understanding how we shape ourselves through our own forms of avowal and practices of the self, and simultaneously how we are shaped, through relations of knowledge and power, into the subjects that we are today. Sexuality plays a central role in this: Foucault's critical project is to expose the way that subjectivity is so deeply and profoundly shaped, within a culture and a particular historical setting, that our own firm conceptions of our deepest selves as desiring subjects begin to feel natural, biological, universal.

We are familiar with the broad strokes of the historical analysis: The ancient Greeks (circa the fifth and fourth centuries BCE) understood sexual relations primarily through the framework of *aphrodisia*, a philosophical understanding that focused on the idea of an ethical self-mastery intended to prevent the subject from being consumed by the pleasures of sexual relations (volume 2, *The Use of Pleasures*). The Greek and Roman philosophers of the early Common Era (circa the first two centuries CE), especially the Stoics, conceptualized sexual relations primarily through the *techniques of the self*, such as the examination of conscience, the memorization of rules of austerity, and practices of penitence (volume 3, *The Care of the Self*). The early Christian thinkers deployed the framework of *lust*, *flesh*, and *sin* as a way to curb and regulate sexual relations (volume 4, *Confessions of the Flesh*). Finally, in modernity, we invented new scientific, medical, psychoanalytic, and juridical frameworks to regulate our sexual behaviors and undergird our judgments of morality, a new set of knowledges that produced the very concept of *sexuality* that had not existed before modern times (volume 1, *The Will to Know*).

In its full completion, *The History of Sexuality* reveals how our contemporary understanding of human sexuality is an artifact of

our times and culture, how it shapes us so deeply, and how it differs so profoundly from earlier ways of living, especially in that
domain that today we call "sexuality." The first volume sketched
how the modern concept of sexuality gave birth to new ways
of governing ourselves, which Foucault described as combin-
ing disciplinary and biopolitical forms of power and resulting in
the governing of populations through the administration of life.
Sexuality is precisely such a crucial space because it is located at
the point of juncture of those two governmental technologies—
discipline and biopolitics. The fourth and final volume exposes
the ambition to integrate the study of the subjective experience
of sexuality back within an analysis of knowledge and power, in
such a way as to reveal both the resilience and the fragility of our
contemporary sexual norms.[15]

In this sense, that other—and also newly published—bookend
is equally revealing. In the final pages of the now-final fourth
volume, *Confessions of the Flesh*, Foucault's intellectual project of a history of sexuality comes full circle and achieves its
long-awaited completion. In those final pages, dedicated to
Augustine's treatment of marital sexual relations, Foucault
reveals the heretofore missing link that now binds his ancient
history of sexual relations to his critique of contemporary forms
of neoliberal governance: Foucault discovers in Augustine's
writings the birth of the modern legal subject and of the juridi-
fication of social relations. Like the final piece of a jigsaw puzzle,
the appearance of the modern legal subject completes Foucault's
critical project and allows us to fold the entire four-volume
series of *The History of Sexuality* back into his critique of contemporary modes of social ordering in the neoliberal age.[16] In
the final pages of volume 4, Foucault points to the direction he
might have taken had his life not been cut short by a pandemic:
to integrate his late work on subjectivity with his earlier theory

of knowledge-power—in effect, to marry the laborious work on subjectivity, knowledge, and power.

Many critics of Foucault complain that the apparent turn at the end of his life to subjectivity, to care of the self, to truth-telling undermines the political force of his philosophy and pushed contemporary critical thought into a complacent apolitical direction. The now-published volume 4 of *The History of Sexuality* should dispel that argument and open the way to integrate those two projects—knowledge-power and subjectivity. That is our challenge today, I would argue: to explore how we have been shaped as subjects in such a way that we implicate ourselves—both willingly and unknowingly—in the social order within which we find ourselves. Only by doing so will we be able to recover philosophical praxis.

*

It is against the backdrop of that other bookend from 1984 that we can better discern the contributions of these early lectures. Of greatest importance, I would urge, is to treat the two texts separately, to understand them as different punctual interventions at different political moments—not only different from 1976 and 1984, but different from each other. It is for this reason that the editor of the French edition, Claude-Olivier Doron, in consultation with the general editor, François Ewald, and the members of the editorial committee, has produced two separate erudite course contexts, which provide fine detail concerning the immediate historical contexts for each of the two lecture series.

Foucault warned about "the paradox familiar to prefaces" in his own foreword to Binswanger's book *Dream and Existence* in 1954. He warned of the temptation to retrace an author's steps, given how important it is to readers, for their own comprehension, to struggle through that process themselves. But here there is value in shedding light on the two lecture series, especially for readers of this English translation, brilliantly executed by Graham Burchell, given our deep familiarity with Foucault's later work on sexuality—his formidable *History of Sexuality*, which exerts such a vast influence across the humanities and social sciences today.

The 1964 Lectures on Sexuality

In 1964, at a time of resurgent heterosexual humanism, Foucault studied the unique cultural formation that he provocatively calls "our culture" and identifies as contemporary Western, European, Judeo-Christian culture. "That is to say," he writes, "a culture marked by patriarchy and monogamy," what he calls elsewhere "European, scientific, rational, and technical culture," with its globalizing tendencies.[17] The regulation and prohibitions surrounding sexuality tend to reveal the contours of culture most powerfully, both because sexuality is the space that is most highly normed and because there are no universal truths about sexuality, no central common core of sexuality with mere social rituals or variances at the edges. What is unique about modern Western culture is the way there arises a troubled consciousness of sexuality and, later, a science of sexuality. It is precisely because of this troubled Western consciousness of sexuality that psychoanalysis becomes, at one time, the foundation and queen of the social sciences.[18]

The cartography of Foucault's theorizing here is at two levels, and they work together. By cartography, I have in mind how he is thinking about this object of study, how he even poses the question—in his words, the "only question." As Foucault emphasizes, introducing his 1964 lectures, "the only question that we have the right to pose in order to begin [our study of sexuality] concerns therefore what sexuality is *in our culture.*"[19]

The first level is borders, limits, and transgression. This is the idea of a space outside our culture that defines the culture itself and its traits. What transgression does is to delineate the boundaries of our culture, previously unnoticed. It demarcates the survey lines. It reminds us of what our culture allows and forbids. And it does a better job of doing that than the notion of the law, or the normal, which are too binary.[20] In this, Foucault is deeply indebted to Bataille, Blanchot, Genet, and Sade—Sade, especially, for he so early and profoundly shook modern society with his transgressive writings. We only see sexuality there, at that limit, at the extreme of our culture. The tension between sex as pure biology and the cultural construction of sexuality gets pushed to that limit, in modernity: as sexuality plays less of a central role as a religious sacrament, and as it is simplified in law as well—with the Napoleonic civil code—it becomes the topic of constant discussion in its scandalous dimension.

The second level is archaeology: unearthing the epistemological formation that allows modern subjects to know sexuality. Foucault describes how, throughout the history of Western culture until the nineteenth century, there were just two ways of articulating sexuality: love and erotics—the first, the positive side of sexuality; the second, transgression. It was only in the nineteenth century that there emerges, with Sade, Laclos, and other transgressives, a new language that triggers research on deviations and perversions, that gives birth to a "science" of sexuality, and that makes possible the birth of the human sciences.[21] "If Western culture is the only culture to have made sexuality an object of science, it is no doubt due to this series of historical and social phenomena," Foucault writes. "In most other cultures, and still in our culture until the beginning of the nineteenth century, sexuality could not be an object [of science] because it was too caught up in silent practices."[22]

This leads Foucault to a fascinating and long development of Freud's writings on perversions and infantile sexuality that shows how important Freud, Anna Freud, Melanie Klein, and psychoanalysis were to Foucault at the time, for that moment, for those struggles surrounding the renewed humanism of sexuality. The reason is that Freud, according to Foucault, began to normalize perversions, put them in continuity with "normal" sexuality—or, in his words, because Freud's work "overturns the ethical relationship that made perversion the deviation of sexuality; it makes sexuality a development of the perversions."[23]

Both of these cartographic elements are deeply opposed to the idea of a humanism of sexuality—or what was often referred to, at the time, as an "anthropology of sexuality"[24]—and to the "science" of sexuality.

At a time when Foucault was excavating the epistemological layers of Western culture from the Renaissance to the nineteenth century in a manuscript published two years later under the title *The Order of Things* (1966),[25] he turned his instruction on sexuality at Clermont-Ferrand into an examination of how his own society crafted and masked its extensive regulation of sexual behavior—of ways of living—through a scientific understanding of sexuality based on the study of supposed deviance and perversions; how, thanks to Freud and psychoanalysis, those perversions began to be reintegrated into the domain of sexuality; but how, in the end, no matter how much we might continue to seek the truth about the biological, medical, or ritual nature of sexuality, what characterized and marked a culture—and "his" in particular—was not a truth about the biological essence of sexuality or its social construction, but the constant interplay, tensions, and contradictions between the two. And where things settled.

The 1969 Lectures on "The Discourse of Sexuality"

Foucault faced an entirely different political landscape and different political struggles in 1969 when he delivered his lectures on "The Discourse of Sexuality" at Vincennes. In the wake of the student uprisings, Foucault conceives a new philosophical praxis he calls the analysis of the discourse of sexuality—or more precisely, a "study" of "discourses that are about sexuality as such."[26] It is an examination of how sexuality became *the* topic, *the* focus of debate and discussion. Almost as if referencing his earlier work from 1964, Foucault underscores that his analytic method is not simply "What are the effects on a culture of the different ways sexuality is structured?"[27] The project now is to explore how sexuality became the focus of discourse, and somewhat recently in Western culture—how it became, in his words, the referential of the discourse: "The way that Sade does not speak of vices and virtues, nor of an imaginary character, but of sexuality."[28]

This entails a historical analysis of discourse—both how it is transformed and how it transforms—which leads Foucault back to political economy and Marxian categories of labor supply, forces of production, and the need of capitalists for a reserve army of workers. Foucault details a political economic process, beginning with a form of primitive accumulation associated with a demographic collapse and leading ultimately to a demand for labor, and the corresponding emergence of new institutions and principles: a whole set of practical effects that include new juridical conceptions of marriage as contract, new ideas of pro-procreative sex, new fields of knowledge about sexuality.

What is key is that these are all practices—*social practices*—and not simply things going on in our heads. They are not just a matter of our consciousness, nor just a matter of the Freudian

unconscious. They are certainly not a matter of false consciousness, and cannot simply be resolved by a claim to truth. They
are the product of social practices that shape the very basis of
how we draw lines and form judgments—including those of
truth, those that separate science from mere opinion or ideology.
In perhaps one of the most important passages from the 1969
lectures, Foucault notes:

> Thus, we should demolish with great care the idea that ideol-
> ogy is a sort of great collective representation that is outside of
> scientific practice [. . .] Ideology is not a matter of conscious-
> ness, any more than it is a matter of science; it is a matter of
> social practice. That is why the ideological struggle cannot be
> merely a theoretical struggle, at the level of true ideas.[29]

This entails the study of what is said and practiced surrounding
sexuality: an analysis of the texts and practices that place sexuality
at their center—a methodological approach that Foucault calls,
at this time in 1969, the "archaeology of sexuality."[30] Foucault
is excavating how it came about and all the different ways that
sexuality was discussed and treated in literature, in biology and
medicine, in the sciences, in psychology and psychoanalysis, in
law and morality, and in everyday exchange. It is through the
regulation and juridical transformation of marriage, for example,
that post-Revolutionary French society facilitated the accumulation of manpower: by readjusting the ease with which people
could marry in order to promote procreation—in other words,
by the interplay of ideas, institutions, and practices.

An "archaeology of sexuality": In focusing on the discourse of
sexuality, Foucault explicitly inscribes his analysis in his archaeological method, but also begins to realize that it may not be fully
adequate to analyze discourse, especially in relation to sexuality.

These 1969 lectures may represent one of the first moments in which Foucault realizes that he may need another method, or a methodological turn, this time toward genealogy, to address both knowledge and power together. It is not an accident that we read here the first of a series of critiques of the traditional notion of ideology that will run throughout his genealogical lectures at the Collège de France during the 1970s: Foucault was also lecturing on Nietzsche at Vincennes and formulating his important essay "Nietzsche, Genealogy, History."[31] His engagement with the notion of ideology at Vincennes clearly points toward his genealogical writings, even if he never utters the word *genealogy* or *dynasty* in these lectures.

In 1969, this is still *experimentation* in an archaeology of sexuality. As Foucault would admit in *The Archaeology of Knowledge*, published the same year, he was still not yet "sufficiently advanced in my task" to be sure whether the analysis of discourse could extend beyond the sciences to a phenomenon like sexuality.[32] In his inaugural lecture at the Collège de France the next year, on December 2, 1970, Foucault identified sexuality as a domain for future investigation. "Later," he declared at the Collège in *The Order of Discourse*, "we could attempt an investigation of a taboo system in language, that concerning sexuality from the sixteenth to the nineteenth century."[33] Later would be 1976: volume 1 of *The History of Sexuality* and the rejection of the repressive hypothesis.

Times change. The philosophical methods change. Even so, when faced with a similar dimension of humanist resurgence—for instance, in Marcuse's writings—Foucault returns to the notion of transgression. In 1969, Foucault critiques Marcuse for his embrace of a humanism that naturalizes a specific conception of healthy sexuality—now allowing homosexuality, but excluding sadism.[34] Foucault underscores how Marcuse uses nature to realign acceptable sexuality. In this context, the concept of "transgression" becomes useful once again, as Foucault returns to Sade and the idea of "transgressive utopias."[35]

*

Times change, indeed. And much as those earlier moments differ from one another—1964 from 1969, from 1976, and from 1984—they differ even more radically, perhaps, from our political times today. The culture wars, in a country like the United States, continue to place sexuality squarely in its bull's-eye, in ways that could hardly have been imagined back then, and to a degree that is inexcusable—or "intolerable," as Foucault would have said.[36]

No less than a month after his inauguration, on February 22, 2017, the president of the United States—yes, the *president* of the United States—thrust himself into the intimate decision of young children across the country as to which bathrooms they should use. The president withdrew protections for transgender students that allowed them to use the sex-designated bathrooms that they felt best corresponded to their gender identity.[37] Overruling his own conservative secretary of education, the president turned children's restroom use into a federal priority, leaving it to states and localities to decide whether transgender individuals could access the bathroom of their gender.

In 2015, the previous administration had clarified the legal rules, through policy guidance, to explain that "transgender students should be treated consistent with their gender identity for purposes of restroom access."[38] That was about the time when the term "transgender" came into the mainstream.[39] Colleges were beginning to design "gender-neutral" bathrooms. College student groups were contesting the term "gender-neutral," preferring the more transgender-positive expression "gender-inclusive."[40] Tension, conflict, and litigation ensued over the required use by transgender students of those gender-neutral bathrooms instead of the bathrooms that most appropriately corresponded to their gender.

Drew Adams, a sixteen-year-old transgender boy who began his junior year at Allen D. Nease High School in Ponte Vedra, Florida, in August 2017, had been living as a boy since 2015 and had been using the boys' restroom since his freshman year without incident, until someone anonymously reported him. He was then required to use the gender-neutral bathroom. Lambda Legal Defense and Education Fund filed a lawsuit on his behalf in June 2017, arguing that the "discriminatory restroom policy sends a purposeful message that transgender students in the school district are undeserving of the privacy, respect and protections afforded to other students."[41] The case reached the U.S. Court of Appeals for the Eleventh Circuit in Atlanta, Georgia, which, in August 2020, ruled that the school must treat transgender students equally in restrooms.

These culture wars would extend far and wide, including to the military. As Foucault noted in 1964, "we now know that sexuality in its mechanisms and meanings is not just confined to sexual practices but extends very much further into behavior apparently very distant from it."[42] Six months into his presidency, on July 26, 2017, the same U.S. president posted a series of tweets in the early morning hours announcing that "the United States Government will not accept or allow transgender individuals to serve in any capacity in the U.S. Military."[43] Thus began another campaign to undo the policies of the previous administration, which had, in 2016, lifted the ban against transgender individuals serving in the military.[44] The following month, August 2017, the president issued a "Presidential Memorandum on Military Service by Transgender Individuals," followed in March 2018 by a new memorandum that had the effect of banning transgender individuals from serving under their identified gender. By means of a subsequent

U.S. Department of Defense directive dated April 2019, and extended in September 2020 through another U.S. Department of Defense order, Instruction 1300.28, "Military Service by Transgender Persons and Persons with Gender Dysphoria," the federal government required that individuals who are transgender and joined the military after April 2019 must serve under whatever sex they were assigned at birth. They may not serve in their preferred gender identity, are not allowed to seek gender-reassignment procedures, must not have transitioned, and must have been deemed by a medical professional to have been "stable" in their biologically assigned sex for more than thirty-six months.

Meanwhile, on other legal fronts, Lambda Legal filed suit on behalf of Sander Saba, a nonbinary transgender New York resident who was seeking an accurate New York driver's license that reflected their nonbinary gender identity. The lawsuit, *Saba v. Cuomo*, filed in July 2020, "challenges New York State's discriminatory policy that categorically prohibits nonbinary people from obtaining an accurate driver's license that reflects their gender identity, instead forcing them to choose either 'male' or 'female.' Saba, a 25-year-old New York University Law School graduate, is seeking an accurate driver's license with an 'X' marker."[45]

Times change. The struggles change. At the time of this publication, in 2021, the culture wars revolve importantly around the daily lived experience of transgender individuals in their most personal and intimate choices. If anything, the term *transgender* is almost already out-of-date. Jack Halberstam has coined the term *trans** with an asterisk to connote a more open-ended and ambiguous transformative ethic and politics.[46] Trans* and other new terms, like *gender nonconforming, gender questioning, nonbinary*, and *neutrois* are becoming more current.[47] And in this context, some advocates and allies, paradoxically, have come to embrace the scientific diagnosis of "gender dysphoria," however uncomfortably, to make possible the types of medical surgery necessary to allow transgender persons to live their lives fully. In these struggles, the earlier stages of Foucault's philosophical praxis become essential.

Listen carefully to Halberstam, one of the leading critical thinkers on transgender matters and the author of *Trans*: A Quick and Quirky Account of Gender Variability*: "Transgender thus became and remains the newest marker of exclusion and pathology to be seamlessly transitioned into a new template for acceptance and tolerance."[48] Or to Halberstam again: "As lesbians and gay men earned recognition and protection from the state, transgender people often came to occupy the newly vacated classifications of disorder and dysfunction."[49] Or listen to Paul Preciado, another leading thinker and the author of *Countersexual Manifesto*: "In this negative sexology, transgression is produced by denying the very grammar that produces sexual signification."[50] Or to Preciado in *Testo Junkie*: "What if desire, excitement, sexuality, seduction, and the pleasure of the multitude were all the mainsprings of the creation of value added to the contemporary economy?"[51]

Notice the terms: exclusion, pathology, acceptance, tolerance, disorder, dysfunction, transgression, surplus value. They are in direct conversation with these lectures of Foucault. Our battles today may be different, but sexuality remains, constantly, at the core of our subjectivity and subject creation. It is precisely for this reason that these early Foucault lectures are of such importance: to help us engage in renewed philosophical praxis for these new and unique times and struggles.

Claiming that a sexual identity or practice is natural, or for that matter a medical disorder, is one of the central ways power functions, and something to resist. In these early Foucault lectures, one can hear the argument that sexuality as identity and scientific knowledge should be replaced by sex as practice and invention. The point is not necessarily to "denaturalize," or for that matter to "naturalize," styles or practices of sexuality, but rather to spotlight how the interplay—one could even say, the dialectic—between what we consider to be natural and what we consider to be socially ritualized is itself the feature that tells us most about our culture and the battles we need to fight. Foucault acknowledged that a claim to nature may be strategically effective at times—for instance, in the context of human rights; but in the end, any strategic deployment is just that—a tactic in struggles of power. There is no point weighing in on the truth of nature or social ritual because there is little to gain in crystalizing social formations in these changing times. But this is, of course, an ongoing conversation—one that can be heard, loudly, still today. It can be heard clearly, I think, when a contemporary like Halberstam writes: "If 'queer' in the 1990s and 2000s was the marker of a politics of sex and gender that exceeded identity and gestured toward a critique of state power and assimilationist goals, we could say the term 'trans*' marks a politics based on a general instability of identity and oriented toward social transformation, not political accommodation. As the term 'transgender' comes to represent the acceptable edge of gender variance, the category of trans* signifies the cost of that level of acceptance."[52]

*

With the inauguration of this new book series, *Foucault's Early Lectures and Manuscripts*, the third panel of a triptych is formed. A new window is opened, alongside the nine principal monographs published during his lifetime and the existing set of published interviews and essays—the famous *Dits et Écrits*—and thirteen lecture series at the Collège de France.

A new vista—but some ground clearing as well. The publication of these lectures immediately belies the overly simplistic, psychologized interpretations of Foucault—that he turned to the history of sexuality and the ancient Greeks late in life as a product of his own radical experimentations and homosexuality. Nothing could be further from the truth, as evidenced so clearly in these early lectures. The history of sexuality, as a way to understand and critique modern Western society, had been a lifelong project. To be sure, as always, there were biographical antecedents to his interests, not the least of which were his own formative life experiences as a gay man. But his theoretical interest in sexuality dates back to the earliest times.

These early lectures also belie the overly simplistic periodization of Foucault's interests, as if he experienced an ethical turn late in life. They provide a corrective to decades of misinterpretation of Foucault—to the aestheticization of Foucault and to the distortions, so often politically motivated, of his work. His was always a quest to understand the political influence of culture and history, time and space, on our subjectivity. These early lectures provide the perfect illustration. They are a window into a lifelong philosophical interest in sexuality as a way to understand *our culture today* and how we are shaped as contemporary human subjects—a lifelong project that, as this new series of lectures before the Collège de France will show, trace back to the early 1950s and his earliest writings on Nietzsche, Husserl, existentialism, phenomenology, and sexuality.

This new series, *Foucault's Early Lectures and Manuscripts*, of which the courses on sexuality from 1964 and 1969 represent the first volume, shines a light on the original problematics, the earliest formulations, the first philosophical praxes. The volumes will explore Foucault's struggles with phenomenology, existentialism, and psychology; his encounter, conversation, and distancing from Nietzsche, as well as Marx; his working of *The Order of Things*; his years in Tunisia. Each volume enriches in innumerable ways the other panels of the triptych and, more generally, the fluorescence of Foucault's thought. I welcome you to this rich trove, little known before.

One word of advice—especially to the wise researcher. It is often thought that the notes at the end of a chapter provide merely citation and reference. But in this volume, so ably annotated by Claude-Olivier Doron, and in the forthcoming volumes, as you will see, the notes are so rich and provide a remarkable bibliography, references, and historical links to many of Foucault's and his contemporaries' related writings. The notes alone are worth the price of admission, in addition to the brilliant course contexts which mine Foucault's unpublished notebooks at the Bibliothèque nationale de France and in the process, provide hidden jewels from those private journals—like, for instance, the list Foucault drew on June 4, 1963, of what he called particularly prophetic cultural formations: "death, decadence, avowal, sexuality, madness."[53]

*

When I set these two lecture series as one bookend, with the fourth and final volume of *The History of Sexuality* as the other, I am left with amazement at how our self-understanding of our sexuality today, no matter how stable, sticky, and natural feeling, is bound to change radically in the twenty-first century—how our sexuality, in the end, is basically written in sand. Just as with that figure of man Foucault identified in the 1960s, our contemporary understanding of sexuality—our own experience and everything we so firmly believe or know about our sexual selves—will wash away and give rise to entirely new ways of being, thinking, and living social, sexual, and political relationships that are practically unforeseeable today.

These works by Foucault reveal not only the iron-fisted hold and resilience of our current imagination of sexuality, but also the openness of sexuality, its fragility and temporality, and its embeddedness in relations of power. As Foucault noted in opening his Clermont-Ferrand lectures in 1964, "if sexuality is quite stereotypical in some of its manifestations, it is extremely plastic in others, and especially in those joined with behavior in general."[54] The plasticity of what is to come is perhaps the most remarkable legacy of this work.

BERNARD E. HARCOURT

*

A special note of thanks to Daniele Lorenzini and Mia Ruyter for lengthy discussions, fruitful comments, and constructive criticism; to Daniel Defert, Claude-Olivier Doron, François Ewald, Henri-Paul Fruchaud, and the other members of the editorial team for their insights and guidance; to Fonda Shen for brilliant research assistance; and to Eric Schwartz and Lowell Frye at Columbia University Press for their foresight, wisdom, and support.

1. Jack Halberstam, *Trans*: A Quick and Quirky Account of Gender Variability* (Oakland: University of California Press, 2018), 3.

2. *Un homme et une femme*, directed by Claude Lelouch, written by Pierre Uytterhoeven, starring Anouk Aimée and Jean-Louis Trintignant (Paris: Les Films 13, 1966). See *A Man and a Woman*, IMDB, accessed January 3, 2021, https://www.imdb.com/title/tt0061138/.

3. For sources regarding Foucault's time at Vincennes, see Stuart Elden, *Foucault: The Birth of Power* (Cambridge, UK: Polity, 2017), 192n22.

4. Michel Foucault, "The Discourse of Sexuality" (1969), in *Sexuality: The 1964 Clermont-Ferrand and 1969 Vincennes Lectures*, ed. Claude-Olivier Doron, trans. Graham Burchell (New York: Columbia University Press, 2021), 176 [21], 161 [13], 161 [17], 190 [27], and 163 [20].

5. Michel Foucault, "The Discourse on Language," in *The Archaeology of Knowledge and the Discourse on Language*, trans. A. M. Sheridan Smith (New York: Pantheon, 1972), 224. For a more recent translation of

Foucault's inaugural lecture at the Collège de France, see Michel Foucault, "The Order of Discourse," in *Archives of Infamy: Foucault on State Power in the Lives of Ordinary Citizens*, ed. Nancy Luxon, trans. Thomas Scott-Railton (Minneapolis: University of Minnesota Press, 2019), 141–73.

6. Michel Foucault, *The Punitive Society: Lectures at the Collège de France, 1972–1973*, ed. Bernard E. Harcourt, trans. Graham Burchell (New York: Picador, 2015), 113. Special thanks to Daniele Lorenzini.

7. Foucault, *The Punitive Society*, 6; see also 2–5.

8. In this, Gilles Deleuze and François Ewald are entirely right. These are philosophical acts that represent "theoretical revolution[s]," in Deleuze's words, acts in relation to political actuality, as Ewald suggests. See Gilles Deleuze, "Écrivain non: Un nouveau cartographe," *Critique* 343 (December 1975): 1212; François Ewald, "Foucault et l'actualité," in *Au risque de Foucault* (Paris: Éditions du Centre Pompidou, 1997).

9. Michel Foucault, "Truth and Juridical Forms," in *Power*, vol. 3 of *The Essential Works of Foucault (1954–1984)*, ed. James D. Faubion, trans. Robert Hurley (New York: New Press, 2000), 32.

10. Daniel Defert, "Chronologie," in *Œuvres I*, by Michel Foucault (Paris: Gallimard/Pléiade, 2015), xxxix.

11. Michel Foucault, *Histoire de la sexualité IV: Les Aveux de la chair* (Paris: Gallimard, 2018).

12. Michel Foucault, *Histoire de la sexualité I: La Volonté de savoir* (Paris: Gallimard, 1976) (back cover); Michel Foucault, *The History of Sexuality*, vol. 1, *An Introduction*, trans. Robert Hurley (New York: Vintage, 1990) (the list is not included here).

13. Michel Foucault, *Histoire de la sexualité II: L'Usage des plaisirs* (Paris: Gallimard, 1984); Michel Foucault, *The History of Sexuality*, vol. 2, *The Use of Pleasure*, trans. Robert Hurley (New York: Vintage, 1990) (I retain the plural "pleasures" in my translation of the title in text to reflect Foucault's ethical and political intervention regarding multiplying pleasures rather than looking inside ourselves for the roots of desire); Michel Foucault, *Histoire de la sexualité III: Le Souci de soi* (Paris: Gallimard, 1984); Michel Foucault, *The History of Sexuality*, vol. 3, *The Care of the Self*, trans. Robert Hurley (New York: Vintage, 1988).

14. Arnold Davidson, Henri-Paul Fruchaud, and Daniele Lorenzini are now editing, for their book series at Vrin, a volume that will collect Foucault's lectures on sexuality at Berkeley and São Paulo in 1975 ("Discourse and

Repression" and "La généalogie du savoir modern sur la sexualité") and his seminar at the New York Institute for the Humanities in 1980 ("Sexuality and Solitude"). In that forthcoming volume, one can watch the metamorphosis unfold before one's eyes.

15. Foucault, *Les Aveux de la chair*, see, generally, Daniele Lorenzini, "The Emergence of Desire," *Critical Inquiry* 45, no. 2 (Winter 2019): 448–70, https://doi.org/10.1086/700997; Stuart Elden, "Review: Foucault's *Confessions of the Flesh*," *Theory, Culture & Society*, March 20, 2018, https://www.theoryculturesociety.org/blog/review-michel-foucault-confessions-of-the-flesh; Lynne Huffer, *Foucault's Strange Eros* (New York: Columbia University Press, 2020).

16. I develop this thesis in detail in an article titled "Foucault's Keystone: *Confessions of the Flesh*: How the Fourth and Final Volume of *The History of Sexuality* Completes Foucault's Critique of Modern Western Societies," *Foucault Studies* (forthcoming 2021); see also Daniele Lorenzini, "La politique du paradis: Foucault, *Les Aveux de la chair* et la généalogie du néolibéralisme," in *Après "Les Aveux de la chair": Généalogie du sujet chez Michel Foucault*, ed. S. Boehringer & L. Laufer (Paris: Epel, 2020), 229–41.

17. Michel Foucault, "Sexuality" (1964), in *Sexuality: The 1964 Clermont-Ferrand and 1969 Vincennes Lectures*, ed. Claude-Olivier Doron, trans. Graham Burchell (New York: Columbia University Press, 2021), 5 [5] and 8 [9].

18. Foucault, "Sexuality" (1964), 16 [21] and 31 [25]; for a detailed discussion of Foucault's relation to Freud and psychoanalysis in these lectures, see note 5 to second lecture, 43.

19. Foucault, "Sexuality" (1964), 5 [4] (my emphasis, though Foucault himself underlines this in his next sentence).

20. Foucault, *The Punitive Society*, 5–6.

21. Foucault, "Sexuality" (1964), 71–72 [70–71].

22. Foucault, "Sexuality" (1964), 86 [76].

23. Foucault, "Sexuality" (1964), 89 [81]. Foucault focuses especially on child sexuality—a theme that he would later develop in his lectures at the Collège de France on *Psychiatric Power* in 1974, in *Abnormal* in 1975, and in the planned volume originally announced in 1976, of which a manuscript exists on *La Croisade des enfants*. Michel Foucault, *Psychiatric Power: Lectures at the Collège de France, 1973–1974*, ed. Jacques Lagrange, trans.

Graham Burchell (Basingstoke, UK: Palgrave McMillan, 2006); Michel Foucault, *Abnormal: Lectures at the Collège de France, 1974–1975*, ed. Valerio Marchetti and Antonella Salomoni, trans. Graham Burchell (New York: Picador, 2004); on the manuscript, *La croisade des enfants*, see note 1 in Foucault, *Sexuality* (1964), fifth lecture 128–129.

24. Foucault writes: "We can call humanist or anthropological philosophy any 'reactionary' philosophy" that, among other things, refuses "to see something other than love and reproduction in sexuality." Foucault, "The Discourse of Sexuality" (1969), 236 [NP/75]. For a detailed discussion of this concept of the anthropology of sexuality, see Foucault, "Sexuality" (1964), note 33 to first lecture, 24–25.

25. At the time Foucault delivered these 1964 lectures, he was immersed in thinking and writing *The Order of Things*, which was published in April 1966. He had already finished a first version of the book manuscript by December 1964, and by April 1965, he had rewritten another three-hundred-page-long version of *The Order of Things*. Defert, "Chronologie," xlix.

26. Foucault, "The Discourse of Sexuality" (1969), 148 [5].

27. Foucault, "The Discourse of Sexuality" (1969), 147 [4].

28. Foucault, "The Discourse of Sexuality" (1969), 148 [6].

29. Foucault, "The Discourse of Sexuality" (1969), 180 [26].

30. Foucault, "The Discourse of Sexuality" (1969), 215 [47/49].

31. Foucault's lectures on Nietzsche at Vincennes will be published as part of this series of *Foucault's Early Lectures and Manuscripts*; for context on Foucault's essay "Nietzsche, Genealogy, History," see Bernard E. Harcourt, "Five Modalities of Michel Foucault's Use of Nietzsche's Writings (1959–1973): Critical, Epistemological, Linguistic, Alethurgic, and Political," *Theory, Culture, and Society* (forthcoming 2021).

32. Foucault, *The Archaeology of Knowledge*, 192; see, generally, 192–94 for a discussion of the archaeology of sexuality.

33. Foucault, "The Discourse on Language," in *The Archaeology of Knowledge*, 232; see also 233–34 for a discussion of how Foucault would approach the study of sexuality.

34. Foucault, "The Discourse of Sexuality" (1969), 268 [11/98].

35. Foucault, "The Discourse of Sexuality" (1969), 263 [15/90].

36. Foucault specifically placed the inquiries of the Prisons Information Group under the label "intolerable." See Michel Foucault and Prisons

Information Group, *Intolerable: Writings from Michel Foucault and the Prisons Information Group (1970–1980)*, ed. Kevin Thompson and Perry Zurn, trans. Perry Zurn and Erik Beranek (Minneapolis: University of Minnesota Press, 2020).

37. U.S. Department of Justice, Civil Rights Division, and U.S. Department of Education, Office for Civil Rights, *Dear Colleague Letter*, by Sandra Battle and T. E. Wheeler II (Washington, DC: 2017), accessed January 3, 2021, https:// assets.documentcloud.org/documents/3473560/Departments-of-Education -and-Justice-roll-back.pdf; Jeremy W. Peters, Jo Becker, and Julie Hirschfeld Davis, "Trump Rescinds Rules on Bathrooms for Transgender Students," *New York Times*, February 22, 2017, https://www.nytimes.com/2017/02/22/us /politics/devos-sessions-transgender-students-rights.html.

38. U.S. Department of Education, Office for Civil Rights, *Letter to Emily T. Prince*, by James A. Ferg-Cadima, accessed January 3, 2021, http://www.bricker.com/documents/misc/transgender_student_restroom _access_1-2015.pdf.

39. Halberstam, *Trans**, 46.

40. See Sophie Rothman, "Restroom Signs Go Gender-Inclusive," *Columbia Daily Spectator*, August 8, 2014, https://www.columbiaspectator .com/news/2013/10/01/restroom-signs-go-gender-inclusive/; Li Cohen, "Federal Court Rules That Transgender Students Must Be Allowed to Use Bathrooms That Match Their Gender," *CBS News*, August 9, 2020, https:// www.cbsnews.com/news/federal-court-rules-that-transgender-students -must-be-allowed-to-use-bathrooms-that-match-their-gender/; see generally Halberstam, *Trans**, 134.

41. "Victory! Federal Court Rules Florida School Must Treat Transgender Students Equally Including Access to Restrooms," *Lambda Legal*, accessed January 3, 2021, https://www.lambdalegal.org/news/fl_20200807_victory -florida-trans-students-bathrooms.

42. Foucault, "Sexuality" (1964), 4 [2].

43. Donald Trump (@realDonaldTrump), "After consultation with my Generals and military experts, please be advised that the United States Government will not accept or allow . . .," Twitter, July 26, 2017, 8:55, https:// twitter.com/realDonaldTrump/status/890193981585444864; Donald Trump (@realDonaldTrump), " . . . Transgender individuals to serve in any capacity in the U.S. Military. Our military must be focused on decisive and

overwhelming . . .," Twitter, July 26, 2017, 9:04, https://twitter.com/real-DonaldTrump/status/890196164313833472.

44. Matthew Rosenberg, "Transgender People Will Be Allowed to Serve Openly in Military," *New York Times*, https://www.nytimes.com/2016/07/01/us/transgender-military.html.

45. Saba v. Cuomo, *Lambda Legal*, accessed January 3, 2021, https://www.lambdalegal.org/in-court/cases/saba-v-cuomo.

46. Halberstam, *Trans**, 4, 50.

47. Halberstam, *Trans**, 10.

48. Halberstam, *Trans**, 46.

49. Halberstam, *Trans**, 47.

50. Paul B. Preciado, *Countersexual Manifesto*, trans. Kevin Gerry Dunn (New York: Columbia University Press, 2018), 71.

51. Paul B. Preciado, *Testo Junkie: Sex, Drugs, and Biopolitics in the Pharmacopornographic Era*, trans. Bruce Benderson (New York: Feminist Press, 2013).

52. Halberstam, *Trans**, 50.

53. Cited by Claude-Olivier Doron in his "Course Context" to 1964 Lectures, note 5, 317.

54. Foucault, "Sexuality" (1964), 4 [2–3].

FOREWORD

TO THE FRENCH EDITION

FRANÇOIS EWALD

From 1952 to 1969, when he was nominated to the chair of the History of Systems of Thought at the Collège de France, Michel Foucault taught in several universities and institutions: psychology at the École normale supérieur (from 1951), Lille (1952–1955), and Clermont-Ferrand (1960–1966), and then philosophy at Tunis (1966–1968) and Vincennes (1968–1969). In addition, in October 1965 he lectured at the University of São Paulo on the subject that is addressed in *The Order of Things: An Archaeology of the Human Sciences* (1966).

Foucault kept only some of the manuscripts of the lectures he delivered during this period. These are deposited in the Foucault collection of the Bibliothèque nationale de France (under NAF 28730). In the same boxes in which the lectures are kept, there are also some texts from the same period, some of which are highly developed. We thought it useful to include them in the volumes that make up this series of "lectures and works" from the period prior to Foucault's election to the Collège de France.

The volumes are edited according to the following rules:

– The text is based on the manuscripts deposited in the Bibliothèque nationale de France. The transcriptions are as faithful as possible to the manuscripts and have been subject to collective review within the editorial team. The difficulties that the reading of some words gives rise to are indicated in footnotes. Only minor modifications have been made (the correction of obvious errors, punctuation, and layout) in order to assist the reading and clear understanding of the text. They are always indicated.

– Quotations have been checked, and references to the texts used are indicated. The text is accompanied by a critical apparatus that seeks to elucidate obscure points and clarify critical points.

– To make the text easier to read, each lecture is preceded by a brief summary that indicates its principal articulations.

– As with the editions of the Collège de France lectures, each volume ends with a "context" for which the editor is responsible: it seeks to provide readers with elements of the context needed for them to understand the texts and situate them in Foucault's published work.

The members of the editorial committee responsible for the project are Elisabetta Basso, Daniel Defert, Claude-Olivier Doron, François Ewald, Henri-Paul Fruchaud, Frédéric Gros, Bernard E. Harcourt, Orazio Irrera, Daniele Lorenzini, Philippe Sabot, and Arianna Sforzini.

We would like to extend particular thanks to the Bibliothèque nationale de France for enabling us to consult the manuscripts on which this edition is based.

FRANÇOIS EWALD

RULES FOR EDITING THE TEXTS

CLAUDE-OLIVIER DORON

This volume brings together two courses on the theme of sexuality.

The first, entitled *Sexuality*, was given by Michel Foucault in 1964 at the University of Clermont-Ferrand as part of his teaching of general psychology. It exists in the form of an autograph manuscript of 121 pages numbered by Foucault and kept in the archives of the Bibliothèque nationale de France (Box 78). This manuscript, extensively prepared, does not present any special editing difficulties.

The second, entitled *The Discourse of Sexuality*, was given in 1969 at the University of Vincennes as part of his teaching of philosophy. It exists in the form of an autograph manuscript of 103 pages partly numbered by Foucault and kept in the archives of the Bibliothèque nationale de France (Box 51). Unlike the earlier course, the manuscript comprises more fragmentary notes, with many crossed-out passages and numerous variants. It required a specific form of editing. To make up for its sometimes limited preparation, we have tried to provide readers with as much information as possible in the accompanying critical apparatus, systematically documenting Foucault's references.

To this end, we have used the important dossiers brought together by Foucault in connection with the course, based on his reading notes on the history of biological knowledge of sexuality, on sexual utopias, and on marriage regulations (Boxes 39 and 45 in the Bibliothèque nationale de France). We have also referred to two typed texts produced from the notes of students who attended the lectures, which are kept in the Bibliothèque nationale de France (Box 78). Extracts from these typed notes have been included in the critical apparatus (designated TN1 and TN2) when we thought this would help clarify the manuscript.

Finally, it seemed appropriate to add, as an appendix to these two courses, an exposition of fifteen sheets that Foucault devoted to the theme of "Sexuality, reproduction, individuality," dated 21 September 1969—that is, three months after the Vincennes course. This document comes from Foucault's green *Notebook*, no. 8, kept in Box 91, which contains Foucault's "Intellectual Journal."

The general rules for editing the texts were the following. As far as possible, we have followed Foucault's page layout, editing, and numbering, with a few exceptions. When a word was missing or a construction was problematic, we have restored the missing word or modified the text, indicating the change by square brackets in the body of the text and giving the reasons for the change in a footnote. Where Foucault himself made a change or crossed out a passage that we considered significant, we have indicated this in a footnote. In the Vincennes course in particular, variants or crossed-out passages that contain significant differences from the rest of the text and are longer than a paragraph have been moved to an appendix to the lecture. Shorter crossed-out passages appear in footnotes. Spelling mistakes have been corrected directly in the text. Sometimes, to make reading easier, short lists with indents and new lines, which Foucault frequently uses in his lecture manuscripts, have been revised into a more compact paragraph. Finally, we have placed Foucault's pagination in square brackets in the left- and right-hand margins; when required by mistakes or the insertion of unnumbered sheets, we note the correct pagination to the right of the number given by Foucault.

CLAUDE-OLIVIER DORON

TRANSLATOR'S NOTE

GRAHAM BURCHELL

In these lectures, Michel Foucault frequently distinguishes between *savoir* and *connaissance*, both of which are translated in English as "knowledge." The University of Vincennes course, "The Discourse of Sexuality," is from the same year as the publication of *The Archaeology of Knowledge* (1969), in which Foucault formulated a clear distinction between the two terms in his work (see especially part IV, chapter 6). Put simply and crudely, knowledge-*savoir* refers to the domain of discursive practices that constitute the necessary conditions for the formation of knowledge-*connaissance* as a rule-governed relation between subject and object. The distinction is less developed in the earlier (1964) course, "Sexuality," although on one occasion Foucault uses the term "discursive knowledge" (*savoir discursif*) in a sense that is close to his later use of *savoir* in contrast with *connaissance*. In these lectures, *connaissance* refers more to a specific content of knowledge or a particular science, and to the notion of knowledge as it figures in the philosophical "problem of knowledge" or "theory of knowledge," while *savoir* refers more generally to a wider, underlying domain of discourses within which a particular science or discipline emerges and exists. No satisfactory or generally accepted English equivalents have been found to mark the distinction Foucault wants to make, and both terms are translated here as "knowledge," followed by the appropriate French word when it was important to note the distinction. The distinction between the two terms is discussed in greater detail in the endnotes and in the "Course Context" by Claude-Olivier Doron.

I would like to offer my sincere thanks to Fonda Shen for her invaluable assistance in completing the work of tracing references and quotations when I was denied access to libraries due to the Covid pandemic.

GRAHAM BURCHELL

ABBREVIATIONS

The following abbreviations are used in the footnotes and endnotes:

BNF   Collections of the Bibliothèque nationale de France

CPW   *The Standard Edition of the Complete Psychological Works of Sigmund Freud*, trans. under general editorship of James Strachey in collaboration with Anna Freud, assisted by Alix Strachey and Alan Tyson (London: Hogarth Press and Institute of Psychoanalysis, 1953–1974).

DÉ, I   *Dits et écrits I, 1954–1975*, ed. D. Defert and F. Ewald, avec la collaboration de Jacques Lagrange (Paris: Gallimard, "Quarto," 2001).

DÉ, II   *Dits et écrits II, 1976–1988*, ed. D. Defert and F. Ewald, avec la collaboration de Jacques Lagrange (Paris: Gallimard, "Quarto", 2001).

EW, 1   *The Essential Works of Foucault, 1954–1984. Volume 1: Ethics, Subjectivity and Truth*, ed. Paul Rabinow (New York: New Press, 1997).

EW, 2   *The Essential Works of Foucault, 1954–1984. Volume 2: Aesthetics, Method and Epistemology*, ed. James D. Faubion (New York: New Press, 1998).

EW, 3   *The Essential Works of Foucault, 1954–1984. Volume 3. Power*, ed. James D. Faubion (New York: New Press, 2000).

IS   L. Bounoure, *L'instinct sexuel: Étude de psychologie animale* (Paris: PUF, 1956).

SI   N. Tinbergen, *The Study of Instinct* (New York: Oxford University Press, 1951).

Sexuality

PART I

Sexuality

LECTURES AT THE UNIVERSITY OF CLERMONT-FERRAND

(1964)

LECTURE 1

Introduction

Questioning the relationships between sexuality and our culture. The opposition between the biology of sexuality and culture is typical of Western civilization. Definition of what is to be understood by "Western culture." A. Synchronically: monogamy and patriarchy. Imbalance of men-women relationships and compensatory mechanisms. Entails a structure and problems that are found whatever the political regime. B. Diachronically: transformations marking our contemporary culture since the nineteenth century. 1. Evolution of compensatory mechanisms for imbalances between men and women: tendency toward a progressive equalization and logic of men-women complementarity. 2. Transformation of the relations between law and sexuality: sexuality ceases to play a central role in marriage as a legal institution. 3. Appearance of a "problematic consciousness of sexuality": sexuality as anthropological theme; sexuality as privileged site of moral and subjective values; sexuality as space of challenge and radical transgression: tragic experience of modern man. Sade, on the threshold of modernity.

What is sexuality in our culture?[a]   [NP/1]

Why this qualification or supplementary limitation: "in our culture"? As if sexuality were not a sufficiently definite anatomical-physiological fact for it to be studied in itself—even if it involves adding some supplementary information about the social rituals

---

a Not numbered.

surrounding it. After all, what does a culture bring to sexuality—apart from some rituals regarding the permanence of the sexual union and some prohibitions regarding sexual objects?

[2]   We may well say that to a very considerable extent sexuality is at the outer edge of culture, what remains irreducible and inassimilable to it. Suffice as proof of this, on the one hand, the constancy, everywhere, of most manifestations of sexual life, and, on the other hand, [the fact] that the rules that societies have always sought to apply to this sexuality, be they social or moral, all remain sufficiently extraneous to it for sexuality to be the most constant site of moral and legal infractions.[1]

Maybe sexuality is our unrecoverable biological limit?

Actually, we now know that sexuality in its mechanisms and meanings is not just confined to sexual practices but extends very much further into behavior apparently very distant from it.

[3]   We also know that if sexuality is quite stereotypical in some of its manifestations, it is extremely plastic in others, and especially in those joined with behavior in general; and that if it eats into culture more than is usually thought, culture, in return, has no doubt a greater hold on it than was previously thought.[2]

So we may wonder whether this isolation of sexuality, this system of disconnection by which we perceive it only at the extreme edge of our civilization, and rather from the angle of our biological destiny, is not just an effect of the way our culture accommodates and integrates sexuality. In other words, this opposition between the biology of sexuality and culture is no doubt one of the characteristics of Western civilization. No doubt it is because we have lived for centuries in a culture like ours that we believe, as if spontaneously, that sexuality is only a matter of physiology, that it only concerns sexual practices, and that ultimately the latter are intended only for the biological preservation of the species—that is to say, for procreation.

In short, all this system of belief, of quasi-self-evidence, is [4] maybe only an avatar in the cultural history of Western sexuality. This is all just hypothesis. But it is [a] hypothesis that at the outset cannot be avoided. So the only question we have the right to pose in order to begin, therefore, concerns what sexuality is in our culture.

*

In this question, we must first of all define what *in our culture*[b] means.[3]

We shall not speak about sexuality solely, but starting from it, with reference to it, and so as to get back to it; it will serve us as ground of evidence. When it looks as though we are talking about man and woman in general, we will not be addressing universal anthropological categories, but those categories, characters, roles, and functions that our culture refers to under these names; and conversely, when we specify that we are talking about it, this does not prove that these categories are valid for other cultural areas.

In any case, we must define what we understand by "our culture" diachronically and synchronically. [5]

A. Synchronically[c]: We will be referring to what is commonly called Western or European culture—that is to say, a culture marked by patriarchy and monogamy. The combination of these two cultural forms immediately entails as consequences:

1. The definition of a fairly simple family cell formed of a parental couple and its offspring. The only complication in relation to this couple comes in subsequent lineage:

þ Underlined in the manuscript.

c Underlined in the manuscript.

- by the multiplication of children, raising the question of the division of goods;
- by the marriage of daughters (i.e., the formation of a new parental couple) and assignation of a share of the family's goods to the daughter's spouse;
[6]
- [by] the integration in the original family cell of couples formed by married sons.

So, an arborescent type of family organization in which lateral relationships create [. . .] few problems, by contrast to vertical problems.[4]

2. A regime of the prohibition of incest that is essentially controlled by this bushy figure of the family cell. The major bans concern father/daughter–mother/son relationships; and brother/sister relationships, but already with a certain margin of tolerance. On the other hand, in our times, prohibitions are very limited outside this family cell. Lateral relationships between first cousins are easily tolerated (and increasingly so as, in these bushy forms, branches are detached from each other earlier and earlier). Moreover, no imbalance between the masculine and feminine sides of the relationship.

[7]
3. A series of controlled imbalances:
a. hereditary transmission of the name and at least a part of the goods through the male line;
b. patrilocal residence of children and their mother, with an unwritten law and biased morality;
c. strongly masculine religion:
  – monotheism in which the masculine figure takes precedence. If there is indeed father and son, the mother does not form part of the Trinity;
  – the essential practices of worship are reserved for men.

d. radical distinction between men's and women's work:

- men's work is outside the home, of which, preferentially, the man is in charge and for which he is morally responsible;
- women's work (tied to the home).

(There are no more women working than at the beginning of the twentieth century.[5])

All of this has resulted in a social and cultural situation   [NP][d]
of women that European law of the nineteenth and at least the beginning of the twentieth century described as "marital power."-"The husband owes his wife protection; the wife owes her husband obedience" (article 213)—this is all there is in the Civil Code.

1. The wife takes the name of her husband (implicitly recognized usage).
2. The husband has the right to supervise his wife.[6]
3. The wife must follow her husband wherever he has to live.[7]
4. The wife cannot perform a valid legal act without her husband's authorization.[8]

e. Finally, to compensate for these inequalities that alter   [8][e]
the homogeneity of monogamy, a series of compensatory mechanisms of an ideological order:

- previously (until the nineteenth century) they concerned the wife's ethical distinctness: chivalry, moral, affective, sexual role;

---

d An unnumbered sheet is inserted here, and sheet 8 follows.
e The initial pagination resumes here.

– they now concern her social homogenization. Demand:
  ° for equal rights
  ° for equality regarding work
  ° for ethical symmetry
  ° for anthropological reciprocity

On the basis of this monogamy and patriarchy, which we share with many other cultures, wherever one of these five characteristics is not found, we will not be able to apply the categories or analyses regarding our culture. [. . . f]

[9] In any case, we can see that this structure, which covers the Judeo-Christian civilizations, now extends very far, identified as it is with European, scientific, rational, and technical culture. It is what is increasingly imposed under the name of civilization *tout court*; it acquires a planetary vocation. In societies that appear to want to distance themselves from this culture, we should not forget that they do little more than strengthen the structures of compensation.

For example, in socialist societies, accentuating the theme of equality between men and women, which comes into conflict with other remaining underlying structures:

– the problem of family work;[9]
– the problem of monogamy and divorce;[10]
– the masculine character of politics.[11]

As for Western societies that seem the most distant from these, the only difference is in the weakness of the compensatory mechanisms: ethical and social inequality between the sexes. But the deep structure is the same.

The anthropological configuration of sexuality is the same in socialist and reactionary countries.

---

f Sentence crossed out: "For example, Arab civilizations."

[This explains the fact that after the dream of a general reform   [NP]ᵍ
of Man, as it was formulated in the nineteenth century, as emancipation of his entire being—including sexuality—the socialist
countries covered over the problem of sexuality:

- with a strict moral conformism taken directly from bourgeois ethics;
- with a systematic refusal of any theoretical problematization
  of sexuality → psychoanalysis].ʰ¹²

*B. Diachronically*ⁱ: what should we understand by "our culture"?   [10]
By defining it geographically by Judeo-Christian culture, we
make it go back a long way. What may be called the "contemporary" period is characterized:

*1. By the transformation of the compensatory mechanisms we were
just talking about*ʲ
a. There was a time when they consisted in a reinforcement,
an intensification of the inequality between the sexes, but with a
game of reverse valorization: in chivalry, courtly love, preciosity,
for example, the reversal of right:

1. Men had the right (of name, property); women appeared
   as creators of bonds (engagement, fidelity, test).
2. Women were forced into marriage, objects of exchange
   between families; they appeared as the inaccessible end
   of desire.
[3. They did not have the right to exercise religious office;
   but they receive religion and have their forms of piety.ᵏ]

---

g We move to a new sheet, not paginated.

h Michel Foucault's brackets.

i Underlined in the manuscript.

j Underlined in the manuscript.

k Originally placed after 4 (which appeared as 3), this paragraph was inserted by Foucault.

4. Women do not have the right to speak (legally, politically); they are inspirers. They inspire what people say.[13]

[11]   This compensation was in turn decompensated by reverse mechanisms, at least at the imaginary level:

- Woman the creator of bonds, above or within the law, is also represented as the destroyer of all bonds, of all obligation. The popular image of the unfaithful wife, the deceived husband, and the matrimonial lie. In the Middle Ages, and up to the eighteenth century, this image is much stronger and more prestigious than the opposite image of the scorned wife.
- The woman who inspires is also represented as the woman who disturbs or destroys society and men's happiness. She is the one who sends misfortune, who sends men to their death.
- The woman of inner piety is also the woman of prohibited religious practices. The witch.[14]

b. Nowadays compensation is directed rather toward a progressive equalization. We can date the culture, at least with regard to sexuality, on the basis of this change in compensatory mechanisms.

[12]   The demand for equality begins roughly in the middle of the nineteenth century. We see evidence for this in a number of socialist utopias or in Comte's religion. Idea of an egalitarian complementarity of men and women, each with precise functions.

- Woman: Order—the Past—Tradition—Memory—cult of the dead.
- Man: Progress—the Future—Science—dynamic values.

With basically the same dream of the Mother-Virgin, that is to say of an abolition of sexuality as source of inequality, but for a radical functional distinction.[15]

However utopian and crazy Comte's final thought may be, it is fairly typical of what actually happened subsequently.

– A search for equality:
- acquisition of the right to vote and participation in political life;[16]
- access, at least by right, to all the professions;[17]   [13]
- access to religious functions.[18]

– At the same time, as compensation, the search for complementarity in psychology, sociology, anthropology:
- description of the affective, libidinal, and character structure of women;[19]
- appearance of a specifically feminine language (of a literary, reflective, or protest language that speaks about women in the first person, on the one hand, and, on the other, in the system of singularities and differences that sets women against the world of men, or rather situates them in that world, but as distinct from it and challenging it).[20]

Woman is the appendage of man but is, however, distinct from him; she challenges him; she is defined as his complement.

2. By the transformation of the relations between law and sexuality[121]   [14]

A little known phenomenon, a bit secret, because it has been overlaid by another, more recent and more striking phenomenon, which is the importance taken by the consciousness and the formulation of sexuality.

In fact, toward the end of the eighteenth century—exactly at the birth of the Civil Code—at a time when the rights of the family are being progressively limited, we see the emergence of

---

1 Underlined in the manuscript.

a definition and legislation of marriage and kinship in which sexuality plays a very low-key role.

    a. European customary and canonical law actually gave a very extensive definition of the family. For example, in the calculation of kinship: counting the number of elements necessary to get back to the common ancestor (on the side of the longest chain). It accorded quite major importance to paternal power (especially in countries of written law, inspired by *patria potestas*[22]). But, at the same time, it gives a definition of marriage especially in relation to its sexual conditions and consequences: whereas Roman Law defined marriage only by *vitae consuetudo, vita consortium,* and *juris communicatio,*[23] canon law orders marriage by reference to procreation:

[15]
- the essence of marriage is consummation (*copula carnalis*)
- impotence as a legal impediment to marriage;
- easy recognition of morganatic marriages outside of authorization;
- fairly extensive definition of incest (seventh canonical degree, which gives fourteenth degree).[m24]

At the same time it becomes indissoluble. A sacralization of sexuality, but defined on the basis of its consequences in procreation.

    b. Now, in comparison with this legislation, the Civil Code appears very low-key with regard to sexuality.

- Portalis gave this definition of marriage: "the society of man and woman who join together to perpetuate their species, to help each other through mutual assistance in bearing the burdens of life and to share their common destiny."[25]

---

m All these dashes are linked by a bracket added in the margin with the following note: "From the tenth century it was the Church that legislated on marriage, celebrated and registered them, and judged matrimonial cases."

— Now, even the perpetuation of the species disappears in favor of the contractual notion. Planiol gave this definition of marriage: "a contract by which man and woman establish a union sanctioned by the law and that cannot be broken at will."[26] Beudant: "the convention by which two persons of different sex unite their destiny for life as spouses."[27]

Sexuality plays no more than a de facto role: [. . .]ⁿ   [16]

- on the side of marriage: impotence is no longer an impediment; marriages *in articulo mortis* or posthumous;[28] [the consequences of marriage: cohabitation, fidelity, assistance (providing what is needed to live), support°[29]].
- on the side of divorce: in 1803 and 1884, the determinant causes of divorce were: adultery, excess or ill treatment; serious offense (nonconsummation of marriage); criminal conviction.[30]

Sexuality ceased to have a positive role in marriage, which had now become a contract between two persons. The desacralization and desexualization of marriage have gone together in Western culture. And by making this transformed marriage a contract, the Civil Code, far from liberating sexuality, rather effaced it and erased it from the institutions. There is a de-institutionalization of sexuality that has entailed a profound modification in Western consciousness: the awareness of sexuality. Sade is the contemporary of the Civil Code.[31]

*3. By the emergence of a problematic consciousness of sexuality*ᵖ   [17]

As if freed by its deinstitutionalization, sexuality becomes a sort of floating theme, such as has never been produced in any other civilization. A cultural theme that appears:

---

n Foucault adds here: "man and woman."

o Passage inserted *a posteriori*.

p Underlined in the manuscript.

a. In the philosophy of nature, where the opposition of the sexes is defined as an interplay of subjectivity and objectivity (see Hegel[32]).

Woman is[q] externalized subjectivity: both his desire manifested[r] (the innermost truth of man is in the woman he loves) and an irreducible objectivity (for woman is[s] the object of desire, the other world, memory, time), but becomes[t] subjectivity (in the form of caprice, feeling, the heart). This externalized subjectivity, this objectivity become internal, these are what are present in the home, in that hollow warmth.

[18]   In that home where man and woman join together and in which they find their destiny. Since from their union children are born, in which the parents' truth become objective is found. Truth that completes them: in the double sense that they kill them (the becoming of children is the death of the parents) and they fulfill them (for the children only ever survive in and from the parents' death). The history that, at the same time, hollows us out and burdens us refers what we are to the whole of the past and reveals us in an irreducible positivity, places us there where we are, is indeed the history in which our parents are dead.

A whole anthropology of sexuality.[33]

b. In the emergence of an everyday, troubled consciousness of sexuality. Freed from the institutions, it will become the privileged site of subjective moral values: of private morality. And since it is desacralized, it will be at the same time what may be

---

q Passage crossed out: "the object of man. But object that is entirely constituted by its subjectivity. Such that she is . . ."

r Read: "to the man."

s Another passage crossed out: "memory, is faithfulness), she is also his future but become object because . . ."

t Replaces "entered into the subjectivity of the man."

constantly talked about. It will be found, therefore, exactly at the surface of contact of the private world of prohibitions (it is therefore cut out to be doubly hidden) and of the public world of the profane. It has become *the*[u] scandal.[34]

- It has become private: all the extralegal constraints, all the unwritten laws, all the usages and traditions press down on it. It is the Sin of a secular civilization.
- But, at the same time, it is still publicized: it becomes the incessant object of everyday literature (comedy, novel). But publicized only in what is bearable in it, that is to say its normal interiority, never externalized (the unmarried couple, mistresses, the lover). Homosexuality, incest, on the other hand, are always excluded from this permanent scandal. [19]

c. In the emergence of the values of challenging sexuality. To the extent that sexuality appears bound up with the concrete forms of a morality, a society, and a culture, the denunciation of this sexuality, the transgression of its most fundamental prohibitions, the bringing to light of the deep scandal of its little scandals—all of this is linked to the critique of society, its values, and its ways of thinking.

And it is in this way that we see, as an integral part of the modernity of our culture, the deployment of a whole questioning language whose theme—both for subject and object—is sexuality. It is what one talks about, but it is sexuality itself that speaks— and it does not speak of happiness, or love, or even pleasures, but of misfortune, suffering, abjection, death, and profanation.

In this sense, Sade appears at the threshold of modernity, as the one who sought out all its negative powers. Freeing the language of sexuality absolutely, letting it and it alone speak. [20]

---

u Underlined in the manuscript.

Saying everything without the slightest reserve. Linking sexuality to all the profanations (incest, homosexuality). Discovering its relationship with death and murder. Attaching it, in short, to the transgression of all morality, every traditional form of thought, all religion, and every society.

Sade had already said what the others were able to say after him.[35]

At any rate, his contemporaneousness with Napoleon, the fact that the Civil Code is written at the same time, in the same ink as *The 120 Days*, no doubt defines quite well what modern sexuality is.

- At the same time what is most private in man—the site of his most basic individuality, the innermost recess of his consciousness, that which is inaccessible to language—and then that on which prohibitions, traditions, and the [most] fundamental laws bear down.

- And this sexuality that is, that ought to be, the site of positive happiness, the point by which man finds in himself the community with other men, the means by which, through the formation of the couple, he joins the whole of humanity; this sexuality is also that which profanes and challenges all that positivity that should be happy.

[21]   It is in this sense that sexuality is the central site of the collapse [of] all morality, the only form of the tragic of which modern man is capable, the ruined temple in which the gods who have been dead for a long time and the profaners who no longer believe in them forever confront each other.

Hence the importance of psychoanalysis. Its sovereign and ambiguous place:

- Since it has shown that this private thing lodged in consciousness was the most unconscious, most collective thing, and that it could only emerge in the dialogue with a strange, anonymous, and faceless doctor.

- That this, at the same time, deadly, challenging thing was, in the most dangerous way, an integral part of the positive values of the family.

In this sense, it has been *the* scandal, but at the same time it has brought out, as a promised utopia, the very thing in which modern man cannot believe and cannot not believe, that there must indeed be a world and a form of existence in which sexuality is happy and reconciled.[36]

*

1. This idea that "at all times as in all places . . . man is defined by having his sexual behaviour subject to rules and precise restrictions" (Georges Bataille, *Erotism. Death and Sensuality*, trans. Mary Dalwood [San Francisco: City Lights, 1986], 50), but that, on the other hand, sexuality and these prohibitions themselves imply their transgression, that human sexual activity is "in essence a transgression" (108), is at the heart of Bataille's reflections on eroticism, which are an essential background for Foucault in this course. It should also be related to the works of Claude Lévi-Strauss in *The Elementary Structures of Kinship*, ed. James Harle Bell, John Richard von Sturmer, and Rodney Needham (Boston: Beacon Press, 1969). Foucault returns to this relationship between rules and transgression in sexuality in the third lecture (see below, pp. 68–72).

2. Foucault is referring here, on the one hand, to the results of psychoanalysis, to which he will return later (see below, lectures 4 and 5), which show the extent to which sexuality goes beyond sexual practices strictly speaking, and, on the other hand, to the research of anthropologists like Bronislaw Malinowski, Ruth Benedict, and especially Margaret Mead, whose works have stressed the importance of cultural factors that include what are apparently the most biological, such as the sexualization of bodies and the stages of sexual development. See notably Margaret Mead's *Sex and Temperament in Three Primitive Societies* (New York: HarperCollins, 2001 [1935]) and *Coming of Age in Samoa* (New York: HarperCollins, 2001 [1928]), or *Male and Female: A Study of Sexes in a Changing World* (New York: HarperCollins, 2001 [1948]). Despite saying that in this course he will deal with "psycho-sociology" and "intercultural divergences" in sexual matters, Foucault does not return to this.

3. In this period Foucault regularly formulated his analyses through the notions of "culture" or "cultural forms," sometimes connecting them with cultural anthropology; see, for example, the second part, "Madness and Culture," in *Mental Illness and Psychology*, trans. Alan Sheridan (New York: Harper & Row, 1976), notably 60–61. This is the case in particular for his historical analyses of madness, in which the episode of the "great confinement" is presented as "of great significance for what it means to do the history of a culture" (in the third of five transmissions on France Culture that Foucault devoted to the languages of madness, "Le silence des fous" [1963], in M. Foucault, *La Grande Étrangère: À propos de littérature*, ed. Philippe Artières [Paris: Éd. de l'EHESS, 2013], 36). This episode appears in fact as a complete restructuring of the relationships between Western culture and madness. This is also the case for "psychology," which is described less as a science than as a "cultural form" ("Philosophy and Psychology" [1965], in *EW*, 1, 249). The course at Clermont-Ferrand is in line with this project, which aims to account for the emergence of a cultural theme as apparently universal as sexuality, and above all for its formation as a possible object of knowledge. Foucault's initial project for his doctoral thesis bore precisely on the problem of culture in contemporary psychology (Didier Eribon, *Michel Foucault*, 3rd ed. [Paris: Flammarion, 2011 (1989)], 73). However, as far as we know, this is the first time Foucault tries to describe more clearly what he understands by "culture"; this effort will be extended in his course in Tunis in 1966–1967 on the way the idea of man appeared and functions in Western culture, a course in which Foucault tries to circumscribe in time and space the "entirely singular cultural form" that appeared at the end of the eighteenth century and that he characterizes as "Western culture" (BNF, Box 58). For more details on the notion of "cultural form," see below, "Course Context," pp. 302–305.

4. Foucault will return to the problem of the division of goods and of the family structure in Western societies in the Vincennes course (see below, p. 142 *et seq.*).

5. This fact is given by Jean Daric, for example, who notes: "For half a century the proportion of women has hardly changed. . . . In all nonagricultural activities we find roughly one woman for two men" ("Le travail des femmes: Professions, métiers, situations sociales et salaires," in *Population* 10, no. 4 [1955]: 677). The proportion of women in employment was thus 33 percent in 1957. See also Jean-Eugène Havel, *La Condition*

de la femme (Paris: Armand Colin, 1961), 101, and Simone de Beauvoir, *The Second Sex*, trans. Constance Borde and Sheila Malovany-Chevallier (New York: Vintage, 2011), who noted that the proportion of active women among those of working age was 42 percent in 1906, as in the middle of the twentieth century.

6. This right is not explicitly present in the Code but is deduced by lawyers from the general principle of the husband's authority over his spouse's person. In particular, the husband had the right to control his wife's relationships and correspondence; see Gabriel Lepointe, "La femme au XIXᵉ siècle en France et dans le monde occidental," in Société Jean Bodin pour l'histoire comparative des institutions, *La Femme: 2e partie* (Brussels: Librairie encyclopédique, 1962), 506.

7. This is article 214 of the Civil Code: "The wife is obliged to live with the husband and to follow him wherever he judges it right to reside."

8. A position that is found again notably in articles 215: "The wife cannot go to law without her husband's authorization" and 217 of the Civil Code: "The wife . . . cannot give, dispose of, mortgage, acquire . . . without her husband's participation in the act, or his written consent." Article 1124 includes, moreover, "married women" among those "unable to enter into contracts."

9. In 1958 women nevertheless represented 45.5 percent of industrial workers in the Soviet Union. See Havel, *La Condition de la femme*, 98.

10. On the evolution of Soviet legislation on these questions, see, for example, Havel, *La Condition de la femme*, 188–92: after a phase tending to reduce marriage to a simple cohabitation without much legal formality and, consequently, making divorce easier, the end of the 1930s and the 1940s saw a strong restriction of the conditions for divorce.

11. Havel, *La Condition de la femme*, 85–88, nonetheless describes women's participation in assemblies and political bodies as being much greater in the Soviet Union than in Western countries.

12. This reading can be compared with Simone de Beauvoir's analysis: "These old patriarchal constraints are exactly the ones the USSR has brought back to life today; it has revived paternalistic theories about marriage; and in doing so, it has asked woman to become an erotic object again . . . [it is] impossible . . . to consider the woman as a solely productive force: for man she is a sexual partner, a reproducer, an erotic object, an Other through whom he seeks himself. Although totalitarian and authoritarian regimes

may all try to ban psychoanalysis and declare that personal emotional conflicts have no place for citizens loyally integrated into the community, eroticism is an experience where individuality always prevails over generality" (*The Second Sex*, 67). But where de Beauvoir founds this necessity on an existentialist anthropology of eroticism, which stresses the "singular situation" of women and an "existential infrastructure," Foucault emphasizes much more the common sociocultural structure underlying diverse political regimes.

13. On these different "compensatory mechanisms" in the Middle Ages, see de Beauvoir's analysis of courtly love (*The Second Sex*, 108–9), which notes, for example: "What is sure is that faced with Eve the sinner, the Church comes to glorify the Mother of the Redeemer: she has such a large following that in the thirteenth century it can be said that God was made woman; a mysticism of woman thus develops in religion." On the other hand, regarding courtly love strictly speaking: "as the feudal husband was both a guardian and a tyrant, the wife sought a lover outside of marriage; courtly love was a compensation for the barbarity of official customs." On courtly love, see also Jacques Lafitte-Houssat, *Troubadours et Cours d'amour* (Paris: PUF, 1950).

14. See the part titled "Myths" in *The Second Sex*, 181–83, where Beauvoir reviews the different myths of woman, "associated with religion and venerated as priestess" but also "devoted to magic" and "regarded as a sorceress"; "the man captivated by her spell loses his will, his project, his future." Similarly, "the Mother dooms her son to death in giving him life; the woman lover draws her lover into relinquishing life and giving himself up to the supreme sleep."

15. Foucault is referring in particular here to Auguste Comte, *Système de politique positive, ou Traité de sociologie, instituant la religion de l'humanité*, vol. 2 (Osnabruck, Germany: O. Zeller, 1967 [1851]), especially 64–65. Women are described here as "superior by love, better disposed to always subordinate intelligence and the universal to feeling" and, in so doing, dedicated to "keeping alive the direct and continuous cultivation of universal affection, in the midst of theoretical and practical tendencies that ceaselessly divert us from it." Women are presented as a "moral garden," composed of "three natural types: mother, wife, and daughter" articulating the "three elementary modes of solidarity, obedience, union, and protection" and the "three modes

of continuity, by binding us to the past, present, and future." The image of the Mother-Virgin refers to the utopia of the Virgin Mother set out by Comte in volume IV of the *Système de politique positive* (Paris: Carilian-Goeury et V. Dalmont, 1854). It aims to "systematize human procreation, making it exclusively feminine" (273), so that women procreate without the contribution of men. Foucault put together a dossier on this theme, titled "Comte. La femme" (BNF, Box 45-C2), on the basis particularly of volumes 2 and 4 of the *Système de politique positive*. He will use this dossier for the Vincennes course, in which he will return to the analyses of Comte from the point of view of the sexual utopia (see below, lecture 7). The other socialist utopias which Foucault touches on doubtless refer to the texts of Fourier, Cabet (which Foucault will return to also in the Vincennes course, see below, lecture 7), but also to the reflections of Saint-Simon, Leroux, Carnot, Flora Tristan, and many others in the years 1830–1850. See also Beauvoir, *The Second Sex*, 130–32, which briefly reviews these works.

16. On this point, see Jean Hémard, "Le statut de la femme en Europe occidentale au XXᵉ siècle," in Société Jean Bodin, *La Femme*, 515–76, which provides the history of the gaining of these rights, from Sweden in 1863 to France in 1944; see also the UNESCO report by Maurice Duverger, *The Political Role of Women* (Paris: UNESCO, 1955), which nevertheless posits the general finding that the participation of women in political assemblies and government is very weak in all countries (in France, in 1951, only 3.5 percent of members of the National Assembly were women) and judges that the situation was even tending to become worse.

17. See Hémard, "Le statut de la femme," 519–26, which describes the historical movement of women's entry into the civil service (general access was recognized in France in 1946), the judiciary (in 1946), and the legal profession (from 1900), and 569–70 for entry to various other professions.

18. This is particularly the case for Protestants. The debate on the general principle of women's access to religious offices is explicitly raised from the 1950s and, in the French Reformed Church, precisely from 1964. Two years later, this results in the de facto recognition that woman may be called to be a minister in the church in the same way as men.

19. Among the many illustrations of this literature to which psycho-analysis has made ample contributions, see Helene Deutsch, *The Psychology of Women: A Psychoanalytic Interpretation*, 2 vols. (Boston: Allyn & Bacon,

1943, 1945); Marie Bonaparte, *Female Sexuality* (Madison, CT: International Universities Press, 1956); and especially Janine Chasseguet-Smirgel, ed., *La Sexualité féminine: Recherches psychanalytiques nouvelles* (Paris: Payot, 1964), which reviews this question.

20. See Beauvoir, *The Second Sex*, and Hélène Nahas, *La Femme dans la littérature existentielle* (Paris: PUF, 1957). In a different style, Frederick Jakobus Johannes Buytendijk's *La Femme, ses modes d'être, de paraître, d'exister, essai de psychologie existentielle*, trans. A. de Waelhens and R. Micha, with a preface by S. Nouvion (Paris: Desclée de Brouwer, 1954), perfectly illustrates an existentialist and phenomenological way of contrasting two ways of being-in-the-world: being-man (marked by work, the knowledge and transformation of nature, the project) and being-woman (marked by caring and looking after others), an analysis that extends Comtean or Hegelian themes.

21. Foucault will take up this analysis of the relations between law and sexuality in the Vincennes course (see below, lecture 4), going into more detail on Christian marriage and its developments and then on the revolutionary period and the transition to the Civil Code. He clearly modifies the analysis put forward here, which is still caught within the interpretation of marriage as a contract advanced by Marcel Planiol, who is Foucault's main source in this course. Planiol's position should be situated in the debates at the beginning of the twentieth century, in connection with the introduction of divorce by mutual consent, which set partisans of the marriage contract against those who challenged its assimilation to a contract. For more details, see below, lecture 4, note 35, pp. 204.

22. Traditionally, lands of written law, that is to say the French Midi, dominated by the influence of Roman law, are contrasted with the lands of customary law, in the north of France, where the influence of Roman law gives way to a multiplicity of regional customs. The importance of paternal power, inherited from the Roman *patria potestas*, in the lands of written law is usually emphasized by jurists who reflect on marriage, from André-Jean-Simon Nougarède de Fayet, *Histoire des lois sur le mariage et sur le divorce depuis leur origine dans le droit civil et coutumier jusqu'à la fin du XVIIIe siècle* (Paris: Le Normant, 1803), préface, 1:xii–xiii (BNF, Box 39-C2), to Marcel Planiol, *Traité élémentaire de droit civil conforme au programme officiel*, 2nd ed. (Paris: F. Pichon, 1903), vol. 3.

23. See Planiol, *Traité élémentaire* 2: "*Individua vitae consuetudo, consortium omnis vitae, divini atqua humani juris communicatio*"; marriage is described as a joint bond for life, a fully shared life, and a union of divine and human law. These are classical expressions of Roman law for defining marriage and to distinguish it from simple cohabitation.

24. Foucault follows Planiol here: *Traité élémentaire*, 5–7, 11 (on impotence), 14 (on incest).

25. Jean-Étienne-Marie Portalis, quoted in Planiol, *Traité élémentaire*, 3. The exact quotation is "the society of man and woman, who join together to perpetuate their species; to help each other through mutual assistance; to bear the burdens of life, and to share their common destiny," in Pierre-Antoine Fenet, *Receuil complet des travaux préparatoires du Code civil*, vol. 9, "Exposé des motifs du projet de loi sur le mariage par le conseiller d'État Portalis, Corps législatif, 7 mars 1801" (Paris: Marchand du Breuil, 1827), 140.

26. Planiol, *Traité élémentaire*, 3.

27. Charles Beudant, *Cours de droit civil français: L'État et la capacité des personnes* (Paris: A. Rousseau, 1896–1897), 1:293, quoted in Planiol, *Traité élémentaire*, 3.

28. See Planiol, *Traité élémentaire*, 5, who notes as well that up until the Revolution, "one hesitated to accept the validity of marriages contracted '*in extremis momentis*,' that is to say, at a moment at which it is certain that consummation can no longer take place."

29. These different effects of marriage are examined by Planiol, *Traité élémentaire*, 67–76.

30. The table of the different grounds for divorce according to legislation is drawn up by Planiol, *Traité élémentaire*, 162, and the different grounds themselves are examined on 165–73. The "voluntary and persistent refusal . . . to consummate the marriage" actually figures among the serious "offensive deeds" justifying divorce (170).

31. Playing on the contemporaneousness of Donatien Alphonse François de Sade and a set of transformations essential to modernity was a fashionable *topos* of the time. Since Pierre Klossowski, Georges Bataille, and Maurice Blanchot, the contemporaneousness of Sade and the Revolution has been stressed (through, notably, the episode of the storming of the Bastille, from which, according to myth, Sade was supposed to have exhorted the people to attack); since Theodor Adorno and especially

Jacques Lacan, the contemporaneousness and closeness of Sade and Kant has been stressed, establishing a parallel between the Kantian categorical imperative and the principle of absolute pleasure in Sade. See Éric Marty, *Pourquoi le XXᵉ siècle a-t-il pris Sade au sérieux?* *Essai* (Paris: Seuil, 2011) for a presentation of these various *rapprochements*. Foucault particularly enjoys this linking game, Sade often serves as a cover name for illustrating what is excluded, the experience of the outside (and sometimes also, consequently, the deep truth) of various founding divisions of modern experience. For more detail on the relations Foucault establishes between Sade and Bichat, Chateaubriand, Kant, and so on, see "Course Context," pp. 315–317. This parallel between Sade and the Civil Code and the reference to Sade in connection with the emergence of a "problematic consciousness," of a discursive knowledge (*savoir*) and at the same transgressive language on sexuality from the beginning of the nineteenth century, will be repeated at a number of points in the course (see below, pp. 31 and 85).

32. See in particular G. W. F. Hegel, *The Phenomenology of Mind*, trans. J. B. Baillie (London: George Allen and Unwin, 1949), 474–78; *Philosophy of Nature: Encyclopedia of the Philosophical Sciences, Part Two*, trans. A. V. Miller (Oxford: Oxford University Press, 1970), 285–303; and *Elements of the Philosophy of Right*, trans. Allen W. Wood (Cambridge: Cambridge University Press, 1991) § 158 *et seq.* The principle that "love, as immediate knowledge of self in the other, finds its unity only in a third term, the child," but [that] the child's coming into being is "the death of the parents" is regularly expressed by Hegel in his philosophy of the family and marriage. [The quotation is from a note in the French translation, *Phénoménologie de l'esprit*, trans. J. Hyppolite (Paris: Aubier, 1941), 2:24n28. The corresponding page in the English translation is 475. —G.B.]

33. This "anthropology of sexuality" was very much alive, in varied forms, when Foucault was giving his course. It is especially marked in the special issue of *Esprit* in 1960 devoted to sexuality and to the "difficulties which make man's existence as sexed existence *problematic*," with an introduction by Paul Ricoeur, "La merveille, l'errance, l'énigme," *Esprit* 28, no. 289 (1960): 1665 (emphasis in the original), which, against the "loss of meaning" and "fall into insignificance" of contemporary eroticism, strives to promote a human conception of sexuality founded on an intersubjective ethics, the interpersonal relationship, and affection (*tendresse*). But this "anthropology

of sexuality" is also found, in 1964, in Abel Jeannière's *Anthropologie sexuelle* (Paris: Aubier-Montaigne, 1964), which came out of a course given at the Institut catholique de Paris and which forms a strange double of Foucault's course. The Clermont-Ferrand course is entirely directed against this anthropology of sexuality, to the double benefit of an archaeology that questions the conditions of emergence and historical contingency of sexuality as an anthropological theme and of an eroticism of transgression inspired by Bataille (see "Course Context," pp. 309–315).

34. Ricoeur also emphasizes the desacralization of sexuality, which integrates it into the order of marriage and of ethical and social constraints; but at the same time sexuality always overflows these constraints: "that is why *putting marriage on trial* is always a possible, useful, legitimate, urgent task . . .; every ethic of constraint engenders bad faith and deception; that is why literature has an irreplaceable function of scandal; for scandal is the scourge of deception" (Ricoeur, "La merveille, l'errance, l'énigme," 1670, emphasis in the original). But we should not confuse these little scandals of light comedies with what Foucault goes on to call the "bringing to light of the deep scandal [of the] little scandals" and the absolutely profaning literature of a Sade or, later, of a Pierre Guyotat (see the private letter from Foucault to Guyotat, published in 1970 in *Le Nouvel Observateur*, "There will be scandal, but . . .", in *DÈ*, I, no. 79, 942–43). Little scandals should be distinguished from the "scandal" in the sense of George Bataille or Maurice Blanchot, which rests on the radical transgression of limits.

35. This analysis should be placed alongside a set of other texts and interventions that, following analyses by Pierre Klossowski, Georges Bataille, and Maurice Blanchot, Foucault devoted to Sade in 1963–1964. See in particular "Préface à la transgression (en hommage à Georges Bataille)," which appeared in *Critique* in 1963, *DE*, I, no. 13, 261–78; "A Preface to Transgression," trans. Donald F. Bouchard and Sherry Simon, *EW*, 2, 69–87, where Foucault stresses how what characterizes the experience of "modern sexuality from Sade to Freud is not its having found the language of its logic or of its nature, but, rather, through the violence of their discourses, having been 'denatured' . . ., carried to its limit" (261; Eng., 69). In the sense that it has been associated with a whole series of limits (of consciousness, law, language) and with the transgression of these limits, "it has become the only division possible in a world now emptied of objects, beings, and spaces

to desecrate . . . it permits a profanation without object. . . . Profanation in a world that no longer recognizes any positive meaning in the sacred—is this not . . . what we may call transgression?" (70). Sexuality, as the fundamental site of transgression, is thus immediately associated by Foucault with the death of God and to that tragic form of experience which, "denying us the limit of the Limitless . . . discloses as its own secret and clarification, its intrinsic finitude, the limitless reign of the Limit" (71). At this time, then, sexuality, along with the experience of death and madness (to which it is intimately linked, particularly in Sade), appears to Foucault as one of the privileged points of the relationship of transgression and limit. This is what for him characterizes "eroticism" in Bataille's sense: "an experience of sexuality which links, for its own ends, an overcoming of limits to the death of God" (72). In this framework, Sade becomes fundamental, since he is the first to link sexuality explicitly to the death of God and to a form of profanation without object, which aims always to transgress the limit. "From the moment that Sade delivered its first words and marked out, in a single discourse, the boundaries of what suddenly became its kingdom, the language of sexuality has lifted us into the night where God is absent, and where all of our actions are addressed to this absence in a profanation that at once identifies it, dissipates it, exhausts itself in it, and restores it to the empty purity of its transgression" (70). It is this dimension of indefinite profanation without object that justifies Foucault's erecting Sade as the "very paradigm of literature," inasmuch as Foucault, in the same period, considers literature to have emerged at the end of the eighteenth century as a particular relationship to language, which pushes language to the limit, profanes it, and transgresses it: "Sade was the first to articulate . . . the speech of transgression; . . . his work is the point that at once gathers and makes possible all speech of transgression" (*La Grande Étrangere*, 86). This reading of Sade should be compared with those given by Klossowski, *Sade, My Neighbor*, trans. Alphonso Lingis (Evanston, IL: Northwestern University Press, 1991), and ᶜspecially Bataille, in particular *Erotism: Death and Sensuality*, trans. Mary Dalwood (San Francisco: City Lights, 1986), and Blanchot, in particular, *Lautréamont and Sade*, trans. Michelle Kendall and Stuart Kendall (Stanford, CA: Stanford University Press, 2004). On this subject, see Marty, *Pourquoi le XXe siècle a-t-il pris Sade au sérieux?* and, for a reading on the relations between Foucault and Sade at the time, see Philippe

Sabot, "Foucault, Sade et les Lumières," *Lumières*, no. 8 (2006): 141–55. The reference to Sade recurs at a number of points in this course (see below, lecture 4, p. 85), and it will be deployed differently in the Vincennes course (see below, lectures 1 and 7). The relationship of the modern experience of sexuality to the "death of God" and to "the only form of the tragic of which modern man is capable" will be developed at greater length in lecture 5 of this course (see below, pp. 121–123).

36. Foucault will return frequently to the place of psychoanalysis—here in relation to the human sciences—in the following lectures. The Vincennes course, in the last lecture, will be concerned more precisely with the theme Foucault evokes here of belief in a form of existence in which sexuality is happy and reconciled, studying the relationship of a certain Freudo-Marxism (that of Wilhelm Reich and Herbert Marcuse) with sexual utopias. We recall that if the theme of the "sexual revolution" only fully asserts itself in France from 1966 (as testify the simultaneous publication of the issue of the review *Partisans*, no. 32–33, devoted to "Sexualité et repression," and some works of Reich by Maspero, edited by Jean-Marie Brohm, *La Lutte sexuelle des jeunes*) it was in the air from the beginning of the 1960s. The issue of *Esprit* of 1960 that has already been referred to, for example, looks at the question of the alienation of sexuality, the demands for a sexual liberation of the young, and the role of psychoanalysis in this popularization of sexuality. Marcuse's seminal work, *Eros and Civilization*, was published in French in 1963.

LECTURE 2

The Scientific Knowledge of Sexuality

*M*odern European specificity of a science of sexuality. Its central place in the human sciences: privileged site of intrication of the psychological and the physiological as well as of the individual and the social. Sexuality occupies the place of the contract and imagination in the classical age, and of religion and sensation in the nineteenth century. This explains why psychoanalysis is the key to the human sciences. Three domains of the human sciences of sexuality: a. psychophysiology; b. psychopathology; c. psychosociology. Sexuality is a negative object here, apprehended in its deviations, except in psychophysiology. 1. The psychophysiology of sexuality: A. Brief history of the biology of sexuality. B. The different modes of sexuality: sexuality is one mode of reproduction among others; the distinction of the sexes is itself complex variable and exists at multiple levels in nature. C. The determinants of sexuality: 1. Hormones: history of their discovery and characterization. 2. Genetic sex: theories of the genetic determination of the sexes. The notion of "sex" refers to two distinct notions (genetic and genital) and brings into play a complex interplay of determinations and differentiations.

Modern European culture is no doubt the only one to have [22] constructed a science of sexuality—that is, to have made the *man/woman*ᵃ relationship an object not only of literature, epic, mythology, and religion, but also of discursive knowledge (*savoir discursif*). Knowledge that has sometimes taken precise institutional forms (M. Hirschfeld, *Institut für Sexualwissenschaft*ᵇ¹) and that, despite or maybe because of its dispersion, occupies an increasingly extensive space in the domain of the human sciences.

This decisive place of sexuality in the human sciences is probably due to several things:[2]

- Firstly, the fact that it is a privileged site of the intrication of the psychological and the physiological. In one sense, sexuality is certainly determined by anatomy and physiology, and, at the same time, it is a set of psychological conducts:

{ – men and women;
  – masculine and feminine.

[23] For Descartes and Spinoza, the fact that we have a soul and a body was established by the fact that we were able to imagine; from Condillac to Helmholtz or Wundt, it was established by the fact that we had sensations; since Krafft-Ebing and Freud, by the fact that we have a sexuality.[3]

- Then, the fact that it is a privileged site of the intrication of the social and the individual.

Nothing is more individual than sexuality since there is choice of partner (and possibility of refusal) [and] since everywhere (save some ritual exceptions) sexual practices are always private and hidden.

And yet nothing is more social than sexuality:

– marriage rules

– rulesofsexualpractice.Strictsanctionsagainsteverything that transgresses.

---

a Underlined in the manuscript.

b Michel Foucault writes in error: "*Sexualforschung.*"

In the seventeenth and eighteenth [centuries], the contract declared the fact that man is both an individual and a social being; in the nineteenth, it was established by the fact that he belonged to a higher organic totality, which was expressed (in an imaginary, mythical, perfect form) in the existence of a religion. From Comte to Durkheim, social man was par excellence the religious man.[4]

So, in our epoch sexuality performs the roles taken by the contract and imagination in the classical age; sensation and the religious bond in the nineteenth century. That man is both singular and collective, physiologically determined and the subject of psychological behavior, is manifested above all in his sexuality. [24]

He owes to sexuality what he is, what he shows of himself, and what constitutes him as an object for scientific discourse. In modern culture, man has become an object of science because he has found himself to be both subject to and subject of his sexuality. That is why psychoanalysis, as the discovery of sexuality at the heart of man's normal and abnormal conduct, is the key to all the modern human sciences.[5] The historical origin and foundation of the human sciences is usually traced back to Weber's and Fechner's laws on the relations between sensation and excitation.[6] In fact, if something like the human sciences is possible in our time, this is due to a series of events, all of which concern sexuality. These are the events that took place between 1790, when Sade, confined in the Bastille, wrote *The 120 Days*, and 1890, when Freud discovered the sexual explanation of hysteria.[7] [25]

The discovery of sexuality made possible the human sciences as they exist today—which does not mean that they are all reduced to the study of sexuality, or that the latter has confiscated them all. In fact, the study of sexuality, if related to all the human sciences, is nonetheless fairly precisely located.

    a. In psychophysiology: the study of the sexual and hormonal induction of behavior.

b. In psychopathology: the study either of deviations of sexual behavior in relation to the norms of our society and culture, or of the relationships between sexuality and those behavioral deviations that we call psychosis, neurosis, criminality, or asocial behavior.

[26]   c. Finally, in psychosociology: the study of the forms of integration, normalization, valorization, and repression of sexual conduct in cultures other than our own.

These are the three fields of study that, in different proportions, will have to concern us. In any case, we need straightaway to note that these studies concern:

- either psychophysiological determinations or correlations;
- or intracultural deviations;
- or intercultural dispersions and divergences.

In other words, there is positivity only on the side of the physiological. For the rest, one can only study abnormalities or differences. Therefore *deviance*:[c] there is no psychology of normal love—but of morbid jealousy, homosexuality, fetishism. Psychology may be a positive science, but it is a positive science of negativities.[8]

[27]   ## ELEMENTS OF PSYCHOPHYSIOLOGY

A. Historical

1. The existence of male and female plants was observed right at the start of the sixteenth century. Pontanus made the discovery in 1505 on palm trees.[9] Then it was noticed that the same plant could have male or female organs. Finally, at the end of the

---

c Underlined in the manuscript.

sixteenth century, Cesalpino noted that some hemp plants were sterile and others became fertile if placed alongside the former. At the end of the seventeenth century, Camerarius (*De Sexu plantarum epistola*) did the first experiments on the artificial fertilization of plants; he identified the male role of the stamens and the feminine role of the pistils.[10] Tournefort and Linnaeus, emphasizing that the most important function of the plant is to reproduce (which is not possible for minerals), proposed classification by flowers and fruit (T[ournefort]), by stamens and pistils (L[innaeus]).[11]

2. For animal sexuality, the problem was obviously not one of discovering the existence of male and female, but of establishing their exact roles.

- Theory of the double seed, still found in Descartes (two   [28] seeds that mix and serve each other as leaven).[12]

- Ovism. Sténon in 1667 put forward the hypothesis that female viviparous animals produce eggs, and these eggs are fertilized by the male seed. Hypothesis verified by De Graaf in 1672, then by Van Leeuwenhoek in 1667 (the spermatozoon).[13]

- Hence the problem: epigenesis or preformation?[14] Until the experiments of Spallanzani, who did the first experiment of artificial insemination on toads (the first experiment on a human being was done in 1799 by Hunter).[15] From that point, the physiological study of sexuality takes on its positivity.

B. The different modes of sexuality[16]   [29]

1. Biologically, sexuality is one of the possible modes of reproduction of the living being. There are others:

- Scissiparity: the living being divides into equal parts, which grow and divide anew; there are no parents or descendants.

- Asexual generation: a part of the individual is detached and grows separately without the intervention of another living being (when there is only one cell, it is the spore).

There is sexual generation when the living being produces a cell that is unable to develop on its own; it has to encounter another cell.

2. But this sexual reproduction is not sufficient to divide every animal species into two categories of individuals, male and female. In actual fact, the male-female distinction may concern:

- *Just some cells:*[d] for example, in algae, such as the *Ulothrix:* it produces numerous zoospores, all apparently alike, each with two flagella which enable them to move in the water. At a given moment, two of them come together, merge into a single cell that stops, loses its flagella, and enters into a phase of rest.[17]

[30]   In another alga (*Ectocarpus*),[e] a zoospore fixes itself to the ground by its anterior cilium. It immediately attracts several others, which fix themselves to it. One of them approaches suddenly and merges. The others follow.

["Fertilization in *Ectocarpus siliculosos*" (Carles, *La Sexualité*, 13]

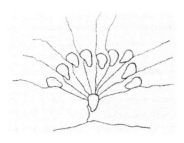

---

d Emphasis added to make the text consistent with the two other points underlined by Foucault.

e Foucault copied on the side an explanatory schema drawn from an illustration in Carles, *La Sexualité*, which we reproduce below.

In some cases, there is a visible difference between male and female cells.[18]

- *The organs:*[f] this is what is found in most plants:
    a. either situated in a single complex organ: there are male and female organs in the flower of the apple;
    b. or situated in a single organ, but self-sterile (so two trees are needed, but each being the male and female of the other; the same for snails).[19]
- *Individuals:*[g] when the individual can only provide the gametes of one sex. This is what is called the primary sex characteristic. Each of the gametes has distinctive features.
    a. the female gamete is *immobile, rich* in nutritious substance (therefore larger), and *fewer;*[h]
    b. the male gamete is mobile, poor in reserves (so generally smaller), and very numerous.[20]   [31]

This must be rectified, moreover, by the [following] phenomena:

1. Relative sexuality: in some algae, we can distinguish individuals that produce strong gametes and others that produce weak gametes. If they are brought together, the latter are always female.[21]

2. Intersexuality—that is, the same individuals have anatomical or physiological equipment that, according to circumstances or after certain modifications, allows them [to adopt] the male or female role.

- Natural [circumstance]. Example: a gastropod mollusk, *Crepidula*, lives in stacks. The oldest form the base of the stack, the youngest the summit. The first are female, the

---

f Underlined in the manuscript.
g Underlined in the manuscript.
h Underlined in the manuscript.

second male; in the middle, they are both. If one takes a young one and isolates it, it becomes female. As the stack ages, they all become female.

There is an annelid that is male when [it] is young (when it comprises less than fifteen segments); it suffices to amputate it regularly for it to remain always male.[22]

[32]   • Artificial [circumstance]:

    a. castration;

    b. hormonal influence.[23]

[33]   *C. The determinants of sexuality*

I. Hormones[24]

History and specification

    a. *Estrogens*[i]

    • The effects of castration were known: alteration of a certain number of organs or organic elements; regression of some others, especially sexual organs (the uterus of the rabbit reduces by half after two or three weeks of regression).[25]

    Galen spoke of an internal force.[26]

    • E. Knauer (1896) shows that on female guinea pigs the atrophy of castration can be compensated for by the graft of fragments of ovaries in various parts of the organism. Therefore, it is not disturbances of vascularization or innervation that cause the atrophy; but that of a product. Hence the idea of a secretion.[27]

---

i Underlined in the manuscript

- J. Halban (1900) shows that on immature guinea pigs, fragments of ovaries provoke the development of the uterus.[28]
- E. Allen (1922) shows that in the mouse, in the period [34] of sexual activity, together with the maturation of follicles on the surface of the ovary we see keratinized cells in the vagina. Now the injection of follicular liquid causes on its own the appearance of keratinized cells. Folliculine (later called estrone):[29]
- Purified by Doisy, studied by Butenandt, this is a derivative of the phenanthrene (cyclopentanohydrophenanthrenic structure). Synthesis by Butenandt, Dodds, Miescher.[30]

b. Likewise, discovery of androgens (the main one of which is testosterone).[31]

c. Discovery of progestogen hormones (which facilitate and protect gestation: they are found especially in the corpus luteum). The most important is progesterone.[32]

d. Discovery of hypophysial hormones. Ablation of the hypophysis in the young individual halts the development of all the sexual organs; in the adult individual, it provokes the degeneration of the sexual apparatus and the disappearance of sexual behavior.

α. Anterior lobe:[j]
- hormones of endocrinal regulation;
- growth hormones;
- hormones of the metabolism;
- hormones of sexuality.

---

j Foucault attaches here the schema copied from an illustration from Carles, *La Sexualité*, which we reproduce here below.

["Schematic sagittal section of the hypophysis of the ape, according to Herring" (Carles, *La Sexualité*, 61)]

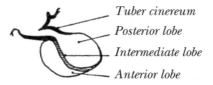

Tuber cinereum
Posterior lobe
Intermediate lobe
Anterior lobe

β. Intermediate: metabolism.[33]

[35]   e. Embryonic hormones. The embryo produces its own hormones:

- since the mother's hormones cannot be determinant;[34]
- since there are phenomena like freemartins;[35]
- since starting from an undifferentiated state there is orientation toward a sex (an orientation that can be reversed).

To sum up, hormones can be defined in the following way: "chemical substances secreted by certain glands which, transported by the blood throughout the organism, can exert a specific action on certain organs, and do so with infinitesimal concentrations."[36] Outside of the organ on which they act, they are harmful to the organism; they are destroyed by the liver or eliminated by the kidney.

[36]   *II. Genetic sex*[37]

Hormones act on the formation, development, functioning, involution, and disappearance of certain organs that have primary or secondary sex characteristics. But what is it that determines that they function and are distributed in such a way that one individual

---

k Foucault writes "*échiuridés*," the accepted term at the time, as "*échiurides*" to describe the echiura group of marine worms.

is male and another female; that, in this difficult equilibrium, the division is made, and in the proportions that we know?

– For a moment, it was thought (this is the epigamic theory[38]) that certain conditions of development could intervene:

Example of a marine worm, the Bonellia, found in the Mediterranean (echiura group).[k] The female is composed of an ovoid body (2–3 cm) and a fallopian tube of one meter. The males, some millimeters long, live within it. The eggs are fertilized passing through; they produce larvae. Some fix themselves to the ground and become females, others fix themselves to females and become males. But it is enough to swap them for the sex to be reversed.[39]

But these environmental conditions cannot explain the statistically equal division. It is probably a matter of relative sexuality.

– We now know that sex is fixed at fertilization: a given individual will be male or female as a result of the gametes that have fused. At the moment of meiosis, when the cells divide, we know that the chromosomes, which duplicate in the cells of our organism, are distributed between each of the two gametes (which live thus in the haploid stage until meeting with another gamete). [37]

Now in some species, when the male cells are divided by meiosis, they do not form two identical gametes; in other species it is the female cells which, in dividing, give rise to two slightly different gametes (male heterogamete—drosophila type—or female—*abraxas* type). It is these differences that found sex difference (with a necessarily equal number of individuals for each of them).[40]

The man is heterogametic in the human species.

The notion of sex corresponds to two distinct notions: [38]

A. Genetic sex:

It is inscribed in the nucleus of every cell of the organism. It is fixed at the moment of fertilization. In the human species, sex is determined by the union of an ovum with a spermatozoon containing an X chromosome. The male sex [by union of an ovum] with a spermatozoon without an X chromosome. This is what is called sex determination.

B. Genital sex:

This is the set of organs and characteristics by which a male organism differs from a female organism.[41] The formation of these organs and sexual characteristics constitutes sexual differentiation. This formation takes place in two stages:

a. During the first month of embryonic life, formation of the glands and of male and female reproductive tracts. *Primary sexual characteristics.*[142]

[39]   b. During the second period (puberty), the organism acquires most of apparent characteristics of the sex to which he/she belongs (that is to say secondary sexual characteristics).[43]

A series of phenomena may occur in the double interplay between determination and differentiation.

• Between determination and first differentiation: in its first stages the embryo has all that will enable it to acquire either sex (it has the preforms of testes and the preforms of ovaries). With the same embryonic elements it may construct one as well as the other sex.

• In the course of differentiation, there are species which pass through a sex which will not be their definitive sex. (Male eels pass through a stage of early feminization: they have ovaries before having testicles).[44]

---

1 Underlined in the manuscript.

- Finally, there are abnormalities which consist in the coexistence of organs and characteristics of both sexes.

*

1. This is the Institute for the Science of Sexuality founded in Berlin in 1919 by Magnus Hirschfeld and Arthur Kronfeld, devoted to research and the diffusion of knowledge about sexuality as well as to marriage guidance and various forms of consultation regarding pathologies linked to sexuality. Active until 1933, it was very harshly repressed by the Nazis.

2. The reflection on sexuality forms part of the broader reflection that Foucault is undertaking at this time on the conditions of emergence and structuration of the human sciences, a reflection that results in the publication of *Les Mots et les Choses: Une archéologie des sciences humaines* (Paris: Gallimard, 1966); English translation, *The Order of Things: An Archaeology of the Human Sciences* (London: Tavistock, 1970). More generally, it is also integrated into the questioning then underway of the status of the human sciences and the place of psychoanalysis at their heart (see below, pp. 31–32 and "Course Context" pp. 308–309). Shortly before Foucault's course, this problem was addressed by Louis Althusser in two lectures within the framework of a seminar on Lacan and psychoanalysis organized at l'École normale supérieur (ENS) in 1963–1964, questioning the place that, in fact and especially in principle, psychoanalysis should occupy in relation to the domain of the human sciences, and to psychology in particular; see L. Althusser, *Psychoanalysis and the Human Sciences*, trans. Steven Rendall (New York: Columbia University Press, 2016). At the end of his second lecture, Althusser examines how psychology is the historically situated by-product of philosophical, moral, or political ideologies that make it possible; within this framework, he refers in turn to theories of error and imagination in René Descartes and Baruch Spinoza, then to sensualist empiricism and the "fundamental problem of sensation," two themes taken up by Foucault further on; see below, p. 31.

3. For Descartes, see, for example, the sixth of the *Meditations*: "when I consider attentively what imagination is, I find that it is nothing other than a certain application of the faculty of knowing to the body which is immediately present to it, and which consequently exists" (René Descartes,

Meditations, in *Discourse on Method and Other Writings*, trans. F. E. Sutcliffe [Harmondsworth, UK: Penguin Books, 1968], 150). The imagination is situated between the senses and access to the external world, on the one hand, and between the understanding and the will, on the other. Similarly, in Spinoza, "knowledge of the first kind . . . or imagination" designates the way the soul knows bodies according to the way, they affect our own body (see in particular, *Ethics*, proposition XVII, scholium). We note that in the years 1952–1955 Foucault devoted a great many reflections to the central place of the imagination in the classical age, presented "as point of arrival, in the body, of nature in its geometrical truth, and as original stratum, in the soul, of its passivity . . . element in which nature is transformed into world" (*Cours sur l'anthropologie*, BNF, Box 46-C1). These reflections form part of his study of the anthropological question at the heart of modern philosophy, as opposed to a classical period dominated by the *mathesis* of nature. Étienne Bonnot de Condillac embodies a radical sensualist position according to which "in the natural order everything comes from sensation," including the "operations of the understanding and the will. Judgement, reflection, desires, passions, etcetera, are only sensation itself which is transformed" (*Treatise on the Sensations*, trans. Geraldine Carr [Los Angeles: University of Southern California Press, 1930], 236, xxxi). Hermann von Helmholtz, *Die Lehre von den Tonempfindungen als physiologische Grundlage für die Theorie der Musik* (Brunswick, Germany: Friedrich Vieweg und Sohn, 1863), and especially Wilhelm M. Wundt, *Beiträge zur Theorie der Sinneswahrnehmung* (Leipzig: C. F. Winter, 1862), among the founders of experimental psychology, deepen the analysis of the way sensations, understood as sensory impressions, are modified in perception and integrated into more complex mental processes—in the case of Wundt, explicitly against a sensualist reductionism. On Krafft-Ebing and Sigmund Freud regarding sexuality, see below, p. 86 *et seq.*

4. See in particular Auguste Comte, *Système de politique positive, ou Traité de sociologie, instituant la religion de l'humanité*, vol. 2 (Osnabruck, Germany: O. Zeller, 1967 [1851]) and Émile Durkheim, *The Elementary Forms of Religious Life*, trans. Carol Cosman (Oxford: Oxford University Press, 2008). From Comte to Durkheim and beyond, religion appears in a holistic perspective, both as the most archaic and the most paradigmatic social bond, and the privileged object of sociology. The references to the

contract obviously echo the various theories of the social contract typical of the end of the seventeenth and the eighteenth century, from Thomas Hobbes and John Locke to Jean-Jacques Rousseau.

5. See note 2, above. Foucault's course takes place in a precise context of the debates of 1963–1964 on the place of psychoanalysis in the human sciences, in connection with the works of Lacan and Althusser (see "Course Context" pp. 308–309). By making psychoanalysis the "key to the human sciences," because it discovers sexuality at the heart of the human condition—a sexuality that the whole course will show is not an intersubjective "human sexuality"—Foucault is clearly taking part in this debate. On the other hand, in contrasting the role of sexuality—from Sade to Freud—in the foundation of the human sciences with the laws of Weber-Fechner (see note 6, below), he also opposes the idea of human sciences reducible to the natural sciences. He situates them rather in a very different project that refers either to a hermeneutics or, in Foucault's case, a semiology that studies the rules, structures, or significations beyond the subject that sexuality takes on. It is useful to compare these analyses with the interview with Alain Badiou, "Philosophy and Psychology," in 1965, *EW*, 2. In this course, sexuality occupies the place that, in the interview, Foucault accords to the discovery of the unconscious: "the simple discovery of the unconscious is not an addition of domains, it is not an extension of psychology, it is actually the appropriation, by psychology [understanding here, psychoanalysis], of most of the domains that the human sciences covered, so one can say that, starting from Freud, all the human sciences became . . . sciences of the psyche" (*EW*, 2, 252). This discovery, Foucault adds, shatters the individual/society division as much as it does the soul/body division. Above all, this psyche is not human consciousness, but the unconscious, itself linked to sexuality seen as "negation of the truth of man". This point was already emphasized by Foucault in 1957, in his analysis of the meaning of the Freudian "scandal": "for the first time in the history of psychology, the negativity of nature was not linked to the positivity of human consciousness, but the latter was denounced as the negative of natural positivity. The scandal [. . . consists] in this, that through psychoanalysis, love, social relations, and forms of interhuman belonging appear as the negative element of sexuality inasmuch as sexuality is the natural positivity of man" ("La recherche scientifique et la psychologie,"1957, in *DÉ*, I, no. 3, 181–82).

6. This is a reference to the discovery by the physiologist Ernst Heinrich Weber in 1834, at the time of his works on the perception of weight, of the existence of a constant ratio between a stimulus of initial intensity I and the intensity ΔI of a second stimulus, for the difference introduced by the latter stimulus to be perceptible. Thus, for this difference to be perceptible, it must reach a certain threshold value ΔI; the relation of this value to the initial stimulus is constant, constituting the constant (k): $\Delta I/I = k$. This equation was established as "Weber's law" by Gustav Fechner, who made it a general principle for describing the relation between sensory excitations and perceptions, a principle according to which "the sensation varies as the logarithm of the excitation." This law is often given as one of the rare laws, expressible in a mathematical form, that is applied to the human sciences, thus seen as an extension of the experimental sciences. It is worth comparing Foucault's position with that of Georges Gusdorf, who also referred critically to the Weber-Fechner laws, given as the origin of the human sciences; see G. Gusdorf, *Introduction aux sciences humaines: Essai critique sur leurs origines et leur développement* (Paris: Belles Lettres, 1960), 16, and especially 402–4. But Gusdorf's criticism is founded on the principles of a humanist phenomenology that denies that "the reality of man in his lived spontaneity conforms to the norms of mathematical formulation" (16), whereas uniting the human sciences to the experience and knowledge of sexuality from Sade to Freud orientates Foucault in an entirely different, clearly anti-humanist direction opposed to the primacy of the subject of phenomenology.

7. The relation established between Freud and Sade, in which Sade appears as a quasi-precursor of Freud, is found in Blanchot, for whom Sade "anticipates (*devance*) Freud" (*Lautréamont and Sade*, trans. Michelle Kendall and Stuart Kendall [Stanford, CA: Stanford University Press, 2004]), 39. Lacan, in his famous "Kant avec Sade," *Critique*, no. 91 (April 1963): 291–313, English translation Bruce Fink, "Kant with Sade," in *Écrits* (New York: Norton, 2007), adopts a position closer to the one taken by Foucault here. If he denounces the "stupidity repeated in works of literary criticism" for which "Sade's work anticipates (*anticipe*) Freud's," he nonetheless affirms that Sade's work is the condition of possibility of Freud's formulation of the pleasure principle: by breaking the bond between pleasure and good, by being the first to assert the theme of "delight in evil,"

"Sade represents . . . the first step of a subversion" which, *in fine*, will make Freud possible. "Here as there, one paves the way for science by rectifying one's ethical position. In this respect, Sade did indeed begin the groundwork that was to progress for a hundred years in the depths of taste in order for Freud's path to be passable"; "Kant with Sade", *Écrits*, 645. In Foucault, it is the relation then established between sexuality and language, the experience of finitude and of the transgression of limits that is involved and in which the line between Sade and Freud can be traced. See "A Preface to Transgression," trans. Donald F. Bouchard and Sherry Simon, *EW*, 2, 69–87.

8. This is a recurring position in Foucault from *Mental Illness and Psychology*, trans. Alan Sheridan (New York: Harper & Row, 1976 [1954]): "It must not be forgotten that "objective," or "positive," or "scientific," psychology found its historical origin and its basis in pathological experience. It was an analysis of duplications that made possible a psychology of the personality . . . an analysis of deficits that led to a psychology of intelligence" (73); through "La psychologie de 1850–1950" [1957]: "Psychology . . . arises at that point where man's practice encounters its own contradiction; the psychology of development arose as a reflection on the delays of development; . . . that of memory, of consciousness, of emotion appeared first of all as a psychology of forgetfulness, of the unconscious, and of affective disturbances. Without stretching things we can say that, in origin, contemporary psychology is an analysis of the abnormal, the pathological, and the conflictual," in *DÉ*, I, no. 2, 149–50; up to "La recherche scientifique et la psychologie" [1957]: "Psychology gets its positivity from man's negative experiences of himself," in *DÉ*, I, no. 3, 181. This position is repeated regularly in this course (see below, lectures 3 and 4, pp. 52–53 and pp. 84–85) and is the basis for Foucault's assertion that the psychological science of sexuality begins with an analysis of perversions. It echoes Canguilhem's analysis in *On the Normal and the Pathological*, trans. Carolyn R. Fawcett (Dordrecht, Netherlands: D. Reidel, 1978).

9. This was the King of Naples' tutor, Giovanni Giovano Pontano or Jovanius Pontanus, who in 1505 wrote a poem, *De Palma Bitontina et Hydruntina*, on the love of two date palms, one male and the other female, the first situated at Brindisi and the second at Otrante, that remained infertile until the moment that, having grown, they caught sight of each other, which enabled fructification (*Eridani duo libri* [Naples: Sigismundum

Mayr, 1505]). Foucault follows closely here the paragraph devoted to the sexuality of plants in chapter 5 on Renaissance botany written by Adrien Davy de Virville, in *Histoire générale des sciences*, vol. II: George Allard et al., *La Science moderne, de 1450 à 1800*, ed. René Taton (Paris: PUF, 1958), 170, from which the references to Andrea Cesalpino are also taken. He returns in much greater detail to the sexuality of plants in the Vincennes course, clearly emphasizing there the break represented by Rudolf Jakob Camerarius (see below, p. 224 *et seq.*).

10. *Ibid.*, chap. 3, "Botanique," 412. On Camerarius, see the Vincennes course, below, lecture 6, p. 232.

11. On the "sexual system" of Carl von Linnaeus, who distributed plants into twenty-four classes according to the stamens and divided them into orders based on the characteristics of either the stamens or the pistils, see Henri Daudin, *De Linné à Lamarck: Méthodes de la classification et idée de serie en botanique et en zoologie, 1740–1790* (Paris: F. Alcan, 1926), 38–39. On Joseph Pitton de Tournefort, whose method rested in particular on the corolla of the flower and the fruit, see Raymond Dughi, "Tournefort dans l'histoire de la botanique," and Jean-François Leroy, "Tournefort et la classification végétale," in *Tournefort*, ed. Georges Becker, preface by R. Heim (Paris: Muséum national d'histoire naturale, 1957), 131–86 and 187–206. Foucault will return to their methods of classification in *The Order of Things*, chap. 5.

12. On the theory of the "double seed" and Descartes's interpretation of it in his *Traité de l'homme* (1664), Foucault relies on Émile Guyénot's article, "Biologie humaine et animale" in the *Histoire générale des sciences*, 2:370–71. According to Descartes, the animal seed "seems to be only a confused mixture of two liquors that serve as leaven for each other" (quoted, 371).

13. Here again Foucault follows Guyénot, "Biologie humaine et animale," 372–74. Usually, the "ovist" thesis, according to which the embryo is preformed in the female's ovum and is fertilized and developed by the male seed, is contrasted with the "spermist" or "animalculist" position, embodied for example in Anton Van Leeuwenhoek, according to which the embryo is preformed in the male spermatozoon ("animalcule"), the ovum serving basically to nourish it. On these theories, see below, Vincennes course, lecture 6, note 33, p. 247.

14. On the epigenesis and preformation opposition, see below, Vincennes course, lecture 6, note 32, p. 246. Preformation presupposes that the animal already exists, "preformed" in the male or female germ, and that it has only

to be developed mechanically through the excitation provoked by the seed of the other sex. Epigenesis entails the embryo's being formed progressively, starting from a relatively unformed material, through the action of particular forces.

15. On Lazzaro Spallanzani, who, in the 1770s, experimented with the artificial insemination of toads, and on the application of these experiments to the human species by John Hunter in 1799, who artificially inseminated a female with the sperm of her husband, affected by a malformation of the penis, see Jean Rostand, "Les expériences de l'abbé Spallanzani sur la génération animale (1763–1780)," *Archives internationales d'histoire des sciences* 4, no. 1 (1951): 413–47.

16. For this and the two following sections, Foucault follows the work of Jules Carles, *La Sexualité* (Paris: Armand Colin, 1953) very closely. The distinction between scissiparity, asexual generation, and sexuality is developed on page 8. With Maurice Caullery's *Les Problèmes de la sexualité* (Paris: Flammarion, 1919), and then again in the 1940s–1950s, there was a significant popularization and diffusion of the biology of sexuality, of which Carles's work is one of many. See Louis Buonoure, *Reproduction sexuelle et Histoire naturelle du sexe* (Paris: Flammarion, 1947), and *Hérédité et Physiologie du sexe* (Paris: Flammarion, 1948); M. Caullery, *Organisme et Sexualité*, 2nd ed. (Paris: G. Doin, 1951); Vera Dantchakov, *Le Sexe, rôle de l'hérédité et des hormones dans sa réalisation* (Paris: PUF, 1949); Étienne Wolff, *Les Changements de sexe* (Paris: Gallimard, 1946). Most of these texts give the same examples and conclusions, which radically complexify the apparent obviousness of sexuality and the natural division of the sexes. Wolff's work in particular gave rise to an important review by Bataille in *Critique* in 1967, "Qu'est-ce que le sexe?" in *Oeuvres complètes*, vol. 11, *Articles 1, 1944–1949*, ed. F. Marmande and S. Monod (Paris: Gallimard, 1988), 210–21, which Foucault probably knew, and which corresponds to his use of these works. Bataille shows how the science of sexuality "ruins" the personal experience and popular representations of the difference of the sexes, the "notion of the individual's fundamental sex-attribute" and of a clear and static separation of the sexes. He shows, rather, that "sex . . . is not an essence but a state," comparable to the liquid or solid state of a body. "Science rigorously eliminates in fact what should be called the 'basic givens' of life . . . it ruins, in short, the construction founded on the feeling of presence, it dismantles individual personal experience into mobile objective representations in

which any substratum has been removed. It withdraws reality and consistency from the personal, apparently immutable notion of sex." This is no doubt how we should understand Foucault's recourse to science (biology and ethology) in lectures 2 and 3 of this course (see below, pp. 63–68); see also "Course Context," pp. 312–315.

17. Carles, *La Sexualité*, 12. Carles prefers to speak of "sexuality reduced to the gametes" rather than to cells.

18. Carles, *La Sexualité*, 13–14. The cases where these differences are visible refer in particular to the *Phaeophyceae* algae.

19. Carles, *La Sexualité*,14–17.

20. Carles, *La Sexualité*, 17–19.

21. Carles, *La Sexualité*, 23–24. The algae in question are notably the *Ectocarpus siliculosus* or the *Chlamydomonus paupera*.

22. On these cases of natural intersexuality, see Carles, *La Sexualité*, 27–28. The annelid concerned is the polychaete *Ophryotrocha puerilis*.

23. This is what Carles calls "experimental intersexuality" (*La Sexualité*, 30–38).

24. Foucault follows the second part of Carles, *La Sexualité*, entitled "The Chemistry of Sex." For a more recent history of sexual hormonology, see, for example, Nelly Oudshoorn, *Beyond the Natural Body: An Archaeology of Sex Hormones* (London: Routledge, 1994), and for a philosophical reflection on the subject, the classical work of Anne Fausto-Sterling, *Sexing the Body: Gender Politics and the Construction of Sexuality* (New York: Basic Books, 2000).

25. Carles, *La Sexualité*, 43.

26. Cited in Carles, *La Sexualité*.

27. Emil Knauer, "Einige Versuche über Ovarientransplantation bei Kaninchen," *Zentralblatt für Gynäkologie* 26, no. 564 (1896): 524–28, cited in Carles, *La Sexualité*, 43–44.

28. Josef Halban, "Ueber den Einfluss der Ovarien auf die Entwicklung des Genitales," *Monatschrift für Geburtshilfe und Gynäkologie* 12, no. 4 (1900): 496–506, cited in Carles, *La Sexualité*, 44.

29. Edgar Allen, "The Oestrous Cycle in the Mouse," *American Journal of Anatomy* 30, no. 3 (1922): 297–371, cited in Carles, *La Sexualité*, 44.

30. On this history, see Carles, *La Sexualité*, 44–53. It ends with the works of the Swiss Karl Miescher (1892–1974), who in 1948 successfully managed the first complete synthesis of estrone.

31. The discovery of the androgens is summarized by Carles, *La Sexualité*, 54–57. It was the result of Arnold Adolf Berthold's experiments in 1848 on castrated roosters onto which testicles had been grafted, and it was Mac Gee who, in 1927, isolated an almost pure male hormone from a bull's testicles. In 1935, Karoly Gyula David and Ernst Laqueur isolated testosterone in this way, by purification. Other hormones (androsterone, adrenosterone) were isolated in the same years.

32. See Carles, *La Sexualité*, 57–60. Adolf Butenandt specified the formula of progesterone in 1934.

33. Carles, *La Sexualité*, 60–61.

34. Insofar as "it is not clear how they could do other than impose their sex," Carles notes. But it is a matter of explaining also the formation of male embryos (*La Sexualité*, 64–65). On embryonic hormones more generally, see Carles, *La Sexualité*, 64–67.

35. The freemartin is a phenomenon that involves fraternal twins of different (genetic) sex, connected to each other in the uterus through the intermediary of the placenta. In this case, the genetic female is born intersexual, because the male hormones of the other embryo have affected it by way of blood through the placenta.

36. Carles, *La Sexualité*, 73. The exact quotation is "Hormones . . . are chemical substances secreted by certain glands, which, transported by the blood throughout the organism, will, in infinitesimal concentrations, exert a specific action on certain organs."

37. Foucault follows here the third part of Carles, *La Sexualité*, "Genetic Sex," 103 *et seq.*

38. The "epigamic" theory posits that the fertilized egg begins development without the sex yet being determined and that it is later conditions of development that contribute to determining it. It was opposed by the "syngamic" theory, according to which sex is fixed at the time fertilization, when the gametes come together (Carles, *La Sexualité*, 103).

39. The example of the Bonellia is explained in detail in Carles, *La Sexualité*, 104–7.

40. For these expositions, Foucault summarizes Carles, *La Sexualité*, 107–13. In the drosophila type, the sex chromosomes are identical in the female (XX) whereas one is different in the male (the Y chromosome). In the abraxas type, it is the male that possesses two identical sexual

chromosomes (ZZ) whereas the female possesses one that is different (the W chromosome).

41. Foucault appears to rely here on Wolff, *Les Changements de sexe*, who gives a similar definition of genital sex: "the set of characteristics by which a male subject differs from a female subject of the same species" (15).

42. Wolff, *Les Changements de sexe*, 19–20.

43. Wolff, *Les Changements de sexe*, 16.

44. On eels, see Wolff, *Les Changements de sexe*, 69–74.

LECTURE 3

Sexual Behavior

*P*sychology *knows sexual behavior only through deviations. Poverty of knowledge about "normal" sexuality and confusion around "sexual normalcy": importance of distortions between frequency and normalcy. The notion of normal sexuality confuses the idea of a biological purpose and a whole network of norms and social prohibitions. Instead of starting from "normal sexuality," taking the whole of sexual conducts in their widest distribution (psychopathology, psychosociology); beginning by problematizing the notion of sexual behavior based upon animal sexuality. I. Animal sexuality: instinctive but profoundly complex, plastic behavior linked to environmental conditions. Definition of an instinctive behavior according to Lorenz and Tinbergen. A. Sexual motivation: hormonal thresholds, external stimuli, effects of group and sociality. B. Unfolding of the sexual act: series of complex conditions that go far beyond the procreative act and introduce relationships to space, others, and the environment. 1. Appetency activity; 2. sexual territory; 3. sexual display; 4. consummatory act. Sexual behavior depends, therefore, on both hormonal control and a system of signals conforming to a code, and so to a message. Intrication of the biological, the environment, and the relationship to others: human sexuality is not a hapax in the biological world. Nonetheless, there are some breaks: the most* *important concerns the relationship of human sexuality to the Law, prohibition and transgression. Clarification of these relationships: human sexual conduct necessarily presupposes a game of rules and prohibitions; it therefore also always entails possible transgression. Paradoxical situation of human sexuality: both nature beneath every rule, the natural foundation of every bond; and always entailing the rule and transgression. Hence the two traditional languages of the experience of sexuality in the West: the lyricism of love and the eroticism of transgression. The twentieth century invents a new language: the psychopathology of sexuality.*

[40]   Strangely, it[a] is only ever apprehended through its deviations, be this because the system of prohibitions to which sexuality is always linked includes a prohibition of knowledge from which we are not free, even in our own time, or because psychology can only ever grasp the negative forms of human experience (deviancies, failures, side effects: forgetfulness rather than memory; stupidity rather than intelligence; fantasy rather than imagination; neurosis, but not successful accomplishment).[1]

Once its determinations have been studied, what is known regarding what is positive, or normal, in sexuality?

1. That it appears in its full exercise only after puberty, in the last stage of sexual differentiation. It clearly manifested itself before this, but in an undifferentiated (not limited to the sexual organs), fragmented (not resulting in the sexual act) form [and] subject to eclipse.

[41]   2. That this appearance is linked to individual, climatic (North and South), and social factors.

---

a Sexual behavior is understood.

3. That once it has appeared, it manifests itself until a determinate age, which is earlier for women than for men.

4. That during this period, it manifests itself in a discontinuous but not rhythmic manner—men and women are not subject to the particular periods of sexual activity that are typical of animals.

5. That this activity, which may be greater or lesser depending on the individual, ends with a sexual act that, if its aim is not procreation, takes place in conditions such that it should be able to bring about procreation. Any sexual act that does not take place in these conditions is regarded as abnormal.

Now, certain things have come to light:

- A series of major distortions between frequency and normalcy, and this in two ways:
  - existence of "sexual minorities" (homosexuals, perversions);
  - frequency, in individual members of the majority, of sexual acts that do not conform to the schema;[2]
  - obligatory passage, before adolescence, through stages in   [42] which sexual activity does not conform to the schema.[3]
- The intrication of certain possibly incompatible, but in any case different elements, in the definition of "sexual normalcy":
  - the idea of a biological purpose that can clearly be seen to rest on a confusion: it is true that procreation takes place only through the sexual act accomplished in certain conditions; but this does not mean that sexual activity is necessarily *normed*[b] by these conditions,

---

b Underlined in the manuscript.

nor that it may not go well beyond the limited series of acts that enable procreation. After all, one feeds oneself through the mouth; but it is also through the mouth that one expresses oneself, speaks, smiles. And in animals, sexual activity, in its real unfolding, goes well beyond the procreative act;[4]

- the idea of a social norm that divides up the permitted and forbidden according to different schemas, but that in certain points confirms the idea of a purpose:

    - prohibition of certain sexual acts;
    - prohibition of sexual activity at certain times of life; in certain circumstances; in certain cyclical periods (seasons, menstruation);
    - prohibition of certain partners defined by age, social function, or degree of kinship.[5]

    Now these prohibitions have been recognized, thought about, and experienced in an ambiguous way: both as imposed by society and as prescribed by the order of things.

    – Hence the interference between this unclear purpose and the ambiguous network of prohibitions. Our culture tends to base the prohibition on the purpose and say that only what is contrary to procreation is prohibited. This is contradicted by the least observation, as much with regard to what is permitted (which is not always because it enables procreation) as to what is prohibited (which is not always contrary to procreation).

    To study sexuality as behavior, we must therefore disso- ciate all these ambiguities. So, not starting with this sexu- ality overladen with ambiguous values, ill-founded limits, and rules that are both strict and poorly thought through,

[43]

[44]

but taking as the area for examination the phenomena in their greatest extension—that is, from the angle of pathological deviations and cultural relativities. Hence the two chapters:

- pathological;
- psychosociological.[6]

But first, animal sexual behavior must be studied as background of the analysis—that is, behavior that appears both entirely controlled by biological (not cultural or ethical) determinations and so spontaneously normalized on the basis of these conditions, without possible deviation.

I. ANIMAL SEXUALITY[7]   [45]

Actually, we realize very quickly that:
- The determinations of sexual behavior are much more numerous and complex than one thinks.
- The development of sexual behavior comprises many more episodes than those that directly prepare and accomplish the sexual act itself.
- Oscillations around the general schema are actually so numerous that automatism is not its exclusive rule.

And yet, sexual behavior is, in the strict sense, what is called instinctive behavior. And the analysis of sexual behavior in animals will show the extent to which an instinctive progression may be linked to environmental conditions, and how plastic it may be. If it is true that human sexuality is much more than a culturalized instinct, we may nonetheless understand on that basis that, while being deeply rooted in the biological, it is totally penetrated by cultural forms.

[46]   The sexual behavior of animals is an instinctive behavior. What is instinctive behavior?

- Behavior that is, for a more or less important part, triggered by a physiological factor of internal motivation.
- Behavior that is subdivided into two segments (according to Lorenz, 1937, and Tinbergen, 1942).[8]

    α. a phase of search or appetent activity. This is characterized:

    - by a number of more or less extensive movements that are subject to the aleatory system of trial and error;
    - by an orientation directed not toward a precise object, but toward a situation.

    β. a phase of execution or consummation. This is characterized:

    - by the fact that it is regulative: its role is to remove the stimulation that provoked it;
    - by the fact that it is triggered by a certain [type] of stimuli, the number and intensity of which modify only its earliness and the strength of its manifestation;
    - by the fact that it is stereotypical, automatic, and rigid.[9]

[47]   Now, environmental stimulations play a role in these two phases of instinctive activity: in the first, as elements encountered by the search; in the second, as elements triggering the act of execution or consummation. They play these two roles in a remarkable way.

- First of all, they are not objects, but sensory elements: the tuning-fork vibration in the spider's web.[10] The method of the "decoy" (Tinbergen)[11] for studying the form/color relationship for the fight behavior of the male stickleback: "sign-stimuli."[12]

- Then, these stimuli form part of a situation: the penguin seizes the fish as prey in the water; out of the water, it does not touch it. Kirkman[c] studied the black-headed gull with regard to its egg:
  - in the nest, it is covered;
  - in the nest, but broken, it is eaten;
  - outside the nest (< 50 centimeters), it is brought back;
  - outside the nest (> 50 centimeters), it is ignored.[13]

  This relationship of stimuli to the situation is called the "*pattern.*"[14]

1. Sexual motivation   [48]

a. Hormonal induction. We know that the presence of sex hormones (essentially, testosterone and estrone) stimulates sexual activity:

- injection outside the phase of activity;
- injection before or after the age of sexual activity.[15]

Now these hormones are neurotropic (= they act through the intermediary of the nervous system); they lower the threshold of excitability of the sensorimotor structures involved in sexual behavior.

This threshold is not the same, however, depending on the structures: in the cockerel, for example, it is quite low for generalized appetitive behavior, then the combative attitude, then song; finally it is especially high for copulation, strictly speaking.[16]

Moreover, this threshold falls with nonexecution of the consummatory act—to the point that the quality of the decoy may

---

c Foucault, following Bounoure, writes "Kirkmann," but the correct name is Frederick Bernulf Kirkman.

drop significantly: Tinbergen observed sexual behavior of the stickleback in an empty aquarium.[17]

b. Induction by physical stimuli

The seasonal periodicity of sexual activity is due to external factors. It disappears in warm countries and is very marked in the north.[18]

[49]   Role of light (known empirically),[19] studied by Benoît (1951), who showed [. . .] the action of the light on the optical paths, which pass through the brain to the hypothalamus, and thereby act on the hypophysis. Orange and red rays are the most effective (due to their shorter wavelength).[20]

c. Induction by group effects

For a long time, it was thought that the social instinct ("the internal impulse that leads the animal toward its kind]")[21] was the development of the sexual instinct; or that the latter was only a specification of the former (the social instinct ensuring specific association with congeners; the sexual instinct ensuring species persistence through descent). In actual fact, there is indeed a relationship, but a very different one, which can be analyzed:

– sexuality and sociality are not direct functions of each other:
  • many animal groups (elephants) are unisexual;
  • many uni- or bisexual animal groups break up when sexual activity begins (sparrows, tits, wolves, reindeer).
– [*In the margin:* "sensory stimulations"] On the other hand, the presence of congeners gives rise to optical, olfactory, and tactile stimuli that, through the play of neuroendocrinal relations, provoke the discharge of hormones.[22]

[50]   • Isolation of the female pigeon stops ovulation, but it starts again if the pigeon is placed in front of a mirror.[23]
  • [*In the margin:* "group incitement"] In animal colonies (seagulls), egg laying occurs earlier if the colony

is large. All the individuals of the same colony arrive simultaneously at the same stage of the reproductive cycle, while there are chronological gaps between different colonies.[24]

- [*In the margin*: "sympathetic induction"] Finally, in addition to this "social incitement," there is a "sympathetic induction." Soulairac (1952) showed that a group of not very sexually active rats were stimulated by the presence of one particularly active individual.[25]

In each of these cases it is not a matter of imitation, for there is no apprenticeship, but of the triggering of an instinctive and innate behavior by behavior of the same type acting as stimulus. Sociality does not act on sexuality through imitation, through "gregariousness," but by the force of precise stimulations.[26]

2. *The procedure of the sexual act*   [51]

In most animals, the procedure of the sexual act is extremely complex. On the one hand, it comprises a whole series of conducts that go well beyond simple fertilization and even the acts that make fertilization possible. On the other hand, along with a very considerable specific stereotype, it presents a certain adaptive margin, due no doubt to the fact that it forms a sequence, that the relays from one phase to another of the sexual act are perceptual stimuli that connect them to the external world.

Ultimately, therefore, a whole relationship to surrounding space, to visual, auditory, and olfactory stimuli, to congeners of the other and the same sex, to objects of the field of behavior, is integrated into the sexual act.

So, we see an uncoupling of hormonal inductions and neuromotor performances. The predominance of a single, universal hormone entails very different behavior in different species. And this uncoupling is increasingly [clearly] manifested as one rises in the scale of beings.

[52]   • On the one hand, because as we look at more advanced animals, the more the neuromotor schema of the sexual act escapes hormonal determinism and the more it is connected to differentiated sensory stimulations.

• On the other hand, because sexual activity changes from obedience of the lower nervous centers to the higher. In the duck, sexual control is above all paleoencephalic (optostriate bodies); in the [cat],[d] control [is] diencephalic; in primates and man, it is cortical.[27]

So we can say that even if sexual behavior in animals is fixed in time by the rutting or heat period, [sexuality][e] manifests itself in general performances of behavior: it puts into operation most of the organism's neuromotor schemas, and in an increasingly marked way as one looks at more advanced species.

[As if it needed the whole weight of our morality to suppose that sexuality must occupy less space as one considers more advanced beings.][f]

[53]   These few clarifications are not unimportant for understanding the meanings of the Freudian discovery.

How does the sexual act take place in its complete melody?

d Foucault omits the word; Bounoure's text, *IS*, 152, enables us to establish "cat."

e Foucault writes "it (*elle*)."

f The brackets are Foucault's.

1. Appetency activity[g] (or Craig's "appetitive behavior").[28]

It especially concerns the male who leaves home "in search of the female," as one says. This activity has a control and a regulation.

The control is internal (the quantity of hormonal secretion) and external: certain environmental factors that act either indirectly (through action on the hormones, like light for ducks) or directly (fresh and oxygenated water for anadromous fish).[29] Regulation takes place through sign-stimuli that guide the search activity and orientate it toward precise aims:

- visual stimuli: which may be a color (stickleback) or a movement as in butterflies (cf. *Eumenis*, which, however, is sensitive to color in the search for food);[30]
- auditory stimuli: birdsong, insect stridulation (example of   [54] Regen in 1913 on the cricket with the telephone);[31]
- olfactory stimuli in many insects that succeed in finding the female even when they are blind.[32]

2. Establishment of a sexual territory[h]

Most of the time, sexual activity includes the establishment of a privileged space in which the next phases of sexual activity and reproduction take place. This space may intersect [other types of territory], but it is neither genetically nor functionally identical to the hunting territory, or to the residence (for example, the bird's nest is not necessarily the sexual territory: for the duck, the two are very distant from each other).[33]

---

g Underlined in the manuscript; Foucault initially wrote "appetency activity phase."
h Underlined in the manuscript.

This territory is an "area defended by a bird which fights against individuals of the *same species* and *sex* [shortly] before and during . . . the sexual act"[i] (Tinbergen).[34]

- It is generally established by the male and serves as rallying point for the female.[35]

[55]
- It is the site of possible fights; Darwin saw this as an instinctive transcription of the old struggle for life. In fact, it has been possible to establish that these fights were rather fictional, a sort of display;[36] that the owner enjoyed a dominance that enables him to resist even those stronger than himself; that, above all, males in the period of sexual activity not only set out a territory, but respect that of others; that it is the young, or those who are not in a phase of activity, who encroach on the occupied [territory[j]].[37]

3. Sexual display[k38]

The immediately prenuptial phase is devoted to dances which are often performed by the male and sometimes by both sexes. This dance can be a more or less violent movement; a presentation of feathers in birds; an offer of food.

This activity presents the following characteristics:

a. It is linked to internal and external stimulations.
b. Contrary to what Darwinians thought, its role is not seduction (generally the female pays it no attention) or rivalry (the fights are sham).

---

i The quotation offered by Foucault is slightly different: Foucault introduces an "and possibly [after?] the sexual act." We reestablish here the quotation from Tinbergen provided by Bounoure, *IS*, 54. Underlining is Foucault's.

j Doubtless by mistake, Foucault writes "characteristic." We restore "territory," which seems more coherent.

k Underlined in the manuscript.

c. It plays a vicarious role: it is more developed as the partner shies away. Waiting activity.[39]

4. Consummatory act[1]   [56]

It has several structures, depending on the species:

- Emission of the genital products (gametes) in the habitat (*milieu vital*), emission that takes place separately for the two sexes (for certain marine invertebrates).
- Fertilization of the eggs by the males.
- Absorption of male gametes by the females who attract them and collect them in their oviduct canal.
- Copulation, i.e., internal fertilization of the female by the male.[40]

N.B.: In most species, copulation takes place with any individual of the same species and other sex. However, monogamous habits are found in some birds (swallow, stork, swan; Tinbergen observed that a seagull recognized its sexual partner in a group of several others at a distance of thirty meters).[41]

In conclusion, we see that animal sexual behavior, as defined   [57] on the basis of present knowledge, appears as a structure of double control.

– One, indispensable but massive, homogeneous, undifferentiated, nonspecific, is hormonal. It applies in the same way for all species, which it divides into only two sexes, giving each some secondary sexual characteristics and general neuromotor themes.

– The other control is, [in] a sense, less indispensable since in some cases, and on the basis of a definite quantitative threshold, the hormonal level may bring about sexual behavior on its own,

---

1 Underlined in the manuscript.

without other stimulation. But this behavior is then not complete, or orientated, or really organized.[42]

To be orientated, organized, and complete, it must be structured around a set of perceptual stimuli that, if they conform to a certain *pattern*, trigger very precise motor responses. Now these *patterns* are formed from successive signaling elements. This means three things:

[58]   1. At each moment in the course of the act, there is a signal whose presence triggers the response and whose absence prevents it. For [example], a red patch on the belly of the male stickleback is indispensable.

2. These signals do not trigger the same response in both sexes. The red patch triggers approach for the female stickleback, fight for the other male stickleback.[43] Vogt (1935) takes a female warbler; it triggers the behavior of copulation in the male, nothing in another female; with a black hood (male attribute), it triggers attack in the male, sexual behavior in another female.[44]

3. These signals are effective triggers when they occur in series. For example, the attacking stickleback's upside-down posture does not provoke any response if the other has not yet established its territory.[45] Conversely, certain links may be skipped if the series of stimulations is fairly continuous. There is a threshold of sufficient saturation.

Now these three characteristics are indeed those of a message—i.e., of signal elements conforming to a code (that is, to a law of correlation with responses) and to a syntax (that is, a law of sequence that gives each element a precise value in the series).

[59]   Sexual behavior thus conforms to an internal hormonal stimulation and to a set of codified perceptual messages that arise from the external world by means of perceptual stimulation. And as hormonal stimulation perhaps also acts on the nervous system in the manner of a codified stimulation, we see that sexual

behavior as a whole is a response to a double, physiological and perceptual, internal and external message. It would conform to the general laws of information.[46]

Now this message linking sexual activity to the external world (including congener) is at the same time what ensures [that] species cannot mix. Contrary to what was thought, anatomically, many species could copulate and, physiologically, crossbreed. In any case, the sexual activity of animals could be completely uncoordinated if it were not triggered by the perceptual message of which only, or almost only, the congener of the other species is bearer.[47] This ensures that, through this message, sexual behavior is linked to perceptual stimulations from the environment and restricted to isomorphous individuals—a strictly specific message that determines and specifies an indifferent hormonal motivation.

What can we conclude from what has been said regarding [60] biological and animal sexuality?

1. That two forms of sexual determination should be distinguished:

  • determination strictly speaking, which is due to the chromosomal structure of the gametes;
  • sexual differentiation, which itself takes place in two stages: the formation of the primary sexual characteristics (embryonic stage); the appearance and development of the secondary sexual characteristics (puberty).[48]

2. That male and female hormones (the formula of which differs little between them) perform their role at three levels:

  • in the formation of primary sexual characteristics (in its earliest stages the embryo can become male or female);
  • in the formation of secondary sexual characteristics, possibly in their dispersion or even total inversion (castration);

- in the instigation of sexual activity, and this in two ways:
  - at the level of triggering (the level of hormones accelerates or delays its triggering, raises or lowers the threshold at which the neuromotor schemas come into operation);
  - they play a role in the intensity of this activity (frequency, duration, completeness).

3. That sexual behavior, if it develops on the basis of these hormonal thresholds, is far from being wholly controlled by such determinations:

- Hormones simply distinguish the sexes (binary and mass differentiation), whereas sexual behavior is very varied in different species and involves a great many motor performances, themselves different in one and the same species. Conducts of nesting, display, fighting, and singing take place on the basis of the same hormone.
- Sexual behavior is connected to a whole set of visual, auditory, and olfactory stimuli; it is linked with spatial conduct, with social and interindividual conduct, with temporal conduct. In short, it seems involved with almost all the stages of individual behavior.

[62]^m   No doubt, in most species, sexual activity is localized in time; but as soon as it is triggered, it involves all of the individual's perceptual and motor structures. And this fact is more evident and supported the higher one rises in the scale of beings.

A purely instinctive model of sexuality was sought in animal biology and psychology; paradoxically, despite the actual instinctive character of this activity, an integrated activity was found that brings into play all the individual's ties to his behavioral milieu.

---

m Manuscript page number 61 is missing from the French edition —G.B.

This has significance, but a limited significance, for human psychology. This consists in human sexuality not being a hapax in the biological world.

- It can be culturalized—that is, adapted to stimuli placed [63] around the individual by society. In this it is [of the] same type as animal sexuality (only the stimuli are of a different kind). Animal sexuality is also sensitive to the behavior of its congeners, or to artificial stimuli like mirrors (provoking phenomena of quasi-jealousy or quasi-narcissism).
- It is spread across behavior; and this is neither unique, nor as paradoxical as it was thought when Freud discovered it. Animal sexuality, like human sexuality, is intricately connected with perception, with motor effectuations—in short, with the whole of behavior.

These are the links that can be established between animal and human sexuality. But we need also establish the breaks.

It is very difficult to make inferences from animal to human [64] behavior. This is true generally: for learning, for perception, even for the phenomena of maturation. There are two reasons for this.

- The corticalization of neuromotor schemas, very strong in humans, involves processes of instigation, inhibition, and cohesion different from those observable in animals, where corticalization is less accentuated.
- The human environment is much more open than the animal environment. Perceptual filtering is narrow in animals (few excitations cross the threshold) because it is subject to subcortical controls; it is wide in man, who "perceives" everything: everything has a meaning, everything is present. So, practically, human behavior carves out what it has to perceive; it can always perceive what falls outside this slice.[49]

[65]   For these two reasons, it is never possible to transpose with
certainty what is observed in the animal to what may be assumed
in man.

But with regard to sexuality there is a supplementary reason. This is that, of all human behavior, sexuality is the most
regulated, the most highly normed. The most strongly subject
to a law, to a division between permitted and forbidden that,
obviously, does not exist in the animal world.[50] Other conducts
are no doubt regulated. Again, it is necessary to mark an essential difference.

1. There are conducts that exist only on the basis of the rule.
    It is the law, the set of rules that founds the possibility of
    the conduct itself. If there were no norms, there would be
    no conduct at all—for example, all political types of con-
    duct, conduct of command, economic conduct. By defini-
    tion, all exchange is rule-governed. If exchange were not
    rule-governed, there would be no exchange. Rule and con-
    duct coexist in a synthetic mode.

[66]   2. There are conducts on which the rule *seems*[n] to be super-
    imposed, as if there were a phenomenon of later super-
    imposition. For [example] feeding. It is regulated by
    prohibitions (on the nature, or mode of preparation, or
    mode of consumption of food); it is also regulated by
    systems of preferential valorization; it is regulated finally
    by forms of community. It remains, nevertheless, that it
    would still exist if it were unregulated. Similarly, sexual-
    ity. Regulated by prohibitions (partner, nature of the act,
    moment of consummation); it is regulated by systems of
    valorization; it is regulated by community forms. And yet
    it, too, would exist.

---

n Underlined in the manuscript.

Which allows us to suppose, and has actually led us to imagine, that the rule came historically afterward. Now it has been found:

1. That no society, however ancient, however crude and little organized, allows these conducts without defining very strict rules. The myth of a primitive and free sexuality is no more than a utopia. Moreover, it seems that the rules are stronger, stricter, and more inviolable the more elementary the society. Liberalization would come later.[51]

2. On the other hand, those conducts that, as one says, [67] answer to a basic need, and on which the law seems only to be superimposed, are generally exposed to much stronger sanctions, to much more violent social reactions, than others when they break the rule.

    Certainly, in some societies, political crimes, disobedience, theft are punished with the death penalty. But the violence of social disapproval is much stronger regarding those that, in archaic societies at least, transgress alimentary or sexual prohibitions. There are even specific reactions that enable transgression to be distinguished from the series crime–misdemeanor (between the two, murder).

    Now this is all very paradoxical: the rules imposed on basic needs seem more inviolable than those that are contemporary [with the conducts]° they give rise to. It is more serious, more horrible to satisfy one of these major functions, like sexuality or feeding, outside the rules than it is to divert social conduct from the rule that makes it possible. To steal, as Kant says, is to contradict the rule of exchange, to radically deny it.[52] Now this is less serious than suspending the prohibition of incest or cannibalism

---

o We add these words, for without them the meaning of the sentence is hardly legible.

in order to satisfy the irrepressible, or anyway biologically founded, demands of sex and hunger.

[68]   A head of state who violates the constitution perhaps commits a crime; no society experiences toward him the horror aroused by the man who rapes his sister. The former, however, contradicts and abolishes the rule to which he owes his existence; the latter satisfies a sexual need inscribed in him by a hormonal determination.

All this [amounts to saying] that sexuality presents itself to experience in a paradoxical and immediately contradictory form.

• Beneath every rule, every prohibition, it is like the dark thrust of a nature prior to law and punishment; it is as if it has an essential positivity outside of all human culture. And that is why we recognize there our link with the animal world, with life in general; it [is] our interspecies link; our synchronic communication with the world; love is experienced as the innocence of spring rather than as an agreed contract. It is also why we recognize in sexuality our link with a history that hangs over us everywhere; it connects us to time as if it were the continuous weft of history beneath any imaginable historical form.

[69]   • And on the other hand, it always appears linked to the rule, experienced and recognized for what it is in the movement of transgression.[53] It is said that there is no happy love. Actually, there is no lawful love. Permitted love is an exception in relation to the essence of sexuality, which is to be prohibited: it is the blank space in the middle of its complex network that allows the grid of prohibitions to appear.

One may well be in favor of free love; but as one might be a partisan of black snow. Contradiction in terms and inexhaustible poetic chimera.

This fundamental contradiction in the experience of sexuality explains why, throughout Western history, we have seen the appearance of only two types of language or formulation for sexuality:

1. A lyricism that finds the resources for its language in the positivity of love: in the link that establishes it at the heart of nature, time, and the world; but such a language only expresses this positivity through the limits imposed on it by the law, hatred, marriage, death.
    Tristan, Romeo, Pelléas.[54]

2. An eroticism that finds the possibility of its language in transgressions: either by the statement of what is pro-   [70] hibited, or by stating what [it] is prohibited to state. But this eroticism only expresses this negativity by referring it back to the force of nature, to the singularity of instinct.

Sexuality was expressed in these two languages until the nineteenth century—until the beginning of the nineteenth century when the quasi-contemporaneousness of de Sade, Laclos, and Rétif de La Bretonne, on the one hand,[p] and Shelley, Goethe, and Lamartine, [on the other], is characteristic of this duality.

Now the nineteenth century discovered a new language on sexuality. A language of neither amorous lyricism nor eroticism. It is a discursive language that cuts across the fundamental themes of lyricism and eroticism.[55]

Since essentially it seeks: [71]

- What relationship might exist between love as feeling and that law of nature, that "instinct," that eroticism always invokes as the raison d'être, justification, and foundation of all its transgressions.

---

p Words crossed out: "and of the pre-romantics on the other."

- What relationship might exist between the prohibitions, the limits constantly encountered by the feeling of love, and the transgressions manifested by eroticism.

These two lines of research, during the nineteenth century, brought about the development of three series of works:

a. Research on the sexual instinct

b. Research on sexual deviations

c. Research on their relationships.

Ulrichs, Krafft-Ebing, Moebius, Havelock Ellis, Magnus Hirschfeld.[56]

*

1. See above, lecture 2, note 8, p. 45.

2. These two points follow Freud's arguments in his *Introductory Lectures on Psychoanalysis*, *CPW*, 15 and 16, chap. 20, "The Sexual life of Human Beings." But they are especially put forward, along with the tension between "frequency" and "normalcy," in the famous reports produced by Alfred C. Kinsey: *Sexual Behavior in the Human Male* (Bloomington: Indiana University Press, 1948) and *Sexual Behavior in the Human Female* (Philadelphia: Saunders, 1953). From the mid-1950s, these two reports provoked intense controversies in France around sexuality and were the object of analyses by, among others, Daniel Guérin, *Kinsey et la Sexualité* (Paris: R. Julliard, 1955) and Georges Bataille, "La révolution sexuelle et le 'Rapport Kinsey' I and II," *Critique*, nos. 26 and 27 (July and August 1958). On the context of the reports' reception in France, see Sylvie Chaperon, "Kinsey en France: les sexualités feminine et masculine en débat," *Le Mouvement social*, no. 198 (2002): 91–110. Kinsey's analysis thus put forward, with the support of statistics, the existence of "sexual minorities," homosexuals in particular—from 3 percent to 16 percent of men are presented as exclusively homosexual. But above all, Kinsey innovates by blurring the binary divisions between categories—homosexuals *versus* heterosexuals—and analyzing instead, on a scale of 1 to 6, the number of homosexual or heterosexual experiences in the population, according to a perspective that varies according to period of life. It is here that we come to Foucault's second point about the "frequency,

in individual members of the majority, of sexual acts that do not conform to the schema": Kinsey shows that sexual practices like homosexual relations, but also masturbation, oral-genital relations, etc., are very widespread in the population, and he analyzes their statistical distribution according to various situations and periods of life.

3. Again, this is a reference both to the results of psychoanalysis, which Foucault will set out in more detail later—see below, lectures 4 and 5, pp. 89–95 and 114–128—which show that human sexuality passes through a set of nongenital stages, through masturbation, and so on, before reaching the genital stage and coitus (see, for example, S. Freud, *Introductory Lectures to Psycho-Analysis*, Lecture XXI, *CPW*, vol. 16, 327 *et seq.*), and also to Kinsey's statistical studies, which emphasize, for example, that 92 percent of the male population masturbate, in particular during preadolescence and adolescence.

4. See below, p. 59 *et seq.* One of the objectives of this lecture is to prove this point through a detailed analysis of the sexual behavior of animals. The refusal to reduce sexuality is obviously characteristic of Freudian analysis (see, for example, Freud, *Introductory Lectures*, *CPW*, vol. 16, 320).

5. See above, lecture 1, p. 4, and below, pp. 68–71. These have been analyzed by Claude Levi-Strauss in *The Elementary Structures of Kinship*, ed. James Harle Bell, John Richard von Sturmer, and Rodney Needham (Boston: Beacon Press, 1969), with regard to the prohibitions affecting kinship, and by anthropologists such as Malinowski and Mead with regard to those directed at certain phases of life.

6. In the end, Foucault will develop only the first of these two chapters, on pathological deviations as the object of psychiatric knowledge (*savoir*) at the end of the nineteenth century and then their study by psychoanalysis (see below, p. 00 *et seq.*). "Psychosociology," which here covers the cultural rules and prohibitions concerning sexuality in different cultures, as found in anthropology and ethnography, will not be studied (see above, lecture 1, note 2, p. 17).

7. Throughout this section, Foucault closely follows Louis Bounoure's work, *L'instinct sexuel: Étude de psychologie animale* (Paris: PUF, 1956); henceforth Bounoure, *IS*.

8. Bounoure emphasizes these two characteristics: instinctive behavior has "for *primum movens* a physiological factor of internal motivation, creator of a specific need and trigger of activity." It is, furthermore, a "complex activity in which two consecutive components must be distinguished: 1°

the appetent activity or research . . . 2° The action of execution or consummation" (*IS*, 14). The references are taken from the same works: Konrad Lorenz, "Über die Bildung des Instinktbegriffes," *Die Naturwissenschaften* 25, no. 19 (1937): 289–300; and Niko Tinbergen, *An Objectivistic Study of the Innate Behaviour of Animals* (Leiden: Brill, 1942).

9. On these two phases, see Bounoure, *IS*, 14–16.

10. This is a reference to the technique employed by, for example, Harold Lassen and Else Toltzin, "Tierpsychologische Studien in Radnetzspinnen," *Zeitschrift für vergleichende Physiologie* 27, no. 5 (1940): 615–30, for differentiating the signification of sensory elements in spiders. If one vibrates its web in contact with the tuning fork, one attracts the spider as if a prey were caught in its web; if one makes the tuning fork vibrate in the layers of air, it flees and even lets itself fall from its web, acting as if an enemy (a wasp, for example) were present. See Bounoure, *IS*, 17.

11. The method of the decoy in ethology, of which the previous case is an example, consists in employing imitations, sometimes extremely rough, which do not have, for example, either the form or the appearance of the natural model (recording of sound, cube of colored wood, here tuning fork . . .) but reproducing a sensory stimulus (sound, odor, color . . .) whose role in releasing an animal behavior one wants to test. Tinbergen employs it on several occasions and formalizes it in order to test the behavior of the male stickleback confronting other male sticklebacks during mating displays. In this way, he shows that it is the color red—embodied by the red belly of the male stickleback in mating color—that triggers the fight: see, for example, Nikolaas Tinbergen, *The Study of Instinct* (New York: Oxford University Press, 1951): 37–40; henceforth Tinbergen, *SI*. The "decoys" rest on a principle that the animal will react to "a relatively simple stimulus . . . meaningful for a situation that is part of the animal's perceptual universe and presenting a functional value for it" (Bounoure, *IS*, 18). It involves, then, the notion of "sign-stimuli" that Foucault evokes later.

12. On "sign-stimuli," see Tinbergen, *SI*, 36. This is how Bounoure describes them: the stimuli of the surrounding world "act on the animal by revealing or evoking the existence of a situation that is of direct interest for the need motivating its instinctive activity: presence of food, movement of prey . . . in this way they function as signs: they are sign-stimuli" (Bounoure, *IS*, 16).

13. These two examples are taken from Bounoure, *IS*, 17. The second refers to Frederick Bernulf Kirkman's studies of bird behavior based on the black-headed gull: *Bird Behaviour: A Contribution Based Chiefly on a Study of the Black-Headed Gull* (London: Nelson, 1937).

14. Bounoure, *IS*, 18: "the animal's conduct is not relative to a world of objects identical to ours; it is related to configurations, "unitary forms" (*Gestalten*) or "patterns," elaborated by the animal on the basis of its perceptions and calling for a determinate action."

15. Bounoure, *IS*, 22, cites, for example, cases of injection of hormones in chicks or capons that induced manifestations of the sexual instinct.

16. Bounoure, *IS*, 23–24.

17. Bounoure, *IS*, 25–26; see also Tinbergen, *SI*, 62.

18. Bounoure, *IS*, 28. According to Bounoure, "the sexual drive is permanent or periodic, according to the species. The former is observed especially in organisms inhabiting warm regions of the globe . . . such beings are able to reproduce all year."

19. Bounoure, *IS*, 28: "an old custom of bird lovers is to expose the males to artificial light in order to get them to sing at a determinate time."

20. Bounoure, *IS*, 29. This is a reference to the work of the endocrinologist Jacques Benoit on the effects of light on the sexual activity of the duck. Bounoure refers to Benoît, *Titres et travaux scientifiques* (Strasbourg: Imprimerie des dernières nouvelles, 1951). The role of the wavelengths of orange and red is demonstrated in J. Benoît et al., "Contribution à l'étude du réflexe opto-hyophysaire gonado-stimulant chez le canard soumis à des radiations lumineuses de diverses longueurs d'onde," *Journal of Physiology*, no. 42 (1950): 537–41.

21. See Bounoure, *IS*, 31. This definition is taken from William Morton Wheeler, *The Social Insects: Their Origin and Evolution* (New York: Routledge, 1928), who speaks of social appetition. The discussion that follows on the relations between social instinct and sexual instinct—the need to distinguish them even though they maintain relationships with each other—and the examples cited are taken from Bounoure, *IS*, 31–32, who himself copies the analyses of Pierre-Paul Grassé, "Sociétés animales et effet de groupe," *Experientia* 2, no. 3 (1946): 78–82; and "Le fait social: ses critères biologiques, ses limites," in *Structure et physiologie des sociétés animales* (Paris: CNRS, 1952), 7–17.

22. Bounoure, *IS*, 32.

23. Bounoure, *IS*, 33. This is a reference to the work of L. Harrison Matthews, "Visual Stimulation and Ovulation in Pigeons," *Proceedings of the Royal Society of London. Series B—Biological Sciences* 126, no. 845 (1939): 557–60.

24. Reference to the work of Frank Fraser Darling, *Bird Flocks and the Breeding Cycle: A Contribution to the Study of Avian Sociality* (Cambridge: Cambridge University Press, 1938), cited in Bounoure, *IS*, 33–34.

25. See André Soulairac, "L'effet de groupe dans le comportement sexuel du rat mâle," in *Structure et physiologie des sociétés animales*, 91–102; cited in Bounoure, *IS*, 35–36.

26. Bounoure, *IS*, 36–37.

27. This passage on the existence of an uncoupling between a single and undifferentiated hormonal factor and the complexity of sexual behavior, as well as on the existence of a hierarchy of neurological control centers according to species, summarizes Bounoure, *IS*, 148–52.

28. See the classic articles of Wallace Craig, "Appetites and Aversions as Constituents of Instincts," *Proceedings of the National Academy of Sciences of the USA* 3, no. 12 (1918): 91–107, as well as Bounoure, *IS*, 41 *et seq.*, and Tinbergen, *SI*, 149–53.

29. See, for example, Maurice Fontaine, "Facteurs externes et internes régissant les migrations des poissons," *Annales de biologie* 27, no. 3 (1951): 569–80.

30. The case of the stickleback was referred to earlier (see above, note 11, p. 74) and is studied in detail by, for example, Tinbergen, *SI*. The butterfly *Eumenis semele* was studied by N. Tinbergen, B. J. D. Meeuse, L. K. Boerema, and W. W. Varossieau, "Die Balz des Samfalters, *Eumenis (= Satyrus) semele* (L.)," *Zeitschrift für Tierpsychologie* 5, no. 1 (1942): 182–226, who show, through the method of decoys, the importance of the contrast and undulatory characteristics of movement in triggering sexual pursuit. See Tinbergen, *SI*, 36, 42, regarding sensitivity to color for feeding, the *Eumenis* choosing blue and yellow flowers to feed on. See also Bounoure, *IS*, 51, and 50–52 for visual stimuli in general.

31. This is a reference to the work of Johann Regen, "Über die Anlockung des Weibchens von *Gryllus Campestris L.* durch telephonisch übertragene Stridulationslaute des Männchens: Ein Beitrag zur Frage der Orientierung bei den Insekten," *Pflügers Archiv—European Journal of Physiology* 155, no. 1

(1913): 193–200, who shows that a female cricket was attracted by the male's song heard through a telephone receiver and attempted to get inside the latter. See Bounoure, *IS*, 47–50.

32. These olfactory stimuli are presented by Bounoure, *IS*, 42–47, who refers to the example of the male *Bombyx mori*, which can find females even though it has been blinded by the application of an opaque varnish, whereas ablation of their antennae, preventing olfaction, makes them unable to do this.

33. Bounoure, *IS*, 61.

34. The exact quotation is taken from Nikolaas Tinbergen, "The Behavior of the Snow Bunting," *Transactions of the Linnaean Society of New York* (1939): "an area that is defended by a fighting bird against individuals of the same species and sex shortly before and during the formation of the sexual bond," translated by Bounoure, *IS*, 54. There are considerable debates on the definition of "territory" in ethology at the time, in particular starting from the definitions put forward by Henry Eliot Howard in the years 1910–1920; see his classic work, *Territory in Bird Life*, illustrated by George Edward Lodge and Henrik Grönvold (London: John Murray, 1920). Tinbergen is part of a criticism of Howard's definition and stresses that it is necessary to distinguish different functions and situations in order to analyze the problem of "territory," which cannot be considered in general. On this subject, see D. R. Röell, *The World of Instinct: Niko Tinbergen and the Rise of Ethology in the Netherlands (1920–1950)*, trans. M. Kofod (Assen, Netherlands: Van Gorcum, 2000), 82–86. Hence the insistence on the specificities of the sexual territory taken up by Foucault, following Bounoure, *IS*, 54–57.

35. Bounoure, *IS*, 54.

36. This criticism of Darwinism is the work of Tinbergen and is taken up by Bounoure, *IS*, 68.

37. See Bounoure, *IS*, 56, who, following Tinbergen, cites the case of the husky: it is "dogs which have not reached maturity [that] often penetrate other fiefs"; "in the week after the first mating, they learn to repel outside dogs and to avoid other territories."

38. The case of sexual display is analyzed in detail in Bounoure, *IS*, 69–103.

39. Foucault here takes up the different general characteristics summarized by Bounoure, *IS*, 99–108. The "vicarious" role, or substitution, in which

the display seems to serve as outlet for excessive sexual motivation, in particular when the female shies away, is illustrated by the male stickleback executing frenetic movements of ventilation of the nest when the female does not respond to his appeals. The term generally used is "displacement activity," rather than waiting activity.

40. These different modes are summarized by Bounoure, *IS*, 104–5. See, more generally, 104–37 for the multiplicity of modes of emission of the genital products and fertilization.

41. See Tinbergen, *SI*, 146–47; and on the monogamy of certain species of birds in general, Bounoure, *IS*, 153–55.

42. Bounoure, *IS*, 145–46.

43. On this subject, see Bounoure, *IS*, 176–78, who analyzes the results of Tinbergen's experiments. The color red, if combined with a special posture (body held in vertical upside-down position), has value as a sign of an attack in the case of a male, to which the defending male responds. Faced with a female, linked to a movement (the zigzag dance), it now has value as a stimulant for preparing for fertilization.

44. This is a reference to the experiment described in Gladwyn Kingsley Noble and William Vogt, "An Experimental Study of Sex Recognition in Birds," *Auk* 52, no. 3 (1935): 278–86, and recounted here by Bounoure, *IS*, 174–75. A stuffed female warbler is placed in the territory of an active male, who makes some attempts at coitus with her; a black paper mask is put on the female, reproducing the most striking sign of males of the species: the male ceases the attempt at coitus and attacks her. But as Bounoure, follow David Lack, notes, this is not a matter of an ability to recognize sex, strictly speaking: "it is not the partner as a sexed "whole"; it is a particular posture or a certain ornamental characteristic acting as stimulus signal for triggering the appropriate response" that is recognized.

45. Tinbergen, *SI*, 37–38.

46. The language of cybernetics, still fashionable at the time, can be detected here. We know that Foucault was very interested in cybernetics, as well as in the notions of signal, code, message, and information, devoting an entire course to them, it seems, at Lille (BNF, Box 42b-C2), and even having thought of devoting his complementary thesis to "The Psycho-Physical Study of the Signal and the Interpretation of Perception" (Didier Eribon, *Michel Foucault*, trans. Betsy Wing [Cambridge, MA: Harvard

University Presss,1992], 128). This interest is found in some later texts, such as "Message ou bruit?" (1966), *DÉ*, I, no. 44, 585–88, where the message is defined in an identical way: "for there to be a "message":—there must first of all be noise . . .;—that this noise is "formed by" or at least the "bearer of" various discontinuous elements, that is to say elements isolable from each other by certain criteria; . . .—finally, that these elements appear linked to each other according to certain regularities. Now . . . the message depends on a 'code' established according to the preceding rules" (586). This interest is found again later in Foucault's reflections on sexuality and heredity with regard to François Jacob's book (see "Course Context," p. 341). In the present case, this analysis is strongly reliant upon the exposition of Bounoure himself and his quotations from Edward Allworthy Armstrong, *Bird Display and Behaviour: An Introduction to the Study of Bird Psychology* (London: Lindsay Drummond, 1947), comparing the sexual behavior of birds to a maritime code, resting on a system of signals, or to a wireless transmitter and receiver set adjusted to the same wavelength (Bounoure, *IS*, 178–79, 194–96; Armstrong, *Bird Display*, 307).

47. See Bounoure, *IS*, 196–202, who makes this one of the purposes of the sexual instinct. For his part, Foucault refrains from any finalism.

48. See above, lecture 2, pp. 39–41.

49. On this point, see the classic work of Jakob von Uexküll, *A Foray Into the Worlds of Animals and Humans: with A Theory of Meaning*, trans. Joseph D. O'Neill (Minneapolis: University of Minnesota Press, 2010 [1934 and 1940]); F. J. J. Buytendijk, *L'Homme et l'Animal: Essai de psychologie comparée*, trans. R. Laureillard (Paris: Gallimard, 1965 [1958]) especially 35–62; and pages devoted to this question by Maurice Merleau-Ponty in *The Structure of Behavior* (Pittsburgh: Duquesne University Press, 1983), chap. 2 and 3.

50. The importance of prohibitions, of the play of the permitted and the forbidden, and consequently of their possible transgression, as constitutive elements of human as distinct from animal sexuality, is at the heart of Bataille's conception of eroticism; Georges Bataille, *Erotism*, trans. Mary Dalwood (San Francisco: City Lights, 1986), 40–71. It is also at the heart of Lévi-Strauss's analysis, since the prohibition of incest defines precisely the transition between nature and culture, inasmuch as it is a universal rule; *The Elementary Structures of Kinship*, ed. James Harle Bell, John Richard von

Sturmer, and Rodney Needham (Boston: Beacon Press, 1969), 12–25. See above, lecture 1, note 1, p. 17.

51. Here again Foucault extends Lévi-Strauss's analysis, which emphasizes the extreme simplicity of the rules of kinship in European societies compared with most so-called "primitive" societies. See C. Lévi-Strauss, *Structural Anthropology*, trans. Claire Jacobson and Brooke Grundfest Schoepf (New York: Basic Books, 1963), chapters 2 and 3, as well as the Vincennes course, lecture 4, p. 191 and note 3, p. 197.

52. Immanuel Kant's position on theft is expressed in the *Métaphysique des moeurs*, vol. 1, *Doctrine du droit*, intro. and trans. A. Philonenko, 3rd ed. (Paris: Vrin, 1985), 215–16; Immanuel Kant, *The Metaphysics of Morals*, trans. and ed. Mary Gregor (Cambridge: Cambridge University Press, 1996), Part I, *The Doctrine of Right*, 474: "Whoever steals makes the property of everyone else insecure and therefore deprives himself (by the principle of retribution) of security in any possible property."

53. The whole of this analysis of the "paradoxical" character of the experience of sexuality should be compared with Bataille's analysis in *Erotism*. Sexuality appears there as caught up in a play of "transitions from continuous to discontinuous or from discontinuous to continuous. We are discontinuous beings, individuals who perish in the midst of an incomprehensible adventure, but we yearn for our lost continuity" (15). Sexuality is a principle of both discontinuity—it is discontinuous beings who encounter each other and discontinuous beings who are produced—and moment, experience of the continuity of being, tending toward disappearance, the fusion of discontinuous beings. Hence, in Bataille, its privileged relationship to death and violence: "What does physical eroticism signify if not a violation of the very being of its practitioners?—a violation bordering on death, bordering on murder?" (17). Which explains, at the same time, the institution of the rule and the prohibition—concerning sexuality in its relation to death and violence—and the fact that eroticism presents itself as "an equal and contradictory . . . experience of prohibitions and transgressions" (36). As Bataille notes, this experience of transgression as emancipation from the prohibition should be distinguished from "a so-called back-to-nature attitude, the prohibition being seen as unnatural. But a transgression is not the same as a back-to-nature movement; it suspends a taboo without suppressing it" (36); it "maintains it in order to benefit by it" (38).

54. On this subject, see the classic work of Denis de Rougemont, *L'Amour et l'Occident*, rev. ed. (Paris: Plon, 1956 [1939]), in which Tristan and Isolde are emblematic of this lyricism of love.

55. This duality of the lyricism of love and the eroticism of transgression, illustrated by the contemporaneousness of Sade or Rétif de La Bretonne and Goethe or Lamartine, can be put in parallel with the duality of literature, emphasized by Foucault in the same period: between the experience of transgression embodied by Sade and that of a death that accedes to meaning by inscribing writing, beyond the grave, in "that kind of dusty eternity of the absolute library," embodied by Chateaubriand, whose contemporaneousness with Sade Foucault stresses (see above, lecture 1, note 31, p. 23, and "Course Context," pp. 315–317). Moreover, the analysis Foucault offers here of the emergence of a new language on sexuality in the nineteenth century—knowledge (*savoir*) about sexuality—and of its relationship to lyricism and eroticism may be compared with what he writes regarding the emergence of a knowledge of death and illness: he links Bichat's pathological anatomy with both Sade's transgressive language and the lyricism of finitude in Hölderlin and Rilke; see Michel Foucault, *Birth of the Clinic: An Archaeology of Medical Perception*, trans. A. M. Sheridan Smith (London: Tavistock, 1973), "Conclusion." One thinks also of the analyses developed by Foucault, since *History of Madness*, on the fact that the emergence of a knowledge (*savoir*) of mental illness as object is coupled with the rejection of the experience of madness at the extreme limit of language, from Sade to Artaud, passing through Nietzsche and Roussel; see *History of Madness*, trans. Jonathan Murphy and Jean Khalfa (London: Routledge, 2006), 532–42. See "Course Context," pp. 299–317.

56. This list refers to a series of classic authors in the emergence of a *scientia sexualis*, focusing on homosexuality and sexual perversions at the end of the nineteenth and the beginning of the twentieth century. Foucault will return to most of them, in particular in *Abnormal: Lectures at the Collège de France, 1974–1975*, trans. Graham Burchell, English series editor Arnold I. Davison (New York: Picador, 2003), when he looks at the emergence of knowledge about sexual perversions. The case of Richard von Krafft-Ebing is developed in the next lecture (see below, pp. 86–87).

LECTURE 4

The Perversions

*T*he very notion of sexuality is formed on the basis of knowledge about perversions. The experience of sexuality is far from
obvious: it is given first of all only through negativities. A. History
of knowledge about sexual perversions: until the eighteenth century,
included in the world of unreason and confinement; at the end of
the eighteenth century, confinement becomes differentiated: patient
or criminal. What status is to be given to sexual quasi-madness or
quasi-delinquency? The case of Sade at Charenton. Sexual transgression has a floating status. It is related to illness without being confused with it. The example of Krafft-Ebing: classification and origin
of perversions. B. At the end of the nineteenth century: intersexual
states and Marañón's theory. C. The Freudian analysis of perversions. Its importance and originality. 1. A formal analysis of perversions according to the object and aim: perversion is not the symptom
of something else; it is, like sexuality, a process with an object and an
aim; 2. An analysis of their content; 3. An analysis of the relations
between perversion, illness, and normal life: elements of perversion
are always present in normal life; relations of signification and
evasion between neuroses and perversions. Congenital perversion
as common base of neuroses, perversions, and normal sexuality:
infantile sexuality.

[72]   The analysis of sexuality was only developed on the basis of perversions. (Even more, the very notion of sexuality was formed only when perversion became an object of knowledge [*savoir*].)[1]

– We tend to think that perversion was only a deviation, an inflection, a derivative form of normal sexuality; the latter would have been known first and then, gradually, with the loosening of modesty, of religious and moral reticence, perversions would have entered the field of knowledge.

– In actual fact, it was exactly the other way round: the perversions were known before sexuality; in truth, the notion of sexuality was formed, it emerged, only through the analysis of perversions.

[73]   A lyrical language of love had existed for a long time; an erotic language of transgression had existed for a long time. Then the perversions began to be studied [as] an object of knowledge (and this roughly coincides with the nineteenth century, from Sade to Freud). And then it is simply with Freud, at the turn of the twentieth century, that thinking is reversed and something like the positive notion of sexuality appeared (*Three Essays*, 1905).[2]

Now, strangely, this historical phenomenon follows the same movement as the formation of sexuality in the individual, according to the account given by psychoanalysis at least. Sexuality in its normal positivity is only the result of a set of partial components that, taken in isolation and their order of succession, appear as so many perversions. We will see later how, for psychoanalysis, oral or anal eroticism, sadism or masochism, and autoeroticism necessarily enter into the composition of a normal, developed, adult—that is, nonpartial—sexuality.[3]

[74]   In remarking on the parallel between history and psychology, between ontogenesis and reasoned and scientific consciousness, I am not taking up one of Piaget's schemas.[4] I am only pointing out that sexuality in its positive form is far from being an

immediate notion, conduct, or experience. It is one of the constant themes of opinion or moral criticism that the modern world is guided by a preoccupation with sexuality. Actually, for the reflexive consciousness of Western culture, as for the individual experience of European man, sexuality only takes shape through negativities.

A. Historically

How was the scientific discourse of perversion formed?

1. Up to the end of the eighteenth century, perversions were not objects of reflection or knowledge, because sexual transgressions were caught up within silent practices, free of any theory. Confinement in the classical age involved, indiscriminately, people like the unemployed, sorcerers, certain categories of religious deviants, the mad, the incapable (feebleminded), and then libertines, the debauched, "sodomites," and so on.[5] So, the singling out of perversion in relation to a prohibition whose supporting surface was far wider than sexual transgression.

2. From the eighteenth century, a problem arises. In fact, [75] the homogeneous and teeming world of confinement begins to break up; detention in the strict sense, which is established at this time, must henceforth involve only the mentally ill: in principle it is a hospitalization. The other categories are split up; either they are purely and simply freed, or they are employed in workshops, or they are recruited by the army, and so on; or, finally, they are handed over to the courts (Penal Code).[6]

Now, we see emerging the case of sexual quasi-delinquency or quasi-madness.

The purest and most famous case is that of Sade. Two assignable sexual crimes. A political crime.[7] The rest of his detention has a strange status: he is transferred from Sainte-Pélagie to

Charenton. But there is protest against his presence at Charenton, Royer-Collard asserting:

- that he is not ill and cannot remain in a hospital;
- that he is affected by a "delirium of vice" and that detention without release should be provided for this incurable case.[8]

[76]   Perversion appears in the naked state through the medicalization of confinement:

– the Civil Code having deinstitutionalized sexuality, as we have seen, and consequently having been "liberal";[9]
– confinement having been, on the other hand, medicalized.

Sexual transgression thus remains without status: a sort of floating phenomenon that, as a result, becomes a scientific and theoretical problem. If Western culture is the only culture to have made sexuality an object of science, it is no doubt due to this series of historical and social phenomena. In most other cultures, and still in our culture until the beginning of the nineteenth century, sexuality could not be an object [of science] because it was too caught up in silent practices.

Throughout the nineteenth century, sexual deviation will thus keep this marginal status, between crime and illness, being neither completely one nor the other.[10] Clearly, scientific reflection will make every effort to relate it to illness; however (this is important), this is not in order to make it a component of illness, but in order to find in illness an abstract and general model that will enable perversions to be classified and explained.

[77]   In other words, perversion is not integrated into illness (or illness into perversion); two parallel series are established that do not communicate, either in substance or in the mode of interaction. The two series are independent; they have only forms in common, principles of explanation, modes of intelligibility.

Evidence of this parallelism without communication is given by the following fact: in the nineteenth century, when doctors curing hysterics by the method of hypnosis saw sexual content surfacing, they stopped the hypnosis, convinced that they were reaching [word missing] that was no longer that of the illness.[11]

However:

1. The only relationship admitted is a general type of causality:
- debauchery leads to mental illness;[12]
- mental illness leads to sexual perversion.[13]

2. There is indeed a common principle, called degeneration: it is only falling outside the normal.[14]

> [. . .]ᵃ   [78]ᵇ
> Krafft-Ebing:[15]   [79]
> - Peripheral neuroses
>   1. Sensory:
>   - anesthesia;
>   - hyperesthesia;
>   - neuralgia.
>   2. Secretory:
>   - aspermia;
>   - polyspermia.
>   3. Motor:
>   - spasms;
>   - paralysis.[16]
> - Spinal Neuroses:
>   - Affections of the erection center:
>   - arousal;
>   - paralysis.[17]
>   - Affections of the ejaculation center:
>   - easy;
>   - difficult.[18]

---

a Words crossed out: "two problems: classification/origin."

b Page 78 is missing. The two sheets that follow (79 and then another not numbered) appear to be taken from a file Foucault made based on the work of Richard von Krafft-Ebing.

– Cerebral neuroses
  • paradoxia: sexual emotions produced outside of the period of anatomico-physiological processes in the genital parts;
  • anesthesia: all organic impulses and all representations leave the individual indifferent;[19]
  • hyperesthesia: exaggerated excitability of internal or external origin;[20]
  • paresthesia: sexual excitation by inadequate object.[21]
    [. . .] "morbid condition of the spheres of sexual representation with manifestation of feelings such that representations that physio-psychologically should usually provoke disagreeable sensations are, on the contrary, accompanied by sensations of pleasure."[22]
    Example. Homosexuality, congenital phenomenon: disposition to homosexuality or bisexuality, which, to emerge, must be influenced by accidental causes.[23]
  • Simple perversion (old age, constraint).[24]
  • *Eviratio* and *defaminatio*: "deep change of character, feelings, and inclinations."[25]
  • Transmutation*sexualis*:feeling,physicalimpression,ofbeing a woman.[26]
  • Paranoiac sexual metamorphosis (hypochondriac and depreciatory delirium).[27]

[80]   *B. At the end of the nineteenth century*

The importance taken on by (or rather the importance uncovered in) homosexuality and the series of discoveries that led to hormonology would bring about a search for the possibility of perversions in the fragility of biological frontiers and for their real origin in the disruption of the imbalance defined as normal.

- Studies of intersexual states (which, in their manifest form, produce hermaphroditism). Theory of balance.[28]
- Studies by Marañón. There is a complete sexual cycle (that of the man); there is a slowed-down cycle, halted very early: the feminine cycle.[29]

C. The Freudian analysis of perversion   [81]

Its importance is said to be due to the fact that it integrated the perversions[c] and normal sexuality in a sort of unity with fluid divisions. In fact, its radically important character is not due to this (Havelock Ellis, Marañón had already done this).

It is important:

- [Because it is] not biological.[d]
- Because it overturns the ethical relationship that made perversion the deviation of sexuality; it makes sexuality a development of the perversions.
- Because for the first time it analyzes the neurosis/perversion relationship according to a schema that is not one of simple parallelism or causality:

  − it does not make perversion an effect of mental illness, although it discovers a component of perversion in every neurosis;

  − it does not make neurosis an effect of perversion, although it discovers the negative of the perversion in neurosis.

- Because for the first time it links perversions to the discovery of infantile sexuality.

---

c Words crossed out: "As components of." Foucault made several corrections to this sentence.
d Added afterward.

These four reasons are what is most important in Freudian doctrine, not the "discovery" of the links, transitions, and intermediate forms between normal and perverse sexuality.

[82]   The Freudian analysis of the neuroses consists:

1. In the formal analysis of the perversions without any search for etiology or psychological characterization. Freud distinguishes different types of perversions.[30]

- According to the object:
  a. inversion (same sex);
  b. children;
  c. animals.
- According to the sexual aim (defined as contact of sexual organs and [emission][e] of seminal fluids or satisfaction of the instinct)[31]:
  a. anatomical transgressions:
    – other parts of the body;
    – overvaluation of the sexual object;
    – fetishism.
  b. fixation of preliminary sexual aims:
    – touching and looking;
    – sadism and masochism.

This simple typology of the perversions is by itself already very significant for two reasons.

1. First of all, because it dissociates perversion, at least provisionally (and especially with regard to homosexuals), from every other abnormal conduct. It is never treated as a symptom of something else, an element in a more complex configuration.

---

e Foucault wrote "emissions," crossed out, then "with," crossed out, and added nothing. We have reestablished "emission."

2. Because it offers a quite singular definition of the sexual [83] object. Object and aim are distinguished. While the aim is defined by the organ, or anything that can be substituted for it, and the act, or anything that can serve it as relay or screen,[32] the object has a much wider, more floating definition: it is a bit the partner, a bit the other person (it is never oneself).[33]

So:

1. Perversion as autonomous phenomenon of sexuality (anyway, having its own forms): it is not the symptom of something else.

2. Perversion and sexuality having an aim and object, being defined consequently in a certain finalized process and by a certain object = x.

2. In an analysis of the contents of perversions:[f] [84]

Generally speaking, we call "tendency (*tendance*)" the psychical equivalent of a source of movement that is internal to the organism [and] that therefore contrasts with external excitations.[34] This tendency is therefore "on the frontier between the physical and the psychical."[35]

Their[g] specificity does not lie in their internal quality but is due to their somatic origin [and] their aim. Now there is a

---

f A version of this page, crossed out, is found on the verso:

"2) In an analysis of the content of perversions

All the tendencies (of which sexuality is a part) are "at the border of the psychical and physical domains"

– either every tendency is of the same type;

– or every tendency can be classified in two orders "according to their chemical nature"

As for its other specifications, they are the different parts of the body."

On "tendency (*tendance*)," see endnotes 30 and 34.

g Understanding "drives (*pulsions*)" or "tendencies" or, in English, "instincts."

tendency whose somatic origin is the sexual organs and whose aim is relief of the organic excitation.[36]

    1.   This tendency may focus on other parts of the body, which cease to be only that and become "parts of the genital apparatus." "Secondary genital apparatus."[37]

        a. This secondary genital apparatus (which often includes the mouth, anus, but [also], in the case of hysteria, many other parts of the body) is the seat of the same phenomena of excitement and satisfaction (or inhibition) as the sexual organs themselves.[38]

        [*In the margin*: "hysterical anesthesia like frigidity of secondary genital apparatus"]

        b. Hence the "partial" character of perversions that take these regions as the only ones.

    2.   It may happen also that the aim is displaced, as in obsession.[39]

[85]   *3. In an analysis of the relations between perversion and illness, on one side, [and] normal life, on the other*

A. Normal life

   – On the one hand, perversion is frequent as an addition to normal sexual activity. "In no normal individual is an element of what may be called perversion lacking, adding to the normal sexual aim."[40]

   – On the other hand, every perversion involves "psychic participation in the transformation of the tendency." "Omnipotence of love" that transforms.[41]

B. Pathology

   – The psychoneuroses are not effects of sexual disturbances; and perversions do not flourish in a privileged way in the climate of psychoneuroses. But "the sexual contribution is the most constant and most important source of energy in the neurosis."[42]

a. Sexual life is expressed wholly or [in] part by symptoms.

b. All symptoms are the expression of sexual life.[43]

   What is this expression? [Not][h] a reflection; not simply [86]
   a coded language; but an evasion. Example of the hysteric who has strong sexual instincts and a strong aver-
   sion due to repressions; solution that avoids conflicts by
   a "conversion of sexual tendencies into morbid symptoms."[44] Avoidance is both a solution and a cover. It
   therefore comes under an analysis in terms of economy
   and in terms of signification.[45]

c. Symptoms that evade (provide a solution but mask)
   are formed at the cost of what? Not normal sexuality.
   Normal sexuality is not what is repressed. But perversion.
   Symptoms are formed at the cost of perversions. One
   becomes neurotic so as to stop being perverse; one ceases
   being perverse to the extent that one becomes neurotic.
   "Neuroses are, so to say, the negative of the perversions."[46]
   (It is easy not to be perverse—which is why morality
   never lacks preachers; but it is not easy not to be neurotic—which is why psychiatrists always have clients.)

Which entails the consequences:[47]

a. The unconscious presence in every neurosis of a perversion in the aim (basically anatomical transgression).

b. The unconscious presence in every neurosis of a perversion in the object (i.e., homosexuality).

c. The presence in some neuroses of other perversions [87]
   (exhibitionism; sadism-masochism).

d. The presence of one of the elements of a perverse duality always entails the more or less apparent presence of
   the other element of the couple.[48]

---

h Foucault appears initially to have written: "less a reflection, less . . . ," then to have corrected the second "less" to "not," forgetting to correct the first. We correct it.

e. In every neurosis there is at least the trace of all the perversions.

Two things should be added to this:

– Should we conclude from this that neurotics are basically perverse? There are many who show no perversion at the apparent level and have never shown any before becoming neuropaths.

– Should we conclude from this that neurotics show no perversion because everything has been evaded?—The example would contradict it, since some are perverse.

We can reply to the second question by the theory of collaterality.[49] When the sexual instincts are repressed, a part of sexuality, without disappearing, will transfer into lateral channels: hence the same type of perversions as those found in the normal adult (an extra of sexuality); but more frequent than normal, because the neurotic only has the extra sexuality [*n'a de sexualité qu'à côté*].

[88]   As for the first question: should we accept that neurotics, even though they have never shown it, are especially perverse, since they have constructed the whole of their neurosis on their perversion?

In fact, there is a congenital perversity[i] to which everyone is subject and which:

- in certain cases becomes [a] determinant factor of— perverse—sexuality. Due to [its] "*intensity*"[j];
- in other cases is repressed and produces neurotic symptoms[k];

---

i Foucault appears to have replaced "congenital perversion" by "congenital perversity," but further on he retains the term "congenital perversion."

j Underlined in the manuscript.

k Foucault added, but then crossed out, "[and] lateral perversions."

- finally, in successful cases, through an "affective repression," a "normal sexual life" is formed.[50]

Perverts	Neurotics (with their perversions)	Normals (extra)
– Non-repression	Repression/derivation	Repression (*repression*)
– Intensity		
	Perversion	

What is this congenital *perversion*[1] on which, as if on a com-   [89] mon ground, the perversity of the perverse, the neurosis and perversions of the ill, and the normal sexuality and normally occasionally perverse (in the extra) sexuality of normal subjects are founded? What is this background noise of perversion, which supports every form of sexuality, whether normal, perverse, or evaded in the pathological symptom?

The sexuality of the infant.

But before examining this, we should note that there are five possible positions of perversion:

- Either understood as sexuality of the infant.
- Or understood as perversion of the pervert.
- Or understood as repressed content of the symptom.
- Or understood as collateral sexuality.
- Or understood as extra sexuality (*sexualité à côté*).

(The last two being really very close, although one is fixed and the other not.)

*

---

1 Underlined in the manuscript.

1. This thesis will be sustained by Michel Foucault in *Abnormal: Lectures at the Collège de France, 1974–1975*, trans. Graham Burchell, English series editor Arnold I. Davison (New York: Picador, 2003), 167–70, and especially 263–90, where it is a matter of the emergence of *scientia sexualis* and, in particular, of considering the irruption of sexuality in medical discourses. This irruption took place first of all through the analysis of the field of abnormalities of instinct. It may be noted that this thesis is purely an extension of the position repeated on several occasions by Foucault that psychology is first of all a knowledge of negativities (see above, lecture 2, note 8, p. 45, and lecture 3, pp. 52–53). For a similar thesis, see Arnold I. Davidson, *The Emergence of Sexuality: Historical Epistemology and the Formation of Concepts* (Cambridge, MA: Harvard University Press, 2001). On the history of the concept of "perversion" in the nineteenth century, see also Claude-Olivier Doron, "La formation du concept psychiatrique de perversion au XIXᵉ siècle," *L'Information psychiatrique* 88, no. 1 (2012): 39–49; Georges Lantéri-Laura, *Lecture des perversions: Histoire de leur appropriation médicale* (Paris: Masson, 1979); and Julie Mazaleigue-Labaste, *Les Déséquilibres de l'amour: La genèse du concept de perversion sexuelle de la Révolution française à Freud* (Paris: Ithaque, 2014).

2. See above, lectures 2 and 3, p. 31 and pp. 70–72. The reference to Freud is to the *Three Essays on the Theory of Sexuality* (1905) to which Foucault will return at length in this and the next lecture.

3. See below, p. 114 *et seq.*

4. See Jean Piaget, *The Origin of Intelligence in the Child*, trans. Margaret Cook (London: Routledge, 2011 [1953]), and *The Psychology of Intelligence*, trans. Malcolm Piercy and D. E. Berlyne (London: Routledge, 2003 [1950]). As Foucault notes, in "La psychologie de 1850 à 1950," 159, "Piaget gives most emphasis to the necessary development of both biological and logical structures; he seeks to show in the development of the first—from those that are irreversibly orientated and concrete up to those that are reversible and abstract . . .—a process that followed in reverse direction the course of the history of the sciences—from Euclidean geometry up to vector and tensor calculus: the psychological development of the infant is just the reverse of the historical development of the mind." The schema would be the same here: the historical discoveries of knowledge of sexuality—from perversions and partial tendencies to the "positive" knowledge of normal sexuality—would follow the various stages of infantile sexual development.

5. See Foucault, *History of Madness*, trans. Jonathan Murphy and Jean Khalfa (London: Routledge, 2006), in particular chapter 3, "The Correctional World," which details the "motley population," "the venereal, the debauched, the dissolute, blasphemers, homosexuals, alchemists and libertines" and beggars, etc., occupying the "correctional world" (101). All of these figures are linked by a common experience of unreason. It is this experience that founds the "homogeneous" character of this world of confinement: "throughout the classical age, there was only one confinement, and all the measures that were taken, from one extreme to the other, hide a common, homogeneous experience" (chapter 4, "Experiences of Madness," 109).

6. See *History of Madness*, in particular part 3, chapters 3 and 4.

7. The two "assignable" sexual offenses refer, on the one hand, to the physical abuses inflicted on the beggar Rose Keller (the case was judged in June 1768 and Sade condemned to six months' detention) and, on the other, to the accusation that Sade gave poisoned sweets to several of his sexual partners during an evening of debauchery in Marseille in 1772 (accused of poisoning and sodomy, he was condemned in his absence to the death penalty). The political crime refers to Sade's condemnation to death by the Revolutionary Tribunal of 8 Thermidor Year 2 for "intelligence and correspondence with enemies of the Republic." He was finally arrested again in 1801 and detained first at Sainte-Pélagie, then at Bicêtre, and finally at Charenton.

8. On this subject, see the letter from Antoine-Athanase Royer-Collard, chief doctor at the Charenton hospice, to the minister of the General Police of the Empire, August 2, 1808. He notes that Sade "is not insane (*aliéné*). His only delirium is that of vice, and this kind of delirium can in no way be repressed in a house devoted to the medical treatment of insanity. The individual affected by it must be subject to the strictest sequestration, both to protect others from his frenzies and to isolate him from all the objects that might excite or support his hideous passion" [in D. A. F. de Sade, *L'Oeuvre du marquis de Sade: Zoloé, Justine, Juliette . . .*, Introduction and notes by G. Apollinaire (Paris: Bibliothèque des curieux, 1912 [1909]), 50]. Foucault refers to Royer-Collard's letter in *History of Madness*, presenting it as the sign that the experience of unreason, which gave unity to the mode of confinement in the classical age, had lost its meaning, giving way to a desire "to turn madness into a positive science, i.e. to silence unreason by listening only to the pathological voices of madness"; "Royer-Collard no

longer understood correctional existence. Having looked for its reason in illness, and failing to find it there, he reverts to an idea of pure evil, which has no reason for existence other than its own unreason" (107). Foucault also returns to this episode in the 1963 radio broadcast which he devoted to the "silence of the mad" ("The Silence of the Mad" in Foucault, *Language, Madness, and Desire: On Literature*, trans. Robert Bononno [Minneapolis, University of Minnesota Press, 2013], 41–45). Royer-Collard appears here as the symbol of a "stuttering" of reason, of a "predicament" of our culture, "which has remained with us since the nineteenth century, in the face of madness and the language of madness." A reasoning madness that "we no longer know exactly where to assign." It is this same predicament, and the institutional in-between, which Foucault will take up in *Abnormal* with regard to the problem posed by monomaniacal homicide and various deviations of the sexual instinct. Saint-Pélagie was a house of correction for women for a long time before becoming, under the Revolution, a remand prison; Sade will pass through Bicêtre—another historic site of confinement in the eighteenth century, which became a *maison de force* in which patients and delinquents coexisted up to the first third of the nineteenth century—before being confined definitively at Charenton, an old *maison de force* that became an asylum for the rather wealthy insane at the beginning of the nineteenth century.

9. See above, lecture 1, pp. 11–13.

10. See *Abnormal*, which goes into this question more deeply.

11. Foucault provides a very different reading of this phenomenon at the end of *Psychiatric Power: Lectures at the Collège de France, 1973–1974*, ed. Jacques Lagrange, trans. Graham Burchell, English series editor Arnold I. Davidson (London: Palgrave Macmillan, 2008). Analyzing the emergence of the "neurological body" at the end of the nineteenth century and making hysteria a point of confrontation and struggle between alienists and hysterics, Foucault reflects on the fact that, in the work of identifying traumas that enable the reality of hysteria to be founded as illness, the neurologists of Salpêtrière constantly encountered sexual content during hypnosis but shied away from it and did not talk about it. His explanation then is that this sexual content is the hysteric's "counter-maneuver" in relation to the doctor's power of injunction; the hysteric takes advantage of the injunction and into "the breach opened by this injunction they will push their

life, their real . . . that is to say, their sexual life." And if Charcot and his students do not admit it, it is because it completely challenges their effort to give hysteria an incontestable and respectable value as illness. "So this sexuality is not an indecipherable remainder but the hysteric's victory cry, the last maneuver by which they finally get the better of the neurologists and silence them" (*Psychiatric Power*, 318–22)

12. This is especially true in the case of general paralysis. On this subject, see the Vincennes course, below, lecture 6, note 7, p. 239; and already in *History of Madness*, where Foucault notes that in general paralysis, "guilt in the form of a sexual fault was clearly designated" (522).

13. For many authors, in fact, sexual perversion may arise from a mental illness and be a symptom of it. During the first debates on the "deviations of the venereal appetite," regarding the case of the soldier François Bertrand, for example, Ludger Lunier maintained the position that the "perversion of the venereal appetite" is only an "epiphenomenon of the illness . . . analogous to those depraved appetites so common in the insane." On this point, see C.-O. Doron, "La formation du concept psychiatrique de perversion au XIXᵉ siècle en France," *L'Information psychiatrique* 88, no. 1 (2012): 44, and Foucault, *Abnormal*, 284–85, which compares the position of Charles-Jacob Marchal and Claude-François Michéa on the subject.

14. The theory of degeneration and the notion of morbid heredity as established in psychiatry with the works of Bénédict-Augustin Morel, *Traité des dégénérescences physiques, intellectuelles et morales de l'espèce humaine et des causes qui produisent ces variétés maladives*, 2 vols. (Paris: J.-B. Baillière, 1857), and Valentin Magnan, *Recherches sur les centres nerveux*, 2 vols. (Paris: G. Masson, 1876–1893), effectively provide a common principle to a set of mental illnesses—from neurosis to idiocy—and to the most diverse sexual perversions. The principle rests on a specific type of hereditary deviation (in the case of Morel) or in a progressive and hereditary imbalance of the nervous centers (in Magnan). For a long time, as Freud himself constantly notes in order to criticize it, the perversions were read as "signs of degeneration" (see, for example, S. Freud, *Introductory Lectures to Psycho-Analysis*). Foucault will return to degeneration, notably in *Psychiatric Power*, 221–23 and 271–72, and *Abnormal*, 291–321. As he emphasizes, degeneration defines the domain of abnormality and its hereditary transformations within which madness and sexual perversions can be fitted. For further clarification, see

notably Jean Christophe Coffin, *La Transmission de la folie, 1850–1914* (Paris: L'Harmattan, 2003) and C.-O. Doron, *Races et Dégénerescence: L'émergence des savoirs sur l'homme anormal*, vol. 2, doctoral thesis of philosophy, directed by D. Lecourt, University of Paris-Diderot, 2011.

15. Foucault here copies, more or less identically, the "Schedule of the Sexual Neuroses" established by Richard von Krafft-Ebing in his *Étude médico-légale*, *"Psychopathia Sexualis": Avec recherches spéciales sur l'inversion sexuelle*, trans. from the 8th ed. by E. Laurent and S. Csapo (Paris: G. Carré, 1895), 50–53; see the authorized English adaptation of the 12th ed. by F. J. Rebman, *Psychopathia Sexualis with Especial Reference to the Antipathic Sexual Instinct: A Medico-Forensic Study* (New York: Physicians and Surgeons, 1935), 49. The next two pages seem to be taken directly from a rough file Foucault made on the basis of Krafft-Ebing's work. They open with a crossed-out passage indicating "two problems: classification/origin," which enables us to retrace something of Foucault's logic. The abstract model of the illness raises two problems: that of etiology (or origin) which was referred to on the previous page (that is, for a long time degeneration provided the etiology of the sexual perversions); and that of classification. It is here that Foucault inserts, as the best illustration, Krafft-Ebing's classification of "sexual neuroses." The importance of the classification in the general model of illness has already been analyzed, in relation to madness, in Foucault, *History of Madness*, 190–98, for the classical age; and for "classificatory medicine," in *Birth of the Clinic*, trans. A. M. Sheridan (London: Tavistock, 1973), chap. 1.

16. Krafft-Ebing specifies pollutions (for spasms) and spermatorrhoea (for paralysis).

17. Arousal actually designates priapism; paralysis is linked to a destruction of the centers or nerve tracts of communication in affections of the spinal cord; or, in a milder form, a form of lessened sensitivity linked to overstimulation or excess (Krafft-Ebing, *Psychopathia Sexualis*, 49–50). Krafft-Ebing adds phenomena of "inhibition" of erection linked to certain emotions (disgust, fear of illness, etc.).

18. Krafft-Ebing, *Psychopathia Sexualis*, 51–52.

19. Krafft-Ebing, *Psychopathia Sexualis*, 52. The exact quotation is "anesthesia (absence of sexual inclination).—Here all organic impulses and visual, auditory, and olfactory sense impressions fail to sexually excite the individual."

20. Krafft-Ebing, *Psychopathia Sexualis*, 52. "*Hyperaesthesia* (increased desire, satyriasis). In this state there is an abnormally increased impressionability of the *vita sexualis* to organic, psychical, and sensory stimuli (abnormally intense *libido*, lustfulness, lasciviousness). The stimulus may be central (nymphomania, satyriasis) or peripheral, functional or organic."

21. Krafft-Ebing, *Psychopathia Sexualis*, 52. "*Paraesthesia* (perversion of the sexual instinct, i.e., excitability of the sexual functions to inadequate stimuli." The set of paresthesias are then described (79 *et seq*).

22. Krafft-Ebing, *Psychopathia Sexualis*, 79: "In this condition there is perverse emotional colouring of the sexual ideas. Ideas physiologically and psychologically accompanied by feelings of disgust give rise to pleasurable feelings." This is the general definition of paresthesia.

23. The case of inversion of the sexual sense or homosexuality is treated by Krafft-Ebing, *Étude médico-légale*, 282 *et seq*. Foucault refers here to 285, where Krafft-Ebing emphasizes that, in the case of homosexuality, the nondevelopment of a "normal" sexual inclination for the other sex is not explained by a bad development of the sexual organs but originates in an "anomaly of psychosexual feeling [that] may be called, clinically, a functional sign of degeneration." Krafft-Ebing notes: "This inverted sexuality appears spontaneously, without external cause, with the development of sexual life, as an individual manifestation of an abnormal form of the *vita sexualis*, having the force of a *congenital* phenomenon; or it develops upon a sexuality the beginning of which was normal, as a result of very definite injurious influences, and thus appears as an *acquired* anomaly. . . . Careful examination of the so-called acquired cases makes it probable that the predisposition—also present here—consists of a latent homosexuality, or, at any rate, bisexuality, which, for its manifestation, requires the influence of accidental exciting causes to rouse it from its dormant state" (285).

24. This is the first degree of sexual inversion, according to Krafft-Ebing, "simple reversal of sexual feeling," "when a person exercises an aphrodisiac effect over another person of the same sex who reciprocates the sexual feeling. Character and instinct, however, still correspond with the sex of the individual presenting the reversal of sexual feeling. He feels himself in the active *rôle*" (*Étude médico-légale*, 289–90). It is difficult to see what Foucault is referring to with the terms "old age" and "constraint," except perhaps to the mechanisms by which this first degree of inversion, presented by

Krafft-Ebing as reversible, can be combated: through external constraints or the person's force of will; or by its disappearing with old age.

25. Second degree of inversion for Krafft-Ebing: "The patient undergoes a deep change of character, particularly in his feelings and inclinations, which thus become those of a female" (*Étude médico-légale*, 297). This degree is particularly characterized by the permanent adoption of the passive role in the sexual act.

26. Correction: *transmutatio sexus*. This is the third degree, which makes the transition toward *metamorphosis sexualis paranoia*. In this case, the "physical sensations are also transformed in the sense of a *transmutatio sexus*" (*Étude médico-légale*, 304).

27. This is the fourth and final stage, that of "delusion of a transformation of sex" (*Étude médico-légale*, 328).

28. This is the theory of genetic balance advanced by Calvin B. Bridges, "Haploid Drosophila and the Theory of Genic Balance," *Science*, no. 72 (1930): 405–6, according to which determination of sex is the result of a balance between a series of genes located on the autosomes, for male, and on the X, for female.

29. See especially Gregorio Marañón, *L'Évolution de la sexualité et les états intersexuels*, trans. J. S. d'Arellano (Paris: Gallimard, 1931). Marañón's position is summarized by Jules Carles, *La Sexualité* (Paris: Armand Colin, 1953), 160–62. For Marañon, physiological sex is not a stable reality, clearly divided between two sexes, but a single process that passes through different phases, evolving sometimes toward the male or female pole. The "normal" man passes very quickly, in infancy, through a preliminary female stage, while the "normal" female tends to reach masculinity only at the end of her evolution, after the menopause. "In the man, the initial feminoid phase is short and not very intense, and the virile phase, highly differentiated, is lengthy. In the woman, the feminine phase is lengthy and differentiated, and the terminal viriloid phase is short and not very vigorous" (Marañón, *L'Évolution de la sexualité*, 243).

30. Foucault here takes up the different categories of sexual perversion as Freud formally divides them up in the first of the *Three Essays on the Theory of Sexuality* (1905), *CPW* 7, focusing on "The Sexual Aberrations," 135–60. Foucault uses a translation of the text that is distinctive in particular for rendering *Trieb* as *tendance* (tendency) rather than *pulsion* (drive).

The English standard edition of Freud's *Complete Psychological Works* (*CPW*) translates *Trieb* as *instinct*. References to Freud's work in the endnotes will be to the English translation.

31. "The normal sexual aim is regarded as being the union of the genitals in the act known as copulation, which leads to a release of the sexual tension and a temporary extinction of the sexual instinct—a satisfaction analogous to the sating of hunger" (*CPW*, 7, 149).

32. See the preceding definition of the "aim," for what concerns the "organs," it being understood that there are a multiplicity of preliminary and intermediary "sexual aims" that are accompanied by a certain pleasure and, at the same time, are supposed to increase tension in order to arrive at the terminal sexual aim; these aims may result in fixations. As for the aim as act, this is the definition Freud gives (*CPW*, 7, 135): the sexual aim is "the act toward which the instinct tends."

33. The sexual object is presented as "the person from whom sexual attraction proceeds" (Freud, *CPW*, 7, 135).

34. Foucault here retranscribes the main elements of part 5, "Component Instincts and Erotogenic Zones," of the first of the *Three Essays*, dating from the 1915 edition, in a translation in which the term "*Trieb*" is rendered by "*tendance* (tendency)" and not by "*pulsion* (drive)." The English *Standard Edition of the Complete Psychological Works* translates "*Trieb*" as "instinct," and the passage referred to here is translated as follows: "By an 'instinct' is provisionally to be understood the psychical representative of an endosomatic, continuously flowing source of stimulation, as contrasted with a 'stimulus,' which is set up by single excitations coming from *without*" (*CPW*, 7, 168)

35. See *CPW*, 7, 168: "The concept of instinct is thus one of those lying on the frontier between the mental and the physical."

36. Foucault literally copies the following passage: "in itself an instinct is without quality. . . . What distinguishes the instincts from one another and endows them with specific qualities is their relation to their somatic sources and to their aims. The source of an instinct is a process of excitation occurring in an organ, and the immediate aim of the instinct lies in the removal of this organic stimulus" (*CPW*, 7 168)

37. *CPW*, 7, 169. In the psychoneuroses (hysteria in particular) and in perversions, "erotogenic zones" like the oral and anal orifices behave like "a

portion of the sexual apparatus", "apparatuses subordinate to the genitals and as substitutes for them".

38. *CPW*, 7, 169–70.

39. *CPW*, 7, 169: "In obsessional neurosis, what is more striking is the significance of those impulses that create new sexual aims and seem independent of erotogenic zones."

40. *CPW*, 7, 160: "No healthy person, it appears, can fail to make some addition that might be called perverse to the normal sexual aim."

41. *CPW*, 7, 161: "It is perhaps in connection precisely with the most repulsive perversions that the mental factor must be regarded as playing its largest part in the transformation of the sexual instinct. . . . The omnipotence of love is perhaps never more strongly proved than in such of its aberrations as these."

42. *CPW*, 7, 163: "the energy of the sexual instinct . . . is the most important and only constant source of energy in the neurosis."

43. *Ibid.*

44. The case of hysterics, regarded as "typical of all psychoneurotics," is analyzed in part 4 of the first of the *Three Essays*, "The Sexual Instinct in Neurotics," 164–69. The quotation is taken from p. 164. See also Josef Breuer and Sigmund Freud, *Studies on Hysteria, CPW*, 2.

45. Foucault attaches a quite specific importance to the fact that "no form of psychology has given more importance to signification than psychoanalysis" ("La psychologie de 1850 à 1950" [1957], 155). In the same period, Foucault evoked Freud's relation to the interpretation of signs—for which the unconscious is both the bearer and the key—in "Philosophie et pscyhologie," 469–71, and in his contribution devoted to techniques of interpretation in Nietzsche, Freud, and Marx at the Royaumont colloquium on Nietzsche in July 1964: "Nietzsche, Freud, Marx" [1967], in *DÉ*, I, no. 46, 592–607; English translation by Jon Anderson and Gary Hentzi, "Nietzsche, Freud, Marx," in *EW*, 2, 269–78. Paul Ricoeur studied in detail the links between the economic ("energetic") and signification in Freud in a series of lectures given in 1961–1962 that form the framework for *De l'interprétation: Essai sur Freud* (Paris: Seuil, 1965).

46. All of this analysis of the relations between neurosis and perversion is found in the *Three Essays*, 165–67.

47. Freud details these consequences on 165–67.

48. When we find a tendency in the unconscious that is capable of coupling with the contrary tendency (active-passive; for example, voyeurism-exhibitionism), a given tendency is always accompanied by its counterpart, one occupying a more or less dominant place in relation to the other.

49. On this theory, see part 6 of the first of the *Three Essays*, "Reasons for the Apparent Preponderance of Perverse Sexuality in the Pscyhoneuroses," 170–71.

50. Foucault is here following part 7 of the first of the *Three Essays*, "Intimation of the Infantile Character of Sexuality," 171–72, from which the various quotations are taken. The choice of the term "perversity" in place of "perversion" however is not Freud's, who is content to note that "there is indeed something innate lying behind the perversions," "innate constitutional roots of the sexual instinct" that are shared by everyone and that, in some cases, give rise to perversions. [Where Foucault quotes "affective repression (*répression affective*)," the *CPW* English translation has "effective restriction." —G.B.]

LECTURE 5

Infantile Sexuality[1]

*I. Long disregard and resistance to the direct study of infantile sexuality. 1. Cultural reasons: history of childhood (eighteenth–nineteenth century). Postulate of the child's purity in the nineteenth century. War and the economic crisis at the beginning of the twentieth century raise the question of pedagogy in a new way. 2. Psychological reasons: amnesia and neurotic relationships to childhood: childhood is always viewed indirectly by adults. 3. Psychoanalytic technique: difficulties raised by the psychoanalysis of children. II. Analysis of infantile sexuality. A. Elements: a nongenital sexuality, focusing on one's own body, linked to different erogenous zones, and made up from partial tendencies. It presupposes intense interpretive activities. Distinguishing interpretations and fantasies. Diverse interpretations. Relationship of knowledge (*connaissance*) and language to sadism and murder. Sexuality and history: relationship to the Law, relationship to others, and tragic experience. B. Forms of organization: 1. oral; 2. anal-sadistic; 3. genital. The question of female sexuality.*

The study of infantile sexuality is a fine expression of the system   [90]
of arguments that Western culture has opposed to the study of
(adult, normal, positive) sexuality itself.

   We have seen that sexuality was [constituted][a] only through
the perversions. It was thought or hoped that this analysis would

---

a We add "constituted."

bring us face to face with sexuality itself. In actual fact, it brought us face to face with a number of negative phenomena (various perversions, various neuroses, lateral sexualities, normal sexuality formed on the basis of a repressed perversion). And then, the basis of all this, a congenital perversion—what the infant brings at birth or, at least, manifests from birth.[2]

For a long time, this study of infantile sexuality, which we must now address, was not carried out directly, and it is doubtful that it can be even now.

[91]   This indirect character of the study of infantile sexuality is marked by a number of facts, some of which doubtless have to do with the history of our culture, others with individual psychology, and the rest, finally, with psychoanalytic technique.

(To tell the truth, these three reasons are connected: individual psychology and cultural history reinforcing each other, determining each other; psychoanalytic technique being linked to these first two reasons.)

A. Cultural reasons[3]

1. Until the end of the eighteenth century, childhood had formed an autonomous entity, a segment of life; but a segment *en bloc*, without internal gradation. One was either inside or outside childhood. There was no internal hierarchy of age groups. (This was expressed pedagogically in indifference to maturation.)[4]

[92]   2. From the nineteenth century childhood spreads out according to age groups (making possible, prescribing a diachronic pedagogy); but, at the same time, it is separated from the adult world, forming a microcosm alongside the grown-up world of mature adults. In truth, a double microcosm: that of early learning [and] that of secondary schools.[5]

3. It is only later, after the war, that the concrete problems of education arise anew:

    a. A number of social upheavals:
- Aichhorn[6]—Makarenko[7];
- Bernfeld: *Kinderheim* for children without parents.[8]

    b. The economic crisis (overproduction) which brings about:
- Mass youth unemployment;
- Need for retraining and training in technical skills.

The problem of childhood arose in a new and urgent way under the pressure of these social transformations.

So, throughout the nineteenth century the postulate of the purity of childhood had reigned. No relationship with sexuality. The child is no more than pure learning.

And as it was in that period that adult sexuality was dis-   [93] covered, one compensated on the side of origins for what was brought to light on the adult's side. Or rather, a sexuality denied for that period of childhood, no longer solely biological and not yet decadent, was fixed on the side of nature and rediscovered on the side of degeneration. The theme of the purity of childhood was protection against the discovery of adult sexual impurity.[9]

B. *Psychological reasons*

1. Infantile amnesia, which concerns the first "6 or 8" years of childhood.[10]

- Amnesia that is so pronounced that no one was astonished by it before Freud, as if there were an amnesia of that amnesia.
- It cannot be regarded as a natural forgetting (due to immaturity of the nervous system), because childhood is the age of learning.

It concerns, therefore, a privileged category of facts:

    a. These facts, as their return in certain circumstances tends to prove, are most important.

[94]   b. They are generally of a sexual nature.

2. Now two things should be noted:

– These facts are forgotten as are, in hysterics, and neuropaths generally, recent events (cf. Dora: the hysterical cough and M[ister] K's kiss at the foot of the stairs).[11]

– On the other hand, these forgotten facts of sexual conduct are of the same nature as those manifested in neuroses:

    • other sexual objects (homosexuality);

    • other sexual aims (partial and derivative aims).[12]

We must be careful here. It is usually said that, for Freud, childhood and neurosis are exactly homogenous and are superimposed on each other. Childhood would be, for him, a sort of precocious neurosis; and neurosis, a childhood halted and fixed on itself. Things are more complex.

    • It is true that there is conduct in children that has the same structure as neurosis; that neurosis, on the other hand, includes infantile fixations.

[95]   • But in fact, what Freud shows above all, what is fundamental, is that the relationship of the adult to the infant they once were is a neurotic type of relationship (i.e., a relationship established according to mechanisms almost all of which are found in neurosis). We were not hysterical, or obsessive, or phobic in our childhood; we are hysterical, or obsessive, or phobic in our relationship to our childhood; and it is when leaving it, in order to leave it, that we set in action *a "certain number"*[b] of phobic,

---

b Underlined in the manuscript.

obsessive, hysterical processes or mechanisms. I say "a certain number," and this is the crucial problem, because this is where the division is made between normal and pathological.

There are a number of mechanisms that are not at work in the normal individual (or are so to a lesser degree: the flight into fantasy; splitting of personality; denial of reality). On the other hand, there is at least one mechanism that is only rarely at work in the ill person, which is sublimation.

On the other hand, a certain number of mechanisms are found in both the normal and the ill: repression (*refoulement*). The theory of repression, with all the enigmas it harbors, is indeed at the heart of Freudian psychoanalysis.

As a result of these "neurotic" mechanisms that structure the [96] adult's relation to his childhood, it is not possible to have direct access to childhood through observation or adult memories.

1. At the level of memory, there is no pure, transparent, immediately delivered recollection of childhood.

2. As for the observations that adults can make of the children around them and, generally, of their own children (or those who act as their substitutes), they too are filtered by those mechanisms transferred from the subject's childhood to the childhood of others. This transfer may be carried out in various ways:

    – either childhood plays the role of sexual object or aim for the adult. For example, we know that the child plays the role of male organ for the mother, operating thus in the structure of castration, which is undoubtedly common to all women;

    – or the child is a way of reactivating infantile situations: it becomes a sexual object; homosexual or Oedipal fixations.

[97]   Relations to the child, even in the case of a normal individual, are part of that collateral sexuality that is commonly part of
adult life. The love one brings to children is fundamentally perverse. The first, the only seducers of the child, are its parents. If
we come out of childhood raped, beaten, homosexual, sadomas-
ochistic, exhibitionist, voyeuristic, [it is] because we had parents.
For years we were the aim and object of adult perversions.

The (normal) adult's relation to childhood enters into the
previous schemas:

- repression (this is the relation to one's own childhood);
- collateral sexuality (this is the relation to other children).

Hence the fact that, for psychoanalysis, no pedagogy is possible:

- "Even before he came into the world, I knew that a little Hans would be born who would love his mother and
  hate his father."[13]
- "Whatever you do, it will be wrong."[14]

So, for all these reasons, the adult's testimony about his
childhood and about children cannot be accepted directly and
without analysis.

[98]   *C. Psychoanalytic technique*

For a long time (and, truth to tell, for all his life), Freud refused
to analyze children. Little Hans, through an intermediary.[15]
Historically, direct analysis of children appeared in 1926, with a
series of lectures by A[nna] Freud at the Vienna psychoanalytic
institute.[16]

- 1927, report by A[nna] Freud at the Tenth International Congress of Psychoanalysis. Regular meetings in
  Vienna start from this date. The International Society
  of Psychoanalysis organizes two clinics, one for children
  (directed by Sterba[17]), the other for adolescents (directed

by Aichhorn[18]). Immediately before the war, experimental crèche for children from one to two years old (with Dorothy Burlingham[19]).

What is the reason for this delay? And what is the reason for the difficulties still encountered for the analysis of children?

– The fact that it is difficult, maybe impossible, to determine the criteria for what is pathological in the child. In fact[20]:

1. The criteria for what is pathological for the adult, the basis [99] on which their awareness of their illness refers to it, is their sexuality and work. Now this cannot be the basis for a decision in the case of the child (reality, pleasure[21]).

2. The adult judges disorders in relation to what will be important for him (anorexia).

3. He judges the pathology through his own disorder. He will consider nocturnal enuresis serious, but a boy's passive femininity a positive sign.[22]

4. The child is not always aware of the illness.[23]

– What is more, a number of difficulties arise once psychoanalysis is underway.

- There is not always a will to get better (it is the parents who get help); and, in addition, more often even than in adults, illness is the only solution in a milieu one does not control.

- No language;

- No structured ego (*moi*).

– Finally, in the course of the analysis itself, one encounters [100] mechanisms of defense that are much stronger than in the adult.

In particular:

- Negation of external reality;

- Amnesia;

- Flight into fantasy;

- Splitting of personality;
- Motor inhibitions.[24]

ANALYSIS OF INFANTILE SEXUALITY

A. The elements

1. It is an activity the sexual nature of which does not have a genital character

Many activities without any relationship with the reproductive system must be ascribed to sexuality. What enables them to be recognized as sexual? A certain number of characteristics:

    a. rhythmicity of the action [. . .[c]];

    b. absorbed attention;

    c. accompaniment with more general muscular tension;

    d. release → sleep;

    e. finally, these activities are sometimes coupled with touching the genital parts.

Sucking meets these five criteria.[25]

[101] ### 2. It is an activity that generally does not concern others but only the child's own body

It is autoerotic (cf. again, sucking). But this autoerotism is remarkable for four reasons:

    a. On the one hand, it is grafted onto feeding behavior: its manifestations, like rhythmicity, etc., are of exactly the same type as nutrition.

---

c An abbreviation, "o", follows; it is difficult to interpret. Freud speaks of "rhythmic repetition."

b. It is thereby attached to actions indispensable to the maintenance of life.[26] This is crucially important:
   – since it brings together the pleasure principle and the reality principle (or rather, they are not yet separated);
   – when the ego is formed (as seat of the reality principle), it will be able to be invested by libido, giving rise to the ego instincts [and] narcissism.[27]

c. This autoerotism is therefore derivative in relation to pleasure that passed through an external object, the maternal breast. And, in a sense, autoerotism is a compensation and substitute for temporary loss of the object.[28] In Freudian analysis, one's own body is perhaps only ever a substitute for the other. I am there if the other is not. I am only the absence of my object. The consequences of which should be noted: [102]
   – To love, as turning from autoerotism to others, is "to give what one does not have".[29]
   – One's own body being the absence of that object, when that object is bad, one disappears: masochism, suicide.
   – The processes of identification are based on an experience of absence.

d. It marks the first separation of the alimentary and the sexual. In this sense, it is as if the sexual, strictly speaking, is detached from an appetite concerning life. One loves because one does not eat.[30]
   This explains how Freud could say that autoerotism is primary (which Anna Freud takes up); and could place the object relation before autoerotism (like Melanie Klein[31]). This is because, in fact, autoerotism [marks the entry]^d into the order of sexuality since the latter only appears with it.   [103]

---

d Foucault forgot the end of the phrase when changing sheets: we have added "marks the entry."

But the condition of possibility for the appearance of sexuality is an object relation; sexuality manifests itself in the gape of this vanished object, and it does so as autoerotism.[32]

3. It is an activity located in various zones of the body [33]

Not sexual, and concerning one's own body, where will it be located?

1st remark[e]: in principle, it may concern any part of the body. The body as a whole may be an erogenous zone. Now if the whole body may be an erogenous zone, it is in the sense that any part may be eroticized; for it is never eroticized all at once and simultaneously in its entirety. Why is this so?

- It is because autoerotism, detached from alimentary behavior, concerns first of all the mouth and hand. And only what can be reached by the mouth or the hand will fall within autoerotism.
- The possibility of complete eroticization of the body would entail three experiences which the child is not capable of:
  [104]   - either a complete relation to others (apart from his mother, when she holds the child on her knee);
    - or perception of another child with which one can identify;
    - or recognition in a mirror.

Now, [of] these experiences, the first confirms the disappearance of the object and, if it unifies the fragmentation, exacerbates it as soon as it disappears. The other two come later. And they are always decisive.[34]

---

e Underlined in the manuscript.

We can see that the fragmentation of the body may appear in these conditions:

  – either in cases of insufficient formation, in the perverse. With an aspect of primary autoerotism and an aggressive aspect;

  – or in cases of serious dissociation of the ego, as in schizophrenia.

These dissociations must be distinguished from the compensatory reactivations of hysterics. These are only collateral forms of sexuality, linked to the repression of genital sexuality. It is the switching off of frigidity. This involves the reactivation of zones of autoerotism.

*2nd remark*f: we can see how anal erotism will be formed on [105] this basis of autoerotism. Since (either by retention or by evacuation) it enables a certain action of the body on itself. It thus has the same structure as oral autoerotism. But, insofar as evacuation brings about pleasure through the disappearance of the object, it will be linked to the bad object (the one that escapes alimentary need). One rejects what one does not eat.

But, on the other hand, since what is evacuated forms part of the body (of the body that is an instrument of pleasure): positive valorization and anxiety before this object that one loses. Hence:

  • ambivalence of anal erotism;
  • the link between aggression and anxiety;
  • the link with sadism (the body one rejects) and masochism (oneself from which one separates[35]).

The obsessional suicide must be distinguished from the melan- [106] cholic suicide (who is genuine), whereas the former is only fantasy.

*3rd remark*g: is that there is no reason to exclude the reproductive system from this erotism by zone, but it does not have

---

f Underlined in the manuscript.

g Underlined in the manuscript.

a privileged position, for the moment at least. It is this auto-erotism that arouses infantile masturbation; masturbation that has particular importance in the case of seduction and that subsequently will be important because it is the forbidden and repressed activity. Hysteria is often due to this repression (and on the basis of seduction). Freud became aware of it in his etiology of hysteria.[36]

4th remark[h]: all this means that the sexuality of the child is characterized by "partial tendencies." This should be understood in several simultaneous senses:

1. The fact that other parts of the body play a role that is just as, if not more, important as the genital parts, at any rate, more basic.

[107]   2. That a number of sexual types of conduct arise without their being integrated as components [or collateral forms (sadism, masochism)[i]] in a genital sexuality.

3. That if it is true that such forms of behavior do not have a privileged sexual object, and one that totalizes them, they are not entirely deprived of an object. Voyeurism, exhibitionism, sadism, and masochism are practiced before or regarding a sexual object. This should not be confused with the libidinal object.[37]

4. That these forms of behavior may be activated, without in any way being created, by seduction. The child then becomes "polymorphously perverse," which differs from the normal only quantitatively. It should also be noted that seduction is a quantitative question (there are parental "seducers"[38]).

This perversion will be able to give either perversity (through lack of repression) or neuroses of repression (hysteria).

---

h Underlined in the manuscript.
i Passage added afterward.

4. They are activities linked to intense interpretive activity [108]

A. It is necessary to distinguish between fantasy and interpretation:

– fantasy: the imaginary actualization of an object with symbolic function, one that covers an anxious experience;

– interpretation: an intellectual activity intended to mask anxious experiences and satisfy affective needs. It is both an insurance system in relation to anxiety and a principle of intellectual systematization.

One is pathological; the other has a positive value. It is an adaptive factor.

It is true that interpretations and phantasies often become entangled: interpretations may link together fantasies (fairy-tale type: the ogre, etc.), and fantasies (the maternal phallus) confirm interpretations. But Melanie Klein is undoubtedly wrong to confuse them or, at least, to establish continuity between them.[39] They work against each other: when interpretation is mixed with fantasies, it is in order to defuse them and make them bearable (the fairy-tale ogre is less dangerous than the castrating father). And, conversely, when the fantasy occurs (the maternal phallus), it is because interpretation has failed (all women have the same genital apparatus as men).

B. What are these interpretations? [109]

They do not focus, in a primordial way, on genitality for the simple reason that this does not have the importance it will have later.

– The first interpretation appears about the birth of children (fear that others should come; that this sexual object, the mother, will disappear and be confiscated). Where do babies come from? (The riddle of the Sphinx.[40]) The interpretation universally given (which may later be repressed or disguised) is the closest to the structures we have already studied: the child is formed from food and is born through the bowel.[41] Which:

- is very "satisfying" since other children who are born will be put in the same category as fecal matter. They are naturally the object of aggression[42];
- authorizes the belief that the two sexes (and possibly the child itself) can have children.

[110] – The second interpretation focuses on the genital apparatus, which is accepted as being identical in everyone:

- Boys assume that girls have a penis. And when they have to submit to the evidence, they interpret it as loss (with an underlying anxiety that may give rise to fantasies).
- Girls think that everyone has the same genital apparatus as them. And when they discover that this is not the case, belief either in castration or in developmental delay. In any case, "penis envy."[43]

– The third series of interpretations focuses on sexual relations between parents. They interpret it always as sadism, and often in connection with urination and defecation.[44]

We see that, in all its themes and structures, this intellectual systematization is akin to sadism, and more particularly anal sadism. The anal-sadistic phase that occurs around the second and third years is the period of great intellectual [systematizations[j]], the acquisition of language, and the first major investigations.

[111] Hence, the well-known fact that obsessional neuroses are peculiar to subjects who are "intelligent", or at any rate intellectual, interpretative, rationalizing.[45] (They differ from paranoiacs in the sense that paranoiac interpretation comprises a whole system of projections concerning the structure of the ego: it is

---

j A missing word: we have reestablished "systematizations."

a psychosis; while here it a matter only of rationalizing experiences of a sexual order, so libidinal: a neurosis.)

Hence also a series of poorly known facts: the relationship of knowledge and language with sadism and murder.[46] A relationship that is found:

- In the great religious themes: knowledge that kills. The tree in Genesis, which should bring knowledge and which, in actual fact, dispels eternal and blessed life. The tree, precisely, that was forbidden by a prohibition. Consider also all the esotericisms: not to reveal, not to know. And the fact that so many sciences developed on the basis of an esoteric ritualization: not revealing in order to know; not revealing what one knows; you will know, if you agree not to know.

- Traces of this relationship are also found in all the prohibitions of language.[47] Words that must not be used. Words that kill. Sacred words that just to reveal would be dangerous. And the theme, which is so widespread, of names that must not be pronounced: either because in doing so one will kill the one whose name [it] is, or because one will be exposed to his blows. Of all our activities, language is certainly the one most receptive to obsessional defenses. It is no doubt from this that it draws its magical power and its capacities for contagion. It is dirty to say dirty things. An obviousness that is only possible against the backdrop of an obsessional defense.

[112]

And if you consider that, in our culture and many others, sexuality is what must not be spoken, as with everything concerning urination or defecation, you can see that we arrive at once at the formation of the language and the anal-sadistic interpretation of sexuality. Hence also the intensity of the scandal (of the pleasure and defense against the pleasure) before the crude swearword or the verbal exposure of sexuality.

[NP]ᵏ [We have seen the general characteristics of sexuality:

- Nongenital
- Relating to one's own body
- Located in different parts of the body
- Linked to important interpretative activities.

That is, sexuality is linked to the constitution of the experience of the body (and its opposite, death) [and] to the constitution of knowledge and language.[48]

But there is a dimension specific to this sexuality. It has a history; characteristic of this history is first being orientated toward a normative end and, second, choosing its objects. That is, it defines the individual's relationship to the Law and to Others. To others who are, at the same time, constituted by sexuality and evade it. Just as that law is what one can transgress.

[NP2] One conforms only to what one can destroy; one loves only what one can lose. It is in this threatened universe that man develops and moves. It is there that he takes on his specific volume.

And sexuality rediscoversˡ Greek tragedy (Others and Destiny). But this tragedy was deeply embeddedᵐ in naturalism. Whereas sexuality (with Freud) brings out from nature the great tragic powers that loom over man.

---

k Sheet not paginated on either recto or verso (following page), with heading (on the verso) "Université de Clermont/Faculté des lettres et sciences humaines/Institut de philosophie." It recapitulates the lecture and was no doubt added afterward. Only the sheet numbered 121 (the final page of the course) is also written on a sheet with the university heading. It is therefore quite possible that Foucault inserted these pages here as a conclusion and that the rest of the lecture was not delivered because, as will be seen, it ends suddenly.
l Foucault first wrote "repeats in reverse."
m Word difficult to read.

We live, we dream, we speak in the tragedy of sexuality. The tragedy that Proust, Genet, or Faulkner have taught us. And if it is said that in the era of the atom bomb sexual tragedy is very weak, the reply will be that tragic experience has always been on the margins of real dangers (the Greeks, Shakespeare[n]).[49]]

B. *Forms of organization*   [113][o]

The partial tendencies, the character of sexuality as either fragmented (in the body) or linked to other activities (like feeding), do not prevent sexual activity from having an "organization." What does Freud understand by "organization"?[50]

1. The most important form of sexual activity + those subordinate activities linked to it + those (nonsexual) activities with which it is associated. It is a nucleus of activity comprising a hierarchy within sexuality, or associations between sexuality and what is not sexual.
2. The definition of the sexual object.
3. The definition of the sexual aim.

These organizations are not directly visible during infancy; they are decipherable only through signs. They appear clearly only in pathological cases—when there is a fixation of the adult to a sexual organization (or rather to a nongenital form of organization, for the genital organization is seen as normative).

a. The first organization is *oral*.[p],[51] This phase is easily charac-   [114]
    terized by:

    • subordination of all sexual activities to that of grasping food (by the mouth and hand);
    • close association of sexual activities with feeding;

---

n The second word is hardly legible but appears to be "Shakespeare."
o We return here to the normal sequence of the lecture.
p Underlined in the manuscript.

- an object, or rather a series of objects—that is, all those that provide food;
- an aim that is incorporation.

The importance of this phase is due [to the fact]:

- that it is very quickly relayed by autoerotism and sucking behavior. That is, in itself it has only a "virtual existence." It is from the outset penetrated and traversed by the disappearance of the object, therefore:
  - by the body's position as sexual object;
  - by dispersion of the body;
  - by the depressive phase of disappearance of the object;
  - by aggressiveness as a way both of finding the object and of destroying it.[52]
- that it is the foundation of identifications. The mechanism of identification will develop on the model of alimentary harnessing, with all the oscillations that may take place. The maternal breast as an active and enriching object is of masculine polarity; now, for the boy, identification with the maternal breast must exclude identification with maternal sexuality. The maternal breast must have the value of the paternal sex, but not in the mode of feminine passivity for the child.[53]

[115]   In this sense, we can say with Melanie Klein that Oedipus takes shape at that point.[54]

b.   The second organization is the sadistic-anal type:[55]

- Associated with bowel activities of retention and evacuation.
- Subordinated to a bipolar sexual activity, not of the different sexes, but of activity and passivity:
  - activity being assured by muscular activity, which entails modification of the child's experience of its own body. The constitution of a unitary experience.

- passivity being represented by the intestinal cav-
ity and orifice, which involves an experience of the
body's interior.

So, two aspects of experience of the body: activity (external
and muscular); passivity (internal, intestinal).

- Importance for the formation of the ego (perceptive-
muscular structure).
- Importance for the formation of hypochondria (strongly
homosexual components).

So, also, importance for the distinction between activity and   [116]
passivity, which does not coincide with masculinity and femininity. That is why the sadistic-anal organization is essential
in the genesis of homosexualities.

• The sexual object is an object within the body but intended
to be ejected, and in this way it also brings about the adult's
(mother's) satisfaction and her seduction.

Hence the opposite structure of the oral sexual object: this
is external to the body but entirely intended to satisfy it (it
therefore combines the pleasure principle and the reality
principle; and it is therefore absorbed in autoerotism). The
sexual object in the sadistic-anal organization is inside the
body but must be ejected, given, in order to satisfy others.

a. It is therefore entirely dominated by the pleasure
principle.
b. This pleasure is ambivalent since loss gives pleasure (to
the other) and retention (displeasure and punishment
for the other) produces pleasure.
c. Hence the intervention of law, which will henceforth
be linked (with the ambivalence of pleasure) to sexual
activity.

• With regard to the sexual aim, it is clear that it is
sadomasochism:

- aggression as retention or release at the wrong time giving pleasure;
- suffering as voluntary loss or retention being rewarded.

This phase is therefore crucial for the organization of the ego, for the constitution of the child's own body (being able to become the object of narcissism), for a bipolar sexual activity (which ignores however the masculine-feminine opposition), through the constitution of sadomasochism.

c. Genital organization:[56]

Subordination to a sexual activity defined by masculinity and femininity. Which involves:

a. sexual organs as privileged erogenous zone (modification of experience of the body);

b. nonindependence of preliminary pleasure (arousal), which is now intended to prepare the "pleasure of satisfaction" (i.e., discharge of genital products)[57];

c. the existence of a particular type of sexual object, the other sex.

[119/118]q   This introduces the problem of the distinction between male and female sexuality.[58]

1. What is libido?[59]

A force that measures processes and transformations in the domain of sexual excitation:

- different from other psychical energies;
- but always positive and active.

So feminine libido is not passive. This explains why the little girl's interpretations regarding her own sex are always of a masculine type.[60]

---

q There is an error of pagination here: there is little doubt that this page directly follows the previous page, yet Foucault writes 119 after having written 117 on the previous page. All the numbers of the last sheets move forward from this. We have put the original number on the left and the correct number on the right.

2. Now feminine libido fixed in the erogenous zone entails a sexual object in relation to which it is passive. Hence:
- a conflict between clitoral and vaginal eroticism;
- a "repression" and a regression;
- a narcissism characteristic of the woman.[61]

3. The third problem concerns the parallelism of libidinal history.   [120/119]
  a. In the first Freudian conception, the libidos being identical and active, the history could not be the same. In particular: castration does not occupy the same position in boys and girls:
- in boys, it concludes Oedipus; attachment to the mother → threat of the father. Formation of the superego—Repression then latency;
- in girls, castration must instead enable attachment to the father[r]: accepting femininity through castration. Castration is the constitutive element of Oedipus. Importance of the clitoris; vaginal pleasure is second.

  b. In the second conception, Freud discovers the girl's attachment to her mother, "like Mycenaean civilization before the Greek."[62]

  c. It is this phase that Melanie Klein analyzes for itself, giving it a privileged importance that enables her to defer   [121/120][s]
castration to the end of Oedipus; thus to reestablish a parallelism between the sexes, but by shifting libido toward passivity and femininity.[63]

---

r A whole passage has been crossed out here: "make the original attachment to the mother (the girl being the father's rival) pass to attachment to the father" and replaced by "enable attachment to the father."

s This is the last sheet, written, like the two previous sheets not paginated (see above, footnote k, p. 122), on headed paper of the University of Clermont-Ferrand.

The desire for incorporation of the penis would come first—
for which feeding would be the substitute—hence:

- early rivalry with the mother (but the phallic mother)[64];
- fear of destruction of the body;
- separation as punitive withdrawal.[65]

Clitoral sexuality would be a substitute. Identification with
the father. Masculine position of libido.[66]

*

1. The theme of infantile sexuality, the importance of which is seen here
in connection with the emergence of a knowledge about sexuality, will
occupy Foucault anew when he takes up the history of sexuality from a
genealogical point of view. Thus, *Psychiatric Power*, trans. Graham Burchell
(New York: Palgrave Macmillan, 2006), is broadly devoted to the psychia-
trization of childhood and to the relation between the figure of the child,
the problem of instinct, and the problem of abnormality (123–42, 201–23).
Abnormal, trans. Graham Burchell (London: Verso, 2003), dwells at length
on the problem of masturbation and infantile sexuality at the end of the
eighteenth and beginning of the nineteenth century as the point at which
sexuality enters medical knowledge, before analyzing the way the *scientia
sexualis* integrated it within a wider knowledge of the sexual instinct and its
perversions (231–321). Finally, we know that the initial project of the *History
of Sexuality* envisaged by Foucault included a volume devoted entirely to
the history of the crusade against infantile masturbation in the eighteenth
and nineteenth centuries and the way it formed a domain at the heart of
which knowledge about sexuality would emerge: "from the medical myth
formulated by onanistics (*l'onanistique*) around 1760–1770, a discourse was
gradually detached . . . which went beyond the discourse from which it
arose. It took sexuality in general as its domain, and gave itself the task of
analyzing the specific effects that could be identified in it. . . . Sexuality as
a domain of knowledge (*savoir*) was formed on the basis of onanistics. . . .
There were a series of numerous, complex transformations in the discourse
of onanistics at the end of which, taking the years 1870–1900 as a reference
point—that is, a century later—a discourse and a technique appeared for

which sexuality was the reference and domain of intervention" (*La Croisade des enfants*, unpublished manuscript, BNF, Box 51, f. 64–65). It will be seen that his rereading in the 1970s goes against the reading given in this course, in particular regarding the supposed hidden character of the sexuality of children prior to Freud's "discovery". See below, note 9, p. 130.

2. See above, lecture 4.

3. It is useful to compare these analyses with those Foucault offered in *Mental Illness and Psychology*, trans. Alan Sheridan (New York: Harper & Row, 1976), regarding how to interpret the fact that mental illness in Western culture is expressed in terms of regression to infantile conditions. As he noted, "evolutionism is wrong to see in these returns the very essence of the pathological. . . . If regression to childhood is manifested in neuroses, it is so merely as an effect." An effect of a specific culture and social history of a society that, from the eighteenth century, clearly separated the child from the adult and was concerned with "constituting for the child, with educational rules that followed his development, a world that would be adapted to him" (80).

4. See Philippe Ariès, *Centuries of Childhood: A Social History of Family Life*, trans. Robert Baldick (New York: Knopf, 1962), especially the second part, which stresses the relationship between the development of mentalities regarding childhood and the development of educational institutions and pedagogical methods.

5. Ariès, *Centuries of Childhood*.

6. August Aichhorn (1878–1949) was an educator specializing in caring for abandoned children in Austria in the period immediately following the First World War. He developed a clinic and psychoanalytic care of juvenile delinquents and abandoned children (see in particular his major work, with a preface by Freud, *Jeunes en souffrance. Psychanalyse et éducation spécialisée*, trans. M. Géraud, preface by S. Freud (Lecques: Champ social, 2002 [1925])). He directed the centers for special education of Oberhollabrunn, then Eggenburg. On Aichhorn, see Florian Houssier and François Marty, eds., *August Aichhorn. Cliniques de la délinquance*, trans. C. Haussonne and A. Zalvidéa (Nîmes: Champ social, 2007).

7. Anton Semenovitch Makarenko (1888–1939), an educator and director of Russian primary schools who was also responsible for setting up special colonies for caring for orphaned children after the First World War, the Revolution, and the Civil War in Russia (the most famous of which were

the Gorky colony, 1920–1928, and the Dzerjinski commune, 1927–1935). His pedagogical works, inspired by collectivism and educational mutualism, were the subject of various publications in French in the 1950s, in particular an article in the review *Enfance*: "L'éducation sexuelle," *Enfance* 3, no. 1 (1950): 457–65.

8. Siegfried Bernfeld (1892–1953), like Aichhorn, was an Austrian educator and psychoanalyst and was also involved in Zionist and socialist movements. Foucault is referring here to the *Kinderheim Baumgarten*, active between 1919 and 1920, a special school camp for homeless children, often presented as one of the first educational experiments inspired by psychoanalysis, but also stressing the manual work and creativity of children in care. See Anna Freud, *The Psychoanalytic Treatment of Children* (London: Imago, 1946), x, which offers a bit of history of the psychoanalysis of children, which Foucault draws on in this lecture. More recently, see Peter Maas Taubman, *Disavowed Knowledge: Psychoanalysis, Education and Teaching* (London: Routledge, 2012).

9. Foucault's position on this question will change radically. Whether in *La Croisade des enfants* or *Abnormal*, he will make the struggle against infantile masturbation from the end of the eighteenth century a key moment in the emergence of knowledge about sexuality. As he notes in *La Croisade des enfants*: "Legend would have it that the sexuality of children has been denied since the eighteenth century. Denied or acknowledged only in monstrous and pathological forms. We would have to wait until the end of the nineteenth century, for Freud and little Hans, for the obvious to impose itself on a puritanism that rejected it; adults needed the purity of their children; or their children's desire aroused fear or shame. Hence, for almost a century and a half, that period of historical latency in which infantile sexuality was systematically pushed back into the shadows. That latency . . . is a myth" (f. 36). The questioning of that myth will be coupled with the more profound questioning of the "repressive hypothesis" that will be taken up in his *History of Sexuality. Volume 1: An Introduction*, trans. R. Harley (New York: Pantheon, 1978).

10. On "infantile amnesia," Foucault follows Freud's analyses at the beginning of the second of the *Three Essays*, "Infantile Sexuality," 179–83.

11. This is a reference to the case of Dora, studied by Freud in his *Fragment of an Analysis of a Case of Hysteria*, *CPW*, vol. 7. Dora suffers from

recurrent attacks of nervous coughing in which Freud sees a hysterical symptom, which he links to forgotten infantile masturbation and especially its repression, around the age of eight, leading to its replacement by the hysterical symptom of nervous dyspepsia. Freud connects this symptom with the fact that she had spied on her parents' sexual activity and was excited by her father's "heavy breathing." The scene of kissing on the stairs refers to the scene, at first forgotten by Dora, when Herr K, a friend of Dora's family, forced a kiss on her and clasped her tightly at the foot of a stairs when she was fourteen. In the disgust Dora then felt, Freud sees a sign of hysteria, linked to a conversion of the oral and genital erogenous zones into hysterical symptoms (disgust and pressure on the thorax), referring to an earlier (infantile) experience of sexuality that she had forgotten.

12. On this point, see, for example, S. Freud, *Introductory Lectures on Psycho-Analysis*, *CPW*, vol. 16, 327–29.

13. This is a rough quotation from the analysis of "little Hans," *Analysis of a Phobia in a Five-Year-Old Boy*, *CPW*, vol. 10, 42: "Long before he was in the world, I went on, I had known that a little Hans would come who would be so fond of his mother that he would be bound to feel afraid of his father because of it." In the courses he devoted to psychoanalysis in the 1950s (BNF, Box 46), Foucault likes to take up this quotation, as much to illustrate "the connection between fear and love, anxiety and eroticism" that characterizes psychoanalysis as to compare it with Saint Paul's expression in the *Epistle to the Romans* 9:11–13: "For the children not yet being born, neither having done any good or evil . . . It was said unto her, The elder shall serve the younger. As it is written, Jacob have I loved, but Essau have I hated."

14. Reference to a phrase, often attributed to Freud (without it being possible to trace its origin), who was supposed to have replied to a mother's question concerning the education of her children: "Madame, whatever you do, it will be wrong." Foucault likes to repeat this quotation, which he takes up again in 1966–1967 in his course at Tunis on the idea of man in modern Western culture (BNF, Box 58), to emphasize again the separation of psychoanalysis and pedagogy.

15. Herbert Graf, "little Hans," was actually analyzed, under Freud's supervision, by his father, Max Graf, a journalist, music critic, and member of the Vienna Psychoanalytic Society. See S. Freud, *Analysis of a Phobia in a Five-Year Old Boy*, *CPW*, vol. 10.

16. All the following information on the brief history of the psycho-analysis of children is taken from the preface to A. Freud, *The Psychoanalytic Treatment of Children*. This work also contains lectures from 1926 and the 1927 report mentioned here by Foucault. For more recent histories, see, for example, Claudine Geissmann-Chambon and Pierre Geissmann, *Histoire de la psychanalyse de l'enfant: Mouvements, idées, perspectives* (Paris: Bayard, 1992), and Xavier Renders, *Le Jeu de la demande: Une histoire de la psychanalyse d'enfants* (Brussels: De Boeck University, 1991).

17. This is Edith Sterba (1894–1986), psychoanalyst and musicologist, companion of the psychoanalyst Richard Sterba, who will analyze Bruno Bettelheim. On this clinic, see A. Freud, *The Psychoanalytic Treatment of Children*, x.

18. See above, note 6, p. 129.

19. Dorothy Burlingham (1891–1979), friend and associate of Anna Freud: during the war they founded together the Hampstead War Nurseries, from which they will draw various observations published in 1943 in *Infants Without Families*. The experimental crèche mentioned here was created in Vienna in 1937. See A. Freud, *The Psychoanalytic Treatment of Children*, x.

20. These different limits seem to be taken from Anna Freud's text "Indications for the Psychoanalytic Treatment of Children," in *The Psychoanalytic Treatment of Children*. A useful summary of the issues raised by the psychoanalysis of children will also be found at the same time as Foucault is writing this lecture in the chapter written by Serge Lebovici, René Diatkine, et al., "La psychanalyse des enfants," in *La Psychanalyse d'aujourd'hui*, ed. Sacha Nacht (Paris: PUF, 1956), 1:163–235.

21. Foucault summarizes here Anna Freud's analyses, *The Psychoanalytic Treatment of Children*, 76–79. In the child, evaluation of the "normal" character of their sexuality is made difficult, on the one hand, because there is not yet maturity and so no possible full enjoyment (*jouissance*) and, on the other, because the relation between narcissistic satisfaction and love directed to external objects is difficult to evaluate. As for the case of work, an analog offered in the case of children could be play, but "Since play is governed by the pleasure principle, and work by the reality principle, the disturbance of each of the two functions has a different clinical significance" (77).

22. The cases of anorexia, nocturnal enuresis, and passive femininity are developed in A. Freud, *The Psychoanalytic Treatment of Children*, 73–76, to illustrate the degree to which the criterion of suffering is not pertinent in the psychoanalysis of children, for it often concerns the parents more than the children themselves.

23. See A. Freud, *The Psychoanalytic Treatment of Children*, 5–6, which is therefore concerned with the means of arousing an awareness of the illness in the child and producing a demand.

24. All these mechanisms of defense are described in A. Freud, *The Psychoanalytic Treatment of Children*, 88–91.

25. For Freud, sucking, in fact, serves as a model of infantile sexual manifestations. The different characteristics listed by Foucault are presented thus: (1) rhythmic action: "rhythmic repetition"; (2) absorbed attention: "Sensual-sucking involves a complete absorption of the attention"; (3) more general muscular tension: "a grasping instinct"; (4) release, sleep: "leads to sleep"; (5) touching of genital parts: "[Sensual sucking] is not infrequently combined with rubbing some sensitive part of the body such as the breast or the external genitalia." See "The Manifestations of Infantile Sexuality," in *Three Essays*, 179–83.

26. "The Manifestations of Infantile Sexuality," 181–83.

27. See, notably, *On Narcissism: An Introduction*, *CPW*, vol. 14, which analyzes precisely this "relation of . . . narcissism . . . to autoerotism" (76).

28. As Freud notes: "the mother's breast [is] the first object of the sexual instinct"; "Sucking at the mother's breast is . . . the unmatched prototype of every later sexual satisfaction" that is later replaced "by a part of his own body." *Introductory Lectures on Psychoanalysis*, *CPW*, vol. 16, 314.

29. This is a reference to Jacques Lacan's famous phrase: "love is giving what one does not have," which dates, in this form, from the 1960–1961 seminar, *Transference: The Seminar of Jacques Lacan, Book VIII*, ed. Jacques-Alain Miller, trans. Bruce Fink (Cambridge: Polity Press, 2015), 33–34: "There are two things in my past discourse that I have noted regarding love. . . . The first is that love is a comic sentiment. . . . The second . . . is that love is giving what one does not have." It refers, in fact, to an older theme in Lacan, found in 1957 in the seminar on the object relation, where love is characterized as the "gift of what one does not have." Love is therefore a relation marked by lack, not by intersubjective communication and

exchange. This phrase will later be completed thus: "Love is giving something you don't have to someone who doesn't want it" (*Les problèmes cruciaux de la psychanalyse, 1964–1965. Séminaire XII*, 2 vols., 1985).

30. On this separation, see, for example, S. Freud, *Three Essays*, 182; and *Introductory Lectures on Psychoanalysis*, 314.

31. On the contrast between Anna Freud and Melanie Klein, at the time of the "great controversies" (1941–1945), see Pearl King and Riccardo Steiner, eds., *The Freud-Klein Controversies 1941–45* (London: Routledge, 1991). For Anna Freud, in fact, autoerotism is primary and precedes any differentiation between ego and object; for Melanie Klein, on the other hand, the child establishes an object relation with its mother from the start and, in particular, with its mother's breast, which takes form as much as the "good object," the good, nourishing, and gratifying breast, as the "bad object," the bad, refused, withdrawn, and persecutory breast. See, for example, Melanie Klein, "Some Theoretical Conclusions Regarding the Emotional Life of the Infant," in *Developments in Psychoanalysis*, by Paula Heimann, Susan Isaacs, Melanie Klein, and Joan Riviere (London: Hogarth, 1952), which summarizes her positions on this subject.

32. The sexual drive (*pulsion*), strictly speaking, is initially satisfied in association with the function of self-preservation (hunger) and through an object (the maternal breast); it becomes independent only through the loss of this object and its replacement by the child's own body as site of the drive's investment. See Jean-Laplanche and Jean-Bertrand Pontalis, "Auto-Erotism," in *The Language of Psychoanalysis*, trans. Donald Nicholson-Smith (London: Hogarth, 1973), for clarification on this subject.

33. As in the rest of this lecture, Foucault follows the different stages of Freud's exposition in the *Three Essays* (here, for example, the part "Characteristics of the Erotogenic Zones," 183–84), adding some personal considerations or issues of other psychoanalysts (Jacques Lacan, Melanie Klein, and Karl Abraham in particular).

34. This is particularly true of recognition in a mirror, analyzed by Henri Wallon in *Les Origines du caractère chez l'enfant: Les préludes du sentiment de personnalité* (Paris: Boivin, 1934), and above all the famous study by Lacan developed in 1936, published notably in "La famille: le complexe, facteur concret de la psychologie familiale. Les complexes familiaux en pathologie," *Encyclopédie française*, vol. 8, *La Vie mentale* (Paris: Larouse, 1938), and taken up again in *Autres Écrits* (Paris: Seuil, 2001).

35. On anal erotism, see S. Freud, *Three Essays*, 185–87. Freud returns on several occasions to this subject, which constitutes the first stage (activity/passivity) of a fundamental polarization in his interpretation of sexuality. According to him, the sadistic dimensions predominate in anal erotism, and he connects it especially with obsessional neurosis; see in particular "The Disposition to Obsessional Neurosis" (1913), *CPW*, vol. 12. Foucault, however, seems to introduce some elements inspired by the reading proposed by Karl Abraham, notably in "A Short Study of the Development of the Libido, Viewed in the Light of Mental Disorders (1924)," in *Selected Papers on Psychoanalysis*, trans. Douglas Bryan and Alix Strachey (Abingdon, UK: Routledge, 2018), which stresses more clearly the ambivalence and aggressiveness of this phase. Abraham distinguishes two sides: one passive, which corresponds to the pleasure of the mucous membrane, and the other active, linked to the muscular contraction; then later, two stages: a first marked by loss of the object and a second marked by retention, to which he connects melancholy and obsessional neurosis, respectively. On the relationship with masochism, see Rudolph M. Loewenstein, "A Contribution to the Psychoanalytical Theory of Masochism," *Journal of the American Psychoanalytic Association* 5, no. 2 (1957): 197–234.

36. Foucault here follows Freud's account in the *Three Essays*, 187–91, regarding the activity of the genital erotogenic zones and various phases of infantile masturbation. Freud himself refers to his article of 1896 on the etiology of hysteria, in which he effectively insists on the role of seduction (by adults or other children) in the resumption of masturbatory genital sexual activity in the child, as in the etiology of hysteria. In the *Three Essays*, he maintains the importance of seduction but emphasizes that it is not always necessary. The question of the place of seduction in the etiology of the neuroses (and above all of Freud's relative abandonment of it after 1897) will give rise to considerable controversy in the period 1970–1980, with Freud being accused of having deliberately turned his back on his theory of seduction in order to deny the importance of sexual abuse. See in particular J. Moussaieff Masson, *The Assault on Truth: Freud's Suppression of the Seduction Theory* (New York: Farrar, Strauss and Giroux, 1984).

37. See S. Freud, *Three Essays*, 191–94, which describes a set of drives (*pulsions*) directed to other persons, who thus play the role of objects but who appear first of all independently of erogenous (*a fortiori* genital) sexual

activity. This is the tendency to expose oneself or, alternatively, of the scopic drive (*pulsion*) and curiosity, as well as the pleasure taken by children in cruelty and mastery. The distinction Foucault makes here with the "libidinal object" seems to refer to the fact that the "objects" to which these partial drives are directed should not be confused with the erogenous zones on which the libido is focused in the different pregenital stages.

38. See S. Freud, *Three Essays*, 191, which notes, in fact, that it is "under the influence of seduction" that the child "can become polymorphously perverse, and can be led into all possible kinds of sexual irregularities."

39. Reference to Melanie Klein's analyses, in particular "The Early Development of Conscience in the Child" (1933), in *Love, Guilt and Reparation and Other Works 1921–1946* (London: Hogarth, 1975), where she sees in "all the monsters of myths and fairy tales that abound in the phantasy life of the child" so many fantasy objects that represent the "children's parents," but laden with a set of anxieties linked to repressed aggressive drives (*pulsions*), and that constitute the early forms of a superego. The "phallic mother" is a recurrent figure in Melanie Klein's analysis, in which the mother appears as having incorporated in herself the paternal penis, which determines feelings of envy as much as of hatred and aggression on the part of children; see, for example, *The Psycho-Analysis of Children* (London: Hogarth, 1975). Foucault's critical remark echoes criticisms of Melanie Klein made in particular by René Diatkine and Serge Lebovic, who regularly denounce this establishment of continuity and confusion between imagos and fantasies, "what is hallucinated phantasy, what is image underlying the phantasy." Behind this criticism, Diatkine and Lebovic are aiming at Melanie Klein's use of material she obtained in games with children, in which she sees an "expression [of the] phantasies" of the child, whereas "one of the essential functions of play is to provide a way out of the phantasy, a solution intermediate between the demands of reality and of the id"; S. Diatkine and R. Diatkine, "Étude des fantasmes chez l'enfant," *Revue française de psychanalyse* 18, no. 1 (1954): 108–59 (passage quoted 117–18); see also R. Diatkine, "La signification du fantasme en psychanalyse d'enfants," *Revue française de psychanalyse* 15, no. 3 (1951): 325–43.

40. Foucault here takes up the different phases of "The Sexual Researches of Childhood," set out by Freud in part 5 of the second of the *Three Essays*, 194–95. The riddle of "where babies come from" is presented here by Freud

as a deformed version of the riddle of the Sphinx addressed to Oedipus. See also "On the Sexual Theories Of Children" (1908), *CPW*, vol. 9.

41. See S. Freud, *Three Essays*, 196.

42. An example can be provided by the case of Erna referred to by Melanie Klein, who in fantasy attacks the inside of her mother's body and, in particular, her feces, which she associates with children. See Melanie Klein, *The Psycho-Analysis of Children* (London: Hogarth, 1975), 79.

43. See S. Freud, *Three Essays*, 195.

44. S. Freud, *Three Essays*, 196.

45. See for example, S. Freud, "The Disposition to Obsessional Neurosis."

46. The close relationship among sadism, violence, knowledge, and language that Foucault finds established in Freud (see "The Instinct For Knowledge," in *Three Essays*, 194) and in psychoanalytic literature (see the pages devoted to this by M. Klein in "The Development of a Child (1921)," in *Love, Guilt and Reparation and Other Works*, 1–53, but also in Bataille, who shows how violence and prohibition, by breaking the contact between subject and object, distancing the object from ourselves, and thereby making it a possible object of knowledge, are the very conditions of the possibility of science (Georges Bataille, *Erotism: Death and Sensuality*, trans. Mary Dalwood [San Francisco: City Lights, 1986], 37–39), plays a considerable role in Foucault's own reflections, throughout his work, up to when it is structured around the Nietzschean theme of the "will to know." Thus, in *Mental Illness and Psychology*, as in the *History of Madness*, Foucault emphasizes that "all knowledge" might be said to be "linked to the essential forms of cruelty . . . in the case of madness, this link is no doubt of particular importance. Because it was first of all this link that made possible a psychological analysis of madness; but above all because it was on this link that the possibility of any psychology was secretly based" (*Mental Illness and Psychology*, 73). The same principle is at work in *Birth of the Clinic: An Archaeology of Medical Perception*, trans. A. M. Sheridan Smith (London: Tavistock, 1973), where it is in fact death and the cadaver that make possible knowledge of life and the individual, which underlines the contemporaneousness of Bichat and Sade: "Is not Bichat, in fact, the contemporary of the man who suddenly, in the most discursive of languages, introduced eroticism and its most inevitable point, death? Once more, knowledge and eroticism denounce . . . their profound kinship. . . . To know life is given only to a

cruel and already infernal knowledge that only wishes it dead" (171 [translation slightly modified —G.B.]). The same theme is evoked in "So Cruel a Knowledge" (1962), trans. Robert Hurley, *EW*, 2, a text almost contemporary with the course, in which Foucault emphasizes that "the initiation story owes its strongest erotic appeal to the link that it intimates between Knowledge and Desire. An obscure, essential link that we are mistaken to recognize only in "Platonism"—that is, in the exclusion of one of the two terms. In actual fact, each epoch has its system of "erotic knowledge" that brings into play (in one and the same game) the experience of the Limit and that of the Light" (57). At the beginning of the 1970s, Foucault takes up this theme again, making it a guideline of his analysis, linked with his reflections on the Nietzschean notions of the "will to know" and "will to truth." As he notes in an interview with Foss Elders on Dutch television, November 28, 1971, "the universality of our knowledge has been acquired at the cost of exclusions, prohibitions, refusals, rejections, at the cost of a kind of cruelty regarding reality." It is indeed this "radical malice of knowledge," which means that behind "knowledge there is a will . . . not to bring the object near to oneself or identify with it but, on the contrary, to get away from it and destroy it" ("Truth and Juridical Forms", *EW*, 3, 11) that will guide Foucault's first reflections on the "will to know."

47. On the question of the prohibitions of language, see "Madness, the Absence of an Oeuvre" (1964) in *History of Madness*, 545 *et seq.*

48. One will have recognized the two major experiences whose formation Foucault was striving to give an account of from an historical point of view: the individual body and death, in *Birth of the Clinic*; language and knowledge (and its other side: madness, which Foucault then linked with the history of the prohibitions of language; see "Madness, the Absence of an Oeuvre," 544–45), in what will become *The Order of Things*. We can see the importance of sexuality, which, through the question of eroticism, is situated at the intersection of language and death. "Death" and "sexuality" will become, with "history," which Foucault introduces a bit later, three notions whose importance for "twentieth-century thought" he will emphasize, as much from the point of view of biological knowledge (*savoirs*) as from that of the humanist "reactions" to which they give rise in philosophy and the human sciences. On this subject, see below, the Vincennes course, pp. 235–236; "Course Context," pp. 339–342; "Cuvier's

Situation in the History of Biology," trans. Lynne Huffer, *Foucault Studies* 22 (January 2017): 235–36.

49. This notion of "tragedy" is at the heart of a set of works of existentialist or Marxist inspiration, in particular in Karl Jaspers or Lucien Goldman (*The Hidden God: A Study of Tragic Vision in the Pensées of Pascal and the Tragedies of Racine*, trans. Philip Thody [London: Verso, 2016]), which Foucault knew well. But it is also at the heart of the Foucauldian project itself: the latter, from the preface to *History of Madness*, is placed entirely "beneath the sun of the great Nietzschean quest," which confronts "the dialectics of history with the immobile structures of the tragic"; "Preface to the 1961 Edition," *History of Madness*, xxx. We can see how much this course aims to extend these analyses on the side of sexuality. On this point, see "Course Context," pp. 302–308. Here again, it should be compared with Foucault's analyses of sexuality in "A Preface to Transgression" (1963), *EW*, 2 (see above, lecture 1, note 35, pp. 25–26), where he notes: "What characterizes modern sexuality from Sade to Freud is not its having found the language of its logic or of its nature, but, rather, through the violence done by such languages, its having been "denatured"—cast into an empty zone in which it achieves whatever meager form is bestowed upon it by the establishment of its limits, and in which it points to nothing beyond itself, no prolongation, except the frenzy that disrupts it." Modern sexuality appears as a "fissure" that "marks the limit within us and designates us as a limit"; the "only division [now] possible" (69–70). When Foucault emphasizes that Freud "brings out from nature the great tragic powers that loom over man," he is referring to the interpretation of Freud that he regularly gave since his courses of the 1950s, making Freud an author caught in a tension between his initial naturalist project—linked to the evolutionism of Charles Darwin or John Hughlings Jackson—and an analysis of significations and their genesis which completely questions this naturalism. According to Foucault, the subject of psychoanalysis becomes, then, a "seat of conflicts" of forces that go beyond him, "caught between a drive (*pulsion*)-will, caught up in the anonymity of instinct, [and] an inhibition-will, which takes shape only in the forms of restriction of the social milieu," a subject that has for freedom "only these two forms of alienation: the freedom of brothels or prisons." This contradiction is "lived by psychoanalysis in the tragic mode. Tragedy, Freud's final tonality" (BNF, Box 46). The Vincennes

course and the appendix "Sexuality, Reproduction, Individuality" will partly extend this reflection: the formation of a biological knowledge of sexuality is here enrolled in an anti-humanist perspective that makes of sexuality a law and a destiny going beyond the individual-subject, which is only its "precarious, temporary, quickly erased extension." Foucault shows here, moreover, the forms in which "humanist philosophy" endeavored to "react" to this tragic experience by reintegrating it in a philosophy of love, communication, and reproduction (see below, Vincennes course, lecture 6, pp. 235–236; "Sexuality, Reproduction, Individuality," pp. 289–296; and "Course Context," pp. 339–342. The reference to the atomic bomb is a direct echo of Karl Jaspers' work, *La Bombe atomique et l'avenir de l'homme*, trans. R. Soupault, preceded by *Le Philosophe devant la politique*, by Jeanne Hersch (Paris: Plon, 1958), which raised precisely the problem of a "limit situation," of tragic form, in which it is a matter of deciding between the possibility of the radical annihilation of humanity by the use of the atomic weapon and the possibility of the death of all human freedom through the triumph of totalitarianism; as well as, perhaps, the critical review Blanchot devoted to this work in *Critique*; "The Apocalypse Is Disappointing," in M. Blanchot, *Friendship*, trans. Elizabeth Rottenberg (Stanford, CA: Stanford University Press, 1997).

50. Foucault follows here Freud's analyses in the sixth part of the second of the *Three Essays*, "The Phases of Development of the Sexual Organization," 197–200.

51. S. Freud, *Three Essays*, 197.

52. This dimension of aggressiveness and depression in the oral organization is the object, in particular, of the works of Karl Abraham, *Oeuvres complètes*, and M. Klein (see, for example, "A Contribution to the Psychogenesis of Manic-Depressive States" [1934] in *Love, Guilt and Reparation*), which stresses frustration and depression linked to loss of the object (the maternal breast) more than the sadistic components in the oral stage.

53. On this subject, see S. Freud, *Leonardo Da Vinci and a Memory of His Childhood* (1910) *CPW*, vol. 11, and M. Klein, *The Psycho-Analysis of Children*.

54. In fact, Melanie Klein distinguished herself very early from the Freudian position by asserting the early existence of an Oedipus complex in children, the first stages of which she situated at the end of the oral phase, toward

six months. Klein initially linked this first moment to aggressive drives and hatred associated with the separation from the maternal breast and the desire to appropriate the father's penis, in the context of exacerbation of the sadistic drives that characterize the end of the oral phase and the anal phase. See, in particular, "Early Stages of the Oedipus Conflict" (1928), in *Love, Guilt and Reparation*, and *The Psycho-Analysis of Children*. Her subsequent work will insist more on attachment and fear of loss of the object, linked to the depressive phase, in the initial formation of the Oedipus complex.

55. See S. Freud, *Three Essays*, 196. On this organization and its characteristics, developed here by Foucault, see above, p. 000; and above, note 35, p. 000.

56. On this point, see S. Freud, *Three Essays*, "The Transformations of Puberty."

57. See S. Freud, *Three Essays*, 207–8.

58. See S. Freud, *Three Essays*, "The Differentiation Between Men and Women," 219–221.

59. See S. Freud, *Three Essays*, "The Libido Theory," which Foucault follows closely here.

60. On this point, see the fourth section of the third of the *Three Essays*, especially 219–220, which emphasizes the always "active" and therefore "masculine" character of libido. Freud insists on the distinction among three senses of the masculine/feminine opposition, either in the sense of the activity/passivity opposition, or in the sense of biological sex, or in the sense of sociological gender.

61. See the fourth section of the third of the *Three Essays*, notably 220–21. For the woman, puberty is marked by a repression of clitoral sexuality, which previously prevailed in infantile masturbatory activity. This psychoanalytic thesis that the sexual maturity of women presupposes a transition from clitoral sexuality to a sexuality focused on the vagina will arouse intense debates in the years 1960–1970. See Sylvie Chaperon, "Kinsey en France: Les sexualités féminine et masculine en débat," *Le Mouvement social*, no. 198 (2002): 91–110 (103 *et seq.*).

62. This is a reference to Freud's text "Female Sexuality" (1931), *CPW*, vol. 21, in which he notes that "insight into this early, pre-Oedipus, phase in girls comes to us as a surprise, like the discovery, in another field, of the Minoan-Mycenaean civilization behind the civilization of Greece," 226.

63. See M. Klein, *The Psycho-Analysis of Children*, especially chapters 11 and 12, which explain in detail the sexual development of the girl and boy. Klein stresses, in fact, the "feminine phase" that the boy passes through.

64. The "phallic mother" appears as the one who has incorporated the paternal penis. Rivalry with this phallic mother is present in both the girl and the boy, according to Klein.

65. Melanie Klein describes separation from the breast as a form of punishment arousing a feeling of frustration and aggression. In this framework, the father's penis will become a substitute for the maternal breast, here again in the girl as in the boy.

66. See M. Klein, *The Psycho-Analysis of Children*, 290–96. Identification with the father, with the sadistic father in particular, is examined at length and in detail here. The clitoris takes on the signification of a penis in the girl's masturbatory fantasies, a role that it keeps throughout the sadistic phase. Klein's position, which maintains the primacy of a vaginal sexuality but makes it the end of a process very different from the one envisaged by Freud, is linked with the "English school," especially Karen Horney and Ernest Jones, and is opposed to the analyses offered in France by Hélène Deutsch, *The Psychology of Women* (New York: Grune and Stratton, 1944), and Marie Bonaparte, *Female Sexuality* (New York: International Universities Press, 1971).

PART II

The Discourse of Sexuality

LECTURES AT THE
UNIVERSITY OF VINCENNES

(1969)

LECTURE 1

The Discourse of Sexuality

*A*nalysis of the discourse of sexuality to be distinguished: 1. from an analysis of the way in which discourse is a site of emergence of or object of investment by desire; 2. from a history of the science of sexuality (biology, psychology, anthropology of sexuality). An analysis of sexuality as possible referential of different discourses (recent historical phenomenon). How was sexuality epistemologized: how did it become a domain of knowledge (savoir) and a field of liberation? Five groups of studies: a. Transformation of the experience of sexuality at the end of the eighteenth century; b. Epistemologization of sexuality; c. Discovery of the sexual etiology of the neuroses; d. Sexuality as referential of literary discourse; e. Theme of sexual liberation.

To be distinguished from several other possible analyses.   [1]

1. Desire and discourse

– Discourse as site of the emergence of desire; site where it takes on its symbolic forms, where it is subject to its displacements, its metaphors, its metonyms; where it repeats itself and where it is repressed.

- One could study, for example, how the child's desire is structured around language:
  - the game of personal pronouns and their use;
  - words (invented, imposed, or deformed) that designate parts of the body or objects of desire;
  - the valorization of expressions, forbidden words, things one does not talk about.[1]

[2] • One could also make comparative studies, showing how this varies according to cultures (Christian ≠ Muslim).

– Discourse as object of investment by desire; the way discourse is eroticized for itself:
  - either through the intermediary of the mouth, as erogenous zone;
  - or as instrument of symbolic satisfaction;
  - or as object belonging to the other (and through which one may receive gratification or prohibition). The discourse[a] of the other is gift and law.[2]

We see that these two aspects of discourse[b] come together in the notion of law. Discourse is the law.

(Language and discourse to be distinguished. What is actually said.)[3]

[3] *2. The science of sexuality*

This would be the study of the way the concepts of a science of sexuality were formed, corrected, purified, and organized.

- One could study the way sexuality was used as a principle of classification:
  - not only binary, male-female (and sometimes for many nonliving beings);
  - but taxonomic for living species.[4]

---

a Replaces "language," which is crossed out.
b Replaces "language," which is crossed out.

- One could study how the science of sexuality
  was formed:
  - the respective roles of male and female in procreation
    (→ ovum and spermatozoon);
  - the process of the development of germs
    (→ embryology);
  - the transmission of specific or individual characteristics
    in sexual reproduction (→ genes)
  - the relation between primary and secondary character-
    istics (→ hormones);

  Physiology—embryology—genetics—hormonology—
  psychology.[5]

- One could also study how a sexual psychology was formed: [4]
  - on the basis of sexual perversions;
  - on the basis of passional states (jealousy, erotomania);
  - on the basis of defects of sexual behavior (neurasthenia,
    hysteria).

  → up to the Freudian conception of libido.[6]

- Finally, one could [study] the themes of a sexual anthropology:
  α. What does being a sexed being mean for man? What
    type of relation to the world is entailed by the fact of
    being sexed?
  β. What do masculinity and femininity mean? What are
    feminine and masculine modes of being?
  γ. What types of sexual behavior are found in different
    forms of culture? What are the effects on a culture of
    the different ways sexuality is structured?[7]

The study undertaken here will not be entirely one or the [5]
other. It situates itself between the following two boundaries.

 1. It does not seek to know how sexuality is invested in discourse, but how sexuality can become an object for discourse.
It is not concerned with discourse as object of desire or as law of
the objects of desire, but conversely with sexuality as object of

discourse. Not sexuality in discourse (or vice versa) but sexuality as correlate of discourse.

Thus, it is not a question of the way, in a given language, sexuality is designated, metaphorized, or metonymized (for example, the twisting of sexual words by children), but of discourses that are about sexuality as such (for example, what is said in Sade or in Freud's *Three Essays*).

[6]   But this must be clarified. What does "discourses that are about sexuality" mean?

After all, what "little Hans" says concerns sexuality; *Gradiva* is about sexuality; the *Three Essays* are about sexuality.[8] But precisely in three different modes:

- In one case, it is[c] what is designated (the referent);
- In another, it is what is connoted (the theme, the horizon);
- In the third, it is the referential, that is to say the general and regular field in which appear:
  - concepts like libido, organizations, objects, partial tendencies;
  - objects (like perversions, masochism, sucking).

It is sexuality as the referential of discourse that will be studied.[9] For example, Sade:

- not what is designated (the different forms of perversion);
- not what is connoted (how sexuality is metaphorized in scenes or how it is presented in philosophical analyses);
- but how it is the referential of the discourse. The way that Sade does not speak of vices and virtues, nor of an imaginary character, but of sexuality.[10]

---

c Foucault adds two illegible words above.

Now this entails an historical analysis, for the establish-   [7]
ment of sexuality as the referential of discourse is not very old.
Certainly, for a long time it was designated (no doubt for all
time); for a long time, it has been conceptualized. But [what is
new is]d that it became the referential of discourses, that there
was a literature that is not only the site of the investment of
desire but that talks about it.

This will be the first point to study: the historical emergence
of sexuality as the referential of a possible discourse. Which
entails two orders of questions:

a. What did sexuality have to be (what did it have to become)
in society; what did its practice and institutionalization have
to be; what did marriage, the division of the sexes, their statu-
tory inequality have to be; what did the law—with its rigors
and transgressions—have to be for sexuality to become the
referential of discourses? While, in European culture, it had
only ever been designated or connoted; it had only ever been
metaphorized or conceptualized.

b. And the reciprocal question: what did literary, philosophi-   [8]
cal, scientific discourses have to become for each of them to
be able to take sexuality as a referential?

Hence a series of studies on the end of the eighteenth and the
beginning of the nineteenth century, on the emergence of sexuality as the referential of discourse.

2. On the other hand, the aim is not to discover how the science of sexuality was organized, but how sexuality was epistemologized—that is, how this discourse of sexuality (this
discourse that had sexuality for its referential) always tended to
be a discourse of knowledge (*savoir*) (and less and less one of

---

d Words in brackets added to complete the sentence.

valorization) and, at the same time, a discourse of transgression (and less and less one of prescription).

In other words, in becoming the referential of discourse, sexuality ceased being connoted by a valorization or designated by a prescription; it became a domain of knowledge and a field of liberation.

[9]   Another series of studies: how did jurisprudence give rise to a knowledge of sexuality; how was psychiatry able to extend its domain to sexuality; how was sexuality able to become a philosophical object; how was an autonomous psychological domain able to be formed; how was the politico-philosophical theme of sexual liberation able to be formed?

Five groups of studies:

   a. Transformations of the experience of sexuality at the end of the eighteenth century:
      1. The practical rules of marriage, regulation of births, and choice of partner in different social classes;
      2. The legal institution of marriage (transition to the contract);[11]
      3. Casuistry.[e]
   b. The epistemologization of sexuality:
      1. Jurisprudence;
      2. Sexuality as object of psychiatry;
      3. Philosophical reflection about sexuality (Schopenhauer, Nietzsche);
      4. Biology of sexuality.[12]
   c. The discovery of the sexual etiology of neuroses in Freud:
      • *Studies on Hysteria*;
      • Letters to Fliess;

---

e "Casuistry" appears at the beginning of this list, but Foucault seems to have added a "3," which suggests that it should be placed where we have put it.

- Little Hans;   [10]
- The *Three Essays*.[13]
d. Sexuality as the referential of literary discourse:
- Sade, [Sacher-]Masoch, Lawrence, Genet.[14]
e. The theme of sexual liberation:
- From [. . .]ᶠ to Hirschfeld, Reich, and Marcuse.
- Sexuality and revolution.[15]

*

1. See above, Clermont-Ferrand course, where the problem of "forbidden words" is referred to with regard to infantile sexuality, lecture 5, p. 121. A set of psychoanalytic references are found there that illustrate what Foucault has in mind. See, for example, Sigmund Freud, "Analysis of a Phobia in a Five-Year-Old Boy" ("Little Hans"), *CPW*, vol. 10, or Melanie Klein, *The Psycho-Analysis of Children* (London: Hogarth, 1975), for two illustrations of the way psychoanalysis studies words invented by children for designating parts of the body and investing them with desire.

2. This is a reference to Lacan, for whom "the unconscious is the Other's discourse," in Jacques Lacan, *Écrits*, trans. Bruce Fink (New York: Norton, 2002), 10. The fact that "one's discourse as a whole may become eroticized" and become the vehicle of gratification is referred to by Lacan in, for example, his Rome discourse, "The Function and Field of Speech and Language in Psychoanalysis," in *Écrits*, 248 with reference to the works of K. Abrahams and W. Fliess. The relation of the discourse of the Other (that is to say, of the unconscious "structured like a language") and the Law, in the sense that it constitutes the law and symbolic order through which the subject is constituted, is at the heart of all Lacanian analysis (see, for example, "The Function and Field of Speech and Language in Psychoanalysis").

3. The manuscript evidences Foucault's initial hesitations between "language" and "discourse" at the start of this text, where at several points "language" is crossed out and replaced by "discourse." From his course in Tunis on the problem of man in philosophical discourse and modern culture

---

f Left blank in the text: maybe it could be Fourier?

(1966–1967), Foucault strove to distinguish "language" and "discourse," but he did so in a different sense than he does here, then contrasting "human language," expressed by a subject and aiming to signify, to represent something, and the "non-human discourse," without subject, "which is not of man but external to him," constituted by a "set of elements . . . conforming to "syntactical rules," to a code (see BNF, Box 58). In other words, at this time Foucault employed the opposition by connecting "discourse" to structural analysis. The distinction established here should rather be compared with pages of *The Archaeology of Knowledge*, trans. A. M. Sheridan Smith (London: Tavistock, 1972) in which Foucault distinguishes the analysis of *langue* and *langage* from that of statements and discourse. If a language (*langue*) is "a finite body of rules that authorizes an infinite number of performances" and possible statements, discourse and statements are, on the other hand, "a grouping that is always finite and limited at any moment to the linguistic sequences that have been formulated" (27). Focusing on statements means taking seriously the "the singular and limited existence" of a set of discursive events. Discourse designates then for Foucault "a group of statements insofar as they belong to the same discursive formation . . . it is made up of a limited number of statements for which a group of conditions of existence can be defined . . . it is, from beginning to end, historical" (117). See also "On the Ways of Writing History" (1967), trans. Robert Hurley, *EW*, 2, in which Foucault stresses that, unlike the structuralists, he is not interested in "the formal possibilities offered by a system such as language (*la langue*) [but] . . . more intrigued by the existence of discourses, by the fact that words were spoken . . . [His] object is not language (*langage*) but the archive, which is to say the accumulated existence of discourses" (289). For a contextualization of this refocusing on the project of an analysis of the discourse of sexuality in the context of Foucault's reflections at this time, see "Course Context," pp. 323–331.

4. See above, Clermont-Ferrand course, lecture 2, p. 33, and note 11, p. 46. This is a reference to the taxonomic method of Carl von Linnaeus, which establishes the taxonomy of plants on the basis of their sexual organs. In *The Order of Things* (London: Tavistock, 1970), Foucault emphasizes, moreover, the modifications of this system at the end of the eighteenth century, through the works of Antoine de Jussieu, for whom the number of cotyledons is fundamental in his natural method of the classification of plants,

this time "because they play a particular role in the reproductive function, and because for that very reason they are linked to the plant's entire internal organic structure" (228).

5. On this series of possible studies, see above, Clermont-Ferrand course, lectures 2 and 3. The first (physiology) refers to the dispute between ovists and spermists from the seventeenth century, which will lead to defining the role of spermatozoa and ova in fertilization. The second (embryology) is related to the debates between the thesis of the preformation and development of germs (*evolutio*) and that of epigenesis, which will lead to the development of embryology in the nineteenth century. On this theme, see Georges Canguilhem, Georges Lapassade, Jacques Piquemal, et al., *Du développement à l'évolution au XIXe siècle*, 2nd ed. (Paris: PUF, 1985 [1962]). The third (genetics) refers to the problem of heredity and the transmission of characteristics, which begins to be posed in natural history in the middle of the eighteenth century and which, through a series of breaks, will lead to the constitution of genetics. Foucault was then particularly interested in the emergence of forms of knowledge of heredity, to which he will return in this course and which will form the basis of his project for the Collège de France (see below, lecture 6, and "Course Context", pp. 326–329). The fourth (hormonology) calls upon the history of hormonology, which was partly considered in the Clermont-Ferrand course. All of these studies were inserted in the Canguilhemian tradition of an epistemological history of concepts, from which Foucault is careful here to distinguish his archaeological perspective. This effort at distinguishing his archaeology of the discourse of sexuality from a conceptual history of the science of sexuality should be compared with the distinctions Foucault makes in the same period between the "*epistemological* history of the sciences," which "is situated at the threshold of scientificity, and questions itself as to the way in which it was crossed on the basis of various epistemological figures. Its purpose is to discover . . . how a concept— still overlaid with metaphors or imaginary contents—was purified, and accorded the status and function of a scientific concept," and the "*archaeological history*" of knowledge (*savoir*), which "takes as its point of attack the threshold of epistemologization . . . what one is trying to uncover are discursive practices in so far as they give rise to a corpus of knowledge, in so far as they assume the status and role of a science" (*The Archaeology of*

Knowledge,190); see also "On the Archaeology of the Sciences: Response to the Epistemology Circle" (1968), *EW*, 2, 297–334. Foucault will return to these questions in lectures 3 and 6 of this course.

6. Here again, see the Clermont-Ferrand course, above, which partly realizes this program by focusing on the genesis of a psychological and psychiatric knowledge of sexuality through the study of sexual perversions and then by focusing on the Freudian analysis of libido. Foucault will take up the question anew in his Collège de France courses, in particular in *Psychiatric Power: Lectures at the Collège de France, 1973–1974*, ed. Jacques Lagrange, trans. Graham Burchell, English series editor Arnold I. Davidson (London: Palgrave Macmillan, 2008), 297–323, on hysteria, and especially *Abnormal: Lectures at the Collège de France, 1974–1975*, trans. Graham Burchell, English series editor Arnold I. Davison (New York: Picador, 2003), 263–318, for the genesis of a psychiatric knowledge of sexuality and the sexual perversions, as well as in *The History of Sexuality. Vol. I: An Introduction*, trans. R. Hurley (New York: Pantheon, 1978).

7. This theme of sexual anthropology was the object of some remarks in the Clermont-Ferrand course (see above, lecture 1 and notes 2, 3, and 33, pp. 17–18, and 24), although Foucault did not, as he initially announced, deal with the "intercultural divergences and dispersions" described by ethnology. In truth, this theme covers two different domains here. On the one hand is anthropology in the philosophical sense, referring, for example, to the anthropology of sexuality which Foucault refers to through the cases of Hegel or Comte in the Clermont-Ferrand course. The problems posed— what does the fact of being sexed entail? what type of relations to the world does this presuppose? what are femininity and masculinity?—refer to questions posed notably in the tradition of German philosophical anthropology around the relation between the essence of Man and sexuality, as dealt with, for example, in Hans Kunz, "Idee und Wirklichkeit des Menschen Bemerkungen zu einem Grundproblem der philosophischen Anthropologie," *Studia Philosophia* 4, no. 147 (1944): 147–69; see BNF, Box 42b, or Max Scheler, "Zur Idee des Menschen" (1914) in *Vom Umsturz der Wert* (Leipzig: Der Neue Geist, 1919), 1:217–312. We know that in his *Phenomenology of Perception*, trans. Donald A. Landes (London: Routledge, 2012), Merleau-Ponty also devoted a chapter to the "body as sexed being" and the way our perceived world is charged with erotic meanings. The same

anthropological theme is found in the work of Buytendijk (*La Femme*) or Jeannière (*Anthropologie sexuelle*) referred to above, p. 24. But on the other hand, sexual anthropology also refers here to the work of anthropologists like Malinowski or Mead (see above, pp. 17–18) as well as, through the reference to the structuring of sexuality, to the works of Lévi-Strauss and the anthropology of the structures of kinship.

8. On "little Hans," see above, Clermont-Ferrand course, lecture 5, p. 112. Gradiva refers to "Delusions and Dreams in Jensen's *Gradiva*," *CPW*, vol. 9, in which Freud analyzes Wilhelm Jensen's short story, *Gradiva*, and its sexual erotics (see Wilhelm Jensen, *Gradiva. A Pompeiian Fancy*, trans. Helen M. Downey [Los Angeles: Green Integer, 2003]). Foucault commented at length on the *Three Essays on Sexuality* in the Clermont-Ferrand course, above.

9. Foucault introduces this notion of "referential" in his reply to the Cercle d'épistémologie of the École normale supériore, in which he asserts that the unity of a discourse is not to be sought in an object to which it refers, but in "the common space in which diverse objects stand out and are continuously transformed"—that is, the pattern of rules that govern the formation and "dispersion of different objects or referents put into play by an ensemble of statements" ("On the Archaeology of the Sciences" [1968], *EW*, 2, 313–14). It will be taken up in *The Archaeology of Knowledge* to designate the correlate to which every statement is referred: not an object or a particular individual, not a state of affairs, but "a 'referential' that is made up not of 'things,' 'facts,' 'realities,' or 'beings,' but of laws of possibility, rules of existence for the objects that are named, designated, or described within it, and for the relations that are affirmed or denied in it" (91).

10. Foucault returns to Sade in detail in lecture 7 of this course; see below. He will take up the question of the relation between Sade's discourse and sexuality and desire in the second lecture he gives in Buffalo in March 1970, "Theoretical Discourse and Erotic Scenes," in Michel Foucault, *Language, Madness, and Desire: On Literature*, ed. Philippe Artières, Jean-François Bert, Mathieu Potte-Bonneville, and Judith Revel, trans. Robert Bononno (Minneapolis: University of Minnesota Press, 2015). But on this occasion Foucault notes that "[Sade's] discourses do not speak about desire, nor do they speak about sexuality; sexuality and desire are not objects of the discourses." But there exists between discourse and desire a connection of a completely different order in Sade: "the discourse functions as the engine

and principle of desire. . . . Discourse and desire . . . trigger each other, without discourse being superior to desire in expressing the truth" (116).

11. This study is carried out in lectures 2 and especially 4 of this course; see below.

12. Of this series of possible studies, Foucault will ultimately retain only the history of the biology of sexuality (see below, lecture 6). The case of sexuality as object of psychiatry was broached briefly in the Clermont-Ferrand course (see above, pp. 84–89) and will be amply considered sub-sequently, as well as, to a lesser extent, jurisprudence (in the matter of the determination of sex, for example), in *Abnormal*; *The History of Sexuality. Volume I: An Introduction*; "Le vrai sexe" (1986), in *DÉ*, II, no. 287, 934–42; as well as in the unpublished manuscript *La Croisade des enfants*. Philo-sophical reflection on sexuality in the nineteenth century will never be the object of a specific study. We note, however, that Foucault was engaged in this analysis through reading the texts of *Naturphilosophie* (in particular the physio-philosophy of Lorenz Oken) and Schopenhauer (BNF, Box 45-C2).

13. Foucault will not return to Freud and the discovery of the neuroses in this course, although, in the same period, he undertakes a detailed reread-ing of Freud on the subject (BNF, Box 39-C2, folders "The first texts [of Freud]" and "Freud. Theory of sexuality"). For an older outline on the sub-ject, see above, the Clermont-Ferrand course, p. 89 et seq., and the numer-ous courses Foucault devoted to Freud in the 1950s (BNF, Box 46).

14. Of these authors, Foucault will refer here only to Sade, from the point of view of sexual utopia (see below, lecture 7), whom he had already referred to at length in the Clermont-Ferrand course and in various texts from the 1960s (see above, lecture 1, and notes 31 and 35, pp. 23 and 25, and lecture 4, p. 85). Genet, who was close to Foucault, is referred to frequently in the same years (see, notably, "Folie, littérature, société" [1970] in *DÉ*, I, no. 82, 987–91, where Foucault takes his distance from sexual transgres-sion in literature, which he judges henceforth dulls real transgression). We know that when he was at Uppsala he devoted a series of lectures to "Love in French literature from Sade to Genet." Leopold von Sacher-Masoch scarcely held Foucault's attention, but in 1967 his *Venus in Furs* was repub-lished, together with a famous essay by Gilles Deleuze, in Gilles Deleuze and Leopold von Sacher-Masoch, *Masochism: Coldness and Cruelty & Venus in Furs*, trans. Jean McNeil (New York: Zone Books, 1989). Deleuze also

devoted a study to D. H. Lawrence, who is a recurring reference in his work: "Nietzsche and Saint Paul, Lawrence and John of Patmos," in *Essays Critical and Clinical*, trans. Daniel W. Smith and Michael A. Greco (Minneapolis: University of Minnesota Press, 1997).

15. This last theme is considered in lecture 7 (see below), in particular through an analysis of Herbert Marcuse, and it is referred to more briefly in lecture 4 (see below, p. 192), in the framework of reference to the criticisms of bourgeois marriage made by Leon Trotski and Alexandra Kollontai. We have seen that Foucault referred to the theme of "sexual revolution" in the Clermont-Ferrand course (see above, lecture 1, pp. 15–17, and note 36, p. 27). The events of May 1968 obviously put the theme at the heart of contemporary reality at the time of Foucault's course at Vincennes (see below, lecture 7, and "Course Context", pp. 342–345).

LECTURE 2

The Transformations of the Eighteenth Century[1]

*T*ransformations of sexuality as practice at the economic level.
*1. Disruption of demographic balances and economic growth.
Fifteenth–sixteenth century: collapse then expansion, which encounters various blocks: de facto Malthusianism, technical innovation,
political centralization. Stagnation-depression. 2. Eighteenth century: economic growth and demographic stagnation: need for labor:
demand for population of one class for another. Consequences: institutions of assistance, statistics, populationist theory, campaign against
celibacy, theme of natural birth rate, control of one's own sexuality by
the bourgeoisie (marriage contract). Sexuality becomes natural science and normative knowledge (*connaissance*). 3. Methodological
comment on ideology/science relations: how to think the articulation
between processes that affect a social formation and the epistemologization of sexuality?*

We can classify them[a] under three rubrics: [11]

- sexuality as practice functioning at the economic level;
- [sexuality] as practice codified by legislation;
- [sexuality] as practice encoded by a morality.

---

a Understanding "the transformations of the eighteenth century."

A. *Breakdown of demographic balances and economic growth*[2]

If we take the broad movements of demography, we have:

1. The great collapse of the fifteenth century (war, plague) which, with the discovery of American gold, was [a] powerful economic stimulant: more goods, more circulation, more technical rationalization (redistribution of labor force).

Hence a big expansion in the sixteenth century but which, from 1570, encounters a number of blocks:
- cultivable land;
- monetary shortage;
- technical inertia (90% illiteracy).[3]

2. These blocks (and the difficulties that ensued) resulted in:
a. At the level of the labor force:

[12]
  - A de facto Malthusianism whose factors were very diverse: natural mortality, late marriage,[4] abortion.[5]
  - And, on the other hand, technical research for new forces of production: agronomy, canalization.[6]

b. At the level of political institutions, the constitution of a central power that responded to the demand of the bourgeoisie (resorption of unemployment, increase of monetary reserves, and increase in production), but that responded in feudal forms: increase of rent, which increased resistance of the blocks. Hence a stability from below, a lengthy depression lasting until the beginning of the eighteenth century.[7]

3. The eighteenth century, period of slow expansion:
a. Accumulation of capital (by increase in rent) and transfers to the bourgeoisie enabling the development of industry.
[*In the margin*: "100% increase in rent; four-year rotation"[8]]

b. The search for new technical means enters the domain of profitability.

[*In the margin*: "—Prices increase by 50 to 60%;—wages stagnate;—the population increases by a third"⁹]

c. But the demographic balance remains relatively stable, because theᵇ peasant's level of life hardly changes.   [13]

Hence a need for labor for the reserve army of capitalism.¹⁰

This demand for population—and this is its specific characteristic—is not linked directly to the expansion of resources, but to a certain type of production that changes the economic and social balances. It is a matter of a demand for repopulation addressed to one part of the population by another. A demand addressed by one class to another. And this is clearly shown in the way the demand is formulated (not only in theory but also in practice).

a. Health, assistance.¹¹

b. A beginningᶜ of statistical calculation.¹²

c. A populationist theory no longer linked to the general theme of the strength of States (and mercantilist enrichment), but linked to the problem of production and consumption [and] raising the problem of regulation (Boisguillebert, Moheau, Bruckner, Grimm, Malthus).¹³

d. A demand in favor of the family and against celibacy.ᵈ;¹⁴   [14]

e. The general ideological theme that all these movements of population, this demanded birth rate, are an effect of nature:

---

b Sheets 17–18 of the manuscript, containing a long passage crossed out by Michel Foucault, a variant of the following sections, are found in the appendix to this lecture (below, pp. 164–165).

c The sign of abbreviation is not clear. TN1 gives: "development of techniques enabling demographic registration (social statistics)."

d A line crossed out follows: "Against or for divorce (see Cerfvol)."

a. Buffon's "scientific" theory. Society is the effect of demographic growth. So long as there were few people, society served no purpose.[15]

b. Moral theme: free birth rate, found in the peasants who, far from the depravity of the towns, are the closest to nature.[e16]

[15]   f. Finally, last element: the bourgeoisie wants to control the effects of demography at its own level (at the level of the distribution of goods). The limitation that, for other classes, it expects from poverty, it wants to control for itself: marriage

[16–17]^f   as contract and the possibility of divorce.[17]

[18]   Sexuality will thus be naturalized. Giving it "citizenship" in a nature that is in fact the ideology of the city. As marriage is made a contract and a civil act.

Comments

1. We find the two terms contract-nature, which have haunted political ideology, but staggered in time:

a. At the time of the development of industrial society, the bourgeoisie has to have it thought that society is not the result of a contract but of an organic bond.

---

e A crossed-out passage follows announcing the analyses Foucault will undertake from page 20 of the manuscript: "Population = morality = nature = spontaneous limitation. Ideological operation that reverses the order of real demands. These: – call for limitation

– which substitutes nature for economic necessity

– which presents a social growth as imperative rule."

f The end of page 15 and the whole of page 16 of the manuscript contain a long crossed-out passage that announces the analyses Foucault will develop in the next lecture, starting from page 21 of the manuscript. Foucault himself indicated "transfer to p. 20." We therefore follow his indication and transfer the crossed-out sheets to an appendix to the next lecture, as a variant of manuscript page 21. See below, pp. 180–181. Page 17 and the beginning of page 18 are entirely crossed out and constitute a variant of pages 13–15. We have therefore chosen to reproduce them in an appendix to this lecture, as variants of these pages. See below, pp. 164–165.

b. In the same period, it has to have it thought that the birth rate it needs is an effect of nature [and] that the concentration of wealth over which it wishes to keep control must be regulated by the contract.

c. There is no contradiction, and an ideology of the family [19] will be developed going from (natural) procreation to the civil contract (as final and completed expression of this great organic urging). The organicist ideology of society, the naturalist ideology of the birth rate, and the theme of the contract that characterizes bourgeois marriage are exactly joined together through the family.[18]

2. This naturalization of sexuality will entail a number of things:

a. It is natural only to the extent that it is procreative (theme that appears in the eighteenth century).

b. It is natural only if it is in keeping with order;

c. and if, consequently, it is the object of the knowledge that is knowledge of its (biological) naturalness and delimitation of what is not natural (normative and repressive knowledge).

Knowledge (*savoir*) of sexuality will be "natural science" and "normative knowledge (*connaissance*)."[19]

3. Methodologically, this does not amount [. . .] to saying [20] either that the knowledge (*connaissance*) of sexuality is ideological, or that the class struggle is its condition of possibility, but of showing four levels of ideological effects:

- How sexuality could be constituted as an object within a determinate social formation and as effect of the processes at work in it.

- How a certain ideology required the implementation of a knowledge (*savoir*) as biological knowledge.

- How it required the knowledge to operate in a certain (normative and repressive) mode.
- How, finally, it imposed themes (such as the natural character of procreation).

So we cannot say *science* against *ideology*.[g] In a given social formation, their interplay is much more complicated.

The hold of ideology on a field of knowledge (*savoir*).[20]

*

APPENDIX TO LECTURE 2

[We insert here page 17 and the beginning of page 18 of the manuscript, which contain a long crossed-out passage by Michel Foucault, a variant of the analyses developed from page 13.]

[17]   c. But the demographic balance remains exactly the same, because the peasants' level of life does not change. Hence a need for labor for the reserve army of capitalism, which manifests itself through:

- Populationist theory
- An ideology of nature (far from the depravity of towns)
- A survey of the health of the population
- A demand for the family and against celibacy.

In other words, for the first time, demographic release is no longer linked directly to the expansion of resources, but to the creation, or at least development, of a certain type of production that changes the social and economic balances. It is a matter of

---

g Underlined in the manuscript.

a demand for repopulation addressed to one part of the population by another; to one class by another.

In fact, the bourgeoisie does not change its own demographic norms. It arranges a marriage contract and a divorce, which should enable it to handle the consequences of its demography economically.

On the other hand, it demands from another social class [18] an effort of population that is not the consequence of an increase of resources, but that should allow an increase of the bourgeoisie's resources. And this increase, which is the effect of a demand, is presented as being the result of a return to nature itself.

*

1. One of the typed texts based on students' notes for this lecture (henceforth designated TN1) has: "Transformation of the regime of sexuality—end of eighteenth century."

2. For this subsection, which represents a significant novelty in comparison with the analysis offered in the Clermont-Ferrand course, Foucault relies on the works of the *Annales* school, whose importance from the point of view of historical analysis he emphasizes in the same period. See "On the Archaeology of the Sciences" (1968), *EW*, 2, 298; "Michel Foucault explique son dernier livre" (1969), in *DÉ*, I, no. 66, 799–807, esp. 801; and especially, later, "Return to History" (1972), trans. Robert Hurley, in *EW*, 2, esp. 426–32. See too the classic works by Emmanuel Le Roy Ladurie, *The Peasants of Languedoc*, trans. John Day (Urbana: University of Illinois Press, 1977), and Pierre Goubert, *Beauvais et le Beauvaisis de 1600 à 1730: Contribution à l'histoire sociale de la France du XVIIᵉ siècle* (Paris: SEVPEN, 1958) and *Louis XIV et vingt millions de Français* (Paris: Fayard, 1966), which Foucault draws on for their results on historical demography. It should be recalled that from 1961 the *Annales* launched a special rubric of inquiries on "material life and biological behavior," in which works on the biological history of populations and on sexual or alimentary behavior appeared regularly.

In 1969, moreover, there was a special issue devoted to "Biological History and Society," in which there is an article by Jean-Louis Flandrin on the history of contraception, "Contraception, mariage et relations amoureuses dans l'Occident chrétien," and another by Jacques Dupâquier and Marcel Lachiver, "Les débuts de la contraception en France ou les deux malthusianismes," *Annales ESC* 24, no. 6 (1969): 1370–90, 1391–1406. As Luca Paltrinieri has emphasized, these works of historical demography and of the biological history of populations, whether of Philippe Ariès, *Histoire des populations françaises et de leurs attitudes devant la vie depuis le XVIIIe siècle* (Paris: Self, 1949), of Jacques Dupâquier and of Jacqueline Hecht at the Institut national d'études démographiques (Ined), or of the *Annales* school, played an important role in Foucault's elaboration of his later reflections on biopower and biopolitics; see, for example, L Paltrinieri, "Biopouvoir, les sources historiennes d'une fiction politique," *Revue d'histoire moderne et contemporaine* 60, no. 4 (2013): 49–75.

3. Foucault here calls on Le Roy Ladurie's analysis in his thesis on the peasants of Languedoc. For Le Roy Ladurie, 1570 represents a cutoff date in relation to the growth of the sixteenth century: "The powerful upswing of the first half of the sixteenth century had definitely spent its force after 1560–1570" (*The Peasants of Languedoc*, 53). On the fifteenth-century collapse and the demographic and economic growth that ensued in the sixteenth century, see 11–83). The block represented by the lack of cultivable land is described notably on 74–76 (see file, "Mouvement de population et régime des naissances sous l'Ancien Régime," BNF, Box 39-C2/F3).

4. TN1 gives in addition: "famine, poor state of health, illnesses; 50% of children do not reach adulthood." All this information is drawn from Pierre Goubert, *Louis XIV et vingt millions de Français* (Paris: Fayard, 1966), 25–29. As Foucault notes in the previously cited file, the birth rate is of the order of 40/100, with pregnancies every twenty-five or thirty months. In total, for families of five children per household, two or three reach adulthood. "Control is obtained:—by death: life expectancy being 25 years, around 25% die in the first year; 50% before the twentieth; 75% before the forty-fifth;—by late marriage;—by conscription by armies." The role of late marriage is also emphasized by Pierre Chaunu, *La Civilisation de l'Europe classique* (Paris: Arthaud, 1966), who recalls that "the age of marriage for girls is the real contraceptive weapon of the classical age."

5. TN1 adds: "moderate contraceptive practices (Le Roy Ladurie records in Languedoc, a pregnancy every 27 months for each woman)." See E. Le Roy Ladurie, *Les Paysans de Languedoc* (Paris: SEVPEN, 1966) 556–57 [This does not appear in the English translation which was based on the abridged 1969 edition; G.B.]).

6. On the development of agronomy from the end of the sixteenth and in the seventeenth century, the fundamental work of André Jean Bourde had recently been published, *Agronomie et Agronomes en France au XVIIIe siècle: Thèse pour le doctorat ès lettres*, 3 vols. (Paris: SEVPEN, 1967). The major works of marsh draining (*Édit pour le déssechement des marais*, 1599) and construction of the main French canals (Briare, Orléans, Deux-Mers) stretch throughout the seventeenth century.

7. TN1 provides a much more detailed account: "We witness also a political institutionalization of nascent capitalism. The latter aims to: 1. overcome European economic stagnation: appearance of a State apparatus the function of which is to stimulate the economy:—the State is made responsible for developing industrial production;—it also takes charge of irrigation;—and of protecting the currency, customs. 2. Artificially maintaining the demographic lock, in order to avoid unemployment, strikes, and riots. In this way a repressive mercantilist State is established; in 1659 [*rectius*: 1699], invention of state police. 3. The mercantilist State is constituted on the feudal political model. The monarchy depends upon the existing classes: the dues that the peasants have to pay the nobles and the Church are increased. Nobility and Church become the guardians of power. As wealth is spent locally and not invested, the bourgeoisie feels thwarted in its political effort, to the advantage of clergy and nobility. *De facto economic closure*:—ground rent increases by 100%;—the price of goods increases by from 50 to 60%;—wages have not increased at all. Real wages are therefore low;—population has increased by 30%. Political effects of this phenomenon:—struggle between bourgeoisie and aristocracy;—the bourgeois revolution is doubled by a popular revolution which does not succeed;—throughout the eighteenth century the bourgeoisie strives to circumvent the obstacles in its way. It is at the origin of:—Physiocracy;—technical research for enabling land to be cultivated;—investment in manufactories. These factors establish a new situation in the context of which capitalism can take off." Foucault returns on numerous occasions to the politico-economic transformations

of the seventeenth century, from *History of Madness*, in which the "great confinement" and the creation of various institutions of internment are closely linked to mercantilism and monarchical institutions (44–77), to *Penal Theories and Institutions*, the first part of which is devoted entirely to the birth of a new repressive State apparatus at the end of the seventeenth century. Foucault, *Penal Theories and Institutions: Lectures at the Collège de France, 1971–1972*, trans. Graham Burchell, ed. Bernard Harcourt with Elisabetta Basso, Claude-Olivier Doron, and Daniel Defert, English series editor, Arnold I. Davidson (London: Palgrave Macmillan, 2019), 1–99.

8. On the 100 percent rent increase, see, for example, François Crouzet, "Angleterre et France au XVIIIᵉ siècle: Essai d'analyse comparée de deux croissances économiques," *Annales ESC* 21, no. 2 (1966): 245–91: "the increase in feudal rent and agricultural profits enriched . . . a not inconsiderable part of the population. . . . Hence a stimulant for commerce . . ., industry, the development of towns, and an increase in non-agricultural revenues" (279).

9. Figures of this order are found in Crouzet's article, which compares English and French growth in the eighteenth century. Thus, the increase of the French population in the period 1701–1781 is estimated at 35 percent; the growth of the "material product" in the eighteenth century is estimated, according to Paul Bairoch, at 69 percent (Crouzet, "Angleterre et France au XVIIIᵉ siècle," 270). Regarding wages, average wages increase in the first part of the century and then stagnate, or rather, in terms of real wages, fall, due to the stronger rise in agricultural prices and rent (279).

10. See Crouzet, "Angleterre et France au XVIIIᵉ siècle," 287–88. The "reserve army of capitalism" is a reference to Marx, for whom the law of the accumulation of capital induces a growing relative overpopulation, which creates an "industrial reserve army" for capitalism: "if a surplus population of workers is a necessary product of accumulation . . . this surplus population also becomes, conversely, the lever of capitalist accumulation, indeed it becomes a condition for the existence of the capitalist mode of production. It forms a disposable industrial reserve army, which belongs to capital just as absolutely as if the latter had bred it at its own cost. Independently of the limits of the actual increase of population, it creates a mass of human material always ready for exploitation by capital in the interests of capital's own changing valorization requirements" (Karl Marx, *Capital: A Critique of Political Economy*, Volume One, trans. Ben Fowkes [Harmondsworth, UK:

Penguin, 1976], 784). This and the following lecture should be linked with Marx's reflections on the law of population peculiar to the capitalist mode of production and his criticisms of Thomas R. Malthus. See below, p. 170.

11. TN1 clarifies: "new social practices: assistance to the poor, to the sick; sharp increase in medical techniques and institutions." On this subject, see Foucault's analyses from *History of Madness* and *Birth of the Clinic* up to "Crise de la médicine ou crise de l'antimédicine?" (1976) *DÉ*, II, no. 170, 40–58, and "L'incorporation de l'hôpital dans la technologie moderne" (1978), *DÉ*, II, no. 229, 508–22.

12. From the second half of the seventeenth century, procedures are established (administrative inquiries, quantifying and tabulating biological, economic, and social phenomena, calculations of probability established on statistical series, etc.) that result in the development of what, at the end of the eighteenth century, is called political and moral arithmetic—that is, social statistics. On the development of these techniques, see the important work of publication and commentary on the classics of demography and political economy undertaken by Ined, at the instigation of Jacqueline Hecht, since the end of the 1950s. See also, more recently, for example, Alain Desrosières, *La Politique des grands nombres: Histoire de la raison statistique* (Paris: La Découverte, 1998); Ian Hacking, *The Taming of Chance* (Cambridge: Cambridge University Press, 1990); or Andrea A. Rusnock, *Vital Accounts: Quantifying Health and Population in Eighteenth-Century England and France* (Cambridge: Cambridge University Press, 2002). Foucault will return to this in greater detail in *Security, Territory, Population: Lectures at the Collège de France, 1977–1978*, ed. Michel Sennellart, trans. Graham Burchell, English Series Editor Arnold I. Davidson (New York: Palgrave Macmillan, 2007) in the framework of an analysis of biopolitics and the establishment of apparatuses (*dispositifs*) of security aiming to know and regulate vital phenomena capable of affecting populations.

13. The authors Foucault mentions here are Pierre le Pesant de Boisguilbert (or Boisguillebert) (1646–1714), an economist critical of the mercantilist policy conducted by Colbert under Louis XIV and the author of, in particular, the *Détail de la France* (1695), often presented as the precursor of French political economy, and to whom J. Hecht had just devoted a work, *Pierre de Boisguilbert ou la Naissance de l'économie politique*, 2 vols., preface by d'A. Sauvy (Paris: Ined, 1966); Jean-Baptiste Moheau (1745–1794), the

author of one of the main treatises on population and demography in the eighteenth century—*Recherches et Considérations sur la population de la France* (Paris: Moutard, 1778)—to whom Foucault will return in *Security, Territory, Population*, 22–23, 27nn; John Bruckner (1726–1804), the author of a *Théorie du système animal* (Leyde: Jean Luzac, 1767), put forward by Marx as one of the first theorists of population and especially one of the precursors of the struggle for existence as a regulatory factor of animal populations. Friedrich Melchior Grimm (1723–1834) was close to Denis Diderot and the encyclopedists and author of an abundant *Correspondance littéraire, critique et philosophique* (Paris: Furne-Ladrange, 1829–1830) and was involved, in particular, in debates against the physiocrats. Thomas R. Malthus (1766–1834) is the author of the famous *An Essay on the Principle of Population*, ed. Anthony Flew (Harmondsworth, UK: Penguin Boks, 1970), in which he posited as a natural law the contradiction between the arithmetic increase in the means of subsistence and the geometric increase in population. From his point of view, this law is a regulatory factor of the human population, leading mechanically to the surplus population—if one deprives it of the artificial help organized by assistance to the poor in England—either disappearing or limiting its reproduction. From Sismondi to Marx, a number of nineteenth-century economists criticize Malthus's reading for making into a natural law what is in reality the result of a particular (capitalist) mode of production that engenders a relative overpopulation specific to it (due to the concentration of capital, and so of the means of production and subsistence). Foucault continues in the vein of these criticisms of naturalization as an ideological operation and strives to situate it in a more complex set of similar operations. The students' notes (TN1) make it possible to clarify the distinction Foucault makes between the problematic of population and its regulation, as it developed in the eighteenth century, and that of the mercantilists: "development of a whole political economy founded on the problem of population. Dialogue between the physiocrats and Ricardo: must a population be strong or weak for the best economic situation? *It is therefore the economic circuit that will determine the value of the population rate.* A problem arises: knowing the optimum demographic development" (*emphasis in the manuscript*). For the mercantilists, the population rate is an essential factor in the wealth and power of a State. The position of the physiocrats is very different: according to them, the population depends on production and, in this case, the growth of the net product of agriculture—the agricultural sector being the only productive sector for the physiocrats. Consequently, the debate effectively begins on the optimum population rate in terms of a set of factors defining the economic circuit—factors of production (land, labor, or capital), consumption, etc. Foucault laid great stress on these transformations of economic reflections in *The Order of Things*, in which, by introducing the question of scarcity as a fundamental anthropological situation, a condition for labor and economic development, Ricardo and Malthus are presented as points of divergence vis-à-vis the "analysis of wealth" typical of the classical age in which the physiocrats are still situated. In *Security, Territory, Population* (68–77), the break takes place clearly between the mercantilists and the physiocrats precisely on the question of population as an object of knowledge and subject of government: if the mercantilists remain on the side of the "analysis of wealth," the physiocrats, by introducing the subject-object population into the theoretical and practical field of the economy, live on the side of "political economy."

14. TN1 clarifies: "Political demand: State control of the status of the family. The civil jurisdiction must no longer be shaped by religious legislation. Demand for measures concerning:—celibacy;—divorce;—large families." This is a reference to the many authors who, from Montesquieu at least, attack celibacy (of priests in particular) as an obstacle to population, encourage measures of assistance to large families and, in the case of Cerfvol in particular, the author of a *Mémoire sur la population* (London, 1768), aim to promote divorce as the best means of increasing and improving the population. On this subject, see, for example, Carol Blum, *Strength in Numbers: Population, Reproduction, and Power in Eighteenth-Century France* (Baltimore: Johns Hopkins University Press, 2002).

15. See, for example, Buffon, "Époques de la nature: 7ᵉ et dernière époque," in *Suppléments à l'Histoire naturelle générale et particulière*, vol. 5 (Paris: Imprimerie royale, 1778), 226–27. Men remained relatively wild so long as they were dispersed: "so long as they formed only small nations composed of a few families, or rather relatives coming from the same family, as we still see today among the Savages. . . . But everywhere [places] or space were confined by seas or closed in by high mountains, these small nations, having become too numerous, were forced to share their land,

and it is from that moment that the Earth became man's domain; he took possession of it through his works of cultivation, and attachment to the homeland followed quickly the first acts of his property: particular interest forming part of the national interest, order, police, and laws had to follow, and society acquired body and strength."

16. This theme, which is classical in physiocratic or medical literature, is present in Rousseau and Rétif de La Bretonne, for example.

17. TN1 notes, somewhat differently: "Ideological theme according to which sexuality is a *phenomenon of nature* that must no longer be entered on the register of sin. And it is by freeing sexuality that all the demographic mechanisms will find their spontaneous regulation. The bourgeoisie, which wants to control the system of this demography, preaches at the same time:—the theme of the peasant family, pure, natural, etc.;—the definition of marriage as a *contract* integrated within the civil jurisdiction. This double theme is profoundly linked; Christian marriage is thereby broken up. *Consequences*: sexuality is different from marriage:—marriage: object of a civil contract;—sexuality: phenomenon of nature" (*emphasis in the manuscript*).

18. Foucault will return to the question of marriage as civil contract and to the organicist ideology of the family in lecture 4 of this course, see below, p. 194 et seq.

19. The two lines of analysis that Foucault will subsequently follow are foreshadowed here. Knowledge of sexuality as "natural science" will be the object of lecture 6 of this course (see below) and extended in the research program announced for the Collège de France. Knowledge of sexuality as "normative knowledge" will give rise in the following years to the research resulting in *History of Sexuality, Volume 1: An Introduction*, in particular through the Collège de France course *Abnormal* and the unpublished manuscript *La Croisade des enfants*.

20. From the typed students' notes no. 2 (hereafter designated TN2) we know that Foucault introduced here two notions, that of episteme (*épistémè*) and that of ideological operations, which are found in the next lecture. Moreover, the two lectures may not have been delivered separately; lecture 3 being a methodological and theoretical interlude before lecture 4 resumes the analysis of the transformations of the eighteenth century, this time from the angle of matrimonial practices and the legal system. TN2 notes: "N.B.: ideology has a hold on knowledge (*savoir*) and not on science → science/ideology

opposition is not pertinent. *Episteme*: that on the basis of which a knowledge (*savoir*) is constituted that is not yet a science. *Ideological operations*: how the dominant class codes, masks, misrepresents the economic needs of the system in which it dominates. The institutions, codes, practices, norms but also knowledge (*savoir*) and science may be considered the expression of these operations" (*emphasis in the manuscript*). The end of this lecture and all of the following lecture should in fact be read as belonging to Foucault's attempts at this time to clarify his criticisms of the ideology/science alternative thematized by Louis Althusser and to refine his own discourse on the articulation between forms of knowledge (*savoirs*), economic relations, and power, a problem he will grapple with in his Collège de France courses, at least until 1976–1977. The "hold of ideology over a field of knowledge" should be compared with the passage in *The Archaeology of Knowledge*, trans. A. M. Sheridan Smith (London: Tavistock, 1972), in which Foucault notes, "The hold of ideology over scientific discourse and the ideological functioning of the sciences are not articulated at the level of their ideal structure . . . nor at the level of their technical use in a society . . . nor at the level of the consciousness of the subjects that built it up; they are articulated where science is articulated upon knowledge (*savoir*)," in the way in which "a science functions in the element of knowledge" (185). See below, lecture 3, where all these questions will be developed further.

LECTURE 3

The Discourse of Sexuality (3)

I. Summary of the previous lecture. How an economic process gives rise to heterogeneous elements (institutions, law, ideological themes, objects of knowledge). II. Methodological remarks. These elements form a functional system. This system presupposes a series of operations that must be analyzed in their contents, forms, and effects. These operations define the "primary ideological coding" of an economic process, which is neither ideology in the strict sense, nor the system of heterogeneous elements, but the rules ensuring their formation. To be distinguished from the "specific ideological effect," that is to say nonscientific propositions produced by this coding; and from the "secondary ideological functioning," that is to say how this specific effect functions in various elements of the system, including the sciences, and not only as obstacle. III. Conclusion. No unitary ideological domain: the ideology/science opposition is not pertinent; the primary ideological coding is neither a set of representations nor an unconscious, but a set of rules put to work by a social class; it is a class practice without a subject. The ideological struggle is not a matter of consciousness nor of science, but of social practices: nonpertinence of the Bachelardian-Althusserian model of the "break" and theoretical work.

[21]   1. We have seen the development of an economic process.

– The formation of a primitive accumulation (thanks to a demographic collapse).

– An economic and demographic development blocked by structural and technical impossibilities.

– The constitution of a political power intended to remove this blockage but that, to some extent, led to locking it (demographically).

Hence:

- capitalist development
- demographic insufficiency.

– The demand for labor.[1]

2. We have indicated how this process gave birth to multiple elements:[a]

- institution → assistance;
- legal principles → marriage, contract;
- ideological themes (only procreative sexuality is normal sexuality);
- finally, an object for possible knowledges: sexuality.

[22]   Some remarks are called for on this subject:[2]

– The economic process does not give rise to something like an ideology, but to a bundle of elements of different kinds, status, and function. The ideological effect is only one of these elements.

---

a In the appendix to this lecture will be found the end of page 15 and page 16 of the manuscript that Michel Foucault indicated should be transferred to page 21 (see above, previous lecture, p. 162). They provide a variant of the passages that follow here.

– These elements are not dispersed or juxtaposed alongside each other, like divergent effects. They occupy precise functions in relation to each other:[3] in particular, the ideological theme:
- strengthens the contract;
- splits (*clive*)[b] the knowledge of sexuality;[4]
- prevents the Malthusianism of the poor classes.

– But for these economic processes to give rise to these effects and not others (free union, for example), a certain operation or group of operations was necessary:

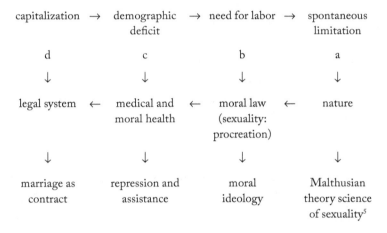

capitalization →	demographic → deficit	need for labor →	spontaneous limitation
d	c	b	a
↓	↓	↓	↓
legal system ←	medical and ← moral health	moral law ← (sexuality: procreation)	nature
↓	↓	↓	↓
marriage as contract	repression and assistance	moral ideology	Malthusian theory science of sexuality[5]

1. In their *content*,[c] this set of operations consists in: [23]
- a: confusion of an economic law and a natural law;
- b: transformation of a class demand into a moral principle;

---

b This is the probable word. TN2 has: "ethical and medical division (*clivage*) of sexuality."
c Underlined in the manuscript.

- c: correction of an economic situation by ethical and medical principles;
- d: translation of economic processes into a legal system.

2. In their *form*,[d] these operations consist in:
- a general inversion of the order of implications;
- shifts of level or order (economy, morality);
- abstract generalizations (economic mechanisms, natural mechanisms);
- translations or misrepresentations (capitalization, legal structure, deficit);
- compensatory mechanisms ([. . .[e]] ethical and medical).

3. In their *effect*,[f] [these operations consist] in getting a set of economic mechanisms and requirements to function as a coherent system going from nature to law, from spontaneity to the institution, by way of morality and medicine.

[24]   This set of operations is what could be called the *primary ideological coding*[g] of an economic process. It is the group of transformations by which a determinate social class (the class holding political, economic, and cultural power) makes possible the formation of an epistemological, moral, legal, and institutional ensemble on the basis of a given economic process. This ideological coding is not an ideology in the strict sense; neither is it the set of institutions, representations, moral and legal rules. It is their historical condition of possibility. It is the set of rules that assures their formation.[6]

---

d Underlined in the manuscript.
e Illegible word.
f Underlined in the manuscript.
g Underlined in the manuscript.

We will call *specific ideological effect*[h] the set of propositions or theories (of a nonscientific character) that are produced by this coding and can be found either in entirely ideological texts (like morality) or in texts that are not entirely ideological (medicine, jurisprudence).

Finally, we will call *secondary ideological functioning*[i] the way this ideological effect is distributed and functions in institutions, juridical systems, and the sciences, playing for example a role of justification (for institutions and juridical systems) [or] a role of obstacle, limitation, but possibly also of stimulus and favorable milieu for a science.[7]

a. These three levels should not be confused, and we cannot [25] speak of a unitary ideological domain.

b. Ideology and science cannot be contrasted en bloc:
- the ideological coding may perfectly well give rise to the object of a possible science, although the operations that enable this object to appear are not scientific operations (i.e., capable of entering into a system that can be formalized).[8] The historical emergence of an object of knowledge is one thing. The determination of an object in an epistemological field is something else;
- on the other hand, if the specific ideological effect is never a science, its secondary functioning may be effectuated within a science, and not simply in the form of an obstacle.

c. The primary ideological coding is neither entirely a system of representations in men's minds, nor entirely an unconscious.

---

h Underlined in the manuscript.

i Underlined in the manuscript.

It is a set of rules employed by a social class in the formation of institutions, discourses, and precepts.[9]

[26]   It is a practice, therefore; but its place is not in a consciousness, nor its point of reference in a subject; it is a class practice that functions in a social formation. It does not have a subject but a site, a distribution, and a functioning.[10]

d. Thus, we should demolish with great care the idea that ideology is a sort of great collective representation that is outside scientific practice and the obstacle from which it has to detach itself by a *break*.[j]

This Bachelardian model is ineffective for determining how ideology operates; it can have only regional value (for showing how a science rids itself of its ideological obstacles).[11]

[. . .][k]

Ideology is not a matter of consciousness, any more than it is a matter of science; it is a matter of social practice. That is why the ideological struggle cannot be merely a theoretical struggle, at the level of true ideas.[12]

*

APPENDIX TO LECTURE 3

[We insert here the end of page 15 and page 16 of the manuscript, which contain a long crossed-out passage that Foucault indicates should be carried over to page 20 and that constitutes a variant of the beginning of this lecture.]

---

j Underlined in the manuscript.

k Paragraph crossed out: "There may be sciences that are really sciences and that function on the basis of a determinate ideological coding."

We see therefore the construction of a whole edifice of very   [15]
different elements:
- social practices (assistance);
- techniques of knowledge;
- economic theories;
- social demands;
- legal reforms;
- moral and literary themes.

Now it is not enough to say that this is all ideology (some elements are not of an ideological kind), but of showing how ideology gets these elements to work and establishes relations between them. Ideology is the functional system of the elements and not the nature of the elements. Ideological operation.[13]

We can see how ideology gets this set to work and what relations it establishes between them.
- Reversing the order of processes:
  Morality → nature → limitation
  [. . .][1]
- It substitutes nature for economic necessity.
- It presents a social demand in the form of a moral rule.
- It divides the social field but creates the appearance of a   [16]
  fictional unity through law.

*

1. Foucault summarizes here the main results of the previous course. "Primitive accumulation" is explained by the demographic crisis of the fifteenth century. According to the typed students' notes (TN1), Foucault pointed out that "economic development in the sixteenth century will be due to this demographic decline . . . the quantity of cultivable land is relatively much more important than it was in the Middle Ages. A primitive accumulation of capital is the consequence of this."

---

1 Crossed out: "Substitutes."

2. These remarks expand on the methodological remarks made in the previous lecture and in the variant in the appendix to that lecture (see above, pp. 162–165). They aim to clarify Foucault's position in the debate on the relations between science and ideology and, more profoundly, between practice and theoretical work, which was all the rage at that time among Marxist-Leninist and Maoist intellectuals, debates that were exacerbated following May 1968. For an analysis of this context, which is essential for understanding the many hidden allusions and references in these few methodological pages, see "Course Context," pp. 331–339.

3. See the variant in the appendix, below, p. 180–181, which stresses this point: "Ideology is the functional system of the elements, not the nature of the elements."

4. This idea that knowledge of sexuality is "split" should be referred back to what Foucault said in the previous lecture (see above, p. 163). On the one hand, a "natural" sexuality, the object of a biological knowledge, and on the other, a delimitation of what is not natural, the object of a normative and repressive knowledge.

5. The typed students' notes (TN2) have the following schema, which is different and clearer:

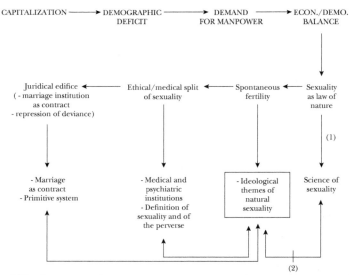

* The formation of a science requires a process that *gives rise* to it and assures a position for the subject who holds the discourse (1) and an episte-mological break (2) that assures its *specification*.

6. The way this primary ideological coding is characterized brings it close to some shifts that Foucault carries out in "On the Archaeology of the Sciences" (1968), *EW*, 2, 297–334, and *The Archaeology of Knowledge*, trans. A. M. Sheridan Smith (London: Tavistock, 1972), when he stresses that it is necessary to shift the analysis of this or that object, style, or element toward the set of rules that assure their formation and dispersion. More precisely, this primary ideological coding is close to the way Foucault was thinking then about *The Birth of the Clinic*, emphasizing that "clinical medicine was just as much a set of political prescriptions, economic decisions, institutional settlements and educational models as it was a set of descriptions," that is of the discursive and the nondiscursive ("On the Archaeology of the Sciences," *EW*, 2, 314). He notes there that it is necessary to analyze "the set of rules that simultaneously or successively made [these heterogeneous phenomena] possible" (315). In fact, the analyses that follow form part of Foucault's effort to pass from a descriptive analysis of discursive systems to what he will call the "dynastic of discourse"—that is, "to see how these types of discourse were able to be formed historically and on what historical realities they are articulated . . . the relation that exists between these major types of discourse observable in a culture and the historical, economic, political conditions of their appearance and formation" ("De l'archéologie à la dynastique" [1973], *DÉ*, I, no. 119, 1274). They will result in 1977 in the notion of "*dispositif*," very close to the way Foucault describes the "primary ideological coding": "a resolutely heterogeneous ensemble, comprising discourses, institutions, architectural arrangements, regulatory decisions, laws, administrative measures, scientific statements, philosophical, moral, and philanthropic propositions, in short: the said as well as the non-said, these are the elements of the *dispositif*. The *dispositif* itself is the network that can be established between these elements" ("Le jeu de Michel Foucault [entretien sur l'*Histoire de la sexualité*]" [1977], *DÉ*, II, no. 206, 299). With a considerable difference, however: if the *dispositif* does have a "dominant strategic function," this is not explicitly linked to a class domination (in 1977 Foucault adopts a nuanced position on this point, see "Le jeu de Michel Foucault," 306–7), whereas the primary ideological coding is clearly the product of a hegemonic social class.

7. Foucault combines two things here that in *Penal Theories and Institutions: Lectures at the Collège de France, 1971–1972*, trans. Graham Burchell, ed. Bernard Harcourt with Elisabetta Basso, Claude-Olivier Doron, and

Daniel Defert, English series editor, Arnold I. Davidson (London: Palgrave Macmillan, 2019), 198, he will distinguish for penal practices: on the one hand, the "ideological operations" understood as "the set of processes by which penal practices and institutions are justified, explained, reworked . . . within systems of rationalization," and on the other, the "knowledge effects" —that is, "the carving out, distribution, and organization of what is given to be known in penal practice"—in other words, how a social practice can define a field and forms of knowledge that potentially constitute a "favorable milieu" for a possible science. The idea that the ideological plays a role of obstacle and limitation for a science, from which it is necessary to free itself by a theoretical work of a break, is recurrent in the analyses of Althusser and his students. Pierre Macherey writes, for example: "an ideological problematic, rather than getting us to know something, is an *obstacle* to knowledge: it prevents the production of a knowledge and at the same time expresses a certain impossibility of thinking" (P. Macherey, lecture no. 6, January 8, 1968, of *Cours de philosophie pour scientifiques*, 3, emphasis in the original; the unpublished manuscript is available online at https://archive.org/details/ENS01_Ms0169). Even Michel Pécheux and François Regnault, who accord a more positive role to ideologies in the formation of a science and put forward "ideological knowledge effects," stress that a science is "preceded by ideologies, systems of representations . . . that are obstacles to it" (F. Regnault, *Cours de philosophie pour scientifiques*, lecture no. 11 [February 26, 1968]: 2). This is because of the way Althusser himself then approached the relation between the ideological and the scientific: an ideological proposition, according to the definition Foucault was familiar with and criticizes in the same period in his notebooks (see below, lecture 6, note 22, pp. 243–244; and "Course Context," p. 331 *et seq.*), is "a proposition which, while being the symptom of a reality different from the one to which it is directed, is a false proposition as it relates to the object to which it is directed" (L. Althusser, *Cours de philosophie pour scientifiques*, "Introduction", November 20, 1967, 4). It therefore necessarily entails an effect of miscomprehension and obstacle vis-à-vis knowledge of that reality. Foucault, on the other hand, constantly stresses that, if one places oneself at the threshold of epistemologization (that is, if one poses the question of the conditions of emergence of a knowledge), ideology has a role of "stimulus" or "favorable milieu" in the formation of this knowledge and, consequently, of a possible science; and that, even within a science, the ideological effect does not have only a negative role as obstacle or threat vis-à-vis the "scientific." On this subject, see *The Archaeology of Knowledge*, 185–86, and below, lecture 6.

8. It is worth stressing this definition of "scientific." For Foucault, the "*threshold of scientificity*" is crossed "when the epistemological figure . . . obeys a number of formal criteria, when its statements comply . . . with certain laws for the construction of propositions." We know, moreover, that this "threshold" may be extended into a "*threshold of formalization,*" when "this scientific discourse is able, in turn, to define the axioms necessary to it, the elements that it uses," etc. (*The Archaeology of Knowledge*, 187). This formalist and axiomatic conception of science, broadly inherited from Jean Cavaillès and Georges Canguilhem, rests on an idealized vision of mathematics as the final horizon of scientificity that Foucault finds it difficult to rid himself of. On this point, see David Rabouin, "L'exception mathématique," *Les Études philosophiques* 3, no. 153 (2015): 413–30.

9. The characterization of ideology as a "system of representations . . . in men's minds" refers to the traditional definition of ideology since *The German Ideology* (1845–1846), in which Marx and Engels contrasted the *reality* of material human relations with the *representations* and *ideas* formed in the consciousness of individuals of their relations to nature, to each other, or about their own nature. These representations were presented as the inverted or deformed reflection of real relations. Such a conception of ideology as a more or less falsified or deformed system of representations lodged in the consciousness of an individual or collective subject ("class ideology," "conception of the world") was still broadly prevalent in the 1960s, particularly in official Marxism. Foucault was always critical of this conception, both because it presupposed as given the knowledge relation between a subject and an object, a relation that economic and social conditions would merely deform or blur (see "Truth and Juridical Forms" [1974], *EW*, 3, 15), and because it focuses on representations and ideas whereas Foucault will stress the fact that relations of power precede the constitution of the conscious subject and pass through bodies (see, for example, "Les rapports de pouvoir passent à l'intérieur des corps" [1977], *DÉ*, II, no. 197; English translation by Leo Marshall, "The History of Sexuality," in Michel Foucault, *Power/Knowledge: Selected Interviews and Other Writings 1972–1977*, ed. Colin Gordon (Brighton, UK: Harvester Press, 1980). In 1969, Foucault is still at the start of the elaboration of his critical reflection on this subject,

which needs to be located in the contemporary debates on the nature of ideology. On this point, see "Course Context," pp. 331–338. In these debates, an alternative position is precisely one that, following Althusser, tries to develop a general theory of ideology consistent with an effort to rethink the subject in the light of Lacanian psychoanalysis and structuralism. Foucault is alluding to this when he points out that the primary ideological coding is "not entirely an unconscious." Since his article on "Freud and Lacan" of 1964, Althusser in fact regularly brings together the symbolic order of the unconscious and the structure of ideology (for more detailed analyses of these points, see Pascale Gillot, *Althusser et la Psychanalyse* [Paris: PUF, 2009]; and "Course Context," pp. 333–334). This parallel is also omnipresent in the works of certain students close to Althusser and Lacan who collaborate in the *Cahiers pour l'analyse* (*CPA*). In Althusser it is coupled with the double thesis that ideology in general, like the unconscious in general, does not have a history and, as Gillot notes, that the "category of the subject," "itself constitutive of all ideology," also "cannot be attributed to a determinate sequence of the history of philosophy" (*Althusser et la Psychanalyse*, 120–21). This thesis enters into tension with other analyses by Althusser, but especially with Foucault's analysis, which accounts for why Foucault characterizes the primary ideological coding as an historically situated set of rules put to work by a definite social class.

10. See the previous note. These comments are aimed at any "humanist" theory that would judge it enough for subjects to become aware of their situation in the world for them to free themselves from alienation. They also echo the reflections of those who, at the intersection of Lacan and Althusser, make the subject's illusion of sovereignty the heart of ideology. For an analysis of this question, see "Course Context," pp. 331–338.

11. Foucault is here explicitly taking aim at the key concept employed by the Althusserians to distinguish what is ideological from what is scientific and to describe the process by which the production of scientific knowledge is carried out. If there is no doubt that Althusser and some of his students would agree that the epistemological break must be analyzed "regionally," since Althusser describes any discourse that speaks of Science in general as "ideological," it remains the case that the Althusserians, following Althusser's propositions in *For Marx* and *Reading Capital* (both published by Maspero in 1965), do erect the Bachelardian notion of "epistemological break" as the general model of the process of production of scientific knowledge and

of the demarcation between the scientific and the ideological. The case of the "break" represented by Galileo constitutes an illustration of this. On this subject, see the set of the *Cours de philosophie pour scientifiques* given at the École normale supérieure in 1967–1968 and, in particular, the course given by François Regnault specifically devoted to "What is an epistemological break?" The same principle dominates contributions to the *CPA*, complete with Lacan's reading of the break in "La science et la vérité," *CPA*, no. 1, 7–28 ("Science and Truth," *Écrits*). As much as Foucault readily accepts the discontinuity entailed by this notion of break (see "On the Archaeology of the Sciences" [1968]), so too he seems to mistrust its function as a general demarcation between science and nonscience: it prevents effective analysis of the formation of forms of knowledge and the way a science is constituted in them (see *The Archaeology of Knowledge*, 184–92); it takes up the division between truth and not-truth (*le non-vrai*) without questioning its historical, political, and social conditions and effects (see *Lectures on the Will to Know: Lectures at the Collège de France 1970–1971, and Oedipal Knowledge,* ed. Daniel Defert, trans. Graham Burchell, English series editor, Arnold I. Davidson (Basingstoke, UK: Palgrave Macmillan, 2013); and it hides the mechanisms of power at work in the formation of forms of knowledge and the constitution of sciences (*Penal Theories and Institutions*). From this point of view, the Vincennes course is the first moment when Foucault distances himself so clearly from the notion of "epistemological break" (see "Course Context," pp. 331–338).

12. In the context of the University of Vincennes in 1969, these phrases mark the critical position taken by Foucault vis-à-vis what was then denounced as Althusser's "theoreticism." In the 1960s, Althusser made theoretical work and the need to provide a theory adequate to Marxist practice the fundamental orientation of his reflections. From 1966 to 1967, this primacy of theoretical work began to be challenged by some of the members of the Union des jeunesses communistes marxistes-léninistes (first and foremost, Robert Linhart), driven by the Maoist model, leading to a split between the *Cahiers marxistes-léninistes* and the *CPA*. This controversy will grow after 1968, marking the evolution of a number of associates formerly close to Althusser at Vincennes and henceforth hostile to his "theoreticism" and "scientism" in the name of the preeminence of practice and political struggle in contact with the popular masses. This evolution is perceptible in various members of the *Gauche prolétarienne*,

as in Jacques Rancière, who writes an article in 1969 remarkable for its critical insights—"On the Theory of Ideology (the Politics of Althusser)" (1969), *Radical Philosophy*, Spring 1974)—before taking stock of this break in his famous *Althusser's Lesson*, trans. Emiliano Battista (London: Continuum, 2011). If Foucault's movement away from the "theoretical" is rather allusive here, it will be considerably strengthened in the following years, in his first courses at the Collège de France as in his political commitments, with the creation in 1971 of the Groupe d'information sur les prisons (GIP) and his relative closeness to the Maoists. For more detail on all these issues, see "Course Context," pp. 331–338.

13. The notion of "ideological operation" that appears here, which Foucault takes up in his analysis of the "primary ideological coding" as set of operations (see above, pp. 176–179) and then in *Penal Theories and Institutions*, is worth comparing with the analyses of Michel Pêcheux (alias Thomas Herbert) who, in striving to distinguish two forms of ideology (empiricist, speculative), also emphasizes that "the *elements* of the field are less important than the *form* of their assemblage" (T. Herbert, "Remarques pour une théorie générale des idéologies," *CPA*, no. 9 [1968]: 77; emphasis in the original). Pêcheux establishes, then, a distinction between two functional modalities of ideology: metaphorical-semantic function, where ideology is "a system of *marks* . . . a system of *signals* that guide the set of effectuable *actions* and *words*" (such a dimension will be found in the "dynastic" developed by Foucault in *Penal Theories and Institutions*); and especially metonymic-syntactical function, where ideology is a "system of operations on the elements," "real structures," "institutions and discourses." Pêcheux describes the various processes of "metaphorical displacements," of "misrepresentation," and of the establishment of coherence at work in these operations, in a way close to the analysis of various operations described here by Foucault (see *"Remarques pour une thèorie gènèrale des idèologies",* 79 *et seq.*).

LECTURE 4

Legal Forms of Marriage up to the Civil Code

Sexuality and marriage exist within a set of regularities. Weak matrimonial rules in Indo-European societies. But, from the Middle Ages, tendency to make marriage more complicated (notably legal constraints); this is coupled with an ideological criticism of marriage and desire for sexual liberation. I. Christian marriage: late, it superimposes the marriage sacrament on Roman marriage; initially, easy marriage without social coercion. II. Increase in the social cost of marriage: Council of Trent: hardening of social controls and constraints; increasing weight of the family. Example of marriage in peasant smallholders (Bourdieu). III. Marriage in bourgeois society: 1. The Revolution: ideological themes and legal measures: the marriage contract and divorce. 2. The Civil Code: marriage is not assimilable to a contract; authorization of divorce is not the result of the contract but of human weakness. Marriage, natural and structuring element of society; sexuality as disturbing threat that has to be framed by marriage and socially excluded.

[27]   *Introduction*

In every society marriage is caught up in a set of regularities.[1] These regularities are linked to two orders of facts, each of which has economic effects:

a. The fact that sexuality involves enjoyment—therefore desire—therefore lack—therefore the object—therefore a good.[2]

b. The fact that sexuality has consequences for the pro- liferation of the species—therefore for demography— therefore for the quantity of both resources and forces of production.

Sexuality [is] on the borders of enjoyment and the forces of production. Sexuality functions in a system of goods; and it modifies the system of goods.

These regularities can be located:

– At the demographic level: marriage may or may not be easy; its fertility may or may not be encouraged.

[NP/28]   – At the level of the circulation of goods: marriage may be accompanied by benefits, i.e., transfer of property.

– At the level of the choices of husband and wife: age, social group.

– At the level of the legal actions accompanying it: monog- amy, dissolution.

Non-Indo-European societies have major matrimonial regu- larities that enable very subtle social balances. Indo-European societies established in Europe do not have such strict rules: the weakest known matrimonial structuration:[3]

• Maybe due to the abundance of resources and to their considerable demographic elasticity.

• Maybe due to the fact that the original tripartition, which in India gave rise to a caste system, gave rise here to essen- tially economic groups.

Now the whole evolution of societies since the Middle Ages   [29]
consists in making marriage more complicated.

- For a long time, the small population, abundance of resources, and high mortality allowed a demography of large cycles. But capitalism had requirements and encountered limitations.
- The economic benefits were weak, but the accumulation of capital entailed the bourgeoisie taking up the "costly" forms found in feudalism.
- Choice of spouse, which was free, has been limited (at least at the level of homogamy).

We passed from a society of easy marriage to one in which it is more difficult. And this was in a society that was "getting richer" and "liberalizing." The increase in the difficulty and, consequently, importance of marriage led:

- to an increasingly heavy legal institutionalization of marriage (social regulation having a legal form in capitalist societies);
- to an uncoupling of the legal forms through which marriage was limited and a consciousness of sexuality as a nonsocial, noneconomic, nonjuridical fact of nature;
- to two systems of recuperation intended to mask this break: [NP/30]
   a. An ideology of love, of free choice,
   b. An institutionalization of the family, which plays the role of apparent reunification (nature → society; sexuality → feeling) and of carefully maintained difference through the repression of sexuality.[4]
- finally [to] a double movement of protest:
   – an ideological reaction, either in favor of a different form of marriage (temperamental combinatorics [*caractérielle combinatoire*] à la Fourier), or in favor of an institutional liberation of sexuality;[5]
   – a revolutionary challenge that has doubtless not even succeeded in producing a coherent formulation (Trotski, A. Kollontai).[6]

[31]   *I. Christian marriage*

1. "Christian marriage" as juridical-religious institution is late (ninth-tenth centuries).[7]
- Originally, Christians allowed the Roman type of marriage. And they accepted its dissolution.[8]
- They double it with a sacrament that consecrates the couple's entry into the group [and] sanctifies nonchastity.[9]
- This doubled marriage involves indissolubility and publication before the community.

The establishment of Christian marriage is a superimposition of Roman marriage and marriage-sacrament.[a]

[NP/32]
- Insofar as it is a civil marriage: consensus.
- Insofar as there is a question of chastity, the sexual act is required: *copula carnalis.*[10]

2. *It is a facilitated marriage.*[b,11]
- − Christian society is a society of easy marriage;
  - a. no economic requirement;
  - b. kinship prohibitions are complex but not very strict.[12]
- − It is a marriage without social coercion:
  - a. clandestine marriages (hence, de facto polygamy);
  - b. marriage of minors without family consent.

This explains why the family had little importance, not being the cell of society.[13]

[33]   *II. Increase in the social cost of marriage*[c]

1. Whether or not they are adopted, the envisaged measures are spread throughout Europe:[14]

---

a Crossed out passage: "a. The contract aspect is never forgotten; b. the rules of the community extended to society. Christian marriage is 'facilitating.' "

b Emphasis in the manuscript.

c There was first of all a "3" (crossed out and replaced by II), and the initial heading was: "The Council of Trent."

- Annulment of clandestine marriages:
  - publicity of marriage;[15]
  - obligation of the parish (with the priest's consent);[16]
  - constitution of a register of civil status.[17]
- Discussion of the annulment of the marriage of children contracted without parental consent. French civil legislation practices it from the sixteenth century.[18] The social cost of marriage increases considerably.[19]

2. At the same time, spread of the system of economic benefits, which was not very common except in the aristocracy.

Example of marriage in peasant smallholders.[d,20]

Whereas in Muslim countries the rule of sharing led to consanguineous marriage,[21] in the West (with individual property), a set of rules [has been established] to maintain the land:

1. Birthright: 2/3, 1/3 or $\dfrac{P}{4} + \dfrac{P - \dfrac{P}{4}}{n}$ [22]   [NP/34]

But replacement of minor shares[e] by money or movable goods.[23] Dowry.

[*In the margin*: "which implies a monetary economy in addition to a subsistence economy"]

2. The dowry circulates:
   - Girls and younger sons get married with this.
   - As it serves to provide a dowry to the next ones (of the family who receives it), it must be bigger as the family is larger.[24]
   - In the case of childless death, the dowry is returnable, so it must not be too big.[25]
   - Finally, the system holds only because the younger marry the older and conversely[26] [and] because the unmarried leave or serve as labor.[27]

---

d Underlined in the manuscript.
e Word difficult to decipher.

[*In the margin*: "very complex system that assures:—the size of properties;—the money/population balance;—the birth of children (in order to avoid the dowry returning to the wife's family);—and then the continuity of the family through time."]

- Hence a system of very heavy restrictions.
- The need to give marriage a very precise legal status.
- The need to make it stable and indissoluble.
- The need to free it from the rules of exogamy.
- The need to consider it as involving the family.
- The need to establish a general social control.

All this explains why

a. Exogamous rules (see all the literature concerning incest in the seventeenth-eighteenth century),[28]

b. the requirement of *copula carnalis*,

fall into disuse.

Apparently a "liberation," in fact additionally the result of a higher social cost.

[NP/35]   *III. Marriage in bourgeois society*[f]
    1. The Revolution[29]

- Themes:
    - Promotion of marriage and struggle against celibacy.
    - Reduction of the limits to incest as far as possible.
    - Making marriage a strictly civil act (neither religious nor sexual).[30]
    - Keeping women in a condition of inferiority (despite the feminist campaigns of Rose Lacombe and Olympe de Gouges).[31]

---

f Not paginated by Foucault, but it appears as the verso of page 35. In his manual numbering, Foucault clearly reversed recto and verso of the page. We restore their logical and chronological order.

– Legal measures:

a. "The law considers marriage only as a civil contract" (1791 Constitution, vol. 2, art. 7).[32]

b. In September 1792, the law authorizes divorce:
  • for a definite cause;
  • by mutual consent;
  • by the will of just one.[33]

c. In Floreal, Year II, divorce for political reasons.[34]

2. *The Civil Code* [g]   [35/
                                                              rectius 36]

We are used to saying that the Civil Code made marriage a contract and permitted divorce. In actual fact, [marriage] cannot be assimilated to a contract either in its content or its form.[35]

a. In its content: not specified: "to provide mutual aid."[36] Regarding its real purpose: "perpetuating the species," it is not sanctioned at the level of the contract.[37]

b. In its form:

1. In what concerns the individuals' will:
    – it is perpetual;[38]
    – young men reach their majority only at twenty-five years;[39]
    – the woman becomes legally incapable.[40] Thus autonomy of the will does not prevail over the effects of the contract.[41]

2. In what concerns the intervention of society: the official of the civil state is not only a qualified witness, he *pronounces*[h] the marriage.[42]

---

g See above, previous footnote.
h Underlined in the manuscript.

[37]   Regarding divorce, it is not the immediate legal consequence of the marriage contract.

- Divorce should not exist. It is an evil, linked to human weakness.
- Divorce must only be tolerated; and tolerated within strict limits.[43]

The drafters of the Civil Code define marriage as:

– Being natural before being civil. Marriage belongs to nature, the consequences of which are:

- That the family is prior to society; that the latter is founded on the family and therefore has no right to dissolve it or any possibility of dissolving it; that its task must even be that of preserving it as its essential and natural core.
- That nature prescribes marriage; that natural, hence normal, sexuality is matrimonial—i.e., monogamous and procreative.[44]

– Having to be the object of a whole social concern, it must have a strict social and legislative framework.

[NP/38]   And this is to avoid marriage being corrupted by the bad nature of individuals. Marriage is the natural, good element of society. Sexuality is the disruptive element of society, what has to be socially repressed.

So, all sexuality as nature is integrated in marriage as contract and in its economic system; and all sexuality as behavior is excluded from the juridico-social system of the family and marriage.[45]

*

1. According to the typed students' notes (TN1), it seems that Foucault began this lecture by referring to the discovery of such regularities in marriage by nineteenth-century social statistics: "1. In the nineteenth century, [Quételet] demonstrates statistically that the frequency of marriage is more regular than the frequency of death. ['Among the facts relative to man,

there is none where his free will intervenes more directly than in the act of marriage [. . . nonetheless] we can say that the Belgian population has paid its tribute to marriage with more regularity than it has to death; however, we do not consult each other in order to die as we do to get married' (Adolphe Quételet, *Du système social et des lois qui le régissent* [Paris: Guillaumin, 1848], 65–66)]. 2. Previously only the abnormal was quantified. 3. The existence of a specifically social reality, referring to nothing else, implies the existence of autonomous normative mechanisms in society."

2. TN1 has "value" in place of "good" and clarifies: "economic implications: the woman is considered as a good." This analysis echoes those of Lacan, on the relationship among enjoyment, desire, and lack, and Lévi-Strauss, who draws a parallel between the exchange of women and the exchange of goods (*The Elementary Structures of Kinship*, ed. James Harle Bell, John Richard von Sturmer, and Rodney Needham [Boston: Beacon Press, 1969]).

3. We find here the analyses developed by Lévi-Strauss in chapters 2 and 3 of *Structural Anthropology*, trans. Claire Jacobson and Brooke Grundfest Schoepf (New York: Basic Books, 1963): Indo-European societies are described here as presenting maximum simplicity in terms of the regulation of marriages (a few negative prescriptions) but social structures organized according to an extremely complex structure (in the form of the extended family); whereas societies of the Sino-Tibetan area, for example, have a more dense and complex system of matrimonial rules with, conversely, a much simpler social structuration organized around clans and lineages.

4. TN1 gives a slightly different presentation: "In ancient and Christian societies, matrimonial requirements were weak. Spontaneous mortality and economic development made possible a practically unlimited proliferation and fertility of marriages. The Church ratified and sanctified *all* marriages that could be contracted; prohibition of all sexual forms that were not susceptible of procreation. In the Middle Ages, there are very few economic benefits for most of the population. Sole exception: the feudal aristocracy. Now the model of aristocratic marriage entailing dowries, etc., is taken up by the bourgeoisie [see below, pp. 192–193]. *Evolution of the choice of spouse*: present-day society appears less liberal than the society of the Middle Ages. *In the Middle Ages*: the rules of exogamy exert very little constraint, due to ignorance within the population of the rules of kinship.

i

The rules of exogamy are much stronger today, due to the multiplication of social groups. *Now*: marriage is a complex social act, approaching the rules observed in so-called primitive societies: a. legal code; b. uncoupling of:—marriage: contract—sexuality: outside contract; c. ideological "recuperation": ideology of love, of passion, which is supposed to ensure individual freedom, the possibility of rejoining marriage through the contract.—Institutionalization of the family. The family in its present configuration is relatively recent. It appears in the seventeenth century. Generations begin to live together in the same house. The child is a justification of this: Appearance of a movement of protest directed toward the lost unity: marriage/sexuality" (emphasis in the original). We can see how the idea that from a certain moment (the end of the eighteenth century), a division took place between marriage (and the legal forms) and sexuality, as natural and outside the contract, joins up with the thesis developed in the Clermont-Ferrand course, see above, pp. 11–13. Foucault took up and developed this analysis in his Tunis course, in which he presents sexuality in the nineteenth century as the "private sphere," which escapes the contract and the "contractual family." According to him, this "de-institutionalization of sexuality" notably induced "a sort of great drive to 'talk' about sexuality" and "a desire to know sexuality as a problem rather than to purely and simply enjoy it."

5. Foucault returns in detail to this in his last lecture; see below, lecture 7.

6. Foucault is referring here to Leon Trotsky's thoughts on the transformation of the family and of relationships between men and women in a series of articles published in *Pravda* in 1923 (notably "From the Old Family to the New," July 13, 1923) and in questions 4 to 12 of the "Family Relations Under the Soviets" (1932/1934); as well as to the analyses developed be Alexandra Kollontai (1872–1952), main promoter of a critique of the traditional family and marriage, defending free union and a radical transformation of relationships between men and women in the new communist society. See in particular *Communism and the Family* (1919) and *The New Morality and the Working Class* (1919), as well as Kendall E. Bailes, "Alexandra Kollontai et la nouvelle morale," trans. M.-J. Imbert, *Cahiers du monde russe et soviétique* 6, no. 4 (1965): 471–96.

7. On the history of Christian marriage as a sacrament, initially parallel to civil Roman marriage, then overlaying it from the ninth-tenth centuries, see Adhémar Esmein, *Études sur l'histoire du droit canonique privé: Le*

mariage en droit canonique (Paris: L. Larose et Forcel, 1891), 1:3–31 (BNF files, Box 39-C2/D12, "La législation du mariage chrétien").

8. See Esmein, *Études sur l'histoire du droit canonique privé*, 2:45 *et seq.*

9. This is a reference to the principle that it is the consummation of marriage (*copula carnalis*), representing the union of Christ and the Church, that founds the absolute indissolubility of marriage. See, for example, Esmein, *Études sur l'histoire du droit canonique privé*, 2:66.

10. On the contractual dimension of Christian marriage, as distinct from its sacramental value, see Esmein, *Études sur l'histoire du droit cano-nique privé*, 2:78–83; on the fundamental role of the *copula carnalis* in the canonical conception of marriage, see Esmein, *Études sur l'histoire du droit canonique privé*, 2:83–85, and more recently, Michel Rouche, ed., *Mariage et Sexualité au Moyen Âge: Accord ou crise?* (Paris: Presses de l'université de Paris-Sorbonne, 2000), 123 *et seq.* As Foucault notes in his files, "the *copula carnalis* [is one of the four elements of the formation of Christian marriage, along with consent, engagement, and nuptial blessing]. Its indispensable character is founded on two texts:—one, apocryphal, of Saint Augustine;—the other: Saint Leon's Epistle to Rusticus. In the latter text, a *non* has been interpolated that changes the meaning of the text. This interpolation is found in Saint Ivo of Chartres. But the text was already interpreted the wrong way in its original state (Hincmar). For Hincmar, a marriage con-cluded but not consummated is not a sacrament." We know that Foucault gave these explanations in the course (TN1).

11. See Esmein, *Études sur l'histoire du droit canonique privé*, 2:85: "Canon law . . . encourages the conclusion of marriages. . . . It made the formation of marriage as easy as it made its dissolution difficult."

12. Foucault presents these prohibitions in the following way in a file in the BNF, Box 39-C2/D12, f. "Canon law encourages marriage": "kinship to the seventh degree; adoption; kinship (seventh degree) of fiancés; spiritual kinship."

13. See Esmein, who, after having cited the case of clandestine marriages as proof of the easiness of marriage, notes: "[Canon law] did even more: in order to facilitate the conclusion of marriages at the age when passions are strongest, it weakened paternal power and familial authority. It dismissed, in matters of marriage, all the civil incapacities to contract resting on age or sex and declared that all pubescent persons were capable of marrying on

their own authority" (*Études sur l'histoire du droit canonique privé*, 2:85–86). TN1 shows that Foucault added the following: "The Carolingian Empire increasingly entrusted the Church with the administrative tasks that gradually replaced civil marriage. Consequence: legal regulation of marriage by theologians:—no marriage without consensus;—necessity of the sexual act;—optional engagement. On this basis, all is permitted. Prohibition of the marriage of priests and of first and second degrees of kinship."

14. These are the various measures adopted during the eighth session of the Council of Trent (1563), which Esmein dwells on in detail; see *Études sur l'histoire du droit canonique privé*, 2:137–240. Foucault also relies directly on Gabriel Du Préau, *Les Décrets et Canons touchant le mariage* (Paris: J. Mack, 1564) in his description of these measures.

15. Esmein, *Études sur l'histoire du droit canonique privé*, 2:170–71. On this point the Council of Trent takes up and clarifies the regulation of the Lateran Council and, in particular, rules that three publications must take place, done by the parish priest.

16. Esmein, *Études sur l'histoire du droit canonique privé*, 2:77. Marriage must be celebrated with the consent of the spouses' parish priest.

17. In this case, it is a matter of a civil measure, linked to articles 50–56 of the Villers-Cotterêts ordinance (1536), which orders priests to keep a register of deaths and baptisms. The Blois ordinance (1579) adds marriages to this. See Esmein, *Études sur l'histoire du droit canonique privé*, 2:203–5.

18. This prohibition will remain a matter of discussion and will not be taken up at the Council of Trent (see Esmein, *Études sur l'histoire du droit canonique privé*, 2:156, 163–65). Esmein notes the role of secular legislation of the sixteenth century in France in the annulment of these marriages (165).

19. TN1 adds: "the family therefore controls marriage. *Marriage becomes a social act. How are marriage and sexuality being invested in economic and social processes?*" (emphasis in the original).

20. To develop this example, Foucault very probably relies on the article by Pierre Bourdieu, "Célibat et condition paysanne," *Études rurales*, no. 5–6 (1962): 32–135, which describes peasant custom in the Hautes-Pyrénées. It is difficult to know if Foucault actually developed this example in the lecture. In the typed students' notes, TN2, we find a somewhat different version that sets out only the general issues of these arguments: "Capitalism and the bourgeoisie made marriage a complex and costly economic act:—problem of the possession of land at the individual level;—

constitution of marriage with dowry. Regime fundamentally linked to birthright: this so as not to undermine property. The circulation of dowries is a condition of this maintenance of property: part of the inheritance that the youngest will be able to take away on marriage, essentially in the form of money. In this way, the inheritance is maintained *to the advantage of an individual.* Thanks to this system, landed property avoided being broken up. This system entails:—a monetary representation of significant wealth—a part of stable movable wealth. The birth of children stabilizes the property, but excessive procreation presents some drawbacks → need for a balance → need for significant monetary circulation → need for significant part of availability. Lavish spending is excluded by the need for capitalization. Formation of a pyramidal family in which generations establish a diachronic bond:—capitalism does not bring about a breakup of the family but, quite the contrary, institutionalizes this type of family;—complication of marriage. The act of marriage is not independent of the family will;—need to marry within a certain *economic range*;—appearance of extremely stable and closed homogamous classes" (emphasis in the original).

21. This is the thesis sustained by Lévi-Strauss in his contribution, "Le problème des relations de parenté," in *Systèmes de parenté: Entretiens pluridisciplinaires sur les sociétés musulmanes* (Paris: EPHE, 1959), 13–20. For Lévi-Strauss, the injunction to marry the parallel cousin, present in Muslim countries, cannot be explained by the elementary rules of kinship alone; to account for it, sociological and economic factors have to be introduced, in particular concerning the inheritance of titles and goods. This position is connected to the broader problem of the relations between structure and history, structures of kinship and modes of production, intensely debated at the end of the 1960s. It is criticized, in particular, by Jean Cuisenier, in "Endogamie et exogamie dans le mariage arabe," *L'Homme* 2, no. 2 (1962): 80–105, who seeks to reassert the relative independence of structures of kinship vis-à-vis economic and social relations, and to reintegrate the apparently aberrant case of marriage of the parallel cousin in a structuralist formalism. Bourdieu, on the other hand, will take up this same case and the analyses of Lévi-Strauss in order to extend them to all the studies on kinship, stressing the need to analyze actual practices of kinship and their insertion into socioeconomic strategies, which he will also do in the case of Béarnais peasants; see Alban Bensa, "L'exclu de la famille: Le parenté selon Pierre Bourdieu," *Actes de la recherche en sciences sociales* 5, no. 150 (2003):

19–26. Foucault's choice to rely on the works of Bourdieu is thus not innocent: for him it is a matter of analyzing the regularities of practices inserted directly into economic and social games, and not the formal rules of an ideal kinship (see "Course Context," pp. 328–330).

22. According to Bourdieu, "when the family had only two children, . . . the local custom was that a third of the value of the property was granted to the younger by marriage contract [this is what is represented here with the schema 2/3 (for the older) 1/3 (for the younger)]. When there were n children ($n > 2$), the younger's share was $\dfrac{P - \dfrac{P}{4}}{n}$, the elder's share thus being $\dfrac{P}{4} + \dfrac{P - \dfrac{P}{4}}{n}$, P designating the value attributed to the property" (Bourdieu, "Célibat et condition paysanne," 37).

23. For example, in Bourdieu's article, the younger girls' share is converted "into 3,000 francs in cash and 750 francs in linen, trousseau, sheets, cloths, towels," etc. ("Célibat et condition paysanne," 38).

24. Bourdieu, "Célibat et condition paysanne," 40: "The choice of husband or wife, of heir or heiress, is crucially important since it contributes to determining the sum of the dowry that the younger sons will receive, the marriage they will be able to make, and if they will be able to marry; in return, the number of younger daughters and especially younger sons to be married weighs heavily on this choice."

25. Bourdieu, "Célibat et condition paysanne," 42: "Every dowry was subject to a right of return (*tournedot*) in the event of the death of the descendants of the marriage in view of which it was constituted, and this over several generations. . . . The *tournedot* placed a serious threat on families, particularly those that had received a very high dowry. It was a supplementary reason for avoiding marriages that were too unequal."

26. Bourdieu, "Célibat et condition paysanne," 45.

27. Bourdieu, "Célibat et condition paysanne," 38: "The inheritance custom actually rested on the primacy of the group interest to which the youngest had to sacrifice their personal interests . . . either by renouncing it completely when they emigrated in search of work, or by passing their life, unmarried, working on the land of the ancestors alongside the eldest."

28. Foucault had collected a set of dossiers on legislation concerning sexual acts and the debates on incest, polygamy, sodomy, etc., in the

seventeenth and eighteenth centuries (BNF, Box 39-C2). It seems he is referring here in particular to Nicolas Fardoil's "Discours ou traité de l'inceste," in *Harangues, discours et lettres* (Paris: S. Cramoisy, 1665), 119–95, and to the reflections of Jacques-Pierre Brissot de Warville on incest, *Théorie des lois criminelles* (Berlin: 1781), both in favor of restricting the prohibition of incest solely to collaterals of the second degree. On Brissot de Warville, see below, note 30.

29. For the revolutionary period, Foucault basically relies on Julien Bonnecase, *La Philosophie du Code Napoléon appliqué au droit de famille: Ses destinées dans le droit civil contemporain*, 2nd rev. and enlarged ed. (Paris: Boccard, 1928) (BNF, Box 39-C2). See also Gérard Thibault-Laurent, *La Première Introduction du divorce en France sous la Révolution et l'Empire (1792–1816)* (Clermont-Ferrand, France: Moderne, 1938), and, more recently, Francis Ronsin, *La Contrat sentimental: Débats sur le mariage, l'amour, le divorce de l'Ancien Régime à la Restauration* (Paris: Aubier, 1990).

30. According to TN2 and the BNF files, to define these various themes Foucault basically relies on the propositions of the future Girondin leader, Brissot de Warville, in his *Théorie des lois criminelles*. Thus, celibacy is the only crime that Brissot classifies as such both in the state of nature and in society. "Celibacy is a crime in nature, it is also a crime in society. . . . It is therefore doubly criminal to observe celibacy" (*Théorie des lois criminelles*, 1:250–51). The position of incest is that it is no way a crime against nature, but varies according to societies: "Let us listen without prejudice only to reason: it tells us that incest permitted in nature is only a crime of society; that the States that prohibit it are right; that those who permit is are not wrong" (1:223). Brissot recommends restricting it only to second-degree collaterals. A purely civil legislation, freed in particular from the "prejudices" and "artificial crimes" invented by religion, is the very meaning of Brissot's project.

31. See Bonnecase, *La Philosophie du Code Napoléon*, 97–110, on which Foucault relies here (file, BNF, "Le féminisme sous la Révolution"). Olympe de Gouges founded the first feminist journal, *L'Impatient*; Rose Lacombe founded the Society of Republican and Revolutionary Women. "Actually, the Convention is hostile. It prohibits the presence of women in the Convention tribunes (May 20, 1798), then in all political assemblies (May 20, 1798)."

32. "The law considers marriage only as a civil contract. The legislative power will establish for all inhabitants, without distinction, the way births, marriages, and deaths will be certified and it will designate the public

officials who will take their certificates" (Constitution of September 3, 1791, art. 7, title II, cited in Ernest Glasson, *Le Mariage civil et le Divorce dans l'Antiquité et dans les principales législations moderne de l'Europe*, 2nd rev. and enlarged ed. [Paris: G. Pedone-Lauriel, 1880], 253). For what follows, see especially Bonnecase, *La Philosophie du Code Napoléon*, 85 *et seq.*, which comments on the work of the Revolution in the matter of family law before comparing it with the Civil Code.

33. This is the law of September 20, 1792, which effectively organizes three different divorces: "one for specific grounds, the other by mutual consent, and the third by the will of just one of the spouses, for reason of incompatibility of temperament" (Glasson, *Le Mariage civil*, 257). More broadly, on the bases and provisions of this law, see 254–59; J. Bonnecase, *La Philosophie du Code Napoléon*, 86. This authorization derives directly from the definition of marriage as a civil contract according to which an indissoluble union is contrary to human freedom.

34. Foucault relies on Bonnecase, *La Philosophie du Code Napoléon*, 86–87, which quotes the statement of grounds by Charles-François Oudot regarding the decree of 4 Floreal, Year II: "Since the Revolution, difference of opinion has caused a multitude of divorces and these are certainly the best founded in reason; for if formerly one said that a bad marriage was the torment of death tied to the living, is not this comparison more striking when it is a case of the bond that ties a slave of tyranny to the fate of a true Republican. The Convention must hasten to facilitate the destruction of the chains . . . of those spouses who, besides the works of the Revolution, have constantly had to combat, in their own home and under the dearest name, an enemy of the Republic." The provisions of the decree of 4 Floreal that can be interpreted in this sense concern the possibility of pronouncing divorce without delay if one can prove, by notarial deed or public knowledge, that the spouses have in fact separated for more than six months, or if one has abandoned the other without giving news, which is aimed in particular at emigrants (this last point will be taken up in the law of 24 Vendémiaire, Year III).

35. From the nineteenth century, the question of the contractual nature of marriage was the subject of numerous debates, in particular during the debate on the introduction of divorce by mutual consent at the beginning of the twentieth century, pitting those who reduce marriage to the general model of contracts between individuals and deduce from this the

legitimacy of divorce and free unions, against those who sharply distinguish civil marriage from other contracts, indeed challenge its assimilation
to a contract, often advancing its socially binding, indissoluble character or
its procreative value. See, for example, Charles Lefebvre, "Le mariage civil
n'est-il qu'un contrat?" *Nouvelle Revue historique du droit français et étranger*
26 (1902): 300–304; Alfred Détrez, *Mariage et Contrat: Étude historique sur
la nature sociale du droit* (Paris: V. Giard et Brière, 1907); Louis Coirard, *La
Famille dans le Code civil, 1804–1904*, doctoral thesis (Aix, France: Mahaire,
1907), 37 *et seq*. Traces of these debates can be found in Émile Durkheim's
texts, "Le divorce par consentement mutuel," *Revue bleue* 44, no. 5 (190):
549–54, and "Débat sur le mariage et le divorce" (1909), in which Durkheim
stresses that marriage cannot be reduced to a simple "contract formed by
the consent of the two parties" that society confines itself to certifying. A
third is added to it—society, the public authority—"which pronounces the
words that bind; . . . which creates the conjugal bond. This bond therefore
depends, in its very formation, on a will, on a power other than the individuals who are joined together" (in *Textes*, vol. 2, *Religion, morale, anomie*,
prés. de V. Karady, [Paris: Minuit, 1975], 206–15). Historically, this opposition is found in the doctrinal differences between the legislation of the
revolutionary period (law of September 20, 1792), which emphasizes the
contractual character of civil marriage and deduces divorce from this, and
that of the period of the Consulate and then Empire, which emphasizes
the particularities of marriage in relation to other contracts and does not
deduce divorce from its contractual nature. We have seen that in the Clermont-Ferrand course, Foucault, relying on Marcel Planiol, broadly took up
the idea that marriage in the Civil Code was a contract that disregarded
sexuality (see above, lecture 1, pp. 12–13 and note 21, p. 22). In the meantime,
he gathered information—drawn in particular from Bonnecase—on "The
Revolution and marriage" and on "Marriage and the Civil Code" (BNF, Box
39-C2/D10-11). This led him to complicate this schema and stress the difference between legislation of the revolutionary period and the Civil Code.
Bonnecase, who is opposed to the interpretation of marriage as a contract,
devotes moreover an entire part of his work to the tension between the
conception of marriage-contract and that of marriage as specific bond outside of the contract (what he calls the "marriage-institution") through the
Civil Code and its interpretations (*La Philosophie du Code Napoléon*, 83–218).

36. This is a reference to chapter 6, article 212, defining the duty of the spouses: "The spouses owe each other mutual respect, fidelity, help, assistance." However, Foucault omits the following articles that clarify these duties, as well as chapter 5 describing the obligations regarding children that flow from marriage. See also the definition given by Portalis: "marriage is the society of man and woman who join together to perpetuate the species, to help each through mutual assistance in bearing the burdens of life and to share their common destiny" (in P.-A. Fenet, *Recueil complet des travaux préparatoires du Code civil*, 9:140).

37. As Portalis states in his speech before the Conseil d'État, 6 October 1801: "Marriage, it is said, is a contract; yes, in its external form it is of the same nature as other contracts, but it is no longer an ordinary contract when one envisages it in itself in its principle and effects. Would one be free to stipulate a term to the duration of this contract that is essentially perpetual, since its object is the perpetuation of the human species? The legislator would blush to expressly authorize such a stipulation; he would shudder if it were presented to him" (Fenet, *Recueil complet*, 9:255).

38. Reference to Portalis's phrase in his *Discours préliminaire sur le projet de Code civil* according to which marriage offers "the fundamental idea of a contract strictly speaking, and of a perpetual contract through its purpose" (Fenet, *Recueil complet*, 1:485). On this point, see Sylvain Boquet, "Le mariage, un 'contrat perpétuel par sa destination,'" *Napoleonica: La Revue* 2, no. 14 (2012): 74–110.

39. This is matrimonial majority, which was fixed at twenty-one years (like civil majority) in 1792, and which, for young men, was raised to twenty-five years by the Civil Code (Civil Code [1804], title V, chap. 1, art. 148).

40. See in particular chapter 6, articles 215 and 217, and the Clermont-Ferrand course, above, lecture 1, p. 7.

41. See Louis Coirard, *La Famille dans le Code civil, 1804–1904* (Aix, France: Mahaire, 1907), 45–50. One of the strongest arguments of the authors challenging the contractual character of marriage is that if, in usual contracts, "agreement of the [individual] wills really and directly produces obligations," this is absolutely not the case in marriage, where the two spouses confine themselves to accepting a state wholly defined, in its modalities and obligations, by the law and the public authority. See also Bonnecase, *La Philosophie du Code Napoléon*, 152–59.

42. This argument in particular is put forward by Lefebvre, "Le mariage civil n'est-il qu'un contrat?," 326. See also Bonnecase, *La Philosophie du Code Napoléon*, 152–59.

43. These are the arguments of Jean-Baptiste Treilhard in the statement of the grounds that he addresses to the legislative body 30 Ventôse, Year XI. Divorce is presented here as pointless in nascent peoples of pure and simple morals, but necessary in people of dissolute morals, when "perversity of the heart . . . corruption of morals" exist. Divorce is thus presented as a "remedy for evil" and must be maintained. On the other hand, it must be strictly regulated in order to avoid abuse. J.-B. Treilhard, "Exposé des motifs," in Jean-Guillaume Locré, *La Législation civile, commerciale et criminelle de la France*, V, *Code civil*, title VI, *Du divorce* (Paris: Treuttel et Würtz, 1827), 289 *et seq*. We recall that it will be necessary to wait until 1816 for divorce finally to be abolished.

44. See J.-É.-M. Portalis, who declares, in his preliminary discourse: "Marriage is a society, but the most natural, the most holy, the most inviolable of all . . . we are convinced that marriage, which existed before the establishment of Christianity, which preceded all positive law, and which derives from the very constitution, is neither a civil act nor a religious act, but a natural act that has fixed the attention of legislators . . . society, in this contract, is grafted on nature: marriage is not a pact but a fact" (in P.-A. Fenet, *Recueil complet*, 1:483).

45. TN2 provides a slightly different version of this conclusion: "monogamous and procreative marriage is a fact of nature that should be accorded a holy and sacred status. It is the duty of society to take up what is necessary and good in nature, and it is its duty to see to it that this association is not dissolved. All sexuality is natural that has the natural form of marriage. If divorce has a place, it is because nature does not exactly conform to the matrimonial model: there exists another nature: *sexuality*" (emphasis in the original). We see, therefore, that if, in the Clermont-Ferrand course, Foucault saw in the Civil Code the moment when sexuality was excluded from juridical forms, kept out of the contract, he now sees in it an operation of the recovery and splitting of sexuality between a natural, monogamous, and procreative form set up as nature protected by laws, and "another nature" that extends beyond and escapes the matrimonial model.

LECTURE 5

Epistemologization of Sexuality

*S*tudying how sexuality was able to become the object of discursive practices. What relations with madness? 1. Some common characteristics: between the organic and the social; objects of different discourses; first person but excluded discourses; development of scientific practices aiming to free them from ideology. The recent theme of a kinship between madness and sexuality derives from these analogies. 2. But also some major differences: a. madness is always excluded; there is a division between tolerated and excluded sexuality; b. synchronic homogeneity of different discourses about madness; synchronic diversity of the rules of formation of discourses about sexuality; c. change of referents of discourses about madness in different periods; the referent of sexuality remains generally the same. Hence different approaches to their archaeology. Place of psychoanalysis in this framework: it claims to give a single referent to madness and to give a discursive homogeneity to sexuality. What must an archaeology of sexuality be?

Previous lecture: [NP/39]ᵃ

Setting sexuality within the economic processes of a determinate social formation.

ᵃ The following sheet (recto and verso) is not numbered in the initial manuscript, after which there is a sheet numbered 39 by Foucault. Moreover, this sheet 39 has the same title as the unnumbered sheet, "Epistemologization of sexuality," but crossed out. Foucault has therefore added a sheet here to which we have given the numbers 39 and 40.

[. . .]^b

This was still only a schema of studies, an identification of possible questions.

• The processes of real exchanges should be studied more closely; and the phenomena of the circulation of goods in relation to the circulation of women. One thing is certain: the rules of marriage are simple, the benefits are substantial. Whereas in primitive societies, both rules and benefits are complex, here only the benefits are; they do not need to rely upon the rules of endogamy. The market economy regulates them.[1]

[NP/40]   • The forms of sexuality, within and outside marriage, should also be studied.

What must be studied now is sexuality in discursive practices. Or rather, the way sexuality was able to become the object of a number of discursive practices.[2]

[39/41]   *Introduction*^c

Relationship with madness^d

a. Here too we are dealing with a complex phenomenon that can be identified at different levels, is caught up in different practices, and is susceptible to different analyses.

• It is a matter of phenomena linked, in part at least, to organic processes and falling within the domain of physiology or pathology.

---

b Paragraph crossed out: "But it is only a matter, after all, of the form of sexuality that is institutionalized by marriage. After all, one could raise the question of other forms of sexuality."

c Foucault here resumes his numbering. The crossed-out title follows: "Epistemologization of sexuality. 1."

d Replaces: "Difference from madness," crossed out.

• But [it is also a matter of phenomena] linked to social practices:

[*In the margin*: "like food and the system of regulation"][3]

– marriage rules and prohibition;

– norms of behavior and exclusion.

• It is a matter of phenomena that emerge simultaneously in different discursive stratifications:

[*In the margin*: "like disease"]

– everyday discourse;

– literary discourse;

– moral, religious, juridical discourse;

– scientific discourse.[4]

• These are phenomena that give rise to discourses in the [NP/42] first person, which are at the same time excluded discourses.[5]

• Finally, they are phenomena to which one tries to give a scientific status capable of freeing them from the ideological, indeed mythological, formations that imprison them, and of giving rise to rational social practices.

> For example, no longer considering madness to be the result of a fault or as shameful, but as an illness; no longer considering sexuality as a sin. Or again, protecting society against madness (both the phenomena of madness and the mad) and against sexuality (against perversion and against the general sexualization of existence).

Now this analogy of the position of madness and sexuality is converted into the now familiar theme that madness is related to sexuality by a causal connection [and] by a connection of reciprocal expression—a fairly recent theme (eighteenth century) that hardly ever appears outside our culture.[6]

b. However, there are a number of major differences: [41/43]

1. Madness is, in any case, something to be suppressed; sexuality is something to be tolerated and integrated.

No doubt, this should be qualified: there is a part of madness that is tolerated, even appealed to (the madness of heroes, the madness of art). And there is a part of sexuality that is not tolerated and doubtless never will be. There is, therefore, a division of madness and of sexuality. But:

- The division of madness is based on a general exclusion, and the margin of tolerance is no doubt a purely ideological figure.[7]
- The division of sexuality is based on a real functioning and integration of sexuality, so that sexuality is really divided.[8]

There is a merely imaginary figure of tolerated madness; there is a real fissure of actually practiced sexuality.

[NP/44]   2. There is a second difference: madness is taken up in distinct (literary, medical, legal) discourses, but according to a continuity that can be reconstructed for each period. For example: what is said in *King Lear*, in medicine at the beginning of the seventeenth century (Du Laurens), in jurisprudence.[9] The rules of formation of the object [of discourse] are similar. The only discourse in which madness is constituted differently is the discourse delivered by madness itself. That is the only heterogeneity.[10]

There is no such continuity for sexuality, but a completely different system of formation for speaking about sexuality: in terms of biology; in terms of psychoanalysis; in terms of morality and law; in literary terms.[11]

Madness is an object of discourse that may not be coherent, but is unitary. Sexuality is not an object of discourse; it gives rise to systems of different objects in different discourses: hormonology, psychoanalysis.[12]

3. This leads us to a third difference: if madness is [a] relatively   [43/45]
unitary object in the discursive practices of a period, on the other
hand the referent varies from one period to another and from
one culture to another.

Possession and witchcraft.[13]

Sexuality gives rise to systems of objects but even so has a
referent, or a single set of referents: the reproductive organs;
individual differences according to the organs; the behavior of
individuals in the activation of the organs. It will doubtless be
said that this domain of reference is not always covered in the
same way by the field of the objects of discourse; for example,
infantile sexuality [was] a late discovery.[14] But the anchor point
of the reference is the same.

So: madness is not a fixed domain of reference but is defined
by an interdiscursive homogeneity. The archaeology of madness
will mean therefore:

- Removing the postulate of a single referent: madness   [NP/46]
in itself and for itself, the same through time and across
cultures, and giving rise (according to tolerance or knowledge) only to diverse reactions or ideas.
- And reconstructing the interdiscursive homogeneity
that means one is talking about the same madness in jurisprudence, literature, and medicine.

On the other hand, sexuality is a fixed domain of reference,
but on the basis of which a discursive heterogeneity erupts. Its
archeology will mean:

- pinpointing the specificity, the mode of operation of
these diverse discourses, and the way sexuality is formed, as
a well-characterized object, in each of them;
- trying [to understand] the principle of this heterogeneity: what accounts for the fact that, in our society at least,

there is no discursive homogeneity of sexuality. What relation, what barrier, what gap—what law of diffraction—is there between the single reference and the polymorphism of sexuality?

[45/47]   N.B.: this last difference between madness and sexuality is one of the factors that may account for psychoanalysis functioning as a theory of the relations between sexuality and mental illness. It tries to give a referential ground to madness: wherever one spoke of madness, it was a matter of sexuality. [And] it tries to give a discursive homogeneity to sexuality. Hence:

1. It functions therefore like the great epistemological mutation in relation to the discourse of madness: it gives it a referent. It thus makes it possible to pose the question of truth within the discourse of madness (and in a specific way, not brought in from outside).
   • Previously, the question of the truth regarding madness was always a matter of analogy:
      1. Does what this individual says resemble what I say and what every normal person says?[e]
      2. Is psychiatry as rigorous as pathological anatomy?[15]
   • Henceforth, the question of truth will be posed for itself:
      1. It is the patient's discourse that tells the truth (hence the fact that it is no longer a sick person as opposed to a [normal][f] person, but someone who suffers and poses the question of their suffering.

---

e   In the manuscript, 1 and 2 are reversed: Foucault begins with 2 (initially numbered 1, but which he corrects), then 1 follows (which replaces a "henceforth," which will come after). It is clear that from the logical point of view, as from his point of view, 1 comes before 2, hence the correction.

f   Foucault writes "sick," which seems contradictory. We have corrected this.

2. The truth of psychoanalytic discourse is specific, not   [NP/48]
directed to another model, but to the process of the cure
and the game of sexuality within it.

2. On the other hand, it is like the removal of the bar that separated the unity of the referent from the polymorphisms of the
discourse. It results in the presence of sexuality itself (in its referential unity) in the world of discourse. It is the presence of sex in
discursive practice, removing the cultural barrier. Hence the fact:

- that it is not foreign to biology (although, and in the
  same measure as, it no longer has to constitute itself on the
  epistemological model of biology or medicine);
- that it can function as a theory for a possible analysis of
  literary, ethical, and religious discourses;
- that it can function as a principle for modification of
  the social and legal, institutional, and traditional forms in
  which sexuality is caught up.[16]

That this is the mode of functioning of psychoanalysis does   [47/49]
not mean that it is psychoanalysis that will bring about these
mutations. Psychoanalysis is only in the space where these mutations are called for and made necessary.

At the end of this introduction, we see that the archaeology of
sexuality—at least at a first stage of the inquiry—will no doubt
have to be deployed in dispersed order. Traversing heterogeneous
discursive levels (biology, jurisprudence, literature) without trying to force them together either in a "collective mentality," in a
"spirit of the time," or in a homogeneous enunciative set.

g Following passage crossed out: "but rather how these differences . . . the nonpresence of
this unity is articulated in different discourses."

Nor should we try to see how each discourse translates the unity of sexuality in its own way (according to a specific code).[g] In particular: the historical processes already analyzed show how the demand for a theory of sexuality came about. But this theory of sexuality (which had its specific concepts) left intact many other levels of knowledge of sexuality.

*

1. See above, previous lecture, p. 191.

2. We find here again the notion of "discursive practices," which is at the heart of Foucault's methodological reflections in *The Archaeology of Knowledge*, trans. A. M. Sheridan Smith (London: Tavistock, 1972), 117, and which here is continuous with other rule-governed practices. The study of the way sexuality became the object of discursive practices extends analyses developed in the Tunis course. In that course, Foucault emphasized that one of the characteristics of modern Western culture was that "the fabric of concrete life is doubled by, intertwined with, penetrable, and to a certain extent transformable by knowledge (*le savoir*)." Where previously there was "a whole set of silent practices that rested on a number of knowledges (*connaissances*), observations, empirical techniques, but that were not reflected in knowledge (*le savoir*)," the whole of daily practices, even the smallest, enter into what Foucault calls "a generalized discursive space" from the end of the eighteenth century. This is expressed notably by the fact that "knowledge (*le savoir*) is formed of domains of objects . . . where one thought it would be beneath the dignity of knowledge to penetrate," such as daily life, dreams, or, precisely, sexuality. The following lecture will examine how certain "silent practices" concerning sexuality become objects of knowledge (see below, p. 221 et seq.).

3. The history of food, between biological phenomenon and sociocultural practices, is at the heart of various works of the *Annales* in the 1960s (see above, lecture 2, note 2, p. 165–166) and notably the research of Jean-Paul Aron, a longtime friend of Foucault. See, in particular, J.-P. Aron, "Biologie et alimentation au XVIIIe siècle," *Annales ESC* 16, no. 5 (1961): 971–77, and *Essai sur la sensibilité alimentaire: Leçon inaugurale au Collège de France, prononcée le 2 décembre 1970* (Paris: Gallimard, 1971).

4. The distinction among these different types of discourse, in particular literary, scientific, and everyday discourse, the analysis of their rules of

functioning, and above all their difference from philosophical discourse, were the subject of an unpublished manuscript of Foucault, *Le Discours philosophique* (BNF, Box 58), which attests his desire, between 1967 and 1970, to work on the particular level of discursive practices that is found in *The Archaeology of Knowledge* and then in "The Order of Discourse," Foucault's Inaugural Lecture at the Collège de France, December 2, 1970, trans. Ian MacLeod, in *Untying the Text: A Post-Structuralist Reader*, ed. Robert Young (Boston: Routledge & Kegan Paul, 1981).

5. For madness, see *History of Madness*, trans. Jonathan Murphy and Jean Khalfa (London: Routledge, 2006), especially "Madness, the Absence of an Oeuvre" (1964), which notes "madness is the excluded language" (546), or the pages Foucault devotes to the "principle of exclusion" of madness in "The Order of Discourse," 53–54. For sexuality, see above, the Clermont-Ferrand course.

6. See above, Clermont-Ferrand course, lecture 4, p. 85 et seq.

7. *History of Madness* was precisely the history of this division and this exclusion, situating it in social practices and discourses from the seventeenth century. In an interview, "Folie, littérature, société" (1970), *DÉ*, I, no. 82, 972–996, Foucault stresses the links between the act of exclusion of madness and the entry of madness as a literary theme at the end of the eighteenth century, and marks the same relation with regard to sexuality, through the figure of Sade: "there is a certain type of system of exclusion that relentlessly fixes on the human entity called Sade, on everything sexual, on sexual abnormality, sexual monstrosity, in short, on everything excluded by our culture. It is because this system of exclusion existed that his work was possible" (*DÉ*, I, no. 82, 977). We again find the link, often put forward by Foucault in the 1960s, between exclusion at the level of social practices and the constitution of madness, death, or sexuality as objects of knowledge, on the one hand, and, on the other, as more or less transgressive literary themes. We can see nevertheless that here Foucault establishes a clear distinction between the case of madness, overwhelmingly excluded and the object of a purely imaginary tolerance, and the case of sexuality, where exclusion rests on a division within sexuality itself, between really tolerated and actually excluded sexuality. The purely imaginary character of the figure of madness tolerated in art (and the weakness of its subversive force) is stressed by Foucault in the same interview and extended to the case of forms of repressed sexuality (986–87).

8. See the previous lecture, which describes precisely this integration and division from the point of view of law; see above, pp. 195–196.

9. The physician André Du Laurens (1558–1609), author in particular of a discourse "Des maladies mélancoliques et du moyen de les guérir," in *Discours de la conservation de la veue: Des maladies mélancoliques, des catarrhes et de la vieillesse* (Tours, France: J. Mettayer, 1594), is referred to briefly in *History of Madness*, 238, to illustrate the resemblance thought to exist between dream and madness up to the seventeenth century, as well as in "Dream, Imagination and Existence: An Introduction to Ludwig Binswanger's *"Dream and Existence"* (1954), trans. Forrest Williams, in *Dream and Existence*, by Michel Foucault and Ludwig Binswanger, trans. Forrest Williams and Jacob Needleman, in *Review of Existential Psychology and Psychiatry* 19, no. 1 (1986): 50, in which Foucault identifies a parallel between the relations between dream and temperament in Du Laurens and the literary discourse of his time.

10. This paragraph asserting the homogeneity of the rules of formation of the object "madness" in different discourses of a period can be compared with Foucault's account in "On the Archaeology of the Sciences" (1968), *EW*, 2, 311–14. The unity of the discourses on madness in a given period is not that of "one and the same object" but of the "set of rules" that account for the formation and dispersion of various objects of discourse on madness in this period. Foucault here nevertheless accentuates the homogeneity of the object in relation to his previous analyses.

11. Foucault will take up this point in the *The History of Sexuality, Volume I: An Introduction*, trans. R. Hurley (New York: Pantheon, 1978), 33–35, founding this discursive heterogeneity on apparatuses of power and various institutions, and emphasizing how much this "explosion of distinct discursivities" broke up and multiplied the "markedly unitary" discourse provided by "the theme of the flesh and the practice of penance" in the Middle Ages. This "regulated and polymorphous incitation to discourse" on sexuality will be contrasted with the general censorship and repression that was supposed to have been imposed on sexuality.

12. These two systems are those analyzed at greatest length in the Clermont-Ferrand course; see above, lectures 2, 4, and 5.

13. Foucault took an interest in possession and witchcraft on several occasions, usually to question the way medicine came to be inserted into

the analysis of witchcraft in the sixteenth to seventeenth centuries—"Les déviations religieuses et le savoir médical" (1962/1968) in *DÉ*, I, no. 52, 652–63, and "Médicins, juges et sorciers au XVIIe siècle" (1969) in *DÉ*, I, no. 62, 781–94)—or, later, to create a tension between witchcraft and possession—*Abnormal: Lectures at the Collège de France, 1974-1975*, trans. Graham Burchell, English series editor Arnold I. Davison (New York: Picador, 2003), 203–15. But this reference should be compared especially with *The Archaeology of Knowledge*, 47–49, in which Foucault distances himself from "an explicit theme of . . . *History of Madness*, and that recurs . . . in the Preface," which is the quest for an original referent, a "primitive, fundamental, deaf, scarcely articulated experience" of madness, which therefore postulates the existence of a single and continuous referent of "madness" more or less recognized and repressed according to the period and the culture. In *The Archaeology of Knowledge*, this quest is linked to those who wonder "whether witches were unrecognized and persecuted madmen and madwomen, or whether, at a different period, a mystical or aesthetic experience was not unduly medicalized" (47). And it is precisely to a critique of these questions, which presuppose the unity of the referent "madness" through different periods and its medical truth, that the article "Médecins, juges et sorciers au XVIIe siècle" is devoted, which appeared at the same time as the Vincennes course and posed a different problem, that of the historical conditions specific to medical knowledge and to its social function, which introduced possession and witchcraft as objects of medical knowledge: "how could the characters of the witch or the possessed, who were perfectly integrated within those very rituals which excluded and condemned them, become objects of a medical practice that gave them a different status and excluded them in a different way?" (DÉ, I, 782). In lecture 7 of this course, Foucault will return to the question of witches, this time from the point of view of the witches' Sabbath as intertwining of utopia and heterotopia (see below, pp. 258–259).

14. See above, Clermont-Ferrand course, lecture 5, p. 107 et seq.

15. This "question of the truth posed to madness" is taken up anew by Foucault in *Psychiatric Power: Lectures at the Collège de France, 1973–1974*, ed. Jacques Lagrange, trans. Graham Burchell, English series editor Arnold I. Davidson (London: Palgrave Macmillan, 2008), 233–95, where he investigates the various techniques employed by psychiatric power to pose the

problem of truth and madness in the nineteenth century (questioning and confession, suggestion and hypnosis, etc.). In this framework, Foucault reconsiders the relation of psychiatry to pathological anatomy through a discussion of the model of general paralysis put forward by Antoine-Laurent Bayle in the 1820s for thinking a correlation between organic lesions and psychical disturbances and the limits of this model for nineteenth-century psychiatry. As Foucault notes, the specific difficulty of psychiatry is to constitute itself as "a medicine from which the body is absent." He distinguishes, on the one hand, pathological anatomy as a "procedure of verification in the form of observation and demonstration" and, on the other, a "test of reality" that aims to make the reality of madness appear through a set of techniques. These two dimensions are then examined from the angle of the distinction between the body of pathological anatomy and the "neurological body," which appears in psychiatry in the period 1860–1880 (297–323). With regard to the procedure aiming to compare what an individual says with "every normal person," this is, for example, the technique generally deployed to identify madness in the framework of a medicolegal expertise, which will be defeated by a series of cases taken up by Foucault in *Abnormal*, in which a reasonable subject who speaks like every normal person has committed an aberrant act.

16. This analysis can be linked with a comparable passage in the Tunis course: according to Foucault, from the beginning of the twentieth century, and notably through psychoanalysis, we witness a "re-institutionalization of sexuality" expressed, among other ways, in its "entry into the universe of discourse. Sexuality is now an explicit signification." Even more, it "appears both as the universal signifier and the universal signified"—a signified that is found "for mental illnesses and dreams; for family and social relationships . . .; maybe even for politics," and a signifier by which our relationship to others, death, and reality is grasped. Psychoanalysis is an essential vector of this transformation.

LECTURE 6

The Biology of Sexuality[1]

*E*xistence of a non-epistemologized knowledge of sexuality linked to multiple practices (human sexuality, agronomy, medicine, religion); verbalized in different forms (ad hoc justification, theories); impossible to oppose true practice and false ideology; the science of sexuality does not emerge as a rational take-up of these practices but has certain relations with them. Maintaining the autonomy of the science of sexuality while locating it within a given social formation. The sexuality of plants as guideline. I. Miscomprehension of the sexuality of plants up to the seventeenth century even though there are practices involving it, the sex of plants is accepted, etc. This miscomprehension is not linked to analogies-obstacles or to a lack of concepts: it is explained by the rules of the discursive practice of naturalists. II. Characteristics of this discursive practice: 1. continuity of the phenomena of individual growth and reproduction: no specificity of sexual function; 2. status granted to the individual: between individuals there are only resemblances and differences: no meta-individual biological reality dictating its law to individuals; 3. the limits between individuals are insurmountable: no meta-individual or individual-milieu continuum. Consequence: impossibility of conceiving of a specific sexual function. More broadly: a discourse is a rule-governed practice, and its resistances are linked to the rules that organize it as practice (versus ideology as representation). III. Transformations: 1. dissociation of male/female characters and individuals; 2. fertilization is not a stimulation but a transfer of elements:

importance of the milieu; 3. reversal of the relation between sexuality and individuals: sexuality is a meta-individual strain that determines the law governing individuals. Conclusion: death, sexuality, and history as constituents of the biological. Discontinuity and limit, fundamental concepts of biology, against the continuum of natural history. Humanist philosophy is a reaction to the epistemological structure of biology in order to give meaning to death, sexuality, and history.

[NP/51]   Before taking its place in botanical or zoological knowledge (*connaissance*), or [a] in a biological type of science, this knowledge (*savoir*) is invested in and functions at other levels, according to particular contexts and modes.

"Before" does not have a chronological meaning here.

With regard to this non-epistemologized knowledge,[2] we can note:

1. The multiplicity of its points of actualization:
- In human sexuality:
  - birth control;
  - regulation of marriage (in terms of kinship);[3]
  - repression of certain forms of sexuality (masturbation);[4]
  - pedagogy of sexuality (prohibition, learning).
- In agronomic practice:
  - animal fertilization (search for pure lines);[5]
  - plant fertilization (date palms).[6]

[NP/52]
- In medical practice (the role of the lack of sexual satisfaction in illness; or again the role of "debauchery" in the etiology of general paralysis).[7]
- In religious and moral practice (the rules of asceticism, techniques for subjugating concupiscence).[8]

---

a From this sheet, Foucault no longer indicates the pagination followed except at rare points, which will be indicated.

2. The multiplicity of its forms of verbalization:

- sometimes it is a matter of almost silent practices, passed on without justification;
- sometimes it is a matter of a specific "ad hoc" rationale that is not enveloped in a theory (fertilization [of] palms);
- sometimes it is a matter of [practice] taken up within a theory (asceticism, in a theory of sin, the body, imagination).

3. The fact that many of these practices are not apposite (that is, not suited to their ends: for example, pedagogical practices or those of sexual repression). We cannot therefore distinguish a practical kernel, with its intrinsic rationality, and theoretical justifications, which are false and ideological.

4. The fact that these practices, which are very stable and have   [NP/53] hardly changed, even in the nineteenth and twentieth centuries, do not constitute the domain in which the science of sexuality has its origin, contexts, and forms. The science of sexuality is not the rational take-up of these practices; it is not their transcription in a more or less rigorous conceptual system. And yet there are a number of precise, regional relations that can be described. For example:

- the theory and practice of hybridization (in the eighteenth century);[9]
- the theory of sexual "energy" and medical practice and pedagogy.[10]

The historical description of sexuality must therefore take into account the role, position, and functioning of human sexuality in the social formation in which this science is developed; taking into account [also] the set of practices in which an effective knowledge of sexuality is invested; but leaving scientific practice its autonomy: the specific mode in which it forms its objects, its models of analysis, its concepts, its theoretical options.

[NP/54]   Analysis will have to focus on these relations between the scientific discourse of sexuality, the position of sexuality in the typical processes of a social formation, and the set of more or less theorized, more or less justified practices concerning sexuality.

[1/55]ᵇ   # THE SEXUALITY OF PLANTS

The fact of plant sexuality was unknown until the seventeenth century: Camerarius recognized the role of the stamen and the pistil.[11] Now this ignorance has a very specific structure.

(The "unspoken" is not a homogeneous and monotonous function; the unspoken, in a case like this, is certainly not of the same type as when it is a matter of human sexuality, or political economy, or philosophy. The unspoken, or the game of the repressed in discourse, should not be considered as general cause or monotonous effect. It exists as a functional principle within a determinate discursive practice.)

    1. [This ignorance] is accompanied by a perfectly established, codified, and passed-on practice:
        a. For diecious plants: date palms.[12]
        b. For monecious plants with separated flowers, panicles with stamens, without which the ears would not give any seed, are not to be removed too soon.[13]

[NP/56]   c. For hybridized plants, artificial fertilization is practiced.
        d. Finally (but maybe this is very late), in cases of cross-fertilization, the stamens are removed from the plants one wants to cross.[14]

---

b The numbering on the left is Foucault's.

2. It is accompanied by a semantic distribution of the terms male and female, and by a nonrandom designation of male and female individuals. Thus, how to use sexual dissymmetry technically was known, [and] the idea of male and female plants was not rejected.[15]

3. It is accompanied by an awareness of analogy between plants and animals (Aristotle-Cesalpino),[16] [or between] seeds and the embryo (Hippocrates).[17]

It could be said:

- that there is a "bad" model, that of the fig and caprification, but it could just as well have been thought that there was a simple mechanism of fertilization in this case, where the phenomenon is much more complex. The problem is precisely why all the cases of simple sexual fertilization were reduced to this very specific case.

- that the notions male and female are employed as metaphors (stronger plants are called male).[18]
  But the problem is why the metaphor; or why a metaphorical usage did not lead to a more precise determination of the sexes;   [2/57]

- that the (inverted plant-animal) analogy (with organs of reproduction at the top of the individual) was a bad analogy and therefore an epistemological obstacle:[19]
  – purely spatial and not functional analogy.
  But we have seen many other analogies vanish. An analogy is not an obstacle in itself. It is not its strength or insistence in imagination that holds the key to its maintenance and accounts for its function as an obstacle.[20]

It could also be said that concepts are lacking: [for example, those] of functions and of life (with the requisites of life).[21]

I would like to show that it is the very disposition (*disposition*)[c] of the naturalists' discourse that constitutes the obstacle. Disposition, i.e., the way in which it forms its objects, enunciations, and concepts. And it is on that basis—of this discursive practice in its specific regularity—that imaginary investments and the organization of ideological themes were possible.

[NP/58] · In particular, the theme of plant innocence and sinful animality. The plant reflects that part of man that is innocent; the animal that part of man that is violent, carnivorous, and sexual.

· Or again the theme that nature is order, adjustment, relative immobility and not movement, growth, spontaneity, and struggle for existence.

That is the basis on which it is impossible to organize and define certain concepts. In other words, the unspoken of a scientific discourse is not the effect of an imaginary masking, or of a conceptual defect, but of the rules specific to a discursive practice and put to work in that practice.[22]

[3/59] *I. This discursive practice is characterized:*

1. By the constitution of a homogeneous series of phenomena that envelops, in the same way, all the processes of growth—that is, the phenomena of the growth of individuals (increase in dimensions, volumes, and weights) as well as the phenomena of the multiplication of individuals.[23]

At a time when mathematics knew only discrete quantities, the transition from small to large and from 1 to 2 were not differentiated.[24] Arithmetic has to count discontinuous quantities; natural science has to account for continuous growths. Biological quantity belongs to the realm of increase.

---

c Replacing "structure," then "configurations," crossed out.

- Hence the idea that the seed is born of the marrow. Food, in its purest essence, goes to the marrow. And the latter, in its development, forms the seed. "Nutrition and fertilization are the work of the same principle, that of the vital force."[25]
- Hence the idea that reproduction is of the same type, that it may be by seed, sucker, or cutting, since in each case new individuals come from a sort of surplus development.[26]

That increase and growth define the great series of facts [NP/60] within the domain of natural history (and not at all individuality) is what confirms:

- the fact that minerals, insofar as they grow, are considered to be living;[27]
- the fact that the animal-plant-mineral division is floating;
- the idea that animal sexuality is also considered as a phenomenon of growth (Hippocrates thought the germ to be a general increase of the organism).

[See File[d],[28]]

There is therefore no specificity of the sexual function. There is not even any sexual function. There are sexual organs only where a complex mechanism is needed to convert growth into reproduction. In natural history, until the eighteenth century, the sexual organs were not organs of the sexual function; but the instrument or organ that transforms intraindividual growth into pluri-individual proliferation. We can say that the sexual function had no place in knowledge (*savoir*).[29]

2.   The second characteristic of natural history—not as sys-   [4/61] tem of representations or concepts, but as discursive practice— is the status accorded to the individual.

---

d Foucault's indication.

[1.] The individual is the bearer of characters that, on the one hand, include it in a kinship[30] and, on the other hand, enable it to accomplish certain ends. These characters are the organs that are both signs and instruments. Hence two faces of natural history:

– the taxonomic face → species, system;
– the teleological face → life, hierarchy.

Hence natural history as science of order.

2. This general functioning of natural history means that there was no individual-to-individual reality other than resemblances. No meta-individual biological reality (outside of the essence understood as form or system of characters), so no identical functions, but similar results through analogous organs. [And] *a fortiori* no function requiring the participation of two individuals for its exercise. *A fortiori* again, no element that may give birth and law to individuals and found a strain (*souche*) while remaining identical to itself in a permanent fashion.[31]

[NP/62] 3. Hence, a series of consequences:

a. If children resemble their parents and belong to the same species, why is this? (epigenesis [or] preformation).[32]

b. If two individuals are indispensable for procreation, why is this? One can only be an adjuvant of the other: ovists [or] spermists.[33]

c. And as a result, far from being the fundamental condition of procreation, sexual union is only a supplementary complication. One can very well conceive of an autonomous proliferation, without either male titillation or female compartment (*habitacle*). This is even the simplest, most immediate form of reproduction—the first reproduction in terms of natural law.

4. Hence, finally, the idea that only mobile or quick living beings have sexual organs (with emission of sperm and production of eggs). The slow or stationary do not.[34]

Sexuality is therefore the form taken by proliferating growth   [5/63] in living species that can move about, and in which one will find two types of individual, each with its role in this growth. But fundamentally, reproduction is parthenogenetic.[35] Male-female union is only a supplementary figure superimposed on the inviolable virginity of nature.

[Sexuality linked to movement; growth is itself a sort of movement, etc.][e]

3. The third characteristic of natural history is to view the limits of the individual as absolute, insurmountable. This is normal when natural history is the science of growth[f] (as distinct from mathematics) [and] the science of resemblances. It therefore only recognizes the continuum within the individual, or the continuum of essences. The biological continuum of individual–milieu is not a possible object for natural history.[36]

- Hence the fact that there can be sexual union where individuals move. But where they do not move about, the milieu cannot be the medium of sexuality.
- Hence the fact that if proximity is necessary for the fruc-   [NP/64] tification of some species, it is only for reasons of affinities or sympathy.[37] See File: *De L'Écluse*.[38]
- Hence the fact that every individual is enclosed in its essence and its role. It is either male or female. It cannot be both. Thus, hermaphroditism is excluded. Where it is recognized, it is monstrosity or sacred.[39]

---

e Foucault's brackets.

f "of the continuous," crossed out.

General consequences of these three characteristics of the discourse of natural history:

- Sexual organs are not the manifestation and instrument of a sexual function, but a particular modality of the function of growth.
- Union of the sexual organs is not the condition of reproduction but the complication of an essential parthenogenesis.
- The sexual organs are linked to the essence of the individual, and the two sexes cannot be found in the same individual.

[6/65]   [. . .]^g

From this we can:

1. See that, more profoundly than ideas and beliefs, it is the practice itself of the scientific discourse that prevents one from conceiving of the sexuality of plants. This practice, considered:

- at the level at which it forms its objects;
- at which it defines its modes of enunciation;
- at which it constructs its concepts.

2. See that what makes a discourse resistant to a real practice, what gives it its impermeability, is not a set of representations; it is not the ideas that might haunt it from within; it is the aspect through which it is itself a practice and a rule-governed practice.

[NP/66]   (Which means that: if the resistance of a discourse to a practice really is linked to a society, or to a class position, a social practice, it is not insofar as it gives rise to ideas in men's heads that are slow to disappear or ideas they have an interest in sustaining, but insofar as this discourse itself is a practice and a social practice.)^{40}

---

g Paragraph crossed out that repeats some elements from the previous page: "reproduction appears as an affinity. It belongs to their essence to need, not their action, but their nearness. See File de l'Écluse. The transfer of an element of one plant to another plant (even though artificial fertilization was practiced) cannot have the status of scientific concept."

3. Finally, we can see what has to change in the naturalists' discourse for the sexuality of plants to be fully conceptualized, and in a scientific mode.

1. First of all, sexuality will have to be dissociated from individuality. And its processes will have to be analyzed scientifically at the level of organs and their reciprocal functions.

2. Sexuality will have to be analyzed within the milieu (and not only as a specific process).

3. Finally, and especially, the growth-reproduction assimilation will have to be decoupled and different vital processes will have to be analyzed in their specificity.

II. *The transformations* [NP/67]

For the sexuality of plants to become the object of a specific knowledge, it was necessary:

• To dissociate the sexual organs from individual characteristics. It had to be discovered that the individual is not male or female as it is big or small, but that a male-female sexual organization exists that may be distributed over one or several individuals.

• To differentiate fertilization from the spatial coming together of male and female, that is to say:
  – establish the indispensable existence of a material element;
  – establish the modalities or instruments of transfer in a milieu.

• To reverse the individuals-sexuality relation: the latter is not situated at the end of the development but in its principle. Sexuality precedes the individual. And it is not the individual who, on arriving at a certain degree of maturity, gains access to sexuality and finds full expression in it.[41]

[NP/68]   *A. Male and female characters* (caractères) *are not characteristics* (caractéristiques) *of individuals.*[H]

> – Natural continuity (which was opposed to mathematical discontinuity) was:
> * the continuity of growth;
> * the continuity of resemblances;
> * the continuity of the cosmos.
> – Now seventeenth-century mathematics gives the schema of a:
> * continuity of variation;
> * continuity of differences;
> * continuity of the table.[42]

Hence, analysis of the most visible elements and the discovery:
* that some plants have similar organs of fructification in all the individuals and all their flowers;
* others have organs of fructification that differ from one flower to another on the same individual;
* that others have two categories of organs of fructification that characterize two types of individual.

Hence the experiments of Camerarius:
* on dioecious plants: mulberry;
* on plants with separate flowers: castor oil, maize;
* on plants with hermaphrodite flowers.[43]

[NP/69]   These experiments are significant.
> – Exemplary value of the history of the sciences:
> * Camerarius's experiments exactly reduplicate an established agronomic practice[:] they say the same thing and employ the same method of verification.

---

h Underlined in the manuscript.

- But they introduce them into a different discursive regime:
  - in which these particularities function as differences;
  - in which the latter function as characters;
  - in which the cosmos functions as a table.

And it is on that basis that the facts can be given an "explanation."

- Epistemological consequences:
  - Sexual organs are generalized. The problem of cryptogams.[44]
  - The male-female polarity falls below the individual scale. It is a process that may be intra- as well as extra-individual.[45]
  - Hermaphroditism enters the domain of the normal. In a sense, it is the most general rule.[46]

B. Fertilization is not stimulation but transfer of material elements[i],[47]   [NP/70]

Here, the transformation does not concern the intersecting of two epistemological fields (science of order) but the possibility of animal-vegetable analogy due to the generalization of sexuality.

1. Structural and functional analogies:
   - Pistil-ovisac: female organization.
   - Stamens-pollen: male organization. The fertilization of plants has the same requisites as the fertilization of animals.
2. But the difference is that plants lack locomotion:
   - Experiments of Sprengel and Knight;[48]
   - Discovery of the milieu.

---

i Underlined in the manuscript.

Here again, epistemological significance:

- the milieu in Buffon and Lamarck: principle of supplementary variation;
- the milieu in the nineteenth century, that which is indispensable to the exercise of a function.

[NP/71]   But this principle, which is still empty in Cuvier, becomes full and positive in botany. Hence the considerations of ecology.[49]

C. Sexuality is not a function dependent on others, nor even on the individual[j]

This transformation, the most important, is due to a redefinition of life. The latter is not a function that develops through living beings, but an intertwining of functions and structures that come into play at the level of an individual and define it. The individual is not a juxtaposition of variables. It is a set of functions, structures, and conditions of existence.

Sexuality will appear as a structural and functional ensemble— no longer subordinated to the great property of growth, but independent and articulated on other functions.

[NP/72]   1. This independence is established by the analysis of the mechanism of fertilization (which, henceforth, no longer appears as stimulation of growth by mechanical and chemical processes). Fertilization is the fusion of two sexual cells: Pringsheim (1855), Strasburger (1884).[50]

2. It [is also] established by the fundamental distinction between cells that constitute an organism [and] those that reproduce it: Nussbaum and Weissman.[51]

As a result, the individual is constructed from sexuality (the sexual cells and the specific properties of hereditary preservation

---

j Underlined in the manuscript.

and fusion) whereas previously sex was produced through the development of individuality.[52] This reversal of the sexuality/individual relations is found again in Freud.[53]

Conclusion [54]   [NP/73]

From the vantage point of the development of biology, it could be said that in the nineteenth century three notions were uprooted from the continuum of natural history.
- Death, which was only an accident which took place in the individual's development.
- Sexuality, which was a function of meta-individual growth.
- History, which was a progress of complication.

These three facts of biology (which were subordinate) become constituent.
- The living is something that can die. The phenomenon of death, the conditions under which one does not die, those that mean that one dies, become constitutive components of life. Death is the individual's limit.
- The living is something that has a sexuality—that derives from a strain of which it is a branch (*dérivation*), and that possesses its principal characteristics. Sexuality and heredity, that is the law of the individual.
- Hence, history: heredity and adaptation. History is no longer a development; it is both the conditions of the milieu and their interplay in relation to the laws of heredity.

That the living is characterized by these dimensions entails   [NP/74]
the use of discontinuity as the fundamental category of biology.
- up to the eighteenth [century], continuity of resemblance and cosmic cohesion;
- up to the nineteenth [century], continuity of difference and ordered succession;

- henceforth, discontinuity through:
  - the limit of death, which isolates the individual;
  - sexuality, which separates the individual from his successors (at any rate, only links it to them through the intermediary of the strain);
  - history, which only connects species together through the difference of conditions of existence and variations.

The individual communicates with its elementary constituents only through the barrier of life and death. It communicates with its descendants only through the identity of the strain (which exists at a meta-individual level). It communicates with other species only through the history of nature, struggle, and variations. The function of anthropological thought is to preserve man from these discontinuities and to put his death, others, and history within his reach.

[NP/75]
- Death and life communicate through signification.
- Sexuality as relationship to others through the family and death.
- History as continuous relationship to the past and future through consciousness and praxis.

We can call humanist or anthropological philosophy any "reactionary" philosophy, any philosophy that reacts to the epistemological structure of biology by trying to compensate for it by mixing it with the epistemological structure of the classical age (continuity and representation) and by refusing:

- to see an absolute and insurmountable limit of the individual in death;
- to see something other than love and reproduction in sexuality;
- to see something other than the continuity of consciousness in history.

*

1. The period 1968–1970 is marked by Foucault's intense reflection on the history and epistemology of biological knowledge of sexuality and heredity. His project of research and teaching at the time of his candidacy at the Collège de France, when he proposed to undertake the history of the "knowledge of heredity" (see "Titres et travaux" [1969], *DÉ*, I, no. 71, 870–74), bears witness to this, as well as a few published texts, in particular, his review of François Jacob's *The Logic of Living Systems* ("Croître et multiplier" [1970], *DÉ*, I, no. 81, 967–72), which Foucault's notebooks show was carefully prepared, and his contribution to the Institut d'histoire des sciences in 1969 on "Cuvier's Situation in the History of Biology" (1970), which contains a number of elements referred to in this course. The archives at the BNF show that Foucault accumulated considerable material on these subjects, of which this lecture forms only a very limited emergent part. We thus have entire dossiers (Boxes 45 and 39 in particular) on the problem of plant sexuality between the seventeenth and nineteenth centuries (discovery of pollination and modes of fertilization, problem of cryptogams, hybridization and agronomic practices . . .), on the birth of a science of heredity and animal sexuality, as well as on the emergence of Mendelian genetics. Foucault's *Notebooks* 8 and 9 (BNF, Box 91), which cover 1969, reflect the double orientation of this interest, which is found in this lecture. On the one hand, the "archaeological" analysis of knowledge of sexuality and heredity enables him to engage in epistemological reflection, in tension with the Althusserian analysis of the relations between ideology and science; to criticize Althusser's definition of an "ideological proposition" through the analysis of Matthias Jakob Schleiden's theory of pollination; to complicate the division between science and nonscience and the characterization of a "scientific problem" through the history of the forms of knowledge of heredity; and finally to put forward his own analysis of the way a science forms levels of different objects, through the history of genetics. This orientation will be translated into the course Foucault gives the following year at Vincennes on the "epistemology of the sciences of life," an outline plan of which is found in *Notebook* 8, dated October 14, 1969—"—what is an epistemological obstacle;—how is a concept (species) criticized;—an epistemological transformation (Mendel);—model and theory (heredity);—science and philosophy (philosophy of nature; unity of the plan. Burdach-Schleiden); politics: Lysenko; anticipation and rediscovery; practice: agronomy, plant

biology"—and, it seems, two lectures focusing on the "scientific error" and "scientific problems" (BNF, Box 70-C5). On the other hand, Foucault is all the more interested in these questions as he links them systematically to the critique of the sovereign subject and of humanism, following Bataille in seeing in the experience of sexuality one of the limit experiences that make of the individual subject, as he notes in a letter to Pierre Guyotat, "a precarious, provisional, quickly effaced extension . . . a pale form that emerges for a few instants from a great obstinate, repetitive strain. Individuals, quickly retracted pseudopods of sexuality" ("Il y aura scandale mais . . ." [1970], 943). The history of biological knowledge of sexuality is then related to a form of radical criticism of the sovereignty of the anthropological subject, and in favor of a general reproductive process of which the individual is only a stage. This reflection, a trace of which is found in this course, is the subject of a passage of eight recto-verso sheets in *Notebook* 8, dated September 22, 1969, under the title "Sexuality, Reproduction, Individuality," which we reproduce in an appendix (see below, pp. 289–296); see "Course Context," pp. 323–349.

2. On this notion of "non-epistemologized knowledge," see above, lecture 5, note 2, p. 216. It refers to a set of knowledges directly forming part of practices that are not "reflected" in discourses that have acquired a form of autonomy and clear delimitation.

3. See above, lecture 4.

4. Foucault will later make the crusade against masturbation that develops in the second half of the eighteenth century the main point of emergence of the "domain of sexuality." It is on the basis of this domain, through a series of uncouplings and displacements, that the *scientia sexualis*, the psychiatric and psychological analysis of sexuality and perversions, will emerge in the second half of the nineteenth century (see *La Croisade des enfants*, BNF, Box 51). Traces of this research are found in the Collège de France course, *Abnormal*, trans. Graham Burchell (New York: Picador, 2003), lectures of March 5 and 12, 1975, 231–90, and in *The History of Sexuality, Volume One: An Introduction*, trans. R. Hurley (New York: Pantheon, 1978), 27–31, 42–49, and 104.

5. Foucault is referring to the attempt to preserve the purity of animal breeds, in particular to produce "thoroughbred" lines in horses, particularly marked at the beginning of the eighteenth century. For the French case, see the works of Nicole de Blomac, notably *La Gloire et le Jeu: Des hommes et*

des chevaux 1766–1866 (Paris: Fayard, 1991); for an analysis of the knowledge and apparatuses (*dispositifs*) of power around heredity linked with horse breeding in the modern period, see C.-O. Doron, *L'Homme altéré: Races et dégénérescence, XVIIIe–XIXe siècles* (Ceyzérien, France: Champ Vallon, 2016), 173–285.

6. See below, note 12, pp. 240–241.

7. The role of sexual abstinence in the development of many illnesses is a commonplace of eighteenth- to nineteenth-century medicine, illustrated, for example, by the case of the priest of La Réole, described by Buffon and constantly taken up afterward. See Tim Verhoeven, "The Satyriasis Diagnosis: Anti-Clerical Doctors and Celibate Priests in Nineteenth-Century France," *French History* 26, no. 4 (2012: 504–23). Debauchery occupies pride of place in the etiology of general paralysis in the early writings of the alienists, before being linked to syphilis and debauched sexual behavior. Masturbation is thus often presented as causing, as one of the many evils it engenders, general paralysis. This is the case in Tissot, *L'Onanisme ou Dissertation physique sur les maladies produites par la masturbation*, 5th ed. (Lausanne, Switzerland: Grasset, 1772), 48–52, cited in Foucault, *La Croisade des enfants*, f. 26; and in Joseph Guislain, *Leçons orales sur les phrénopathies* (Gand, Belgium: L. Hebbelynck, 1852), 2:61–62, cited in Foucault, *La Croisade des enfants*, f. 28, which notes that "the habit of solitary touching gives rise to a crowd of evils: . . . mental alienation, melancholy, mania; suicide, dementia with paralysis especially."

8. Foucault became interested very early on in the way concupiscence was treated in the casuistry and moral theology of the seventeenth century (for example, in the *Theologia Moralis* of the Jesuit fathers Hermann Busenbaum and Claude Lacroix, 1710). The question will be treated very differently starting from *Abnormal*, 168–230, and *The History of Sexuality: Volume One*, 115–22, where it will form part of an analysis of the procedures of confession and examination, marking the emergence of the problem of the body of pleasure and desire within penitential practices. Foucault will then try to undertake the genealogy of this problem through the analysis of the theme of the flesh and of ascetic practices linked to it since early Christianity. See, for example, "The Battle for Chastity" (1982), trans. Anthony Forster, in *EW*, 1, 185–97, and *Les Aveux de la chair*, ed. F. Gros (Paris: Gallimard, 2018).

9. The history of the problem of the hybridization of plants in the eighteenth–nineteenth centuries is studied by Herbert Fuller Roberts in *Plant Hybridization Before Mendel* (Princeton, NJ: Princeton University Press, 1929) and Robert C. Olby in *Origins of Mendelism* (London: Constable, 1966). Its relations with the Mendelian science of heredity have been discussed with the tools of historical epistemology by Jacques Piquemal, "Aspects de la pensée de Mendel" (1965), in *Essais et Leçons d'histoire de la médecine et de la biologie*, pref. Georges Canguilhem (Paris: PUF, 1993), 93–112 (BNF files), who stressed Mendel's radical departure, in terms of research problems and concepts, from the earlier reflections on hybridization, from Joseph Gottlieb Kölreuter to Charles Naudin.

10. The theory of "sexual energy" refers, in particular, to the conception of sexuality developed in various works of Sigmund Freud, Wilhelm Reich, and other sexologists.

11. Between 1691 and 1694, Rudolf Jakob Camerarius (1665–1721), professor of botany at Tübingen, conducted a series of experiments the results of which will be compiled in *De sexu plantarum epistola* (1694), in which he identifies the stamens as male sexual organs and the ovary and the style as female sexual organs in plants. See É. Guyénot, *L'Évolution de la pensée scientifique: Les sciences de la vie aux XVIIe et XVIIIe siècles: l'idée d'évolution* (Paris: Albin Michel, 1957 [1941]), 320–22; Julius von Sachs, *Histoire de la botanique du XVIe siècle à 1860*, trans. H. de Varigny (Paris: C. Reinwald, 1892), 398–404; J.-F. Leroy, *Histoire de la notion de sexe chez les plantes*, lecture of December 5, 1959 (Paris: Palais de la découverte, 1960), 10–11 (BNF files).

12. The case of date palms is a commonplace of the literature of the history of botany on the problem of plant sexuality. Date palms are diecious, that is to say, male and female flowers are on different plants and the sexes are therefore clearly separate. Since antiquity, in Mesopotamia, fertilization of dates was practiced by spreading the pollen of the male plants on the spadices of the female plant. See George Sarton, "The Artificial Fertilization of Date-Palms in the Time of Ashur-Nasir-Pal B.C. 885–860," *Isis* 21, no. 1 (1934): 8–13 (BNF files). This kind of operation, already described by Hérodote, is called "caprification," "by analogy with the method employed to ripen the fruit of the domestic fig. Fruit from the wild fig or *Caprificus* were hung in the branches. Insects came out of the fruit and carried out pollination." See É. Guyénot, *L'Évolution de la pensée scientifique*, 314; see

also J.-F. Leroy, *Histoire de la notion de sexe chez les plantes*, 8. Many details about these practices are found in Alphonse de Candolle, *Introduction à l'étude de la botanique* (Paris: Roret, 1835), 1:341–43 (BNF files).

13. The information is taken from de Candolle, *Introduction à l'étude de la botanique*, 1:345, which notes: "in plants where stamens and pistils are separate on the same plant (monecious), like corn, it is well known in practice that the panicles with stamens, without which the ears will not produce seed, must not be removed too soon."

14. These details on artificial and cross-fertilization are given by de Candolle, 1:346: "in our time a mass of varieties are obtained . . . by the cross-fertilization of different species. One takes care only to remove the stamens of the flower one is working on, before opening their locules."

15. Von Sachs, *Histoire de la botanique*, 392–93, and Guyénot, *L'Évolution de la pensée scientifique*, 316–17, analyze these male/female divisions and their rules in Théophraste, and then in the authors of the sixteenth century (Cesalpino, L'Écluse, etc.). As Guyénot notes, "it is important to imagine that in this period . . . the terms male and female are used to designate different qualities of two individuals, like we would say big and small, short and long, strong and weak, without these words involving any necessary relation with reproduction" (316). In Cesalpino, for example, they refer first of all to different "temperaments," the females being more tepid and males hotter. Foucault also calls upon the work of Arthur-Konrad Ernsting, *Historische und physikalische Beschreibung der Geschlechter der Pfanzen* (Lemgo, Germany: Meyer, 1762), 1:35–37, in which the latter analyzes the male/female mode of designating plants in antiquity. Thus, when two plants are similar, but one is bigger and stronger and the other weaker and tender, then the former is male and the latter female. Similarly with color (red = male; blue, yellow, white = female) (BNF, Box 45-C1).

16. For Cesalpino, see von Sachs, *Histoire de la botanique*, who recalls Cesalpino's analogies between the ovaries of plants and the eggs of animals (393). But the analogy to which Foucault is no doubt referring via Aristotle and Cesalpino is the "old analogy of plant to animal (the vegetable is an animal living head down, its mouth—or roots—buried in the earth)" that Cesalpino strengthens and multiplies, according to Foucault, "when he makes the discovery that a plant is an upright animal, whose nutritive principles rise from the base up to the summit, channelled along a stem

that stretches upward like a body and is topped by a head" (*The Order of Things: An Archaeology of the Human Sciences* [London: Tavistock, 1970], 21). This analysis is inspired by Émile Callot, *La Renaissance des sciences de la vie au XVIe siècle* (Paris: PUF, 1951), 136–38. See below, note 19.

17. See Hippocrates, *Generation,* in *Hippocrates, Volume X,* Loeb Classical Library 520, ed. and trans. Paul Potter (Cambridge, MA: Harvard University Press, 2012). Foucault summarizes: "The seed that grows in the soil is like the embryo developing in the womb" (BNF, Box 45-C1).

18. See above, note 15. This is the view of Guyénot and von Sachs.

19. This is the view of Callot, for whom the analogy "becomes . . . the source of endless errors which engender each other"; he takes as example precisely the problem of sexuality, emphasizing that the denial of the sexuality of plants, in Aristotle and then Cesalpino, derives from this analogy (*La Renaissance des sciences de la vie,* 138).

20. The notion of epistemological obstacle refers to the epistemology of Bachelard and its take-up by Althusser. By stressing that the obstacle consists neither in the force of an image nor in the absence of certain concepts, but in the organization of naturalist knowledge, how it functions and constructs its objects, Foucault extends the Bachelardian principle that it "is at the very heart of the act of cognition that, by some kind of functional necessity, sluggishness and disturbances arise . . . that we shall call epistemological obstacles"; Gaston Bachelard, *The Formation of the Scientific Mind: A Contribution to a Psychoanalysis of Objective Knowledge,* intro., trans., and anno. by Mary McAllester Jones (Manchester, UK: Clinamen Press, 2002), 24. Here, the epistemological obstacle occupies a specific place within the functioning of naturalist knowledge.

21. This is a general position: thus, for Guyénot as well as von Sachs, male/female characters are not distributed according to a specific function (reproduction), and the latter is confused with nutrition (see also Callot, *La Renaissance de la sciences de la vie,* 139–40). "Requisites" should be understood here as what is needed or what is lacking for the presence of a concept of life in terms of a typical Canguilhemian analysis of the history of concepts. Foucault explains what he means by this in his preparatory notes to his review of Jacob, *The Logic of Living Systems*: "Cf. . . . all the terminology of requisites. What is needed; what one lacks; what is insufficient; what is necessary" (*Notebook 9,* October 27, 1969).

22. We find here a recurring position taken by Foucault of seeking to situate science in the more general field of knowledge (*savoir*), that is, of discursive practice subject to rules that can be accounted for positively: "instead of defining between [knowledge (*savoir*) and science] a relation of exclusion or subtraction (by trying to discover what in knowledge still eludes and resists science . . .), archaeological analysis must show positively how a science functions in the element of knowledge" (*The Archaeology of Knowledge*, trans. A. M. Sheridan Smith [London: Tavistock, 1972], 185). By placing a science in the interplay of the rules that order it as discursive practice, one shows the "positive" character of certain errors, obstacles, or impossibilities. Which Foucault will note with regard to botany in "The Order of Discourse": "botany and medicine are made up of errors as well as truths, like any other discipline—errors which are not residues or foreign bodies but which have positive functions, and a role that is often indissociable from that of the truths" (p. 60). This point, regarding the characterization of a scientific error and a scientific problem, was developed in more detail in the course Foucault devoted to "the epistemology of the life sciences" the following year at Vincennes (BNF, Box 70-C5). Foucault envisages the relation between ideology and science within this framework (see *The Archaeology of Knowledge*, 184–86) and criticizes the Althusserian definition of an "ideological proposition." In his notebooks, taking the example of Schleiden's theory (the embryo transmitted to the ovule through the pollinic tube), which he describes as a "disciplined error" in "The Order of Discourse" because "in accordance with the rules of biological discourse" (61), Foucault emphasizes that in truth, every scientific proposition, as every ideological proposition, is the "symptom of a reality other than that at which it is aimed," inasmuch as they all involve respecting certain discursive rules, a certain state of knowledge (*connaissances*) and techniques, and various sociopolitical and institutional conditions, etc. As Foucault notes, "the second characteristic of the ideological proposition, being "symptom of another reality," is probably true for every scientific proposition; the only difference between a scientific and an ideological proposition is the difference between truth and error. Now only science can determine this difference. Consequently, a scientific proposition is an ideologically true proposition; an ideological proposition is a false scientific proposition. One will not get out of this as long as one superimposes the science/ideology

problem and the truth/error problem. We have to get rid of Spinoza" (*Note-book* 8, October 2, 1969). We can see from this that "to tackle the ideological functioning of science . . . is to question it as a discursive formation; it is to tackle . . . the system of formation of its objects, its types of enunciation, its concepts . . . It is to treat it as one practice among others" (*The Archaeology of Knowledge*, 186). See also above, lecture 3, p. 180, where a comparable position is asserted.

23. Foucault develops comparable analyses to describe the living in natural history in "Cuvier's Situation in the History of Biology," trans. Lynne Huffer, *Foucault Studies* 22 (January 2017): "in the end it is growth that characterizes the living . . . 1. To grow in size. The living is that which is subject to increase in size . . . 2. To grow according to the variable of number. This growth through the variable of number is reproduction" (234). More generally, the whole of this lecture should be related to that lecture and the discussions that followed it, in which whole fragments of the manuscript are found.

24. Foucault appears to be referring here to the absence of a differential calculus before the seventeenth century. See below, note 42, p. 248.

25. This is Aristotle's view (see von Sachs, *Histoire de la botanique*, 389; BNF files; Guyénot, *L'Évolution de la pensée scientifique*, 315; Callot, *La Renaissance des sciences de la vie*, 147), which is taken up by Cesalpino (*De plantis*, libri XVI, 1583). According to Cesalpino: "in animals, the seed (*semence*) is a product of the secretions of a part of the heart, from the most perfect . . . these seeds (*semences*) are made fertile by the vital principle and natural heat; just as in plants, the substance from which the seeds (*graines*) will come later must be separated from the vegetal part in which the principles of natural heat reside, that is to say . . . from the marrow. For the same reasons, the marrow of the seeds (*graines*) is formed from the most humid and purest content in the nutritive principles." This view is still found in the eighteenth century in, for example, Johann Gottlieb Gleditsch, "Remarques abrégées sur quelques traces de confromité entre les corps du règne végétal et ceux du règne animal," in *Mémoires de l'Académie royale des Sciences et Belles Lettres de Berlin*, vol. 14 (1758); French ed., 2:374–75, who notes that the seeds are formed "by means of an extension of the marrow whose delicacy is incomprehensible. There are as many young plants which, when they have attained their perfection, separate from the mother and no longer receive any food. The seeds contain, therefore, in an invisible

form, the whole plants" (BNF, Box 45-C1). Gleditsch's view illustrates well the continuity of growth and reproduction Foucault refers to.

26. Foucault, "Cuvier's Situation," 234: "for a long time it was believed that reproduction, through cuttings or sexuality, was a phenomenon of growth. Sexuality was not granted any real independence in its physiological functioning."

27. Foucault, "Cuvier's Situation," 234.

28. Foucault seems to be referring here to the file he created on "Hippocrates and Human Reproduction" (BNF, Box 45-C3), in which the production of the seed is effectively described as a general increase coming from the whole organism:

> The sperm from the human male comes from all the fluid in the body . . . there are veins and nerves that extend from every part of the body to the penis. When as the result of gentle friction these vessels grow warm and become congested, they experience a kind of irritation, and in consequence a feeling of pleasure and warmth arises over the whole body. Friction on the penis and the movement of the whole man cause the fluid in the body to grow warm: becoming diffuse and agitated by the movement, it produces a foam, in the same way as all the other fluids produce foam when they are agitated. But in the case of the human being, what is secreted as foam is the most potent and richest part of the fluid. (Hippocrates, *The Seed*, in *Hippocratic Writing*, ed. G. E. R. Lloyd [London: Penguin Classics, 1983], 317)

29. See "Cuvier's Situation," 235: "sexuality was considered to be a kind of supplementary apparatus through which, having reached a certain stage, an individual shifted toward another mode of growth: no longer increase in size, but multiplication. Sexuality was a kind of growth alternator." A similar passage is found in the manuscript "Sexuality, Reproduction, Individuality", reproduced as an appendix to this course; see below, pp. 289–296.

30. The "kinship" involved here does not involve any idea of genealogical relation and common descent: it is a matter of "natural kinship" in the sense of the "methodists"—that is, "plants that could be deduced from a fundamental ideal form that presented a same type, a same plan

of symmetry, were considered to be related" (Guyénot, *L'Évolution de la pensée scientifique*, 28). The individuals-characters relation in the taxonomic game of natural history was the object of Foucault's analysis in *The Order of Things*, 138–45.

31. We will see (below, p. 234 et seq.; "Sexuality, Reproduction, Individuality," pp. 000–000; and "Course Context," pp. 289–296) that for Foucault, in fact, the constitution of sexuality as an object of knowledge presupposes thinking this strain that gives birth and law to individuals and remains identical to itself (the *germen* in Weismann's sense). It therefore presupposes, as he notes in a rough draft of the time (BNF, Box 45-C1), a "total deindividualization of sexuality." According to Foucault, this deposition of the individual is fully realized in the discovery of DNA, in which a "code," a "program," "controls us," while "the birth and death of individuals are only enveloped ways of transmitting heredity" (see *Notebook* 9, October 29, 1969, and "Croître et multiplier" (1970), 968–69).

32. See above, Clermont-Ferrand course, p. 33. Preformation and epigenesis are the two opposed theories of generation between the end of the seventeenth and the beginning of the nineteenth century to account for, in particular, the reproduction of the specific form across generations as well as the resemblance of children to their parents. Preformation, as embodied in particular in the theory of the nesting of germs, assumes that the germ— the form—of each individual is contained in the seed (ovum or spermatozoon) and is, through mechanical forces (the impulse given by the other seed during reproduction) developed in stages, according to a process of *evolutio*. This view is found in Swammerdam or Leibniz, for example, and will be reasserted, in a more refined form, by Haller in the 1750s. Opposed to this is an "epigenetic" theory that assumes particular forces (Buffon's "internal mold," the affinities and instincts of Maupertuis, Wolff's "*vis essentialis*," Blumenbach's "*Bildungstrieb*") at work during reproduction that impose an organic form—the specific form and that of the parents—on the material. On this subject, see Guyénot, *L'Évolution de la pensée scientifique*, 296–312, or especially Jacques Roger, *Les Sciences de la vie dans la pensée française du XVIIIᵉ siècle: La génération des animaux de Descartes à l'Encyclopédie*, 2nd ed. (Paris: Albin Michel, 1993 [1963]), and, later than Foucault's course, François Jacob, *The Logic of Living Systems: A History of Heredity*, trans. Betty E. Spillmann (London: Allen Lane, 1974 [1970]).

33. The "ovists" thought that the reproductive element was lodged solely in the eggs of the maternal organism, the masculine seed serving strictly as a stimulant for implementing it. The "spermists" or "animalculists," on the other hand, thought that only the sperm contained the reproductive element, the ovules playing solely the role of compartment for its development. See Guyénot, *L'Évolution de la pensée scientifique*, 240–78, and Roger, *Les Sciences de la vie dans la pensée française*, 255–325.

34. This was already Aristotle's view: "Animals that do not move, and animals that remain stuck to the place where they were born, have an existence similar to that of plants; they are neither male nor female" (quoted in von Sachs, *Histoire de la botanique*, 390). For Aristotle, only animals possessing locomotion are endowed with sexual organs. This is taken up in the seventeenth century by Van Leeuwenhoek, for example, who notes with regard to the relations between plants and animals in reproduction, "we shall not find any other difference between *Plants* and *Animals*, than that the first wanting a locomotive Power, cannot couple as Animals do" ("A letter from Mr. Anth. Van Leeuwenhoek *concerning the Seeds of Plants, with Observations on the manner of the* Propagation *of* Plants *and* Animals," *Philosophical Transactions* 17, no. 199 (1693): 704; see BNF, Box 45-C1).

35. This is Réaumur's view when he analyzes the parthenogenesis of aphids in 1742: "It is quite natural to think that . . . the embryos develop in the aphid's body when it begins to grow . . . far, it seems to me, from finding it difficult to agree that the generation of aphids could take place in such a simple way, one can only be embarrassed that, to carry out the generation of other animals, a more composite way has been taken by the one who could not fail to choose the most perfect and suitable means" (R.-A. F. de Réaumur, *Mémoires pour servir à l'histoire des insectes*, vol. 6 [1742], 548, quoted in Roger, *Les Sciences de la vie dans la pensée française*, 382).

36. The history of the concept of "milieu," in the sense Foucault uses it here—that is, marking a close correlation between the organism and its sphere of existence—is given by Canguilhem in "The Living and Its Milieu," in *Knowledge of Life*, trans. Stefanos Geroulanos and Daniela Ginsburg (New York: Fordham University Press, 2008 [1965]). See also below, p. 234; and note 40, p. 250–251.

37. "Affinities" and "sympathy," two notions for accounting for relations of resemblance between natural beings before natural history, are analyzed by Foucault in *The Order of Things*, 23 *et seq.*

38. The file in question is taken from von Sachs, *Histoire de la botanique*, 392. This is its exact content: *"De L'Écluse.* He calls flowers with stamens male, and those that enclose an ovary female. 'It is claimed that some mysterious affinities join each of the plants to the other [this is "male" and "female" flowers of the *Carica papaya*], so that the female plant does not bear fruit if the male plant is separated from it by an extended space rather than being close to it'" (*Curae Posteriores*, 42) (BNF, Box 45-C1).

39. Foucault will return to hermaphroditism, seen in terms of monstrosity or the sacred, but this time from the point of view of juridical teratology, in *Abnormal*, 63–75. See also on this subject, Valerio Marchetti, *L'invenzione della bisessualità* (Milan: Mondadori, 2001).

40. This section should be compared with the analysis of ideology as practice developed by Foucault in lecture 3; see above, p. 180–181.

41. In the BNF archives (Box 45-C1), there is a variant that explains some of these conditions: "—to separate the sexuality/growth relation from a scale of the organ to the elements (determination of the specific elements: pollen-spermatozoon (*spermaton*) and ovaries-ovules);—to differentiate the sexuality-movement relation and to effectuate the transition to the meta-individual (to the milieu). In short, it involves a general deindividualization of sexuality; or again, a relativization of the individual, removal of its absolute limits, identification of the systems to which it belongs and from which it is itself constituted."

42. These are the essential elements of differential calculus and the *mathesis universalis* (on the question of the table, see *The Order of Things*). We recall that Michel Serres' thesis on *Le Système de Leibniz et ses modèles mathématiques* (Paris: PUF, 1968) was published in 1968, the first chapter of which in particular refers to the themes broached here by Foucault.

43. These examples are given in von Sachs, *Histoire de la botanique*, pp. 399–401. With regard to dioecious plants, Camerarius observes first of all that female mulberry trees bear fruit even when they are not near male mulberry trees, but that these fruit contain only hollow and empty seeds, which Camerarius compares to unfertilized birds' eggs. An experiment on another dioecious plant, mercury, confirms his analysis. In the case

of monoecious plants (maize, castor oil), Camerarius removes the male flowers of the castor oil plant before the anthers have developed, without touching the ovaries already formed, and observes the formation of seeds that do not develop fully and are sterile; he similarly cuts the stigma of a maize plant and completely prevents the formation of maize seeds. Regarding hermaphrodites, Camerarius, taking inspiration from the work of Jan Swammerdam on the hermaphroditism of slugs, reckons that it is a matter of a common rule in plants.

44. Phanerogamic plants, the reproductive organs of which are apparent and serve moreover as bases for classification, are distinguished from cryptogamic plants, whose reproductive organs are hidden. The "problem of cryptogams" (algae, lichens, ferns, fungi) will haunt the first two thirds of the nineteenth century (see von Sachs, *Histoire de la botanique*, 451 *et seq.*, and especially J.-F. Leroy, *Histoire de la notion de sexe chez les plantes*, 17–24) until the discovery in them of the alternation of generations, which will lead to a more general re-elaboration of the theory of fertilization. Foucault put together a very important dossier (BNF, Box 45-C1-2-3) on the problem of the sexuality of cryptogams in the nineteenth century, its resolution in the alternation of generations, and its extensions in the biology of his time.

45. This point is illustrated perfectly in, for example, the first part of Karl Friedrich Burdach's *Traité de physiologie* (Paris: Baillière, 1837), which Foucault read closely, and which lists the set of different modes of sexuality.

46. This thesis was already present in Camerarius. We find it, for example, clearly stated by Meyer in K. F. Burdach, *Traité de physiologie*, 1:252–57 (see file titled "The Normal Hermaphroditism of Plants", BNF, Box 45-C1). According to Meyer, dioecious plants are not the most perfect and closest to animals but, rather, "mutilated plants that present a rudiment of the sex they are lacking" (252). In other words, "hermaphroditism is the highest degree that the plant can reach" (256).

47. What is at issue here is as much the discovery of the material element (pollen) as its modes of transfer (by way of insects or the milieu, for example) and the way fertilization is carried out (with, in particular, the identification of the pollen tube and the micropyle, through which fertilization is carried out in seed plants). Even if it is not apparent in this course, Foucault studied these different aspects extensively, reading the works of

Stephano-Francisco Geoffroy, *An hominis primordia, vermis* (1704); Sébastien Vaillant, *Sermo de structura florum* (1718); Patrick Blair, *Botanick Essays* (1720); Richard Bradley, *Nouvelles Observations Phisyques* [sic] *et pratiques sur le jardinage et l'art de planter* (1756); Joseph Gottlieb Kölreuter, *Vorläufige Nachricht von einigen, das Geschlecht der Pflanzen betreffenden Versuchen un Beobachtungen* (1761); Wilhelm Friedrich von Gleichen, *Découvertes les plus nouvelles dans le règne végétal, ou Observations microscopiques sur les parties de la génération des plantes renfermées dans les fleurs* (1770); Johann Gottlieb Gleditsch, "Remarques abrégées"; Adolphe Brongniart, *Mémoire sur la fécondation et le développement de l'embryon dans les végétaux phanérogames* (1827); and many others concerning the discovery of pollen, the pollen tube, as well as the modes of fertilization of plants.

48. Christian Konrad Sprengel (1750–1816) and Thomas Andrew Knight (1759–1838). For Sprengel, see von Sachs, *Histoire de la botanique*, 430–35; for Knight, see J.-F. Leroy, *Histoire de notion de sexe chez les plantes*, 13. Sprengel emphasized in particular cross-fertilization (allogamy) between plants and stressed the role of mechanical factors of the milieu (wind, watercourses . . .) and especially insects for pollination. In addition, he studied how the general form and structure of flowers are explained by their relationship with pollinating insects: "the first attempt to explain the development of organic forms by the observation of the relations between these forms and the surrounding milieu," notes von Sachs, *Histoire de la botanique*, 430. Knight extends his analyses on the need for cross-fertilization and the role of insects in the transport of pollen.

49. In "Cuvier's Situation," 229, Foucault takes up this same distinction between the notions of influence or milieu in the eighteenth century, "meant to account for an excess of variety; they were concerned with factors of additional diversification; they served to account for the fact that one type could become another"; and the notion of "conditions of existence" in the nineteenth century, which was "concerned with the eventual impossibility of an organism continuing to live if it were not as it is and exactly where it is; it refers to that which constitutes the limit between life and death." This distinction should be linked to Foucault's analyses in *The Birth of the Clinic* and especially *The Order of Things*: what characterizes the break between natural history and biology is the introduction of the problem of death and of the limit: "the object of biology is that which is

capable of living and subject to dying." For Foucault, these conditions of existence refer both to internal systems of organic correlations—on which, for example, Georges Cuvier founds his classification of living beings— and to "conditions of existence understood as a threat coming from the milieu or a threat to the individual—of no longer being able to live—if the milieu changes. Biology is articulated through the analysis of the relations between the milieu and the living, that is, through ecology." For Foucault, this latter articulation is carried out most clearly in Darwin, but we know that it is precisely Darwin who will highlight Sprengel's work, referred to previously.

50. Foucault here calls on Leroy in particular, *Histoire de la notion de sex chez les plantes*, 24–25, (BNF, Box 45-C1). Nathanael Pringsheim "in 1855, shows not only that [antherozoids attach themselves to spores] but that they penetrate the spore; and that a membrane is then formed that prevents access to the egg of any other spermatozoon. So, fertilization can be defined precisely: *fusion of two material parts, the sexual cells.*" This mode of fertilization is "first established in the cryptogams" by Pringsheim. It is then extended by Eduard Adolf Strasburger in the phanerogams: "in 1884 [he] observes the fusion of one of male nuclei with the nucleus of the egg cell (since 1875 it was known that, for animals, there was fusion of the spermatic nucleus and the nucleus of the ovule)." Foucault in addition compiled a whole dossier, later it seems, on Strasburger (BNF, Box 45-C2), no doubt in preparation for his project for the Collège de France.

51. Here Foucault calls upon, notably, the fourth volume of *Introduction à la biologie* (Paris: Herman, 1967) entitled *Sexualité: Lignée germinale, spermatogenèse*, by Charles Houillon, 17–18, in order to trace the "discovery of the germ line." "There is a fundamental distinction between:—the cells that make up the organism—and those that reproduce it. The former have exhausted their possibilities; the others have conserved their original potentiality and can reproduce individuals. This distinction poses two problems:—that of the segregation of the germen and soma: existence in the course of development of a particular cellular material evolving on its own behalf. Hence the idea of a continuity of the germ line and of the potential immortality of the germ.—that of the independence of the germen vis-à-vis the soma and of the inheritance of acquired characteristics. It is Nussbaum (around 1880) who makes the first observations. In frogs

he observes large cells that keep their embryonic aspect for a long time: they preserve for a long time their reserve of vitellin and are situated in the region of the future gonads. For Nussbaum, this was the continuous strain of the species. Weissmann (in 1885) conceived not a strain, but an immortal substance passing from one generation to another. A part of this "germ-plasm" would be put in reserve in germinal cells in order to assure following generations (BNF, Box 45-C1). See also Yves Delage, *L'Hérédité et les grands problèmes de la biologie générale*, 2nd ed. (Paris: Schleicher frères, 1903 [1895]), 196–203 (BNF, Box 45-C3). The idea that the "germplasm" defines sexuality as a general function, subjacent to individuals, which are reduced to the state of "excrescence" or "quickly retracted pseudopods," is constantly emphasized by Foucault, in a clearly "anti-humanist" vein (see above, note 31, p. 246; "Cuvier's Situation"; "Il y aura scandale, mais . . .," 943; "Croître et multiplier," 968–70; and see below, "Sexuality, Reproduction, Individuality," pp. 211–216 and "Course Context," pp. 339–342).

52. "The individual is itself no more than an excrescence on the continuity of the germinal strain. Sexuality, instead of appearing at the point of the individual as the moment when growth becomes proliferation, becomes an underlying function in relation to this episode that is the individual" ("Cuvier's Situation," 235).

53. See in particular the beginning of chapter 26 of *Introductory Lectures to Psycho-Analysis*, in which Freud, elaborating the distinction between ego instincts and sexual instincts, notes that "Sexuality is . . . the single function of the living organism that extends beyond the individual and is concerned with his relation to the species. It is an unmistakable fact that it does not always, like the individual organism's other functions, bring it advantages, but, in return for an unusually high degree of pleasure, brings dangers that threaten the individual's life and often enough destroy it. It is probable, too, that quite special metabolic processes are necessary, differing from all others, in order to maintain a portion of the individual life as a disposition for its descendants. And finally, the individual organism, which regards itself as the main thing and its sexuality as a means, like any other, for its own satisfaction, is from the point of view of biology only an episode in a succession of generations, a short-lived appendage to a germplasm endowed with virtual immortality—like the temporary holder of an entail which will outlast him" (*CWP*, vol. 16, 413–14; BNF, Box 39-C3).

54. This whole conclusion should be compared with the discussion that follows "Cuvier's Situation," 236, which offers an analogous but even more explicit exposition concerning what he calls " 'reactions' in the strong sense of the term, that is, in its Nietzschean sense" provoked by the eruption of death, sexuality, and history as biological facts, which makes it possible to see clearly to whom his criticisms are addressed—that is, at the same time, Hegelianism, phenomenology, existentialism, and a certain humanist Marxism. On the one hand, his target is those who assert (after Heidegger but especially Sartre) that "death is the fulfilment of life . . . in death, life finds its meaning . . . death transforms life into fate"; on the other, those who declare (after Hegel, Ricoeur, and a whole "anthropology of sexuality"—see above, Clermont-Ferrand course, pp. 13–14) that "through sexuality the individual can . . . develop itself, overflow itself, and enter into communication with others through love, within time, and through lineage"; and finally a whole philosophy of history, from Hegel to Sartre, that aims, through "the use of a certain form of dialectic . . . to give it the unity of a meaning and the fundamental unity of a free consciousness with its project" (236). These analyses may be brought together with the Tunis course of 1966–1967, in which Foucault similarly evoked "all those great blows to man's narcissism of the discovery of biophysiological determinations, the determining character of sexuality," etc., and how these blows were "compensated for by an exaltation of man as origin and center of all significations. Since he knows that he must die, that he is not free, [and] that the largest part of himself escapes him, he consoles himself by thinking that it is his existence that gives meaning to everything." Foucault's project at this time, in the lineage of Bataille, seems rather to be to mobilize the "knowledge" of sexuality to destroy these consolations: "knowledge is not made in order to console: it disappoints, disturbs, incises, wounds" ("Croître et multiplier" [1970], 967). See "Course Context," pp. 339–342.

LECTURE 7

Sexual Utopia

I. Distinguishing utopias and heterotopias. Sexual heterotopias: heterogeneity of sexual norms in different places in society. Primitive societies and ours: some institutions are alternators of sexuality. Sometimes linked to utopian themes: the witches' Sabbath as mixture of utopia and heterotopia. II. Summary of introduction: relations between utopias and heterotopias. Homotopic and heterotopic utopias. Sexual utopias: importance of the sexual theme in utopias (Sade, Campanella); either integrative utopia: return to a normal sexuality prevented by society; or transgressive utopia: a radically de-normalized sexuality (Sade, The Story of O*). Presence of these utopian elements in Marcuse and Reich. III. Comparative analysis of transgressive and integrative utopias: 1. desire-difference-subject: sovereignty of desire instituting an absolute difference (Sade,* The Story of O*) versus harmonious distribution of differences suppressing desire (Comte, Fourier, Rétif de La Bretonne); 2. law and disorder: asocial and unnatural, asymmetrical, and disordered law in the transgressive utopia versus restitution to sexuality of its natural law in which conduct sticks to the rule in the integrative utopia. IV. The problem of sexual revolution: Marcuse or the double utopia. Liberating normal sexuality alienated by society. Criticism of different postulates of Marcuse: how they diverge from Freudian analysis.*

[1/76]^a   *1. Distinguishing utopias and heterotopias*¹

– Utopias: placeless places; acts of discourse; conduct inter-mediate between criticism, reform, and reverie.

– Heterotopias: regions of space, institutions involving a number of specific conducts, divergent from everyday conduct. Roman thermae, fairgrounds, prisons.² (Likewise, heterochronies like festivals).³

There is a study to be made of sexual heterotopias.

Some comments:

– Sexual behavior is doubtless among the most sensitive to change of place (and time), and most tied to the spatiotemporal conditions in which it is carried out:

- maybe there is a physiological or psychological normal-ity of sexual behavior;

[2/77]
- in fact, there is [not] *one* but *a number* of quite different sociological normalities.^b Sexual behavior (in the broad sense: forms of approach and seduction; sexual practice; subsequent relations) is not the same at home and out-side: in military service and in civilian life; on holiday and during the year . . .

– This spaatiotemporal heterogeneity of sexual behavior has perhaps a fairly universal value for it to be found in most cultures:⁴

- houses for the young where boys are sent at puberty;
- places where unmarried young people can make love;
- system of closure or reclusion for women who cannot make love (during menstruation, pregnancy);

---

a The figures on the left indicate Foucault's numbering.

b Foucault appears to have omitted part of the sentence: we reestablish "not." Underlined in the manuscript.

- taboo periods after death;[5]
- festivals.

– There are elements in our system that are isomorphous to   [3/78]
elements found in primitive societies:

- young people who "want to enjoy themselves": exogamy.
  Sexuality outside one's home, at once explicit, extolled
  in words, and no doubt not very active (it is no doubt
  not found in countries with strong endogamy like Arab
  countries);
- military service: period of sexual and civic initiation
  (the three great training institutions established by the
  bourgeoisie: primary school, barracks, brothel).[6]

– But whatever the analogies, we have a very complex spatiotemporal system of sexuality:

- which modifies the major prohibitions: homosexuality (prisons, colleges, some but not all forms of military communities); incest (father-daughter in the
  country);[7]
- and which defines fields or spaces of specific sexual
  normativity.

– Anyway, in this heteromorphism, we need to distinguish   [4/79]
regions specifically intended to change sexual behavior: military service or hospitals are not intended to produce this change
(although there is a very specific hospital sexuality). This change
is entailed solely by the link between sexuality and military service or illness. On the other hand, there are institutions whose
function is precisely to introduce this change: the love courts,[8]
brothels. These institutions function as alternators of sexuality.
They are sexual heterotopias.

- Sometimes they are mixed with other institutions:
  or rather there are institutions with mixed functions:
  Roman thermae, holiday villages.[9]

- Sometimes they are found mixed with or underpinned by imaginary formations that play the role of program or privileged expression:

[5/80]
  - literature of love, courtly romances in the courts of love: they are, in a sense, their product or expression, and they serve as their program. It is a matter of giving life to this fictional character;
  - the themes of chivalry in homosexual societies of the sixteenth and seventeenth centuries.[10]

This mixture of institution and the imaginary, of ritual and fantasy, achieves its most enigmatic form with the witches' Sabbath: practice[c] dreamily recounted, really condemned. The witches' Sabbath is between utopia and heterotopia.[11]

- Its utopian character is proclaimed:
  - by the systematic reversal to which it subjects the real institution of the mass;
  - by the fantastical character of the episodes: animal metamorphoses, spatial transports;
  - by the role of discourse: "literary tradition."
- Its heterotopian character:
  - by the semi-institutionalized group form probably taken by the witches (association, tradition, recruitment, formula);

[6/81]
  - by the regularity of forms and places;
  - by the reactions of the milieu (which excludes witchcraft).

The intertwining of the utopian and heterotopian is marked even more deeply by the fact:

- that the "other place" of the Sabbath is reached by the "utopian" means of diabolic transport;

---

c The following terms crossed out: "dreamt, execrated, condemned and maybe practiced."

- that the utopia is strengthened, if not constituted, by procedures of exclusion, acts of accusation, forced confessions, and condemnations.

Introduction   [7/82]ᵈ

1. Heterotopia and utopia

a.   Heterotopias are real places, but they are often underpinned by ideological structures. And with, as an intermediate element, as a shifter of ideology on the institution, *utopias*.ᵉ,[12]

– This is not always the case: barracks as heterotopia with their class functioning [and] their rationalist and egalitarian ideology (opposed to the revolutionary idea of the nation in arms). Practically no utopian elements. But the Foreign Legion functions with a utopian relay: city of outcasts; community without memory; civil fraternity.

   – There are heterotopias with a strong utopian content:
   - familial utopia in asylums at the end of the eighteenth century;[13]
   - vacation villages;
   - gardens and animal collections.[14]
      Ideology is present above all through the utopia.   [8/83]
   – There are heterotopias that are the exact realization of utopias:
   - Cabet;[15]
   - Californian utopias;[16]
   - prophetic or millenarian groups.[17]

---

d The end of page 6 is blank, and one passes on to a new sheet marked 7, which summarizes and extends the preceding exposition. As it is not, strictly speaking, a case of a variant, we have included the sheets that follow in the rest of the text.

e Underlined in the manuscript.

b. Conversely, there are heterotopian utopias as opposed to homotopian utopias.

- Homotopian utopias: those that present themselves as the equivalent, alternative, or transformation of society: a different society, similar to ours, in which all the elements are found again, but displaced and in a different system of relations (Swift,[18] A[uguste] Comte[19]).
- Heterotopian utopias: those that represent a heterotopian place, that is to say external to our society, but present within it, at any rate, alongside it (Sade, *The Story of O*).[20]
- Utopias that imagine a transition from one to the other. Fourier: the Phalanstery, which is the first transition to the member state (*l'état sociétaire*) that will itself give rise to H[armony].[21]

[9/84] So there is an intertwining of utopia and heterotopia.

Spatial difference as the site of imaginary precipitation. Whereas for a long time this was assured by temporal difference, loss of the past (N.B.: the eighteenth and nineteenth centuries as moment of confrontation of the heterotopian imaginary and the heterochronic imaginary: at the beginning of the nineteenth century, the terror novel and historical novel. *Le Château des Pyrénées*).[22] It seems that today the heterotopian system of the imagination prevails in science fiction and the detective or spy novel (a different world in the same place; other social relations beneath the apparent ones).

[10/85][f]
[11/86] *2. Sexual utopias.*[23]

a. Most heterotopias include a modification of sexual behavior: from suppression (convent) to exaltation (brothel) by way of

---

f Page 10 contains a variant of the section that follows on page 11, but entirely crossed out. We have included it as an appendix to this lecture (see below, pp. 000–000).

natural sexuality (see the "treatment" of vacation villages).[24] And they often include utopian elements: a model of perfect social functioning:

- the pure city of minds in the convent;
- man in the state of nature, the vacation village ("Adamic retraining").

   b. Most utopias include sexual elements:

- either as the main element: Sade;[25]
- or as component. Campanella:
- the magistrate Amour who sees to the beauty of the race;[26]
- freedom of sexual relations, except for reproduction;[27]
- mothers put in rooms with statues of great men. Astrological time of mating.[28]

These elements of sexual utopia may function in two ways.   [12/87]

- As criticism of real society inasmuch as it does not allow a normal sexuality. That is to say, a sexuality that is happy for individuals [and] adapted to the requirements and functioning of society. [Real] sexuality is criticized as the point at which society and the individual become enemies of themselves and each other.

  Hence the following process in these utopian elements: a reform of society that modifies sexuality; hence a sexuality that makes individual-society relations transparent and easy; hence, finally, a good social functioning. Sexuality is society in the bodies of individuals; or it is the individual immediately and fully socialized. For example: the voyage of Bougainville is the integrative utopia.[29]

- But they may also function as a challenge to so-called nor-   [13/88]
  mal sexuality, inasmuch as this normality is fixed arbitrarily by society (its regulations, prejudices, its religious and moral laws). These utopias bring to light a de-normalized,

de-socialized sexuality; which becomes, on its own, the law of reconstruction of interindividual relationships.

- Sade: where disorder becomes the rule:
  ° of individual behavior (anyone who refuses disorder, or even hesitates, is condemned);
  ° of interindividual behavior (one must be able to do and suffer all that the others desire);[30]
  ° of the pact whereby sovereigns lay down the rule of disorder between them.[31]
- *The Story of O*:
  ° in which the conduct of enslavement, gift, agreement, and established or accepted regulation are elements of eroticism;
  ° on the basis of which a fantastic and secret society is formed, with its signs of recognition, hierarchies, and places.[32]

[14/89]   This is the transgressive utopia.[33]

These are only some "pure" elements. In fact, in most utopias these elements are mixed. With, at exactly midway, the figure of a society that is "normal" due solely to the fact that sexuality is de-normalized in it. Nonmonogamous, nonreproductive, nonheterosexual sexuality → and society becomes perfect.

Example. J[acques] Sadeur and hermaphrodite society.[34]

It is important to clarify how these elements function since they are found in Marcuse and Reich:

- use of Marxism: in order to show that it is society that prevents the functioning of a normal sexuality;
- use of Freud in order to show that what is called normal sexuality is in fact not determined by a law peculiar to sexuality, but by society.

Marcuse and Reich do not go through utopian themes in order
to constitute a theory of sexuality; they use epistemological fields
in order to constitute utopias.[35]

Comparative analysis of transgressive and integrative utopias   [15/90]

1. Desire, difference, and the subject

   a. Transgressive utopias include:
- A sovereign subject in relation to whom the utopia
  is implemented. It is set out around him, and it is his
  desire—in its singularity, in its limitlessness—that constitutes its law:[36]
  - the four masters of the *120 Days*;[37]
  - the anonymous subject of the *Pornographe*;[38]
  - the double system of *The Story of O*: around the mas-
    ters [and] around O.[39]
- Which implies an irreversibility of relations, without
  equality or complementarity. It is not difference that
  gives rise to desire, it is desire that gives rise to difference. As soon as I desire you, you are the heterono-
  mous correlative of this desire. Hence, at the end, death,
  whether the sovereign desires death, or desire disappearing, its correlate just has to disappear.
  [*In the margin*: "see the second possible end to *The Story
  of O*."][40]

   b. On the other hand, integrative utopias: [16/91]
- no sovereignty but horizontal distributions of complementarities and choice.

      a. Free choice. Rétif. The Megapatagons in *La Découverte
  australe*.[41] The male/female division, each side of a barrier; the day of the festival: two lines, and one chooses.[42]

b. Complementarity: Fourier, Comte.

Woman	Man
Domestic life	Theoretical
Religion	Practice
Intrafamilial	Extrafamilial
Feeling	Intelligence
Sympathy	Synthesis
Induction	Deduction[43]

Reciprocity of two great axioms: no society without government → man; no government without religion → woman.[44]

- Consequently, desire is not the differentiating element; it is difference, [the play][g] of oppositions, of complementarities, that gives rise to desire. So that desire occurs only in difference. And the arrangement of differences, their exact distribution in a table, or in a stable figure, suppresses desire.

[17/92]   See the voyage of a harmonious tribe, the festival of the Megapatagons.[45]

- And finally, the elision of desire: in Comte;[46] in Foigny and the myth of the hermaphrodites.[47]

Integrative utopia: the system of differences as site of the elision of desire;

[Transgressive utopia][h]: sovereignty of desire as constitutive moment of irreversible differences.

2. Law and disorder

Sexual utopias are never anarchic (not even in the most benign, immediate, and natural form, as in Diderot, where there is honor,

---

g The word written here is illegible. We have added "the play" out of concern for readability.
h Our addition, for balance with the preceding sentence.

the rule of hospitality, the obligation to have children).⁴⁸ But this non-anarchy does not function in the same way in the transgressive and the integrative utopia.

a. In the transgressive utopia   [18/93]

– It is inaugurated and continued through a series of breaks regarding nature:

- Spatial break: *Pornographe*, *The 120 Days*.
- The gift in *The Story of O* (so that love is eradicated).⁴⁹
- Sexual practice systematically diverted away from its natural forms. And this is imposed as a law. So that this sexuality is not a return to an animal nature but a systematically developed non-animality.
- A sort of constructed monstrosity (the owl at the end of *The Story of O*).⁵⁰

– So we are dealing with a regulation that is neither of nature nor of animality. A regulation that is not calculated for society, that is both imposed and accepted by sovereigns as well as subjects.

The villain,⁵¹ for Sade, is someone who lays down the rule for himself and others, the rule that seizes hold of him, runs through him, commands him, determines him entirely, and is the rule of his disorder. The victim is the one who accepts as the rule for himself the disruption of every rule: I shall be what you will want me to be.

Hence the appearance of a strange law of sexuality: [19/94]

- both strict and disordered;
- not homogeneous for oneself and others. Nontransferable;
- not conforming to nature, or to society;
- closer to death than to life, to monstrosity than to nature; to aberration than to reason.

[The interest for psychoanalysis of which they form something like the anticipation.]⁵²

b. The integrative utopia

– This is the return of sexuality to nature: either plant and animal nature (see *Voyage de Bougainville*); or human nature, calculated in its temperamental components (Fourier). In any case, for reproductive ends: eugenics or preservation of society (Comte).[53]

– Thus, returned to its natural law, sexuality appears as that which cancels the rule as rule. Sexual rules are internalized without being repressive. See Fourier's combinatorial system.[54] As a result, social rules are integrated as pleasure.

[20/95] The man of the integrative utopia is someone for whom regulation no longer functions as a rule. But as determination of his individuality, and which, consequently, makes sexuality function as a calibrated moment.

The result of integrative utopias is that the moment of desire and the instance of the rule are removed from sexuality—thanks to which nature and society can communicate in the individual. The result of transgressive utopias is to bring out desire as an absolutely differentiating principle, and the rule as an element that is not internal to nature, society, or the subject.

In other words, integrative utopias constitute a synthetic subject that joins nature and society in the form of the individual without desire. Transgressive utopias establish the irreducibility of the desiring subject in a system of rules that belongs neither to nature nor to society.

[9/96][i] [We can see how what will be one of the major difficulties of the problem of sexuality-revolution takes shape.

• The theme of an alienated, perverted sexuality to which future society will restore normal functioning.

---

i There is a sudden change in the numbering here. Foucault wrote "9" then crossed it out. The following page has "10" not crossed out, and the one after an "11" crossed out. It is certain anyway that these sheets form a unit. Moreover, Foucault marked out this section (*a posteriori*, it seems) by putting it in square brackets.

- The theme that bourgeois society, through its institutions (marriage, family), has defined norms of sexuality that are seen as the truth of its nature.

Hence the ambiguity: is sexuality, in its currently "normal" form, an institution naturalized by an ideological operation and coding? Or are its perverse, neurotic, and abnormal forms the result of a social relation in which the individual is alienated?

These two themes are found intertwined in many texts that are more utopian, at least more ideological, than political. An example: Marcuse:

- The presently accepted limits of sexuality (marriage, procreation) are defined by a society in which human labor is exploited. Thus, a whole range of sexual behaviors that are abnormal only in relation to this delimitation are condemned as perverse. This is surplus-repression.[55]
- But what will we find when these limits are removed (and   [10/97] this will only happen in a new type of society)? A society that tolerates all perversions, like sadism and necrophilia? No, but a sexuality freed from these perversions, a non-sadistic sexuality, etc. In short, normal. Let's say: a sexuality broadened on the basis of its own norms.

Marcuse, the double utopia in a single discourse:

- How must society be transformed so that it no longer imposes its arbitrary norms on sexuality?
- How, in such a transformed society, will [sexuality]ʲ rediscover itself and do so through a sort of right of nature, a normativity that will no longer exclude but really suppress perversions?

---

j Foucault writes "society."

Hence the quasi-explicit splitting of perversions in Marcuse.

[11/98]
- The "good" perversions that, as a result of bourgeois society, currently fall outside the limits of normal sexuality. These must be reintegrated: they will disappear as perversions but will figure as real practices in normal sexuality. Homosexuality.
- The "bad" ones that are excluded by bourgeois normal sexuality only insofar as they are produced by it and its illegitimate limits (sadism). These will really disappear as practices and, if by some chance they occur, they will still retain their status as perversion.]

[NP/99][k]   *Marcuse's postulates*

1. No antinomy between work and the pleasure principle (but between the pleasure principle and a reality principle whose form and content are determined, for the most part, by the performance principle).[56]
Postulate of social ethics.[1]
[*In the margin*: "this against the Freudian theme: unhappiness and work"]
2. No antinomy between polymorphous sexuality and genitality (but between a genitality that has been made exclusive and partial formations).[57]
Postulate of psychobiological normality.
[*In the margin*: "this against the Freudian theme of exclusion of the instincts"]
3. Correlation between several systems of differences: repression/surplus-repression; modification/exclusion; pleasure/suffering.

---

k This is a final separate sheet, recto-verso, with the title "Marcuse's postulates."
1 Replaces "hedonism," crossed out.

Anthropological postulate: there is a socio-natural truth of man [. . .].[m]

[*In the margin*: "this against the Freudian theme of repression"][58]

4. Correlation between disappearance of destructive instincts and strengthening of Eros.

Economic postulate.

[*In the margin*: "against the theme of the interweaving of Eros and aggression"].[59]

Now, in all of these theses we see: [NP/100]

• The critique of a society unable to ensure the happy functioning of sexuality (but this assumes a core of normality, implicitly defined).

• The reverse critique of a normal sexuality that is only the result of social pressure.

*

APPENDIX TO LECTURE 7

[The following is page 10/85, which is a variant of page 11/86 (see above, p. 260). In the manuscript, the whole page was crossed out.]

1. Sexual heterotopias and utopias:

A. Every heterotopia involves a more or less profound modification of sexual behavior:

– disappearance: convent;

– Exaltation: brothel.

(Hence the overemphasized character of the convent brothel.)[60]

---

m Passage crossed out: "4. Distinction between a generalized sexuality and perversions (costly for society) like sadism."

- Heterotopias often include a sexual utopia:
  - Desexualized fraternity of the convent: relationship to God, to Christ, to the mother;
  - Sexual utopias in the brothel: slave society;
  - Utopia of natural sexuality in vacation villages.
- Most utopias have a sexual component:
  - either as the main element: *The 120 Days of Sodom*;
  - or as a particular element: Fourier, Campanella.

*

1. This lecture on utopias and heterotopias extends Foucault's reflections of 1966–1967 on the concept of heterotopia as distinct from utopia. In his preface to *The Order of Things* (London: Tavistock, 1970 [1966]), Foucault introduced the notion of heterotopia with reference to Jorge Luis Borges's text on the Chinese encyclopedia and contrasted heterotopias, which "are disturbing . . . because they secretly undermine language" by introducing radical differences, ruining the common place on which language relies, and utopias, which console and "permit fables and discourse: they run with the very grain of language" (p. xviii). This notion of heterotopia is developed at the same time, and always in tension with that of utopia, in two radio talks for France Culture in December 1966: "Le corps utopique" and "Les hétérotopies" (*Utopies et hétéropies: Deux conférences radiophonique diffusées sur France Culture les 7 et 21 décembre 1966*, CD, Bry-sur-Marne, INA, 2006; see "Les utopies réelles ou lieux et autres lieux" and "Le corps utopique," in M. Foucault, *Oeuvres* [Paris: Gallimard, 2015], 1238–57); then in a lecture "Des espaces autres" (*DÉ*, 2), given at the Centre d'études architecturales on March 14, 1967 (trans. J. Miskowiec, "Of Other Spaces," *Diacritics* 16, no. 1 [Spring 1986]). On this occasion, utopias and heterotopias are contrasted insofar as the former are "sites with no real place" ("Of Other Spaces," 3), a "place outside any place" ("Le corps utopique," 1249), whereas heterotopias are "real places . . . formed in the very founding of society. . . . Places of this kind are outside of all places, even though it may be possible to indicate their location in reality" ("Of Other Spaces," 3–4), "utopias that have a precise and real place" and play a role of "counter-spaces," "absolutely

different places" present in every society ("Les utopies réelles," 1238–39). The whole of the following passage is inspired by these lectures, stressing the question of sexuality, which, in the context of post–May 1968, was not at all innocent (see "Course Context," pp. 342–345). On the notion of heterotopia in Foucault, see, for example, Daniel Defert, "Foucault, Space, and the Architects," in *Politics/Poetics: Documenta X. The Book* (Ostfildern-Ruit, Germany: Cantz, 1997), 274–83; Peter Johnson, "Unravelling Foucault's "Different Spaces," *History of the Human Sciences* 19, no. 4 (2006): 75–90; Mariangela Palladino and John Miller, eds., *The Globalization of Space: Foucault and Heterotopia* (London: Pickering and Chatto, 2015).

2. Prisons will be the object of an obviously very different treatment, forming part of an analysis of disciplinary power and penal institutions in *Discipline and Punish: The Birth of the Prison*, trans. Alan Sheridan (London: Penguin, 1977), and *The Punitive Society: Lectures at the Collège de France 1972–1973*, trans. Graham Burchell, ed. Bernard E. Harcourt, English series ed. Arnold I. Davidson (London: Palgrave Macmillan, 2015). In the typology put forward in "Of Other Spaces," Foucault places them among heterotopias of "deviation." He mentions hammams, saunas, and fairgrounds (7).

3. On heterochronies, see "Of Other Spaces," 6–7.

4. This observation is part of the more general project that Foucault assigns to "heterotopology," which places it in a structuralist perspective: every society entails heterotopias ("there is probably not a single culture in the world that does not constitute heterotopias"); societies can be classified in terms of certain types of heterotopia ("Of Other Spaces," 4).

5. These heterotopias correspond to what Foucault calls "crisis heterotopias" ("Of Other Spaces," 4). The "houses for the young" (*bukumatula* in Melanesia), where young adolescent boys are sent at puberty with their "sweethearts," is described by Bronislaw Malinowski in *Sex and Repression in Savage Society* (London: Kegan Paul, Trench, Trubner, 1937), 67, and *The Sexual Life of Savages in North-Western Melanesia* (New York: Readers League of America, 1929), 69 *et seq.*

6. See "Of Other Spaces," 4.

7. In Malinowski, for example, *Sex and Repression in Savage Society*, 66n1, we find the idea that father/daughter incest is fairly frequent among peasants in Western countries.

8. On love courts, see Jacques Lafitte-Houssat, *Troubadours et Cours d'amour* (Paris: PUF, 1950).

9. Vacation villages ("Club Méditerranée") are referred to in several places in "Of Other Spaces," 7, and "Les utopies réelles," 1243–44, where they are presented as a "temporal (*chronique*) heterotopia" mixing "two forms of heterotopia," that of the festival and that of "the eternity of accumulating time." We recall that the Club Méditerranée was created at the beginning of the 1950s.

10. Foucault is no doubt alluding to the various homosexual societies formed in the seventeenth century, such as the society founded around 1681 by the Chevalier de Lorraine, Biran, Tallard, and others (described in the publication by Jean Hervez, alias Raoul Vèze, of the *Anecdotes pour servir à l'histoire secrète des Ebugors: Statut des sodomites au XVIIe siècle* [Paris: Bibliothèque des curieux, 1912], 3–32; BNF files), which in fact took the form of knightly orders, publishing statutes, requiring vows, with initiation procedures, grand masters of the Order, etc. Sometimes the valorization of devotion between lovers was added to this organization modeled on the knightly orders. For the eighteenth century, see also by Jean Hervez, *Les Sociétés d'amour au XVIIIᵉ siècle: Les Sociétés où l'on cause d'amour, académies galantes . . .* (Paris: H. Daragon, 1906). Foucault appears to have been interested very early on in homosexual culture between the sixteenth and eighteenth centuries, creating a dossier on the subject (BNF, Box 42a-C1) titled "sodomy," in which he compiled a whole set of documents on homosexuality at the court of Henry III, pamphlets and epigrams of the eighteenth century, information on secret homosexual societies, but also on representations of "sodomites" and their repression.

11. Foucault looked at the problem of witchcraft and the witches' Sabbath on several occasions (see above, lecture 5, note 13, pp. 218–219). On this question, see Robert Mandrou's study, which had recently appeared, *Magistrats et Sorciers de France au XVIIᵉ siècle: Une analyse de psychologie historique* (Paris: Plon, 1968), and especially Carlo Ginzburg, *Ecstasies: Deciphering the Witches' Sabbath*, trans. Raymond Rosenthal (Chicago: University of Chicago Press, 2004 [1989]).

12. The relation between ideology and utopia, two themes at the heart of the Vincennes course, constitutes the fundamental problem of the work of Karl Mannheim, *Ideology and Utopia* (London: Routledge & Kegan Paul,

2002 [1936]). Although Foucault makes no direct reference to this work, we should bear in mind that it was then an obligatory reference in political debates on utopia and revolution, in particular in connection with the reflections of Marcuse (see, for example, "The End of Utopia" in *Five Lectures*, trans. Jeremy J. Shapiro and Shierry M. Weber [Boston: Beacon Press, 1970]). Moreover, Foucault's analysis here of the relations among utopia, ideology, and heterotopia can be compared to what Mannheim says about this in the part "Utopia, Ideology, and the Problem of Reality" in *Ideology and Utopia*.

13. See how Foucault describes the Retreat founded by the Quakers in England at the end of the eighteenth century: as a contractual coalition that, at the same time, "took its place in the myth of the patriarchal family . . . a rigorous family, without weakness or complacency, but fair, in accordance with the great image of the biblical family" (*History of Madness*, trans. Jonathan Murphy and Jean Khalfa [London: Routledge, 2006], 474). In *Psychiatric Power* (ed. Jacques Lagrange, trans. Graham Burchell [London: Palgrave Macmillan, 208], 123, and more broadly, 93–142), Foucault distances himself from this "rather loose hypothesis, which I have myself maintained, that the asylum was constituted through the extension of the family model," to rework in a more complex way the relations between family and asylum, "sovereignty of the family" and "asylum discipline."

14. On gardens, see "Of Other Spaces," 6; the garden is described here as a "sort of happy, universalizing heterotopia" whose vocation is to represent the whole world in its symbolic perfection. See also "Les utopies réelles," 1242.

15. Foucault is referring to Étienne Cabet (1788–1856), member of the Charbonnerie, deputy for the Côte-d'Or, founder of the workers' paper *Le Populaire*—which, under the name Francis Adams, published his work describing a communist utopia (*Voyage et Aventures de Lord William Carisdall en Icarie*, 2 vols. [Paris: Hippolyte Souverain, 1840])—who then tried, from 1847 to 1848, to realize his utopia in the United States. On this subject, and more generally on the utopian communities of the nineteenth century inspired by Cabet, Fourier, and others, see Jean-Christian Petitfils, *Les Communautés utopistes au XIXe siècle* (Paris: Pluriel, 2011). Foucault compiled a whole dossier on the problem of sexuality and marriage in Icarie (BNF, Box 39-C4), drawing on Cabet's texts (*Voyage et Aventures* . . .; and

Colonie icarienne aux États-Unis d'Amerique: Sa constitution, ses lois, sa situation matérielle et morale . . ., Paris: Author, 1856).

16. This refers in particular to the various "hippy" communities that flourished in California in the 1960s, such as Gorda Mountain, Hog Farm, and Esalen, which are part of the long history of utopian communities in the American West since the nineteenth century. On this subject, see Robert V. Hine, *California's Utopian Colonies* (San Marino, CA: Huntington Library, 1953) and, on the communities of the 1960s, Timothy Miller, *The 60s Communes: Hippies and Beyond* (Syracuse, NY: Syracuse University Press, 1990). Foucault consulted Hine's work and analyzed, particularly from the point of view of the sexual question, the colony of Fountain Grove founded in 1875 by T. Harris (BNF, Box 39-C4). Harris thought that a golden age had existed, founded on the union of man and woman—a lost golden age, but one that could be found again by calling upon the "pivot man," that is to say himself, through whom God revealed himself. For Harris, God is bisexual, and man can rejoin God through sexuality in its most spiritual aspects. It was on this principle that the Fountain Grove community was founded; it organized purely spiritual unions, forbidding any carnal relationship between the couples (Hine, *California's Utopian Colonies*, 12–32).

17. Mannheim made these millenarian groups (in particular the Hussites, Thomas Müntzer, and the Anabaptists) an essential turning point in his study on *Ideology and Utopia*, presenting them as the "first form of the utopian mentality." Foucault will return to these prophetic and millenarian groups of the end of the Middle Ages and the beginning of the modern period in *Security, Territory, Population*, ed. Michel Sennellart, trans. Graham Burchell (New York: Palgrave Macmillan, 2007), 191–226, when he will develop the concept of "counter-conducts" opposed to pastoral power. On these groups, see notably Norman Cohn, *The Pursuit of the Millennium: Revolutionary Millenarians and Mystical Anarchists of the Middle Ages* (London: Pimlico, 2004 [1957]).

18. Jonathan Swift, *Gulliver's Travels* (London: Benjamin Motte, 1726). *Gulliver's Travels* works, in fact, both as criticism of English society of the time and as a reservoir of possible utopias. Foucault was particularly interested in marriage in the Houyhnhnm, where the institution is organized above all for the preservation of the color and beauty of the race; neither seduction nor financial questions are involved in the marriage, which is

subject solely to the will of the parents and friends of the future couple (BNF, Box 39-C4)

19. On August Comte, see above, p. 263 et seq.; for the sexual dimension, see René de Planhol, *Les Utopistes de l'amour: L'amour sentimental des platonisants et des précieuses* . . . (Paris: Garnier frères, 1921), 238 *et seq.* Foucault worked on the question of the status of women and the role of sexuality and the family in Comte's utopia from [the time of] his Clermont-Ferrand course (see above, lecture 1, p. 10, and note 15, pp. 20–21). Furthermore, he had compiled a dossier on this theme, entitled "Comte: La Femme" (BNF, Box 45-C2) based in particular on Comte, *Système de politique positive* (Osnabrück, Germany: O. Zeller, 1967 [1851]), vols. 2 and 4.

20. On Sade and *Histoire d'O.*, revised and corrected edition with preface by J. Paulhan (Paris: Pauvert, 1972 [1954]); English translation, *The Story of O* (New York: Ballantine Books, 2013), see below. *The Story of O* is a novel published in 1954 by Pauline Réage (pseudonym of Anne Desclos, alias Dominique Aury), set around three main characters—O and her masters, René and Sir Stephen—in a sadomasochist universe in a Roissy chateau and in Paris. *The Story of O* was published by Pauvert, a publisher involved at the same time in the publication of the *Oeuvres complètes* of Sade, and was the object of, in particular, a preface by Jean Paulham, editor of *La Nouvelle Revue française* (*NRF*) and Dominique Aury's lover, as well as an analysis by Georges Bataille, "Le paradoxe de l'érotisme," *NRF* 3, no. 29 (1955): 834–39, which compared it with the work of Sade and Pierre Klossowski's novel *Robert ce soir* (Paris: Minuit, 1953). In his analysis, Bataille describes *The Story of O* as the very example of what Foucault initially understood as "heterotopia": a form of radical alterity—that of eroticism and transgression—which undermines language and considers it in the alternative of repetition or silence—final, deceptive silence, which in *The Story of O* is embodied in the novel's relatively brutal halt or, in the alternative end offered by the author, in O's death.

21. On Charles Fourier, see below, p. 263 et seq., and de Planhol, *Les Utopistes de l'amour*, 208 *et seq.*, for the sexual questions. For Fourier, in fact, the application of his principles of organization of society, and of the phalanstery in particular, should enable a transition from social chaos to "universal harmony." Foucault compiled a whole dossier on the sexual and passional dimensions of Fourier's reflections (BNF, Box 39-C4), which

draws in particular on *L'Harmonie universelle et le phalanstère* (1849), the *Théorie des quatre mouvements et des destinées générales* (1808), and the *Théorie de l'unité universelle* (1841–1843). At the time, Foucault was interested in Fourier from the point of view of sexual utopia, putting it in tension with Sade; Fourier was the object of renewed interest in this sense on the part of several authors close to Foucault. Between 1967 and 1970, Roland Barthes published his studies on Sade ("L'arbre du crime," *Tel Quel* 28 [1967]), Loyola ("Comment parler à Dieu?" *Tel Quel* 38 [1969]), and Fourier ("Vivre avec Fourier," *Critique*, no. 281 [1970]), which he will bring together in *Sade, Fourier, Loyola*, trans. Richard Miller (Berkeley: University of California Press, 1989 [1976]). René Schérer, Foucault's colleague at Vincennes, has been interested in sexual utopia in Fourier since 1967: he published an anthology of Fourier's texts, *L'Attraction passionnée* (Paris: Pauvert, 1967), and since then has constantly reflected on sexual liberation as a key element in the realization of utopias: *Charles Fourier ou la Contestation globale* (Paris: Seghers, 1970). In 1970, a special issue of *Topique* on Fourier appeared, with a preface by Maurice Blanchot and a contribution from Pierre Klossowski on "Sade et Fourier." This revival of interest owes much to the work undertaken from 1966 by Simone Debout, who edited Fourier's *Oeuvres complètes* in Anthropos (1966–1968) and brought to light a fundamental text in his work, devoted precisely to sexual and amorous relationships, *Le Nouveau Monde amoureux* (published in 1967 with a long preface by Debout), which will play a key role in the mobilization of Fourier in the debates on sexual liberation and feminism after 1968. See, for example, Simone Debout, "Le désir et la boussole: Le système sociétaire chez Charles Fourier," *Cahiers internationaux de sociologie* 43 (1967): 159–68, and, on the context of the publication and reception of this work in 1968, Michel Bozon, "Fourier, le *Nouveau Monde amoureux* et mai 1968: Politique des passions, égalité des sexes et science sociale," *Clio: Histoire, femmes et sociétés* 22 (2005): 123–49.

22. This is not Fréderic Soulié's novel *Château des Pyrénées*, but the novel *Romance of the Pyrenees*, by Catherine Cuthbertson, long attributed to Ann Radcliffe, published in England in 1803 (BNF, Box 39-C4). This novel was analyzed by Pierre Macherey in *A Theory of Literary Production*, trans. Geoffrey Wall (London: Routledge & Kegan Paul, 1978), chap. 6, "Front and Back." Victoria, orphan of Count Ariosto, is captured by bandits and taken, through a desolate landscape in which steep rocks and dark forests make a

break with the rest of the world, and then through a cave over fast-running water, to a very old castle built by Catalan princes at the time of the Arab conquest. Foucault formed a dossier, "Places (*Lieux*)," in which he compiled a set of examples of spatial differences invested by the imagination between the end of the eighteenth and the middle of the nineteenth century (inn, castle, convent, and prison, glacier and mountain, etc.) (BNF, Box 39-C4).

23. Foucault compiled an important dossier on these sexual utopias, as much in the literature of the seventeenth to nineteenth centuries, and the social theory of the nineteenth century (Charles Fourier, Étienne Cabet, Auguste Comte, Flora Tristan), as in Herbert Marcuse (BNF, Box 39-C4). He no doubt also consulted René de Planhol's *Les Utopistes de l'amour*, which makes an inventory of the various sexual utopias in France between the Renaissance and the end of the nineteenth century. He may have been familiar with the article "Les utopistes et la question sexuelle," written by Émile Armand and Hugo Treni for the *Encyclopédie anarchiste* (1934) and reprinted in *Les Utopistes et la Question sexuelle: Le symbolisme sexuel de Sade: non conformiste et libre-penseur* (Orléans, France: L'en-dehors, 1935), which carries out a similar review. In the immediate post-1968 context, the theme of utopia in general and of sexual utopia in particular was intensely debated, particularly with reference to the work of Marcuse, who proposed revolutionizing the political force of utopias to think in terms of a radical qualitative break with the present system (transition from an unfree to a free society) and stressed the need to envisage a new anthropology in which vital (particularly sexual) needs would be completely freed from repression, and of founding a society on the liberation of these needs. Foucault's course forms part of the criticism of these positions. See below, note 35, p. 280–281, and "Course Context," pp. 342–345.

24. See "Of Other Spaces," 7: "Quite recently, a new kind of temporal heterotopia has been invented: vacation villages, such as those Polynesian villages that offer a compact three weeks of primitive and eternal nudity to the inhabitants of the cities."

25. Foucault subsequently returns in detail to the case of Sade. On Foucault's analyses in the 1960s regarding Sade and the question of sexuality, see above, the Clermont-Ferrand course, pp. 23–26. Shortly after the Vincennes course, in March 1970, Foucault gives two lectures on Sade at the University of Buffalo ("Why Did Sade Write?" and "Theoretical Discourses and Erotic

Scenes," in *Language, Madness, Desire*, ed. Philippe Artières, Jean-François Bert, Mathieu Potte-Bonneville, and Judith Revel, trans. Robert Bononno (Minneapolis: University of Minnesota Press, 2015), which take up the analysis of the Sadean oeuvre in the light of Foucault's problematics at the time, both on the question of the relations among desire, sexuality, and discourse (see the second lecture; and above, lecture 1, note 10, p. 155–156), and on the problem of truth in Sadean discourse. He returns again to the case of Sade, from a perspective quite close to that adopted in this course, in his interview with Giulio Preti, in which he presents Sade as "the one who tried to introduce the infinite force of desire into the combinations of representation" (an opposition akin to that established here between integrative and transgressive utopias; see below, p. 261 et seq.) and was thereby "obliged to take away the subject's privileged position" and to describe "a type of sexuality that goes beyond the subject, that is found . . . behind the self, that exceeds it" ("Les problèmes de la culture: Un débat Foucault-Preti" [1972], in *DÉ*, I, no. 109, 1244). We know that Foucault slightly changed his view of Sade some years later, making him a "sergeant of sex" who formulated "an eroticism proper to a disciplinary society" ("Sade, Sergeant of Sex" [1975], trans. John Johnston, *EW*, 2, 226–27).

26. In Tommaso Campanella's utopia in *The City of the Sun*, "the magistrate *Amour* is specially responsible for the care of generation, that is to say with ensuring that sexual unions are such as to produce the most beautiful offspring possible"; *La Cité du soleil* [circa 1613], in *Oeuvres choisies de Campanella* (Paris: Lavigne, 1844), 168–69. The aim is to "produce a well-formed race" (183) through the optimal arrangement of different temperaments.

27. This is a very relative freedom. In order to avoid satisfaction being obtained with unnatural means, men and women, from a certain age, are allowed to satisfy themselves with sterile or pregnant women, with "matronly mistresses and old masters," in order to avoid any possible fertilization (Campanella, *La Cité du soleil*, 182).

28. "Fine statues of illustrious men are put in the bedrooms so that the women look on them and ask the Lord to grant them beautiful progeny. The man and woman sleep in separate cells until the time of union; a matron opens the two doors at a set time. The astrologist and doctor decide on the most propitious hour; they are tasked with finding the precise moment

when Venus and Mercury, to the east of the Sun, are in a propitious section with regard to Jupiter, Saturn, and Mars, or completely outside their influence" (Campanella, *La Cité du soleil*, 183).

29. It is difficult to determine whether Foucault is referring here to Bougainville's *Voyage* itself, the voyage around the world undertaken by Bougainville between 1766 and 1769, the report of which appeared in 1771, or to the *Supplement to Bougainville's Voyage* written by Diderot between 1772 and 1778. Both present New Cythera (Tahiti) as a sort of integrative utopia. On both of them, from the point of view of the sexual utopia, see de Planhol, *Les Utopistes de l'amour*, 151–57. Foucault analyzed the *Supplement* as a sexual utopia (BNF, Box 45-C4), and it is most likely that he is referring to this.

30. See, for example, *Justine, or Good Conduct Well Chastised* (1791), chap. 3, where these two points are well illustrated (in Marquis de Sade, *Justine, Philosophy in the Bedroom and Other Writings*, trans. Richard Seaver and Austryn Wainhouse [London: Arrow Books, 1991]).

31. See, for example, *The 120 Days of Sodom* [1785], in *The 120 Days of Sodom and Other Writings*, trans. Richard Seaver and Austryn Wainhouse (London: Arrow Books, 1990), "Introduction," 192: "For above six years these four libertines, kindred through their wealth and tastes, had thought to strengthen their ties by means of alliances in which debauchery had by far a heavier part than any of the other motives that ordinarily serve as a basis for such bonds."

32. The conduct of enslavement, gift, commitment, and regulation Foucault refers to form the heart of the erotic *dispositif* of *The Story of O*. Thus, O is a slave successively to René and various masters in the Roissy chateau, before being given to Sir Stephen by René; each time it is with her full agreement, just as is René's toward Sir Stephen. The most characteristic sign of recognition remains the iron ring with triple spiral that is imposed on O during her initiation at Roissy and that will serve as the sign of her enslavement. The sadomasochist world described in the novel is saturated with interwoven hierarchies: thus, in the château, there are masters and valets, each with particular clothes; similarly, there is a quasi-feudal hierarchy between René and Sir Stephen. With regard to places, the most emblematic is the château, which is itself broken up into a number of places—bedroom, library, cell, park, etc.

33. On transgression, see the Clermont-Ferrand course, above lecture 1 and notes 31 and 35, pp. 23–24 and 25–26.

34. This is Gabriel de Foigny's *La Terre australe connue, c'est-à-dire la description de ce pays inconnu jusqu'ici, de ses mœurs et de ses coutumes par Mr Sadeur* (Vannes, France: Verneuil, 1676). The narrator, Jacques Sadeur, himself a hermaphrodite, following a shipwreck, stays in the southern land whose population comprises solely hermaphrodites and presents all the characteristics of a perfectly ordered, uniform society where everything is equal and balanced. Having two sexes is described as "necessary for perfection," enabling man to be radically differentiated from animals, and making their love purely spiritual. In addition, the Australians are never ill, do not fear death, have a perfect language, etc. (BNF, Box 39-C4).

35. On Marcuse, see below, p. 268 et seq. Foucault appears to be referring here to Marcuse's principle that "we must face the possibility that the path to socialism may proceed from science to utopia and not from utopia to science" ("The End of Utopia," in *Five Lectures: Psychoanalysis, Politics, and Utopia*, trans. Jeremy J. Shapiro and Shierry M. Weber [London: Allen Lane, 1970], 63) in his revaluation of utopia as a principle of radical political transformation (see above, note 23, p. 277). Foucault does not come back to the work of Wilhelm Reich here. The reflection on sexual utopias and heterotopias forms part of a first version of Foucault's constant critical view of Freudo-Marxism, accused here of producing utopias through a conception of a "natural" sexuality, which is curbed and repressed by social relations, and which should simply be liberated by developing a society in accordance with that nature. Situating Freudo-Marxism in the long tradition of sexual utopias is also a way of showing the extent to which, contrary to his claims, Marcuse does not propose a radically new anthropology that breaks with history (see "The End of Utopia"). As Foucault will note in 1972 in his interview with G. Preti: "I think Marcuse tries to use the old themes inherited from the nineteenth century to save the subject, understood in the traditional sense" ("Les problèmes de la culture", 1245). This critical perspective is found in a different form in *The History of Sexuality, Volume 1: An Introduction*, together with a radical challenge of the "repressive hypothesis." It joins, moreover, Foucault's broader criticism of all humanist analyses that wish to found social transformation on a "human nature" or a deeper "original nature," a very marked criticism in his argument with Noam Chomsky

("Human Nature: Justice Versus Power," in Fons Elders, ed., *Reflexive Water: The Basic Concerns of Mankind* [London: Souvenir Press, 1974]) or in the irony with which he evokes the "anti-medical bucolism" of anti-medicine, its dream of a "kind of natural hygiene" ("Crise de la médecine ou crise de l'antimédecine" [1976], *DÉ*, II, no. 170, 57).

36. This analysis of the Sadeian subject is found both in Blanchot, who emphasizes the "absolute solitude" and radical singularity of every Sadeian subject (*Lautréamont and Sade*, trans. Michelle Kendall and Stuart Kendall [Stanford, CA: Stanford University Press, 2004], 10), and in Bataille, who contrasts Sade's "sovereign man," asserting sovereignly his desire in the unlimited, to the "normal man" (*Erotism*, trans. Mary Dalwood [San Francisco: City Lights, 1986], part two, chap. 2 and 3). The same principle leads Lacan to compare Sade and Kant, seeing in Sade the affirmation of a categorical and unconditional imperative, that of enjoyment (*jouissance*): "The crux of the diatribe is, let us say, found in the maxim that proposes a rule for jouissance, which is odd in that it defers to Kant in being laid down as a universal rule. Let us enunciate the maxim: 'I have the right to enjoy your body,' anyone can say to me, 'and I will exercise this right without any limit to the capriciousness of the exactions I may wish to satiate with your body.'" ("Kant with Sade," in *Écrits*, trans. Bruce Fink, in collaboration with Héloïse Fink and Russell Grigg [New York: Norton, 2006], 648). Nevertheless, Lacan stresses that in reality the Sadeian subject is himself subject to the law and that his transgression, apparently absolute, is the best proof of this. Similarly, in Bataille, absolute sovereignty ends by leading to the negation of self in the movement of an endless transgression. In his first lecture on Sade at Buffalo in 1970, "Why Did Sade Write?," which questions the relation between truth, discourse, and desire in Sade, Foucault takes up the idea that Sadeian writing allows "desire [to] become itself its own law; it will become an absolute sovereign embodying its own truth, its own repetition, its own infinity, its own means of verification" (in *Language, Madness, Desire*, 113). Likewise, in the second lecture, "Theoretical Discourses and Erotic Scenes," invoking the "irregular individual" (which echoes Bataille's sovereign man) to characterize Sadeian heroes, Foucault notes that the "irregular individual" is "an individual who recognizes no sovereignty above himself: not God, not the soul, not the law, not nature. It is an individual who is at no time connected to any eternity . . . any

obligation, any continuity, and who would surpass not only the moment of his life but of his desire" (*Language, Madness, Desire*, 120).

37. These are the Duc de Blangis and his brother, the Bishop of ***, the financier Durcet, and the president de Curval, the former two presented by Sade as those who "were the first to hit upon the debauch we propose to chronicle, and having communicated the scheme to their two friends, all four agreed to assume the major roles in these unusual orgies" ("Introduction," in *The 120 Days of Sodom*, 191).

38. Foucault is referring to the *Pornographe ou Idées d'un honnête homme sur un projet de règlement pour les prostitutes* (London: Nourse, 1769) by Rétif de La Bretonne (see also de Planhol, *Les Utopistes de l'amour*, 182 *et seq.*). The "anonymous subject" probably alludes to the fact that the women must submit to the desires of the men who observe them from a hidden wing before choosing them and who may appear masked (but the women also observe them and may refuse them). But it may also simply refer to the very general administrative subject who produces the utopia and the rules of the *Parthenions*, that is to say the public convents-brothels that the gentleman author of the text proposes to establish.

39. The system "around the masters" refers to O's different successive "masters"—that is, in the first place, the "masters" to whom she is enslaved in the Roissy château: "you are here to serve your masters. . . . Your hands are not your own, nor are your breasts, nor, most especially, any of your bodily orifices, which we may explore or penetrate at will . . . if anyone desires to use you in any manner whatsoever, he will use you, unmasked" (*The Story of O*, 15), and, particularly, René. Then, from René's gift of O, Sir Stephen: "when René had surrendered her to his friend the surrender had been absolute. . . . Sir Stephen's slightest desires took precedence over René's decisions as far as she was concerned" (*The Story of O*, 101–102). The system "around O" no doubt refers to the last part of the novel in which O, having been marked with Sir Stephen's signs, acquires great pride in her enslavement and, after donning the mask of an owl, is exhibited, naked, kept on a leash by a young woman totally devoted to him, during a party organized by another character (the "Commander") to whom Sir Stephen has loaned her. She becomes the center of attention to a whole set of couples and an object of a contemplation stamped with respect and fear.

40. This alternative end was mentioned in a chapter of the original edition of 1954 that was later suppressed. "There exists a second ending to the story of O, according to which O, seeing that Sir Stephen was about to leave her, said she would prefer to die. Sir Stephen gave her his consent" (*The Story of O*, 196). Bataille also emphasizes the necessity of death or silence in *The Story of O* as the culminating point of eroticism captured by discourse: "This book goes beyond the language (*parole*) that is in it inasmuch as, on its own, it tears itself apart, resolving the fascination for eroticism through the greater fascination for the impossible: for the impossible that is not only that of death, but that of a solitude that encloses absolutely" ("The Paradox of Eroticism," trans. Romana Byrne, *Textual Practice* 29, no. 6 [2015], 1048).

41. N. E. Rétif de La Bretonne, *La Découverte australe par un homme-volant, ou Le Dédale français* (Leipzig: 1781), vol. 3, esp. 525 *et seq.* On Rétif and the sexual utopia, see de Planhol, *Les Utopistes de l'amour*, 176 *et seq.*

42. In the Megapatagons, encountered by Victorin and his son (the two Flying Men who are the heroes of Rétif de La Bretonne's text), marriages last for one year. Every year, the married couple separate ("thus, the two sexes were divided into two nations which no longer had any relation with each other") and, for thirty days, are "separated by a barrier," so that they strive to seduce by sight, without contact. Then a big collective festival is organized, during which the men choose the women who suit them.

43. This play of complementary oppositions is especially perceptible in Comte, in the *Discours sur l'ensemble du positivisme* (Paris: L. Mathias-Carsilian-Goeury, 1848), fourth part, "Influence féminine du positivisme," 198 *et seq.*, and in volumes 2 and 4 of the *Système de politique positive*. This is how René de Planhol summarizes him in *Les Utopistes de l'amour*, 244–45: "the two sexes have clearly distinct roles . . . to men belong the exercise of intelligence and will, the priesthood, and government. Women, on the other hand, are privileged with the qualities of the heart. As such, 'they are responsible, first as mothers and then as wives, for the moral education of humanity.' They will fulfill this task especially in marriage, where they will develop the affective and moral feelings of their husbands and children."

44. These are the two axioms of positive politics: no society without government, no society without some kind of religion. See BNF, Box 39-C2 (dossier on "Comte-woman"), in particular the file "The Political Theory of Marriage": "marriage verifies the fundamental axiom of any sound politics:

society can no more exist without government than government without society." In this framework, men must command and women obey. But in addition, marriage "verifies the complementary axiom: every government presupposes a religion to consecrate and regulate command and obedience." Women play an essential role from this point of view; see A. Comte, *Système de politique positive*, 2:193–94.

45. On the festival of the Megapatagons, see above, note 42. The reference to the "voyage of a harmonious tribe," which refers to Fourier, is more obscure: it may refer to the episode entitled "Arrival of a horde of knights-errant at the Gnide maelstrom: Capture of an outpost and recovery of the captives," in *Le Nouveau Monde amoureux* (Paris: Anthropos, 1967), 156 *et seq.*, in which Daffodil "hordes and bands assembled in Indostan" launch themselves on a great voyage that leads some of them to Gnide, where one of their groups is captured. Fourier then describes the meeting of the captives' redemption, which conforms to a system of strict distribution and combination. There is a comparable description of the love courts between a caravan of travelers and the Gnidians in "Note C: Préliminaire de sympathie omniphile," in *Théorie de l'unité universelle*, III, in *Oeuvres complètes* (Paris: À la librairie sociétaire, 1841), 4:380–85. A system in which different tribes, each composed of a hundred or so persons divided into nine groups, some exclusively male, others exclusively female, are distributed into separate units, in distinct buildings, in which their members devote themselves to their occupations. Between the different buildings there is a network of covered galleries that allow the members of the tribes to travel and exchange, notably for sexual pleasure. In this way, a stable figure is established (the different tribes distributed in distinct buildings) with a system of exchanges and dynamic equilibrium founded on the journeys of tribe members to other tribes (see *Théorie des quatre mouvements*, I, in *Oeuvres complètes*, 1: 172–84.

46. As Comte writes, "positivism makes . . . the theory of marriage independent of any physical purpose, representing this fundamental bond as the main source of moral improvement and, consequently, as the essential basis of true human happiness, public as well as private. . . . All the personal and social effectiveness of marriage can thus be realized in a union that, albeit more tender, will always remain as chaste as the fraternal bond. . . . Provided that the renunciation [of sexuality] is sufficiently motivated on both sides, it encourages greater mutual attachment" (*Discours sur l'ensemble du positivisme*, 234–35). On this subject, see de Planhol, *Les Utopistes de l'amour*, 248–49.

47. We, the true men, explains an Australian, "live without feeling any of those animal ardors for each other, and we cannot even hear them spoken about without horror . . . we are entirely sufficient to ourselves; we have no need of anything to be happy" (de Foigny, *La Terre australe*, 69).

48. On this subject, see the Tahitian Orou's reply to Bougainville's chaplain, who refuses Orou's offer for him to sleep with one of his daughters in the name of the duty of hospitality: according to Orou, he would thus refuse "bringing into the world one of your own kind . . . repaying a gracious host" ("Supplement to voyage of Bougainville, or dialogue between A and B on the inappropriateness of attaching moral ideas to certain physical actions that do not accord with them," in Denis Diderot, *Political Writings*, ed. and trans. John Hope Mason and Robert Wokler [Cambridge: Cambridge University Press, 1992], 47). Furthermore, he would dishonor Orou's family and his daughter. As for the obligation of having children, it is actually essential in the social organization of the Tahitians, who do everything to encourage men and women to produce children as soon as they are of age.

49. Foucault is no doubt referring to René's absolute gift of O to his half-brother, Sir Stephen, in the second part of *The Story of O*. Throughout the first part, even though René has handed O over to different masters in the Roissy château, O and René constantly declare their love for each other. In the second part, René completely surrenders O to Sir Stephen: "this time it was apparent that she had been given with no strings attached" (87); "the surrender had been absolute" (101) and ends by completely eradicating O's love for René: "'Well,' thought O, 'the day I was so afraid would arrive, the day when I'd merely be a shadow in René's past. And I'm not even sad; the only thing I feel for him is pity . . . it was enough for him to have given me to Sir Stephen for me to be detached from him" (180).

50. See above, note 39, p. 282. At the end of *The Story of O*, O dons a mask of an owl before being exposed naked at a party.

51. Sade frequently uses the notion of villain to describe his characters: thus, in *Justine*, Saint-Florent is often described as the "villain." Klossowski adopts the expression to describe Sade himself as the "philosopher-villain"; see Pierre Klossowski, *Sade My Neighbor*, trans. Alphonso Lingis (Evanston, IL: Northwestern University Press, 1991).

52. Lacan in particular, who notes, in "Kant with Sade," that Sade played an inaugural role in the "groundwork" that, throughout the nineteenth century, enables the relationship between pleasure and evil to be thought

about, making possible eventually Freud's enunciation of "*his* pleasure principle without even having to worry about what distinguishes it from the function of pleasure in traditional ethics" (*Écrits*, 645, emphasis in original). On the relations between Foucault's and Lacan's reading concerning Sade, see above, the Clermont-Ferrand course, p. 45. We have seen that Foucault himself made Sade an inaugural moment in an archaeology of sexuality.

53. For Comte, the family is the first constitutive unit of society, "the most spontaneous" form of society, most resistant to social dissolution—the decomposition of society into individuals being, for Comte, doomed to anarchism (*Système de politique positive*, 2:180–82). But it is above all the condition of the transformation of egoistic instincts into social instincts, "the only natural transition that as a rule can detach us from the pure personality in order to raise us gradually to true sociability"; consequently, it is essential for the preservation and reproduction of society (*Système de politique positive*, 2:183–84).

54. Foucault is referring here to the combinatorial system developed by Charles Fourier in his "Abrégé sur les groupes ou séries passionnelles," in *Théorie de l'unité universelle*, III, in *Oeuvres complètes*, 4:337 *et seq.*; see BNF, Box 39-C4. Fourier describes a combinatorial system of "groups or elementary modes of social relations," with major passions (friendship, ambition) or minor (love, family), which may be dominant or invigorating. Harmony presupposes an artful combination of these groups. To this is added a theory of balances of the passions, based on a play of combination between different classes of passion (affective, sensory, distributive) with a view to a perfect balance. This balance derives particularly from what Fourier calls "rallying agreements," which unite antipathetic and divergent classes (see "De l'équilibre passionnel," in *Théorie de l'unité universelle*, IV, in *Oeuvres complètes*, 5:378 *et seq.*). The case of the "love rallyings" is developed particularly in pages 461–70. As Fourier notes, through his combinatorial system, one arrives without constraint "at the aim advanced by moralists . . . to make the spiritual principle called sentimental affection, celadony prevail in love . . .; to prevent the excessive influence of the material principle or lustfulness, which, when dominant on its own in love, degrades the human species" (461–62). It is in truth the unnatural regulations of civilized societies (and particularly marriage) that induce these vices.

55. On the notion of surplus-repression in Marcuse, see below, note 58, p. 287.

56. See Herbert Marcuse, *Eros and Civilization: A Philosophical Inquiry Into Freud* (Boston: Beacon Press, 1966), 47n45: "The irreconcilable conflict is not between work (reality principle) and Eros (pleasure principle), but between *alienated* labor (performance principle) and Eros" (emphasis in original). The opposition between the pleasure principle and work in Freud is described by Marcuse in this way: the reality principle is supposed to refer to the fundamental fact of scarcity, the fact that reality falls short of satisfying human needs; satisfaction entails work and sacrifice, "pleasure is "suspended" and pain prevails" (35). Marcuse, taking up Marx's criticism of Malthus's law of population, accuses Freud of applying to "the brute *fact* of scarcity what actually is a consequence of a specific *organization* of scarcity" (36, emphasis in the original) characteristic of the social formation of modern society, determined above all by the "performance principle." Every social organization, with its characteristic mode of domination, entails differences in the form and content of the reality principle, and for Marcuse "the performance principle" is the "prevailing historical form of the *reality principle*" (35). On the definition of this principle, according to which "society is stratified according to the competitive economic performances of its members" (44), see Marcuse, *Eros and Civilization*, 44 *et seq.*, or 81.

57. According to Marcuse: "The organization of sexuality reflects the basic features of the performance principle and its organization of society" (*Eros and Civilization*, 48). The primacy of genitality and repression of the partial instincts are the result of a process of centralization and concentration of libido "in one part of the body, leaving most of the rest free for use as the instrument of labor" (48). In this framework, perversions "thus express rebellion against the subjugation of sexuality under the order of procreation, and against the institutions which guarantee this order" (49). Even more: "Against a society which employs sexuality as a means for a useful end, the perversions uphold sexuality as an end in itself; they thus place themselves outside the domination of the performance principle and challenge its very foundation" (50).

58. Marcuse (*Eros and Civilization*, 35–37) thus distinguishes between "basic repression," or "modifications" of the instincts constitutive of and necessary for any human civilization, and "surplus-repression"—that is,

"restrictions necessitated by social domination" that have a determinate sociohistorical value (where the general principle of repression in the Freudian sense is judged to be ahistorical). In this way, he makes a distinction between "basic restrictions," which distinguish man from animals, and "surplus-repressions," modifications of instinctual energy specific to a given social formation (38). He adds: "the 'containment' of the partial sexual impulses, the progress to genitality belong to this basic layer of repression which makes possible intensified pleasure . . . [a] normal and natural maturation of pleasure"; on the other hand, surplus-repression, linked to the specific organization of the desexualization of partial impulses in collaboration with a specific mode of social domination, may be used "against gratification" and induce suffering.

59. The interweaving of Eros and destruction or death in Freudian theory is discussed by Marcuse in *Eros and Civilization*, 27–32 and 42–44. As Foucault notes (BNF, Box 39-C4), Marcuse identifies two contradictory positions in Freud: one in which sexuality appears as incompatible with society, where the emphasis is on the strict bond between Eros and destructiveness; and one in which Eros appears as an important factor in the social relationship. Marcuse's solution for reconciling these positions is that "*free* Eros does not preclude lasting civilized societal relationships—that it repels only the supra-repressive organization of societal relationships under a principle which is the negation of the pleasure principle" (50, italics in the original). In Marcuse's eyes, far from being inextricably bound to them, only Eros can triumph over aggressiveness and destruction: "Strengthened defense against aggression is necessary; but in order to be effective the defense . . . would have to strengthen the sex instincts, for only a strong Eros can effectively 'bind' the destructive instincts. And this is precisely what the *developed civilization is incapable of* doing because it depends for its very existence on extended and intensified regimentation and control" (80–81, italics in the original).

60. Foucault compiled a dossier (BNF, Box 39-C4) on convents and abbeys in the imaginary of English novels of the end of the eighteenth and the beginning of the nineteenth centuries (those of Ann Radcliffe, *The Monk* by Mathew Gregory Lewis, or Charles Robert Maturin's *Melmoth the Wanderer*). The figure of the convent brothel is found, for example, in Rétif de La Bretonne's *Pornographe*, and also in novels like *Les Délices du cloître ou la None éclairée*, by the Abbé Du Prat, attributed to Jean Barrin (Cologne, Germany: Sincère, 1748).

APPENDIX

Extract from *Notebook* No. 8, Green

September 1969

[*The files kept in the archives of the Bibliothèque nationale de France attest to the fact that Michel Foucault accumulated considerable material on the history and current state of the biology of sexuality. This reading was accompanied by numerous reflections regarding the epistemology of the life sciences, the birth of a knowledge (savoir) of heredity, and the transformations of naturalist knowledge (savoir) at the end of the eighteenth century. Furthermore, Foucault sketches out a problematization of the way the relations between individuality, reproduction, and sexuality are reconfigured by the biology of sexuality. This sketch—found at the beginning of* Notebook *no. 8 (Box 91), dated September 21, 1969—appears in the form of a continuous exposition of eight sheets, recto and verso: we have decided to reproduce these here, insofar as they clearly extend Foucault's reflections in lecture 6 of the Vincennes course.*][a]

*

21/09/1969   [1]

Sexuality, Reproduction, Individuality

I. One of the postulates (archaeological, epistemological?—to be examined later), is a certain subordination of these three terms:

---

a See above, p. 231 *et seq.*, and "Course Context," pp. 339–342.

1. The individual living being has the property of reproducing, and of doing this, at least in several types of individual, through sexuality.

Two other theses are connected to this postulate:

2. An individual begins when the cycle of the same begins *again*.[b] Either the first individual disappears so that another individual that is the same appears. Or the individual, without disappearing, gives rise (outside it, or at one of its extremities, through budding and branching) to another similar individuality. The individual is that which reproduces.

[2]   3. Sexuality is a mode of reproduction: more complex than others, which may take the place of others (animals) or be juxtaposed with others (plants).

What the theory of sexuality (and particularly plant sexuality) showed in the nineteenth century is that this subordination had to be viewed differently.

1. The individual is not what reproduces but what figures within a cycle of reproduction. In other words, it is not just that reproduction (of the same) is not a function of biological individuality, but the individual is not even sufficient for a cycle of reproduction. It has to be accepted that, in a given cycle of reproduction, there may be several, completely different individualities.

It was known that a single individual could reproduce several times. It was known that a single process of reproduction (going from the same to the same) could give rise to several individualities.

[3]   2. As a result, sexuality is not simply one of the possible modes of reproduction. It may be one of the phases of reproduction. Previously it was thought that reproduction was or was not sexual. Now we know that one and the same cycle of reproduction may

---

b Underlined in the manuscript (*re*commence).

be sexual and nonsexual. Sexuality is then a phase of reproduction, characteristic of certain individuals.

3. Inasmuch as sexual reproduction is defined by the fusion of two nuclei, and nonsexual reproduction by the division of a nucleus, there can be the formation of two different types of individualities: an individuality that carries the gametes and another that carries the spore.

We are obliged to subordinate the three notions in the fol- [4] lowing way:

- the reproductive cycle—the sexual or nonsexual mechanism of reproduction—the individuality defined by this.

Of course, it was known that an individual living being is what can be obtained by reproduction on the basis of one or two other individuals of the same species. But this reproduction characterized the birth. It was not a process within which the individual was placed. We now know that all individuals can be distributed in the larger process:

- sporophytic stage → gametophyte stage (with meiosis).

And that, according to circumstances, one of the stages may be reduced, completely reduced or diminished; that they may give [rise] either to a single individual in which they are combined, or to two individuals in which they are distributed either more or less equally, or completely unequally.

The individual to which our familiarity is accustomed (the [5] sexed individual who, thanks to this sexuality, can reproduce) is only a particular case: a sort of shriveling of the gametophytic stage within the sporophytic stage—which has enveloped and covered the first (a bit like, in the higher vertebrates, the telencephalon has covered and enveloped the mesencephalon: but this is only a comparison, it is not a biological analogy). This covering creates the impression that sexuality is a characteristic of certain biologically sophisticated individuals that permits them (or condemns them to) a certain mode of reproduction. But, in fact, there are certain cycles of reproduction that occur in such a way that the conjunction of gametes gives rise to a sporophyte (with $2n$ chromosomes) and the gametophytic phase (with n chromosomes) is entirely reduced.

[6]   It is, therefore, the general structure of the type of reproduction, and the place meiosis occupies within it, that defines "typical" individuality for us.

In its most general biological unfolding, the individual is defined by the cycle of reproduction and when the gametophytic phase of sexual reproduction takes place.

We see, incidentally, the necessary reversal of the great theme that was current up to, and even beyond, the nineteenth [century]: that of sexuality appearing late in biological evolution, and assuming increasing importance. The simplest beings are not sexed; then they are bisexual; finally, unisexual. And the importance of sexuality constantly grows since, strictly limited to cycles or periods in animals, it is diffuse in man.

[7]   In fact, taking a wider biological scale (the eukaryotes or even just the the archegoniates), we can show on the contrary that the (gametophytic) sexual stage constantly contracts and the sporophytic stage increases. We are mushrooms upside down. We are exaggerated ferns. Constant diminution of sexuality. Whereas there are individuals in whom meiosis has already occurred: which are therefore composed of elements with n chromosomes; which are therefore entirely devoted to the production of gametes; which are immense sexual cell machines. In these, yes, sexuality is important. We are beings of involuted sexuality.

It is not society that has reduced the part of sexuality that evolution had developed in us to the extreme.

[8]   In the archegoniates we are, it is the play of biological structures that reduced the moment of the sexual phase. It needs

very little—some groups of cells enclosed in our organism—for the rest of the sexual phase to be entirely resorbed. We are just gigantic sporophytes, and have kept only some gametophytic cells. Biologically, we are successful sporophytes that carry some stunted gametophytes.

[It is typical that man should claim for his species the final blossoming of a sexuality that, before him, was sketched out and partial; or rather, that he is the result of a process of reproduction in which the gametophytic phase is absolutely reduced.

Freud's and, generally, modern man's mixture of narcissism [9] and moralism. Everything is sexuality in us, they say: in other living individuals, sexuality is localized, limited, when not entirely absent; we are the only beings for whom sexuality is omnipresent—in all our bodies, in our language, in our imagination. This may be true, but only inasmuch as the *psyche* reinvests in the body a sexuality that has been biologically expelled from it. It is not because our whole body is sexualized that the *psyche* is too; it is because our body is biologically desexualized that, perhaps, the *psyche* is so sexualized and that it can resexualize the body only by a gigantic hysterical process. Hysteria as fantastic resexualization of the body is at the origin of the contemporary theme of sexuality.

And it is here that Freud's moralism comes into play. Indigna- [10] tion, basically, at being only sexuality. Rejection of that sexuality. Attempt to master it, to limit it, or at least to transform it.

We are[c] indeed derisory and, to tell the truth, nonexistent in front of the sexual happiness of a fern's prothallium.][d]

In any case, we know the epistemological task facing the biology of sexuality when it had to reverse the relations of

---

c "Sexually," crossed out.
d Foucault's square brackets.

reproduction and individuality. In other words, to take reference points that were no longer those of the individual but of a cycle that may be meta-individual, the decisive moments of which are nuclear processes. Double change of scale, since it had to look over the individual's shoulder at the whole cycle; and since it had to reach an extremely tenuous level in comparison to that individual. The individual must no longer be the absolute reference point. The intranuclear processes determine meta-individual scansions.

[11]   For this it was necessary:

– to generalize sexuality to the maximum—to find it even where it did not appear (cryptogams);

– to define the position and specificity of nonsexual reproduction (reproduction by spore);[e]

– to determine in what the male's fertilization of the female consists (that is, the fusion of the nucleus of the spermatozoon with that of the oosphere);

– to determine the nature of the elements so combined[f] (chromosome reduction).

The last two points lead to the questioning of the second major postulate of the science of living beings before the nineteenth century.

[12] *II. Second postulate*

The processes of reproduction are a continuation of the processes of growth. Sexual reproduction is a certain form of growth, characterized:

  • by the fact that it gives rise to an individual separated from the first;

---

e This line appeared at the end of the list, but an arrow added by Foucault indicates it needs to be moved to this level.

f Foucault wrote first: "of the sexual cells."

- by the fact that the conjunction of two individuals is necessary.

The theme is that the living individual is essentially capable of growth. And that this growth encounters two limits: death and reproduction.

Death is the limit of growth that has reached its end and has run out. It is the stop on itself, the relapse, a sudden or slow decline.

Reproduction, on the other hand, is growth that, having [13] arrived at a certain limit, crosses it and gives rise to a new individuality capable, in turn, of growth. This excess growth can, in the simplest form, give rise to an individual similar to the first but remaining connected to it (this is how another branch can grow on a branch that has completed its first growth—a new individuality that remains linked to the first); in another form, growth gives rise to a detachable individual (layering). In a third form, growth gives rise to an element that, without resembling the first (in appearance at least), frees itself from it and reproduces the image of the first (germ). Finally, in a fourth form, growth gives rise to elements that, in themselves, would remain blocked and unable to grow, in turn, without the intervention of a special mechanism of excitation or fertilization.

Sexual reproduction is a complex growth. Sexuality plays the [14] role of an alternator in the processes of growth: the mechanism that concentrates growth in some specific products and that cannot develop without a certain mixture.

- This thesis presupposes absolute homogeneity of the sexual products and the organic elements constituting the individual. No specificity of the sexual as such. Sexuality is the expression of the individual itself.
- It presupposes its proximity to death: sexuality is what enables an individual to grow beyond its own limit without dying. And, thereby, to reconstitute another identity beyond death. Sexuality avoids and circumvents death.

[15]   The epistemological task of the nineteenth century is to isolate the specificity of sexual reproduction. Its radical difference from growth. The previous conception assumed an action of a substance on a substance and then the separation of the product from the mother. That the action is a fusion, and that this fusion is preceded by a physiological division within each product, had to be discovered. That it is a divided product that is passed on.

There must be reduction before fusion. This is the specific characteristic of sexuality. This is what makes these processes unassimilable to those of growth.

CLAUDE-OLIVIER DORON

Course Context

SEXUALITY

Lectures at the University of Clermont-Ferrand

(1964)

A masked philosopher?

The course that Michel Foucault gave in 1964 on the theme of sexuality formed part of his teaching in the philosophy department of the University of Clermont-Ferrand. From the autumn of 1960, in fact, Foucault taught psychology there, first as assistant professor and then, after the defense of his thesis on *Folie et Déraison* (*History of Madness*) in May 1961, as full professor from 1962. "His specialty is psychopathology," notes the report of the dean who proposed he be given tenure.[1] In truth, from 1962 Foucault had obtained the recruitment of two assistants (Nelly Viallaneix and Francine Pariente), which allowed him to concentrate on the single course of general psychology. This is the course we have made available for readers in this volume.

Its first interest is to illustrate how Foucault conceived of his teaching in psychology. A quick overview could give the impression that it is a conventional exercise, presenting successively, after an introduction on sexuality and culture, the facts of biology, ethology, and then psychoanalysis. Such lessons were then classical, and we only have to look at the courses on child psychology and pedagogy given by Maurice Merleau-Ponty in 1949–1952[2] to see that, at first sight, Foucault's course does not break new ground in its themes and references. As a university course, its function was, first and foremost, to pass on to students a certain number of facts and to give an account of the current state of knowledge about sexuality. This is even clearer if we compare it with the course on sexual anthropology given shortly before by the Jesuit philosopher Abel Jeannière at the Catholic Institute of Paris.[3] This looks like a veritable humanist double of Foucault's course: it starts in the same way, putting the topical nature of the sexual question, the evolution of marriage, and the status of women in perspective; it questions the relativity of the sexes through biology; it goes through the question of animal sexuality and then psychoanalysis; and it ends with a reflection on an authentically human sexuality founded on the relationship to the Other and conjugal ethics. But precisely the formal similarity between these two courses makes it possible to bring out all the originality of Foucault's course and to understand how, far from being just an academic exercise, it is in fact fully part of the general project Foucault is developing at this time: to awaken philosophy and the human sciences from their "anthropological slumber";[4] to question, through the history of sexuality as a cultural formation, as he had done through that of madness and that of death,[5] the historical conditions of the divisions at work in our culture—which, on the one hand, exclude a certain experience of sexuality as transgression, and, on the other, reduce it to a possible object of certain forms of knowledge. In short, to undertake an archaeology of sexuality.

Questioned in 1965 by Alain Badiou about how he would teach psychology in a philosophy class, Foucault suggested he would wear a mask and disguise his voice to present the findings of psychology, before removing it and taking up his own philosopher's voice to show the impasse in which psychology, caught up in the anthropological circle, found itself.[6] Reading the Clermont-Ferrand course, one becomes aware that, rather than this binary game of mask and actor, a more complex intertwining of voices has to be disentangled. Some occasionally surprising links emerge, for example, between some fundamental themes of Foucault's later works and propositions taken from psychoanalysis. For example, the intrication of knowledge, violence, and cruelty, that "radical malice of knowledge,"[7] which Foucault will stress from *Lectures on the Will to Know*, but which is at the heart of his reflections from the beginning of the 1960s: it appears here at the intersection of Sigmund Freud's analysis of the drive to know and Georges Bataille's theses on the necessary violence and breakdown in communication underlying the reduction of an experience to an object of knowledge.[8] Also, there is continuity between the fundamental thesis that guides Foucault in the *Abnormal* lectures—that sexuality first became an object of knowledge in the form of the perversions and negativity—and both Foucault's recurring position on psychology as a science of negativities and the Freudian theory of sexuality.[9] As well as, finally, the central role Foucault accords to the problem of infantile sexuality in the development of knowledge about sexuality, in which in this course we note he has a particular interest, and which he poses first of all in psychoanalytic terms of lack of knowledge and repression, drawing a parallel between cultural reasons for the prevalence, until the end of nineteenth century, of the myth of the child's purity and psychological reasons for the repression of infantile sexuality.[10] We can see the extent to which the distance he will take from this thesis in the *Abnormal* lectures and in the unpublished manuscript of the *La Croisade des enfants*—rejecting as a myth the idea that the sexuality of children was ignored until its discovery by Freud at the end of the nineteenth century and making it, rather, one of the main domains from which something like a *scientia sexualis* emerges—was a criticism addressed to himself and a necessary precondition for his broader rejection of the repressive hypothesis in the history of sexuality.[11]

Such intertwining between the voices of the philosopher and the psychology teacher are found at every level in the course. So that, if some long passages give the impression of Foucault delivering impersonal didactic content to his audience, we can see that they are actually taken up in an intellectual project, some key themes of which need to be identified, situating them in the context of their enunciation.

The archaeology of sexuality and the project of an archaeology of the human sciences

It is 1964 and, following on from his *History of Madness*, Foucault has just completed work on *The Birth of the Clinic*. He is also preparing a book on the archaeology of the human sciences, which will become *The Order of Things*. What links these works is the constancy of an archaeological project that in these years Foucault is striving to define in his *Notebooks*.[12] Archaeology takes on multiple faces: first of all, it is a specific way of analyzing "cultural formations." The notion of cultural formation recurs in the methodological reflections recorded in his *Notebooks* in 1963,[13] as well as in various texts from 1963 to 1965. It reminds us that Foucault then situated his works in a "history of [our] culture."[14] The Clermont-Ferrand course is no doubt the only one, along with that of Tunis in 1966, in which he tries to clarify diachronically and synchronically what he means by "Western culture," here in the case of sexuality taken as a particular cultural formation. The *Notebooks* identify several analytical principles that are applied in the course, in particular the principle that a cultural formation does not fall within the domain of "the history of an idea, of a concept, or of an institution": it has an "impalpable body" and is "multilinear." "It is concept, myth, institution, silent practice, principle of classification of individuals and phenomena." It is a matter of reconstructing what gives coherence to this heterogeneity. A cultural formation entails therefore: "a. [a] principle of classification of individuals; b. [a] ritualization of conduct (silent sedimentations); c. [a] variable scale of verbalization and [a] fixing of limits."[15]

But archaeology is not just any way of studying a cultural formation. Foucault notes that archaeology is a "science of *archai*," that is to say, of "what begins and what governs (*régit*). The opening that makes possible and constantly keeps open the field of possibilities"; in short, he adds, an "historical *a priori*."[16] Archaeology makes it possible to combine a "chronological eidetic" founded on the historical examination of the conditions of possibilities of a cultural formation; a morphological analysis that "deciphers its isomorphisms"; and—assuredly the most essential—an "uncovering of the original structures," that is to say, of those obscure gestures that institute a field of possibility and, at the same time, trace a limit. In other words, archaeology is situated at the point of intersection of an historical analysis and an excavation of the fundamental structures and divisions of a given cultural formation.[17] It is the "science of divisions," of those "gestures[s] that open up differences" and that constantly recur and reverberate in a culture.[18] We recognize here an echo of the preface to *History of Madness* from 1961: "We could write a history of limits—of those obscure gestures, necessarily forgotten as soon as they are accomplished, through which a culture rejects something which for it will be the Exterior . . . in the region of which we would speak, it makes its essential choices, operating the division which gives a culture the face of its positivity."[19] For (we will see the importance of this point for sexuality), against phenomenology, which, after coming closest to the critique of anthropology, finally returned to the anthropological slumber due to its reflection on the "original," Foucault, in a slanted reading of Bataille, constantly invokes the "return to Nietzsche, that is to say taking seriously the origin as transgression"[20]: the original structures, what Foucault elsewhere calls the positivities constituting the unthought of knowledge, rest on the establishment of limits and refer to the transgression of these limits.[21] For this reason, "the science of the archai is also discovery of limit-experiences."[22]

The Clermont-Ferrand course should be seen as belonging to the continuation of this project. It is indeed a matter of advancing the hypothesis that the rejection of sexuality as nature, as our "biological destiny," and the "cutoff system" by which we make it the external border of culture, is in fact only one "of the characteristics of Western civilization."[23] Foucault strives to examine the historical conditions and effects of this characteristic, as much from the point of view of the tragic experience of sexuality thus constituted (for what constitutes modern sexuality is that it "marks the limit within us and designates us as a limit"[24]) as for the emergence of a new form of language on sexuality: a discursive knowledge (*savoir*) of sexuality. With *History of Madness*, Foucault showed how, by breaking the communication that existed between the experience of madness and common experience, the "great confinement" of the seventeenth century, by violence and exclusion, made possible the constitution of madness as an object of knowledge at the same time as it rejected the experience of the limits of language in a transgressive discourse.[25] With *The Birth of the Clinic*, Foucault described how, by constituting death and disease as objects, by "ceaselessly reminding man of the limit that he bears within him," clinical anatomy authorized a "rational language" on the individual, a "knowledge . . . that was not simply of a historic or aesthetic order," while opening the way to "a lyrical experience that sought its language from Hölderlin to Rilke," an experience of a world "placed under the sign of finitude, in that irreconcilable, intermediate state in which reigns the law, the harsh law of the limit."[26] Similarly, in this course, he studies the conditions through which sexuality is "detached from the institutions," ejected from society into a nature or as a floating theme, a "problematic consciousness" that becomes both "the central site of the collapse of morality, the only form of the tragic modern man is capable of," the space of profanation par excellence, and the possible object of a "new language on sexuality" that is neither lyrical nor transgressive: a discursive knowledge of sexuality. And, as we shall see, the figure of Sade, as the contemporary of Kant, Bichat, the Civil Code, and asylum institutions, will serve as the marker common to these different divisions.

Reading this course alongside other texts of the same time attests to the fact that sexuality, along with the problem of death, of language, and of madness, occupies at this time a central place in Foucault's reflections on the question of the limit and the anthropological problem. One detects a strong resonance of Bataille's analyses, all the more so as Foucault had just contributed to the editing of his works and to the tribute to him.[27] Sexuality is presented here as the site par excellence of the limit. While it is often believed that "sexuality has regained, in contemporary experience, its truth as a process of nature" that may "at last emerge in the clear light of language," to the same extent as it has been "liberated," Foucault stresses that we should rather say:

> What characterizes modern sexuality from Sade to Freud is not its having found the language of its logic or of its nature, but, rather . . . its having been "denatured"—cast into an empty zone in which it achieves whatever meagre form is bestowed upon it by the establishment of its limits. . . . We have not in the least liberated sexuality, though we have, to be exact, carried it to its limits: the limit of consciousness . . . the limit of the law . . . the limit of language.[28]

Let us note this opposition, for it will be found again in another form in the Vincennes course: against those who believe in a natural (human or psychobiological) truth of sexuality that needs to be liberated, and who sometimes find in psychoanalysis a support for their belief, Foucault invokes a different vision of sexuality (and of psychoanalysis), as that which radically inscribes the limit within man, "discloses as its own secret and clarification, its intrinsic finitude, the limitless reign of the Limit" and brings it back to the necessary transgression of that limit.[29] On this point, the Clermont-Ferrand course and "A Preface to Transgression" are perfect echoes of each other: sexuality is the only tragedy of which man is capable in a world without God because it dooms him to a profanation without object. "A rigorous language, as it arises from sexuality, will not reveal the secret of man's natural being, nor will it express the serenity of anthropological truths, but rather, it will say that he exists without God."[30] But behind the death of God is hidden a more profound event, a "much more threatening gaping openness" against which nineteenth-century anthropological thought is formed in reaction: what Foucault, from 1963, describes as the death of man. "It is already because man no longer existed that he thought of the death of God."[31]

So, through the case of sexuality, we find again the double, tragic, and critical meaning of the notion of limit that Foucault explains in his *Notebook* on August 28, 1963. On the one hand:

> the limit as experience (in madness, death, dream, sexuality): this is the experience based on a division and that constitutes it as division. Division that, in one sense, takes place within an experience . . . and that, on the other hand, only designates the other side of all the positivities: the nonexperience, that which remains outside experience. The necessary streaming of the outside.

Foucault is referring to this experience when he evokes, in the course, the tragedy of sexuality, which he develops later in "The Thought of the Outside."[32]

> And then this other meaning: every positivity forms its own *découpage*, its limits and its bounds. It has to be illuminated from within. . . . It is nothing beyond itself. And even if it projects itself beyond itself as a knowledge to be developed, an institutional form to be maintained, etc., this project is of course part of itself and enclosed within the borders of this positivity. . . . There is archaeology where one discloses the articulation of these limits specific to every positivity, or those constitutive limits of positivity in general of the culture. . . . The limit experience in the first meaning (*au sens no. 1*) necessarily entails a transgression, that is to say those things such as madness, disease (death in life), sexual frenzy. . . . In the second meaning (*sens no. 2*) the limit does not play the same role in relation to the positivities. These are drawn up against transgression: they take it over and defend themselves from it, that is to say they are themselves transgressions, but in the form of the unthought. And thought is everything that, reviving these forgetful transgressions, goes back to those fundamental divisions in which culture (and the thought of which it is the thick body) constantly begins.[33]

The whole art of archaeology is in this work: showing how the positivities on which forms of knowledge are founded (in this case, the human sciences) are both constitutive and reactive. They establish limits that make possible a certain form of knowledge but that, at the same time, repress an experience beyond the limit. Sexuality, along with death and madness, offers a perfect example of this. Hence its importance in the Foucauldian project of an archaeology of the human sciences.

This importance is marked in the course by the central place Foucault gives to sexuality and psychoanalysis in the configuration of the human sciences. "In modern culture, man has become an object of science because he found himself to be both subject to and subject of his sexuality. That is why psychoanalysis . . . is the key to all the modern human sciences."[34] This reflection on the place of psychoanalysis as knowledge of sexuality at the heart of the human sciences is situated within a precise context. On the one hand, the recent split of the Société française de psychanalyse and Lacan's creation of the École française de psychanalyse (École freudienne) in 1963–1964. The split concerned, in part, the problem of the relation of psychoanalysis to other human sciences, and in particular to psychology. Daniel Lagache was in favor of an integration of psychoanalysis within psychology; Jacques Lacan argued for a radical distinction. The Lacanian position sought to include psychoanalysis in the reworking of relations between subject and structure, drawing on linguistics and anthropology.[35] On the other hand, the renewal of philosophical interest, particularly by way of Louis Althusser, in a psychoanalysis that would provide a theory of the subject beyond the sovereignty of the psychological subject or intersubjectivity.[36] Foucault's position takes this approach. If psychoanalysis occupies a central place, it is certainly not because it discovers the deep nature of the human subject that must be brought to light and liberated. To be sure, it puts sexuality in a language, but this language denaturalizes it and removes it from the sovereignty of the speaking subject. Through it, man discovers, "next to himself, . . . the existence of another language that also speaks, and of which he is not the master . . . that in the location from which a subject had traditionally spoken in philosophy . . . a void has been hollowed out in which a multiplicity of speaking subjects are joined and severed, combined and excluded."[37] To be sure, it places sexuality within the game of the rule, prohibition, and transgression, but while making it a law empty of all positive content and destined to an indefinite transgression.

Foucault's reading at this time, like much of the way in which psychoanalysis or a certain erotic literature was making sexuality speak, like biological or ethological knowledge about sexuality, seems turned against a certain "anthropology of sexuality" that seeks to give sexuality a human meaning, to make it part of a dialectic and ethics of intersubjectivity, or to ground it in nature. His is indeed a project of "denaturalizing sexuality" directed against any naturalist reduction looking to biology for confirmation of a cramped, ultimately "too human" conception of normal sexuality, and against a humanist project emphasizing the irreducible character of human sexuality and seeking to give it an anthropological value and a reassuring philosophical meaning.

The forms of knowledge (savoirs) of sexuality against the anthropology of sexuality

Before recalling the forms taken by this sexual anthropology, we need to return to some points of context that enable us to better situate what is at issue in the course. As Foucault noted in 1963, we analyze a cultural formation only insofar as it enters into crisis and closure: "our perception is made possible by and identifiable with the movement that breaks what was open and closes it." This principle of "closure and recurrence" (in the sense that it conditions the *a posteriori* recovery of a cultural form) presupposes "the possibility of discovering the point of a critique of the recurrence" in present reality. Thus, what makes it possible to speak of the birth of clinical medicine is the fact that it is currently being called into question. And Foucault adds: "what makes it difficult to speak about sexuality is that there is doubtless no closure or, at any rate, we don't know where it is."[38] Nevertheless, in the years preceding the course, there are signs that attest to sexuality being called into question: if the politicization of the sexual question may seem typical of the late 1960s, it actually began to be asserted, on several fronts, from the 1950s.[39] The echo of several of these fronts can be heard in Foucault's course. First of all, the question of the status of women: in addition to the repercussions of Simone de Beauvoir's *The Second Sex*, published in 1949, the beginning of the 1960s is marked by strong discussions on the question of women and work (the model of the working woman then beginning to be established) and on control of their sexuality, regarding abortion and unwanted pregnancies (there were several campaigns on this subject from the middle of the 1950s), as of contraception (the contraceptive pill being discovered in the United States in 1956 and its distribution prohibited in France).[40] Then, from the beginning of the 1960s, there was a more explicit promotion of free love or of sexual relations outside marriage on the part of young people. Finally, following the publication of, in particular, the second report of Alfred Kinsey on sexual behavior (the first report having had only a limited impact in France), there were occasionally animated discussion of the norms of sexual behavior, homosexuality, and female pleasure.[41] We recall, moreover, that the first works of Herbert Marcuse appear in French in this period.[42] On a different level, and in the wake of Jean-Jacques Pauvert's publication of Sade's *Oeuvres complètes* (and the legal action brought against it in 1956),[43] we should add the development of a whole transgressive erotic literature (including the works of Georges Bataille and Jean Genet).

These phenomena bear witness to what Foucault describes in his lectures as the emergence of a "problematic conscious-ness of sexuality," about which the least one can say is that it will become more pronounced from 1966, confirming the diag-nosis. There are a number of testimonies of this. One is the spe-cial issue of the review *Esprit* in 1960 on *Sexuality*, edited and introduced by Paul Ricoeur. On the one hand, the tone of the issue and Ricoeur's introduction illustrate perfectly an attempt to "not evade any of the difficulties that make man's existence as sexual existence *problematic*,"[44] reviewing the relation of human to animal sexuality, the question of men-women relationships, the problem of the place of sexuality in human psychology, its alienation, and so on. On the other hand, they express a desire to denounce the "loss of meaning," the "fall into triviality" of con-temporary eroticism, and to promote a humanist conception of sexuality founded on an intersubjective ethics, the interpersonal relationship, and tenderness. Following Max Scheler, Ricoeur thus proposes to look for a "new sacred in contemporary con-jugal ethics" and, undoubtedly with the discourse of the likes of Bataille or Blanchot in mind, denounces the "intense despair of eroticism," of a meaningless and groundless eroticism. We have here an example of the very actual (and multiform) place of the sexual question at the beginning of the 1960s, as of the human-ist reactions and efforts to recapture sexuality in a philosophy of meaning, of the human subject and the intersubjective relation-ship of which it can be the object. The Jeannière course is another: for Jeannière, it is a matter of completely separating human from animal sexuality, of criticizing any attempt to reduce sexuality to a scientific approach in order to found a specifically human sex-uality tied to freedom, free choice, and recognition of the other: "sexuality reveals to man his fundamental dimension: he is for the other or he does not exist; human love reveals to him that

he is nothing outside of intersubjectivity."[45] "A whole anthropology of sexuality," Foucault notes in his lectures, which connects
it to the old Hegelian and Comtean themes of the nineteenth
century. This anthropology tends to identify what having a sexed
existence and body signifies for men and women, and what relations to the world and others this induces, in a way that may be
marked by a phenomenological or existentialist style of analysis.
We may think of the works of Simone de Beauvoir or Maurice
Merleau-Ponty,[46] or of the philosophical anthropology of Max
Scheler,[47] or of Hans Kunz, which Foucault was familiar with.[48]
This anthropology is often concerned to distinguish human sexuality from the facts of biology, stressing the clear break between
them; but it may also claim, on the contrary, to derive vital principles for human sexuality from "natural differences" between
the sexes.[49]

   In contrast with these approaches, Foucault carries out a
double sidestep in these lectures. On the one hand, rather than
invoke a strict break between biology and human sexuality, he
makes the break itself (and the relations of determination or, on
the contrary, the radical distinction that one seeks to establish
on the basis of it) a specific characteristic of sexuality as a modern Western cultural formation, whose historical conditions of
appearance he is studying. And he chooses to work on naturalism from within, showing how the results of biology and ethology, far from founding the common, "too human" conceptions
of the difference of the sexes or of sexual conduct reduced to the
procreative act, shatter and radically challenge them. We discover
here, especially in lectures 2 and 3, an alternaturalist Foucault,[50]
which initially surprises and one would be tempted to explain
by the particular character of this university course. But reading
the Vincennes lectures, the appendix "Sexuality, Reproduction,
Individuality," and various texts from 1969 to 1970, invites us to

take this stance very seriously.[51] Far from objecting to the results of the science of sexuality (biology or ethology), Foucault, like Nietzsche, seems to call on a "certain form of biologism" in order to be released from the anthropological slumber.[52] He takes up a strategy comparable to that adopted by Bataille in his 1947 article, "Qu'est-ce que le sexe?" In this article, Bataille shows how biology destroys the intimate experience and common representations of the difference of the sexes, the "notion of the individual's basic sex-attribute," and the idea of a clear and static separation between the sexes. On the contrary, it reveals that "sex . . . is not an essence but a state," comparable to the liquid or solid state of a body:

> Science in fact rigorously eliminates what should be called the "basic facts" of life . . . it destroys, in short, the construction founded on the feeling of presence, it dismantles intimate individual existence into moving objective representations in which any substratum is concealed. It removes the reality and consistency of the intimate, apparently immutable notion of sex. . . . The problem of being dissolves in these shifts.[53]

This strategy, which consists in employing the facts of biology or ethology, not in order to found some positive truth about man, but in order to destroy the illusions of a natural norm or human essence, is in line with how, since the course he devoted to "Problems of Anthropology" in 1955, Foucault understood Nietzschean naturalism (and, it should be added, a certain Freudian naturalism) as opposed to classical naturalism: a means of dissolving objectivity and determinism, undoing man's relationship to the truth, and freeing him from the problem of his essence. "It is the questioning of anthropological comfort, the discovery of those multiplied horizons which, before and behind him, hide man from himself."[54] Foucault proceeds in the same way here in mobilizing the facts of the science of sexuality. The aim is not to mark a radical break between human sexuality and the biology of sexuality, but to decenter the former by putting it in a broader perspective so as to shatter its self-evidence; showing that "human sexuality is not a hapax in the biological world,"[55] but without being able to draw other than negative lessons from this (on its indeterminacy, complexity, and fluidity). A paradoxical naturalism, therefore, since it aims to radically denaturalize sexuality.

This does not prevent Foucault from emphasizing the particular character of human sexuality, but, here again, in a way that is above all negative, since it is that of the relation to prohibitions and the transgression of rules.[56] Again we find the importance of the rule—which, along with the norm and system, will be emphasized in *The Order of Things*[57]—at the heart of human sexuality. But in a particular way, since the rule is inseparable from conduct without referring to a norm or a nature beneath it (which gives it its meaning) and refers to the empty form of the limit and its transgression. Such is the second sidestep Foucault makes: far from seeking the human meaning of sexuality in a philosophy of love, an ethic of intersubjective relations, or a dialectic of man-woman or parent-child relations, Foucault identifies what characterizes human sexuality in the naked confrontation of the rule and prohibitions, and their necessary transgression, in the empty game of the limit and its profanation. The reference to Georges Bataille and Claude Levi-Strauss, as much as to Jacques Lacan, is transparent here. This analysis refers, in addition, to the problem of limits and transgression, which then constitutes, as we have seen, the correlate of Foucauldian archaeology. From this point of view, far from being a "fall into triviality" or "loss of meaning," contemporary eroticism speaks volumes about what sexuality is for us as a cultural form. It reveals that it constitutes a limit-experience that, with others, captures the drama unfolding in Western thought since the end of the eighteenth century.

Sade and his doubles

This drama is regularly embodied in the multiple forms of contemporaneity of the Sade event highlighted by Foucault. We have seen that playing on the contemporaneity of Sade and a set of founding events of modernity was a typical move at the time.[58] Foucault tends to multiply them. In the lectures, Sade is contemporary with the Civil Code—in the sense that he embodies the deinstitutionalization of sexuality, expelled from marriage as a nature external to society; contemporary with the predicament of institutions of confinement confronted with a wild sexuality that does not enter into the binary division (criminal or sick) that breaks up the unitary figure of unreason; contemporary, finally, with the formation, alongside a transgressive language of sexuality, of a scientific language taking sexuality and its perversions as objects. What Sade always serves to illustrate is the other side of the division by which a positivity is founded. Reflecting in his *Notebooks* on the conjoined emergence of the human sciences at the end of the eighteenth century, Foucault notes that these sciences are "surface phenomena" of which it is necessary to reconstruct the "concrete conditions of possibility" (that is to say, the institutional transformations: asylums, hospitals, etc.), but above all to identify the "complex structures," what he then calls positivities that are the "unthought of knowledge," at work in these transformations (the "insertion of death between sickness and health," the "disappearance of the binary structure of reason and unreason," and above all, the wider positivity, the "anthropological structure"). It is not difficult to give names to these positivities: Bichat, Pinel, and Kant are no doubt the most appropriate. And all of them have Sade as their other side. As Foucault notes:

> This positivity constituting anthropology had both a constitutive and repressive role. . . . Maybe all these positivities formed at the end of the eighteenth century were limits denied, limits thought of as nature, finitudes reflected as properties. Which means that to do the history of the positivities is at the same time to do the critical history of limits, therefore bringing them back to life, confronting them with transgression (madness; death in the twentieth century). In general terms, the meaning of the Kant-Sade couple is there.[59]

It is certainly not the only couple that finds its meaning here, even if it is the most encompassing. Sade serves, in fact, as a cover name for the set of what is ultimately expelled, in those gestures that both constitute and repress. This is the case in *The Birth of the Clinic*, where Foucault stresses the contemporaneity of Sade and Bichat,[60] and even more in a manuscript text of 1962:

> Sade and Bichat, strange and twin contemporaries, put death and sexuality in the body of Western man; these two experiences so unnatural, so transgressive, so charged with a power of absolute challenge and on the basis of which contemporary culture has founded the dream of a knowledge that will make it possible to display *Homo natura*.[61]

Whereas Bichat introduces death into the order of a discursive knowledge, Sade places it at the heart of a transgressive language. There is the same contemporaneity of Sade and Chateaubriand, the "two exemplary figures" of the emergence of literature at the end of the eighteenth century. The former represents "transgressive speech," putting transgression at the heart of language and thus constituting the "very paradigm of literature." The latter strives to go beyond death by placing himself in the eternity of the book.[62] Contemporaneity, above all, with Kant, inasmuch as both place the game of the limit—of finitude—and its transgression at the heart of modern experience: "the experience of finitude and being, of the limit and transgression."[63] It is indeed this same movement of constitution of a discursive knowledge and of a tragic and transgressive experience of sexuality that appears in these lectures through the figure of Sade and his multiple contemporaneity.

*

1. Didier Eribon, *Michel Foucault*, 3rd ed. (Paris: Flammarion, 2011 [1989]), 130; on the context of Foucault's teaching at Clermont-Ferrand, see more generally 128–30.

2. Maurice Merleau-Ponty, *Child Psychology and Pedagogy: The Sorbonne Lectures 1949–1952*, trans. Talia Welsh (Evanston, IL: Northwestern University Press, 2010).

3. Abel Jeannière, *Anthropologie sexuelle* (Paris: Aubier-Montaigne, 1964). It is ironic that the second edition of this book appeared in 1969, at the same time as the Vincennes course.

4. "Philosophy and Psychology," *EW*, 2, 259.

5. On June 4, 1963, Foucault drew up that particularly premonitory "list of cultural formations": "death, decadence, confession, sexuality, madness" (BNF, Box 91, *Notebook* no. 3, yellow, 1963).

6. "Philosophy and Psychology," 258–59.

7. "Truth and Juridical Forms," *EW*, 3, 11.

8. See above, Clermont-Ferrand course, lecture 5, pp. 121–123, and note 46, pp. 137–138.

9. Clermont-Ferrand course, lecture 4, p. 83 et seq., and note 1, p. 96.

10. Clermont-Ferrand course, lecture 5, p. 107 et seq., and notes 1 and 9, pp. 128–129 and 130.

11. Clermont-Ferrand course, lecture 5, p. 107 et seq., and notes 1 and 9, pp. 128–129 and 130.

12. Foucault's *Notebooks*, kept at the Bibliothèque nationale de France, attest to his intense work, from 1963, on the notion of archaeology itself as well as on the more precise project of an archaeology of the human sciences, focused at that time especially on problems of language (innumerable notes on the question of signs) and death (in connection with *The Birth of the Clinic*). See in particular *Notebooks* 3, 4, and 5.

13. See in particular *Notebook* 3, yellow, starting from May 28, 1963.

14. "Le silence des fous," in *Le Grande Étrangère: À propos de littérature*, éd. Philippe Artières (Paris: EHESS, 2013 [1963]), 36. See above, Clermont-Ferrand course, lecture 1, note 3, p. 18, for the importance of the notions of cultural form (or formation) and culture in Foucault's analyses at this time.

15. *Notebook* 3, May 28 and 30, 1963. See also *Notebook* 3, July 14, 1963, Foucault's analyses devoted to "what is an analysis of cultural formations in relation to the science of archai."

16. *Notebook* 3, July 13, 1963.

17. *Notebook* 5, September 10, 1963. He adds, December 22, 1963: "Only the archaeology of positivities can be a discipline in which there is at once history and conditions of knowledge."

18. *Notebook* 5, August 27, 1963.

19. "Preface to the 1961 edition," *History of Madness*, trans. Jonathan Murphy and Jean Khalfa (London: Routledge, 2006), xxix. Furthermore, Foucault includes the "history of sexual prohibitions" and the "mobile and obstinate forms of repression" "in our culture itself," as one of the histories of divisions to be written "to reveal, as a limit of our Occidental world and the origin of its morality, the tragic division of the happy world of desire" (xxx).

20. *Notebook* 5, August 17, 1963.

21. To go back to the limits and to the founding divisions is to recover the constitutive affirmations of a positivity, as Foucault makes clear in the *Notebook* 3, July 16, 1963: it is not a matter of undertaking "a critique of the positivity of forms of knowledge by questioning, bit by bit, . . . each positive content; but [of] restoring to the positivity as such its power of affirmation. What is positive in the positivity is not the transcendental act that gives meaning, it is, in the things themselves . . . the affirmation. The affirmation

that denies nothing, but decides and divides. This (moving back from the positivity to its kernel of affirmations) is" archaeology. This conception of archaeology as aiming to grasp, in a culture, a practice, or a field of knowledge, the series of affirmations that make it possible and organize it, the play of postulates that constitute it, will endure in Foucault well beyond the valorization of the theme of the limit: it runs through his reflections up to the beginning of the 1970s.

22. *Notebook* 3, July 16, 1963.

23. See above, Clermont-Ferrand course, lecture 1, pp. 3–5.

24. "A Preface to Transgression," *EW*, 2, 70.

25. *History of Madness.*

26. *The Birth of the Clinic,* trans. A. M. Sheridan Smith (London: Tavistock, 1973, xiv, 198.

27. He contributes to the editorial board of the review *Critique* and to the special issue devoted to Bataille in 1963.

28. "A Preface to Transgression," 69–70.

29. "A Preface to Transgression," 71.

30. "A Preface to Transgression," 70.

31. *Notebook* 5, July 16, 1963. As he clarifies, "the constitution of anthropological thought" in the nineteenth century is a form of reaction to "the very thing that makes it impossible and derisory"; "it required all of Nietzsche's courage to rediscover, behind the dialectical event of the death of God, the nondialectical sudden appearance of the higher man (*surhomme*) (which makes all anthropology impossible)." This principle, according to which anthropological thought is a reactive philosophy faced with radical limit experiences (death, sexuality, history), is found again in the Vincennes course. See above, Vincennes course, lecture 6, pp. 235–236, and below pp. 339–342.

32. "The Thought of the Outside" [1966], trans. Brian Massumi, *EW*, 2.

33. *Notebook* 3, August 28, 1963.

34. See above, Clermont-Ferrand course, lecture 2, p. 31.

35. For the context of this, see Annick Ohayon, *Psychologie et Psychanalyse en France: L'impossible rencontre, 1919–1969* (Paris: La Découverte, 2006 [1999]), 387–91.

36. See the two talks from Althusser's seminar devoted to Lacan and psychoanalysis at the École normale supérieure in 1963–1964, in Louis

Althusser, *Psychoanalysis and the Human Sciences*, trans. Steven Rendall (New York: Columbia University Press, 2016).

37. *A Preface to Transgression*, 79.

38. *Notebook* 3, May 28, 1963. This passage clearly formulates the principle of a necessary diagnosis of actuality as a condition of identification of a given cultural formation, which we know Foucault will put at the heart of his philosophical activity from 1966.

39. For an effective summary of the context concerning sexual questions from 1950 to the beginning of the 1960s, see Michelle Zancarini-Fournel and Christian Delacroix, *La France du temps present: 1945–2005*, ed. d'H. Rousso (Paris: Belin, 2010), 149–54.

40. Foucault was all the more attentive to this as one of his assistants, Francine Pariente, was involved in the Movement for Family Planning at Clermont-Ferrand (I am grateful to Daniel Defert for this information).

41. See above, Clermont-Ferrand course, lecture 3, note 2, p. 000; and Sylvie Chaperon, "Kinsey en France," *Le Mouvement social* 1, no. 198 (2002): 91–110.

42. With a still fairly limited distribution, however. On this first period of the reception of Marcuse in France, see Manuel Quinon, *La Réception en France d'Herbert Marcuse (1956–1968): Phénoménologie d'une conscience critique*, paper of DEA, ed. J.-M. Berthelot, University of Paris IV–Sorbonee, 2003.

43. See Jean-Marc Levent, "Un acte de censure 'scélérat': Sade en procès (1954–1958)," *Lignes* 3 (2000): 109–26.

44. Paul Ricoeur, "La merveille, l'errance, l'énigme," *Esprit*, no. 289 (1960): 1665 (emphasis in the original).

45. Jeannière, *Anthropologie sexuelle*, 199.

46. In his *Phenomenology of Perception*, trans. Donald A. Landes (London: Routledge, 2012), 137 *et seq.*, Merleau-Ponty devotes a chapter to "The Body in its Sexual Being" and to the way in which our perceived world is charged with erotic significations.

47. Max Scheler develops both a reflection on the difference of the sexes within his anthropology (see, for example, "Zur Idee des Meschen") and a theory of specifically human "sexual love" that goes beyond the instinct of preservation and elevates it by integrating it into a system of choice and values. On this, see Gabriel Mahéo, "La question de l'amour

chez Max Scheler: par-delà l'activité et la passivité?," *Bulletin d'analyse phénoménologique* 8, no. 1 (2012): 478–98.

48. Foucault took detailed notes (BNF, Box 42b-C1) on Hans Kunz's text, "Idee, Wesen und Wirklichkeit des Menschen." In the framework of a phenomenological reflection on what constitutes the essence of man, Kunz wondered about the status to be given to sexuality and the difference of the sexes.

49. Nothing illustrates these different strategies better than the analyses of Simone de Beauvoir, *The Second Sex*, and F. J. J. Buytendijk, *La Femme*. On Buytendijk's analysis, see Marina Paola Bachetti-Robino, "F. J. J. Buytendtdjik on Woman: A Phenomenological Critique," in *Feminist Phenomenology*, ed. Linda Fisher and Lester Embree (Dordrecht, Germany: Kluwere, 2000), 83–101.

50. To adopt Thierry Hoquet's expression in "L'alternaturalisme: Comment travailler le naturalisme de l'intérieur?," *Esprit*, no. 411 (2015): 41–51, which summarizes this strategy well.

51. See below, pp. 339–342. From this point of view, one can only be struck by the continuity between lectures 2 and 3 of the Clermont-Ferrand course, lecture 6 of the Vincennes course, the expositions on "Sexuality, Reproduction, Individuality," and texts like the review of François Jacob or the letter to P. Guyotat ("Croître et multiplier" [1970] and "Il y aura scandale mais . . ." [1970]).

52. *The Order of Things* (London: Tavistock, 1970), 342.

53. Georges Bataille, "Qu'est-ce que le sexe?," in *Oeuvres complètes*, vol. 11, *Articles 1, 1944–1949*, ed. F. Marmande and S. Monod (Paris: Gallimard, 1988).

54. "Problèmes de l'anthropologie" (BNF, Box 46). The same remark goes for Freud, as Foucault notes in 1957 when he emphasizes that the Freudian scandal is that sexuality, "nature, as negation of the truth of man, becomes for and through psychology, the very ground of its positivity" ("La recherche scientifique et la psychologie" [1957], 182).

55. See above, Clermont-Ferrand course, lecture 3, p. 67.

56. See above, Clermont-Ferrand course, lecture 3, p. 68 et seq.

57. *The Order of Things*, 355–66.

58. See above, Clermont-Ferrand course, lecture 1, note 31, pp. 23–24.

59. *Notebook 5*, December 22, 1963.

60. *The Birth of the Clinic*, 195.

61. Daniel Defert, "Chronology," in *A Companion to Foucault*, ed. Christopher Falzon, Timothy O'Leary, and Jana Sawicki (Oxford: Blackwell, 2013).

62. "Literature and Language," lecture at Saint-Louis University, Brussels, 1964, in *Language, Madness, and Desire*, ed. Philippe Artières, Jean-François Bert, Mathieu Potte-Bonneville, and Judith Revel, trans. Robert Bononno (Minneapolis: University of Minnesota Press, 2015), 52–56.

63. "A Preface to Transgression," 77.

THE DISCOURSE OF SEXUALITY

Lectures at the University of Vincennes

(1969)

The second course we publish was given in the first semester of 1969 at the Experimental University, Vincennes, where Michel Foucault was a lecturer in the philosophy department. In 1966, shortly after the appearance of *The Order of Things*, Foucault leaves Clermont-Ferrand to give some philosophy courses at the University of Tunis. He remains there until June 1968, in particular devoting a course to the place of the idea of man in modern Western culture, giving various lectures, and writing a still unpublished manuscript titled *Le Discours philosophique*.[1] These productions all indicate his refocusing in these years on discourse viewed as a set of rule-governed practices. "The Discourse of Sexuality" bears the strong mark of this shift that we see in *The Archaeology of Knowledge* (1969).

Foucault returns to France in June 1968, when the May events are almost coming to an end. He then declines a chair in psychology at the University of Nanterre to join the "coopting nucleus" of lecturers responsible for recruiting the teams of teachers for the Experimental Center of Vincennes, created, following May 1968, between August and October 1968, which opens its doors in January 1969.[2] Among the team recruited by Foucault are many of Althusser's old students or people close to him, particularly from the Epistemological Circle of the École normale supérieure

and the group *Cahiers pour l'analyse*, with whom Foucault had
an exchange in 1967, in an interview "On the Archaeology of
the Sciences," published in 1968, and who had moved toward
Maoist positions.[3] We will see the importance of this context:
"The Discourse of Sexuality" in fact forms part of the debates on
the relations between ideology and science and between theory
and practice that are common in these movements after 1968.
In addition to the course on sexuality, in 1968–1969 Foucault
gives a course on the "end of metaphysics." The following year he
devotes one course to Nietzsche and another to the "epistemology of the sciences of life," which extends the epistemological
reflections developed in lectures 3 and 6 of this course.[4] Teaching
takes place in a fairly chaotic atmosphere: packed lecture theaters
(almost six hundred persons attend his course in 1969), interventions and animated discussion during the teaching, demonstra-
tions, blockades, and confrontations with the police. Foucault
will leave Vincennes at the end of 1970 after his election to the
Collège de France. The project he proposes at the time of his
election attests to the importance of his teaching at Vincennes in
the maturing of his thought: to undertake a history of heredity in
the nineteenth century that takes this knowledge as a set of rule-
governed practices, an "anonymous social knowledge (*savoir*)
that does not take individual or conscious knowledge (*connaissance*) as a model or foundation"; to consider "the elaboration of
this knowledge into a scientific discourse" and analyze how it is
inserted into a given social formation.[5] But above all, thanks to
his *Notebooks*, we know that having barely finished his course on
"The Discourse of Sexuality," Foucault, doubtless in connection
with the course he is preparing on Nietzsche, engages in a dense
reflection on "will-knowledge (*vouloir-savoir*)" and on "how, in a
culture, knowledge becomes power? Where this power is located,
who exercises it and in what form? . . . Conversely, how power

defines the place of the formation, delimitation, and transmission of knowledge."[6] A path that certainly opens up promising perspectives and, from 1971, will become the heart of his teaching at the Collège de France.[7]

From archai *to the archive: discourse as rule-governed practice*

From 1966, following the publication of *The Order of Things*, and in the framework of the debates raging around structuralism and humanism, Foucault's archaeological approach undergoes a series of inflections. From "science of the *archai*," archaeology becomes "description of the archive," that is to say it is concerned with the "set of discourses actually pronounced" in a culture. Above all, it views discourse "in its manifest existence, as a practice that obeys certain rules—of formation, existence, coexistence—and systems of functioning."[8] These inflections lead him to pay less attention to the original gestures of division and exclusion than to discourses viewed in their specific density and existence, as singular, rule-governed practices whose historical conditions of formation, regime of enunciation, mode of functioning, and delimitations need to be studied. Foucault's reading in Tunis of Anglo-Saxon analytical philosophy plays a role in this refocusing. The reorientation is perceptible in the unpublished manuscript *Le Discours philosophique*, in which Foucault looks at the different "modes of being" of everyday, literary, scientific, and philosophical discourses.[9] In the same period it is found in his course at Tunis and in various texts collected in *Dits et Écrits*,[10] and it will be clearly asserted in *The Archaeology of Knowledge* and then in "The Order of Discourse." The Vincennes course is an integral part of this reorientation. Foucault here distinguishes discourse (the "things actually said")[11] from language, a distinction regularly made at this time to separate his analysis of discourses as rule-governed practices, in their concrete functioning, from the structuralist approach of "the formal possibilities afforded by a system such as language."[12] Thus he is concerned with the historical conditions through which sexuality became the referential of a set of heterogeneous discourses at the end of the eighteenth century and strongly emphasizes that an archaeology of sexuality must give an account of the polymorphism of these discourses on sexuality, of their specificities (regarding the rules of formation of their objects, for example), and of their relations, without confusing them with each other. These principles are found again in 1976 in the first, introductory volume of *The History of Sexuality*.[13]

This refocusing on discursive practices has two consequences. On the one hand, from the epistemological point of view, it involves situating scientific statements and concepts, obstacles and errors, in the wider framework of the discursive practices within which they operate. This is the whole thrust of the sixth lecture of the course: viewing natural history as a collective discursive practice that conforms to certain postulates and rules; studying the transformations that affect this practice in the eighteenth-nineteenth centuries and make possible the formation of specific knowledge about the sexuality of plants and heredity. The consequences of this shift from an epistemological level (which carries out the internal analysis of a scientific discourse, its theories, and its concepts) to an archaeological level (which places the scientific discourse itself in a form of "positive unconscious of knowledge": a set of rules and postulates that order the practice of discourses, define the mode of formation of their objects, the place of their subjects, and the conditions of demarcation of the science itself in the field of knowledge [*savoir*])[14] are the object of important expositions on

Foucault's part in this period, in connection with the publication of *The Archaeology of Knowledge*. Thus, strictly contemporaneous with lecture 6, on May 30–31, 1969, Foucault takes part in the "Journées Cuvier" of the Institute for the History of Science and in an exchange with François Dagognet.[15] Dagognet emphasizes Georges Cuvier's secondary and erroneous positions for the development of biology (as opposed to the central role Foucault attributes to him in *The Order of Things*), assigning him at best the role of epistemological obstacle. To the problem of truth and error in the scientific field, Foucault, on the other hand, opposes the more fundamental question of the epistemological transformations affecting the rules of the constitution of objects, concepts, and theories in natural history viewed as practice.[16] Some typical themes of Bachelardian-Canguilhemian epistemology (and of their Althusserian appropriation), such as scientific error, epistemological error, or scientific problem, are thus rethought in terms of their place within a field of knowledge viewed as a system of rule-governed practices. Scientific error is placed within the set of collective rules that organize a field of knowledge: it takes on meaning and value within these practices and may, paradoxically, have a positive role in the transformation of the rules organizing these practices, giving rise to a different configuration of knowledge (*savoir*). The epistemological obstacle is viewed in the same way, as opposed to a reading that reduces it to a purely negative role in the process of producing knowledge (*connaissances*). With regard to scientific problems, Foucault characterizes them as "categories of will-knowledge (*vouloir-savoir*)"; that is, unlike the concepts and theories internal to a science, they constitute unconscious collective postulates that determine and orient discursive practices. They entail our viewing science not as a language, Foucault points out, but as a *will*, identifying "singular, isolated, individualizable forms of will-knowledge."[17] But it is a matter of a will "that has nothing to do with intention or the project,"[18] the subject of which remains undetermined: "the problem of the subject arises: it is not at the origin, the source of this will that the subject is found: man, class, society."[19]

Foucault clarifies these questions in the course he gives the following year at Vincennes on the "epistemology of the life sciences." From the archives, it appears in fact that Foucault undertook considerable reading around the history of forms of knowledge about sexuality and heredity (biological but also juridical), which he saw as a new way of posing epistemological questions on the history of forms of knowledge viewed in their practical dimension (discursive practices but also inserted in a set of social practices). This project finds expression in his initial program for the Collège de France. But there are few published traces of it apart from the review of François Jacob's *The Logic of Living Systems*,[20] which the *Notebooks* show Foucault prepared with care. The interest of the Vincennes course is that it offers a general view of this project. The *Notebooks* make it possible to gauge its importance. We can see a whole historical epistemology taking shape that, through cases in genetics or biochemistry, examines how a science emerges from a "problematic field" followed by the formation of a "body of discipline (*corps de discipline*)"; how, in interaction with other sciences and with the help of technical and conceptual tools, this science constructs distinct "object planes (*plans d'objets*)," Foucault attempting to establish a differentiated typology of these epistemic objects. As he points out:

> the object, no less than the subject, must be dissociated. There is, in fact, a whole layer of objectivity. It should not be defined by a set of laws or limits but by a whole layer of rule-governed

practices. These strata are no doubt not the same for different regions of knowledge, nor at different times. Objectivity is
not a general norm that is valid in the same way for all forms
of knowledge.[21]

Behind this project is the attempt to fundamentally examine
the historical co-formation of the subject and object of knowledge on the basis of the forms of will-knowledge that determine
their constitution: in other words, to get free from the theory
of knowledge (*connaissance*) to the advantage of an historical
analysis of the forms of will-knowledge (*vouloir-savoir*).

But this refocusing on discursive practices has another effect
that is very perceptible in this course.[22] If discourse is a set of
rule-governed practices, then:

> [it appears] in a describable relationship with a set of other
> practices. Instead of having to deal with an economic, social
> or political history that encompasses a history of thought . . .,
> instead of having to deal with a history of ideas attributed . . .
> to extrinsic conditions, one would be dealing with a history
> of discursive practices in the specific relationships that link
> them to other practices.[23]

This is the advantage of taking a distance from the formalist ambition of an analysis of structures. Studying discourse historically, as a set of rule-governed practices, embeds discourse in
the more general field of rule-governed practices: matrimonial
practices and juridico-moral regulations, economic practices and
sociopolitical strategies. From this point of view, sexuality offers
a fertile terrain. In the first place because, at precisely this time, a
number of studies are being developed (including those of Pierre
Bourdieu used in the lectures) that analyze the matrimonial

strategies and rules organizing alliances and reproduction, not from the perspective of a strict structuralist formalism but in the concrete thickness of practices and their history.[24] And then also because, from the beginning of the 1960s and in light of this history, a research program is created within the *Annales* school focusing on "material life and biological behavior" that studies the history of alimentary and reproductive behavior with the tools of historical demography and statistics, linking them with economic movements. In 1969, this work results in a special issue on the theme of "Biological History and Society."[25] Foucault was familiar with this work, regularly referring to the *Annales* school from the middle of the 1960s: he makes wide use of it in the course.[26]

The conjunction of these two lines of analysis gives a particular coloring to this course: that of an historical materialism that is made clearer here by Foucault's adoption of a perspective based on the class struggle (a position found again later, but more muted, in the first courses at the Collège de France). If sexuality becomes the referential of a set of discourses at the end of the eighteenth century—if, above all, it is split between a natural sexuality taken up, ambiguously, via the Civil Code, in the institution of marriage, and a deviant, abnormal sexuality—this is partly the result of an economic and social process regarding the productive forces (contradiction between economic growth and demographic obstacles) and class relations. On the one hand, Foucault endeavors to show how the "discursive explosion" around sexuality at the end of the eighteenth century is bound up with the development of productive forces and relations of production—which at this time he explicitly links to a "class demand," whereas subsequently, in the first volume of the *History of Sexuality*, the same phenomenon will be related to a broader and anonymous development: "the entry of life . . . into the order of knowledge and power, into the sphere of political techniques."[27] On the other hand, he particularly undertakes to consider the relationships between these economic and social processes and the emergence of a knowledge of sexuality without treating them in the binary mode of ideology and science, or, as he says in an interview, in the mode of reflection and "pure and simple expression," as if concepts and discourse were only the mechanical expression of underlying "pre-discursive economic and social formations."[28] For Foucault, the economic and social processes presuppose a certain "primary ideological coding" that defines the place of a knowledge of sexuality (here, a knowledge of sexuality as *nature*), and this knowledge could eventually become a science. Above all, this ideological coding determines the functioning of this knowledge, which is both normative—procreative sexuality becomes the norm—and repressive—expelling a set of conducts from normal sexuality.

The question of ideology

By posing, with regard to sexuality, both the epistemological problem of the relations between science and knowledge (*savoir*) and the problem of the articulation between forms of knowledge of sexuality and the material processes affecting a social formation, Foucault takes up a position in a controversy that needs to be explained because it is omnipresent, in sometimes allusive form, in particular in lecture 3 of the course. The debate bears as much on the nature of ideology and the relation between ideology and science as, more broadly, on the relations between theory and practice.

The problems raised by an analysis that opposes ideology and science run through Foucault's works up to the middle of the 1970s.[29] The criticisms of this opposition developed in this course, and of recourse to the Bachelardian model of the epistemological break, echo the objections raised by Foucault regarding Althusser and some of his students. The latter made the model of the epistemological break a paradigm of the process of production of scientific knowledge, the general principle being that scientific knowledge emerges only through theoretical work that presupposes the radical critique of a set of ideological elements that play the role of ideological obstacles preventing the establishment of an adequate knowledge of reality.[30] Foucault's criticisms should be read as extending the interview he gave to the Epistemological Circle of the École normale supérieure in October 1967 (published in the *CPA* in summer 1968),[31] as well as of some pages devoted to the relations between science, knowledge (*savoir*), and ideology in *The Archaeology of Knowledge*.[32] It is important not to reduce this debate to a head-on opposition because the Althusserian reading of the relations between ideology and science is rich and complex: it shares some dimensions with the reading proposed here by Foucault. A systematic comparison of the third lecture of the course with the article by Michel Pêcheux (alias Thomas Herbert), "Remarques pour une théorie générale des ideologies,"[33] would show this. Moreover, *The Archaeology of Knowledge* declares that the problem of the relations of science to ideology should be posed at the level of "its existence as a discursive practice and of its functioning among other practices":

> To tackle the ideological functioning of a science . . . is to
> tackle not the formal contradictions of its propositions, but
> the system of formation of its objects, its types of enuncia-
> tion, its concepts, its theoretical choices. It is to treat it as one
> practice among others.[34]

This is the task to which Foucault devotes himself in the course, trying to develop a sort of theory of ideology as a rule-governed system of class practices without reference to a subject: a collective system of operations and codings that articulate heterogeneous elements and get them to function together—institutions, ideological themes, juridical principles, and also sciences.[35] Actually it should be noted that, for Foucault, the criticism of traditional models of ideology (ideology as false consciousness or ideology opposed to science) does not mean abandonment of the notion, which is put to work here at several levels: "ideological operations" or "primary ideological coding"—these will be found again in *Lectures on the Will to Know* and *Penal Theories and Institutions*.[36]

We shall try nonetheless to outline some points of tension between the position adopted by Althusser and that proposed by Foucault. First of all, we should stress the points where they are close to each other. The most essential is that Althusser, like Foucault, tries to free himself from what, since Marx, has been a standard conception of ideology as false consciousness produced by erroneous representations that must be corrected.[37] Like Foucault (and following Antonio Gramsci on this point), Althusser stresses that ideologies are not reducible to representations but have a practical dimension (what he calls precisely "practical ideologies"). Here "notions-representations-images" are shaped "into behaviour-conduct-attitudes-gestures. The ensemble functions as practical norms that govern the attitude and the concrete positions men adopt towards the real objects and real problems of their social and individual existence, and towards their history".[38] As such, they form part of the ensemble of social practices. This reflection results in the thesis of the materiality of ideology and of its functioning in institutions (the ideological state apparatuses) in the article

Althusser published on this subject in 1970.[39] But above all, Althusser endeavors to develop a general theory of ideology consistent with his attempt to rethink the subject in the light, in particular, of Lacanian psychoanalysis. It is this articulation of the theory of ideology and a theory of the subject that is expressed in the 1970 article through "the interpellation of individuals as subjects" by ideology. Foucault is alluding to this when he points out that the primary ideological coding is not "entirely an unconscious."[40] In fact, after his 1964 article on "Freud and Lacan," Althusser regularly brings together the symbolic order of the unconscious and the structure of ideology.[41] This parallel is also omnipresent in the works of students close to Althusser and Lacan who collaborate on the *CPA* and who make the connection between ideology and belief in a sovereign conscious subject a decisive element.[42] In Althusser, this position is coupled with the double thesis that ideology in general, like the unconscious in general, has no history and that the "category of the subject," "constitutive of all ideology," "cannot be assigned to a determinate sequence of the history of philosophy."[43] It goes without saying that if Foucault can only endorse the approach that consists in getting rid of the conscious (or sovereign) subject and of representation as the site of ideology, he does not share the assertion—historically and philosophically somewhat abstract and problematic—that establishes ideology (in general) as unconscious and connects it, formally and ahistorically, to the category of the subject. Here again we find a situation comparable to the sidestepping vis-à-vis structuralism: Foucault readily takes up the critique of the subject of *praxis* and history, but without being satisfied with the formalist analysis of the elementary structures of language or kinship; he seeks to place himself in between, in an historical practice without subject (and, in the case of ideology, a *class* practice).[44]

The same goes, even more profoundly, for the knowledge relation defined as an adequate relation between subject and object. This is where we should locate Foucault's hostility to the opposition between science and ideology and to the general (not local) recourse to the model of the epistemological break and epistemological obstacle for thinking about the relation between science and ideology. Foucault criticizes this type of approach for "assuming that the human subject, the subject of knowledge, and forms of knowledge themselves, are somehow given beforehand and definitively."[45] One is thereby prevented from questioning the knowledge relation itself at the root, the fact that "knowledge (*connaissance*) asserts its rights over every activity of knowing (*savoir*)."[46] This reticence begins very early in Foucault, since its trace is found in his reading of *Reading Capital* in 1965–1966. He is already wondering about the autonomy of theoretical work and the definition of ideology in Althusser, emphasizing that "if, in this domain [of the theoretical], something is produced that qualifies as a knowledge (*connaissance*), how can this product qualify as truth?"; and he points out that Althusser's attempt aims "to ensure that knowledge of history avoids being compromised in its object (historicism)" and to save "the subject of knowledge (*connaissance*) [at least the act of knowing]" from history, as Edmund Husserl tried save the "object of knowledge (*connaissance*)."[47] This double difficulty is found again subsequently: the problem of the criterion of truth as division of ideology and science is at the heart of Foucault's criticism of the Althusserian definition of the ideological proposition as "a proposition that, while it is a symptom of a reality other than that of which it speaks, is a false proposition to the extent that it concerns the object of which it speaks".[48] As Foucault shows, using his research on plant sexuality, which serves as his point of departure in this epistemological reflection, every scientific proposition is also "symptom of a reality other than that to which it refers," precisely because it is governed by a certain discursive practice, a certain state of techniques, philosophical themes, and institutions; science has an "ideological" functioning as practice inserted in other practices.[49] So that what constitutes the division of the ideological and the scientific in Althusser is ultimately nothing other than the separation of truth and error, which can only be decided by science (and within a given science). In other words—this point will be developed in greater detail in *Lectures on the Will to Know* and *Penal Theories and Institutions*—the division between ideology and science presupposes accepting the truth value of science and not examining the mechanisms of demarcation, of distinction, as well as the insertion of science in the more general field of knowledge and in social practices.[50]

We come here to a deeper criticism, which is directed, in a general way, at all the analyses trapped in what Foucault calls a "theory of knowledge (*connaissance*)" to which he opposes his conception of knowledge (*savoir*).[a] The criticism is directed as much at Kantian idealism as at a materialist theory of knowledge (*connaissance*) or phenomenology. "Within a philosophy of knowledge (*connaissance*), it is not possible to avoid the relation to the object. A dialectic of subject and object will also always remain within the element of ideality." The analysis of knowledge (*savoir*) as an anonymous set of rule-governed discursive practices situated within other social practices, on the other hand, makes it possible "to cross to the other side of the subject-object relation . . . enables one to escape the horizon of ideality." Better, it frees one from the subordination of knowledge-*savoir* to the "legislation of knowledge-*connaissance*." The problem that

---

a See Translator's Note.

will guide Foucault in his Collège de France lectures appears
here in 1969:

> the Greeks did not invent rationality . . . but knowledge-
> *connaissance*: that subject-object relationship of possession
> and identification. . . . The struggle against the Sophists is
> the struggle to replace the practice of knowledge-*savoir* and
> its immediate powers with the rights of knowledge-*connais-*
> *sance*. . . . But this should not mean that all knowledge-*savoir*
> must strive for knowledge-*connaissance* as its final vocation and
> that knowledge-*connaissance* is the truth of knowledge-*savoir*.[51]

The division of ideology and science is condemned to accept
this principle and, ultimately, to reproduce it and conceal the
historical conditions and forms of its appearance.

We touch here on a second marked criticism by Foucault in
the course, which focuses on the importance accorded to the
practical dimension of ideology. By defining ideology above
all as a "matter of social practices" and emphasizing that the
"ideological struggle cannot be just a theoretical struggle at
the level of true ideas,"[52] Foucault adopts a position against
the "theoreticism" and "scientism" Althusser was accused of by
some people. In the 1960s, in fact, Althusser made theoretical
work and the need to give an adequate theory to Marxist practice the fundamental orientation of his reflections. However, it
should be noted that, from Althusser's point of view, theory is
a practice like others—that is, a process of the transformation
of a given raw material into a determinate product (knowledge-
connaissance), a transformation effectuated by a determinate
human work, employing determinate means of production. But
it is a relatively autonomous practice and essential for orienting
political action.[53] (Scientific) theoretical practice thus consists in

"transforming an ideological product into theoretical knowledge by means of a determinate conceptual work."[54] This theoretical work presupposes a constant exercise of demarcation between the ideological and the scientific, which is performed by philosophy. This primacy and autonomy of theoretical work will found the involvement of a group of students around Althusser in the 1960s, who take part in his seminars, which seek precisely to provide an adequate theory of Marxism (the principal result of which will be *Reading Capital*), or who take part in the work of theoretical formation of various publics, either through the theoretical formation schools of the Union of Young Communists (Marxist-Leninist)—UJC(ml)—or through philosophy courses for scientists, or again who publish in the *Cahiers marxistes-léninistes* (*CML*, founded in 1964) or the *CPA* (founded in 1966).[55] Beginning in 1966–1967, the autonomy and primacy of the theoretical begin to be challenged by some members of the UJC(ml), under the banner of the Maoist model. After 1968, this criticism will grow significantly, marking the development of Althusser's old associates at the University of Vincennes who are now hostile to his "theoreticism" in the name of the primacy of practice and political struggle in contact with the popular masses. This trend is noticeable in the various members of Gauche prolétarienne and in Jacques Rancière, for example, who in 1969 writes an article that is remarkable for its critical insights,[56] before making his assessment of this breakup in his famous *La Leçon d'Althusser* (1974). If the critical distance Foucault takes from the theoretical is fairly allusive in this course, it is considerably strengthened in the following years, both in his first courses at the Collège de France and in his political commitments (with the creation of the Groupe d'information sur les prisons—GIP—and his relative closeness to the Maoists).

Sexuality, humanism, and utopia

Continuing his reflection aimed at rescuing knowledge-*savoir* from the primacy of the subject and knowledge-*connaissance*, in his *Notebooks* Foucault adds that there are "two paths of access to this knowledge-*savoir*": on the one hand, the study of discourse as a set of rules independent of a founding subject, and on the other, "the experience of a thought that crosses to the outside, crosses its own limits":

> On the one hand, knowledge-*savoir*, and on the other, non–knowledge-*savoir*? But it is rather a matter of non–knowledge-*connaissance*: Bataille's transgression is not breaching the rules and advancing in a sovereign fashion into freed land; it is shaking off the constraints on the basis of which the subject is constituted.[57]

This remark reminds us that at this time Foucault's epistemological reflection continues to be linked to an analysis of limit-experiences and the concern to call into question the sovereignty of the subject. In the Clermont-Ferrand course, we saw that, from this point of view, sexuality played a central role and that it was possible to mobilize (biological or psychoanalytic) forms of knowledge of sexuality against the sovereignty of the subject, and against a narrow conception of sexuality. The same strategy appears at the end of lecture 6 of the Vincennes course and in the text "Sexuality, Reproduction, Individuality," published here as an appendix to the course, as well as in several articles from the same time: biological knowledge about sexuality is presented as providing a truth that mortally wounds the narcissism of the human subject and calls into question the primacy accorded to the sovereign individual-subject. Nowhere better than in the letter he writes in September 1970 to Guyotat in support of *Eden, Eden, Eden* does Foucault summarize what he claims to draw from this knowledge about sexuality:

> you reach . . . what has long been known about sexuality, but what is carefully kept at arm's length in order to protect the primacy of the subject, the unity of the individual, and the abstraction of "sex": that something like "sex" is not at all at the limit of the body, or a means of communication from one individual to another, or even the individual's fundamental or primal desire, but the very fabric of its processes largely preexists it; and the individual is only its precarious, provisional, quickly erased extension . . . a pale form that shoots forth for some moments from a great, stubborn, repetitive strain. Individuals, speedily retracted pseudopods of sexuality.[58]

It might be thought that this is just an isolated literary phrase in Foucault's reflection: reading the courses of Clermont-Ferrand and Vincennes and various texts of the time show a constant interest in a biological sexuality that "is no longer subjugated" and shatters all anthropological self-evidence. The Vincennes course focuses precisely on the conditions of appearance of this biological knowledge (*savoir*) of sexuality and how it involves the reversal of the subordination of reproduction to the individual, to its growth and death. He shows how the biology of the beginning of the nineteenth century reveals three transgressive experiences in the field of knowledge (*savoir*): death, sexuality, and historical discontinuity. These experiences radically challenge the sovereignty of the subject, introducing an opening, a gap to which the humanist philosophy of the nineteenth-twentieth centuries sought to react, "in the strong sense of the term, that is in its Nietzschean sense."[59]

On the one hand, then, knowledge (*savoir*), which "is not meant to comfort: it disappoints, disturbs, cuts, wounds":[60] fundamental cruelty of knowledge (*savoir*), which systematically destroys human consolations and fictions. The biological knowledge of sexuality offers a perfect example of this, which Foucault will deepen through his review of François Jacob's book, which allows him to review all the ways in which "genetics wounds us":

> It is often said that, since Copernicus, man suffers from knowing that he is no longer at the center of the world. . . . Biological disappointment . . . is of a different order: it teaches us that the discontinuous not only delimits us but passes through us: it teaches us that we are governed by the dice.[61]

Or again, as he puts it in his *Notebooks*, "a line governs us," that of DNA viewed as a program preceding all language and meaning. The genetic program is primary with respect to any form of language and "the emergence in the animal series of conditioning, signals, signs, and finally language coincides [. . . with] an expansion (*détente*) of the program"; a purely accidental expansion, the "two great reasons" for which are "the appearance of sexuality and death."[62] Biological knowledge of sexuality, therefore, is enrolled in this more general battle against "man" or "human nature," which Foucault has far from abandoned at this time. This is because, in fact, at the same time, faced with the radically transgressive notions of biology, a reactive humanist philosophy is developed which endeavors to recover death in a philosophy of meaning, sexuality in an intersubjective ethics of communication with the other, and the discontinuity of history in "the unity of meaning" and the "continuity of consciousness."

Now, if there is one principle that Foucault maintains up to the middle of the 1970s, it is indeed that of radically challenging these references to the human subject, to human nature, and to a philosophy of meaning and consciousness. As he notes in a series of interviews in 1966, "our task is to free ourselves definitively from humanism," from "all those wordy undertakings" that advocate "saving man," exalt the "human person," and promise happiness when "the human being . . . will become authentic and true" and rediscover his previously alienated or denied nature.[63] For Foucault, this humanism is both a cheap consolation, a way of "resolving in terms of morality, values, and reconciliation problems one could not resolve at all," and a "negative, harmful" theme "since it permitted the most diverse and dangerous political operations."[64] It has no critical value, and its political meaning cannot be trusted. This will still be Foucault's position in 1968 (with a denunciation of those philosophical-political systems that in the nineteenth century promised to make man happy by restoring his nature to him) and again in 1971, in the debate with Noam Chomsky on human nature, for example.[65] We also note that Foucault had all the more reason to return to this in the Vincennes course, as in March 1969 he was invited to London to give lectures on "humanism and anti-humanism" (which will be transformed into an open debate with English students on their practical commitments).[66]

But there is another reason that makes the question of humanism very topical in 1969, in particular in connection with the sexual question: this is the pervasive theme of sexual liberation, the struggle against the supposed alienation and repression of sexual desire, and the exaltation of utopias after May 1968. Devoting his last lecture at Vincennes in 1969 to sexual utopias and heterotopias is certainly not neutral. Of course, we know that Foucault began thinking about utopias and heterotopias in 1966,[67] and we have also seen that the Clermont-Ferrand and Tunis courses already showed an interest in nineteenth-century utopias claiming to reconcile the sexual nature of men and women with social structures. But since 1964, the "problematic consciousness of sexuality" that Foucault had diagnosed has intensified to the point of crystallizing into a fundamental political issue.[68] This crystallization gives rise to a set of utopian projects inspired by a particular humanist and dialectical reading of Marx and Freud—the "Freudo-Marxism" of Wilhelm Reich and especially Herbert Marcuse[69]—or by nineteenth-century sexual utopian literature (in particular Charles Fourier, whose work enjoyed a successful revival at this time).[70] These projects seek to liberate human sexuality from the alienation or surplus-repression linked to social organizations based on performance and consumption, and to found new societies adapted to man's sexual nature and desire. After May 1968, these utopias acquire a particular political meaning. As Jacques Julliard notes in an article published in *Esprit* in February 1969:

> The May movement put an end to two myths: that of the death of ideology and that of the depoliticization of the French. In the past there was no lack of sensible people claiming that projects without concrete means for their realization, projects not situated in the field of the immediately possible, were not "credible" and were politically prehistoric. Utopia has been rehabilitated—not utopia as dream or means of escape, but utopia as regulative idea of a real politics.[71]

Against the possibilism that "confines the possible within present-day reality," the "effective role of utopia is to expand the field of the possible, not by attacking economic or political structures, but by attacking *mental* structures."[72] In this framework, the question of the struggle against the repression of sexual instincts linked to capitalism, the appeal to an anthropology and a psychology that envisage vital, especially sexual, needs completely freed from repression and that found a new society on the liberation of these needs, becomes fundamental. Marcuse in particular stresses the political force of utopias in the collective work *La Fin de l'utopie*, published in 1968. As he notes, in a phrase directly echoed by Foucault in the course, "we must face the possibility that the path to socialism may proceed from science to utopia and not from utopia to science."[73] The break with the present system—the transition from an unfree society to a free society—must be radical and presupposes a clear qualitative leap, which is that of utopia. In other words, Marcuse claims, on the one hand, to build on science to found a new vision of man that really corresponds to his free nature and, on the other, to revalorize utopian thought that can conceive of a radical qualitative leap within society in order to think of the radically new social forms finally adapted to that nature.

Foucault's response is cruel and paves the way for his criticisms in 1976 of the Freudo-Marxist use of the "repressive hypothesis" with reference to the history of sexuality.[74] Far from "passing through utopian themes in order to constitute a theory of sexuality," Reich and Marcuse are perfect illustrations of a reactive thought in relation to the profoundly transgressive experience of sexuality introduced by forms of knowledge of sexuality (both biology and Freudian analysis, Marcuse's divergence from which Foucault shows).[75] They remain prisoners of a classical anthropology at the same time as they reactivate the division between "normal" and deviant forms of sexuality (the latter attributed to social institutions), constitutive of the sexual question since the end of the eighteenth century. They do not propose a radically different anthropology, nor free themselves from the dialectic between natural sexuality and social institutions that was forged in the nineteenth century. Foucault, then, sees in Marcuse no more than a new version of the nineteenth-century utopians, briefly analyzed in the Clermont-Ferrand course and then in the Tunis course, who inherit divisions peculiar to modern Western culture (private versus public life, individual freedom versus social determinism, natural sexuality versus institutions-contract) and dream of their reconciliation: "the dream of a form of society or culture in which private life and public life, freedom and determinism, would properly fit together."[76] As he recalls in an interview with Giulio Preti, "Marcuse is trying to use the old themes inherited from the nineteenth century to salvage the subject, understood in the traditional sense."[77] In other words, he is entirely on the side of what Foucault describes as "integrative utopias," both because he dreams of the perfect match between social relations and a finally freed sexual nature, and because he desperately maintains the primacy of the human subject. Against these integrative utopias, Foucault invokes—one more (and last) time[78]—the transgressive power of Sade, who illustrates at the same time the dissociation of the subject, the total asymmetry of relations in sexuality, and a form of asocial as well as denaturalized sexuality: what he describes in the course as "transgressive utopias."

Beyond archaeology, groundwork for a history of sexuality

The Clermont-Ferrand and Vincennes courses attest to two important moments in what is already a "history of sexuality." Foucault had been pursuing the project from the beginning of the 1960s, alongside an archaeology of the human sciences; it takes on a clearer form at the end of the 1960s. In his Tunis course, Foucault notes the fact that, in Western culture, everything has become a possible object of knowledge (*savoir*) and explicit discourse and takes the case of sexuality as an example of this indefinite extension of the domain of knowledge. However, he remains a prisoner of the myth of a Victorian watershed in the nineteenth century, when sexuality became "what one does not talk about," as opposed to the "talkative sexuality" before the nineteenth century or the fact that, since Freud in particular, it has once again become an "explicit signification."[79] From this point of view, the Vincennes course marks a turning point and announces what will become the heart of the history of sexuality that Foucault takes up again in 1974–1976. Henceforth, the challenge is to give an account of how "a steady proliferation of discourses concerned with sex" occurred, "specific discourses, different from one another both by their form and by their object: a discursive ferment that gathered momentum from the eighteenth century onward";[80] against a reading that thinks about the history of sexuality in terms of the censorship of discourse, this involves analyzing the intense "putting sex into discourse (*'mise en discours' du sexe*)" of the seventeenth-eighteenth centuries. And it also involves emphasizing that there is not "*a discourse on sex*" but "a multiplicity of discourses produced by a whole series of mechanisms operating in different institutions."[81] This is the thrust of the five groups of studies Foucault announces at the start of the Vincennes course, of the importance he gives to the fact that archaeology must pay attention to the heterogeneity, the multiple points of actualization and forms of verbalization, of knowledge concerning sexuality. At this double level—interest in how sex is put into discourse and the proliferation of these discourses since the eighteenth century; study of the polymorphous character of these discourses and of the centers of their formation—a continuous line can be traced between the Vincennes course and the first volume of *The History of Sexuality*.

However, the Vincennes course is barely finished when the project seems to be left in abeyance. Apart from a few references, Foucault does not really return to the question of sexuality until, in 1974–1975, *Abnormal*, the unpublished manuscript of *La Croisade des enfants*, and the lectures in São Paul in the autumn of 1975 on the history of modern forms of knowledge concerning sexuality (in which he invokes the model of confession as opposed to repression), as well as various contemporary interviews.[82] This reemergence of the question of sexuality results in the project of a history of sexuality, the first volume of which appeared in 1976. Clearly, in the meantime, the analytical framework was profoundly transformed. If the study of the "discursive fact" of sexuality[83] and its constitution as domain of knowledge remains at the heart of the project, Foucault adds two levels that were relatively absent from the Vincennes course. First, the level of "polymorphous techniques of power": the plurality of institutions and apparatuses (*dispositifs*) that produce and involve discourses on sexuality. The Vincennes course raises the very broad question of the relation between ideology and knowledge and social and economic process, rather than the polymorphous forms of power-knowledge that besiege sexuality. The course was part of the approach Foucault embarked on at this time to clarify the "links between prediscursive economic and social formations and what appears within discursive formations," while dispensing with a Marxist model that considers these relations in terms of expression or reflection.[84] This attempt to analyze the relations between the discursive and extra-discursive will lead him to view power relations autonomously and to situate the formation of forms of knowledge within diverse strategies of power, from either the dynastic or genealogical perspective.[85] More precisely, the study of the *dispositifs* of disciplinary power—developed in *The Punitive Society* and *Psychiatric Power*—leads to his interest in power relations that directly invest the body and, among other corporal phenomena, sexual activities.[86] For example, the crusade against infantile masturbation and the emergence of the problem of infantile sexuality are caught up in the "strategic development . . . of a struggle" around the sexual body.[87]

This strategic analysis of the links between techniques of (in particular, disciplinary) power and the formation of knowledge concerning sexuality leads Foucault to clarify his position on another problem, which constitutes the third level evoked in the first volume of *The History of Sexuality*. This is bringing out "the 'will to know' that serves as both . . . support and . . . instrument" of the "discursive productions" and "effects of power" on sexuality.[88] In other words, what is at issue is questioning the will—understood as the dominant strategic function—that orientates the *dispositif* of sexuality. As we have seen, the Vincennes course has barely finished when this problematic of the will to know, this concern with identifying historical forms of "will-knowledge," becomes the heart of the Foucauldian project. In the present case, on the sexual question, this means Foucault once again crossing swords with a Freudo-Marxist reading that, following Reich, Marcuse, and Van Ussel,[89] interprets the history of sexuality in terms of the repression-alienation of desire and its necessary liberation; an interpretation according to which "Freud and psychoanalysis, by speaking of sexuality [. . . perform] unreservedly a work of liberation."[90] We saw that in the Vincennes course Foucault is skeptical vis-à-vis the general theme of sexual alienation and liberation. On the one hand, his analyses of disciplinary power and the control of sexual bodies might give the impression of adherence to an approach that sees the repression of desires as necessary to the development of capitalism. Thus, he is led to clarify his position. This involves demonstrating, against the repressive hypothesis that reduces discourses and powers regarding sexuality to a great imperative of censorship and repression, how the prohibitions, censorships, and controls should themselves be grasped in a more general economy of discourses and techniques of power marked by an intense desire to know sexuality, to "obtain the confession (*aveu*) of sexuality"[91]—techniques of confession and examination being at the heart of the forms of will-knowledge concerning sexuality—and, since the eighteenth century at least, by a concern to govern life positively and maximize the forces of the body. Problem of sexuality, confession, and truth; problem of biopolitical techniques aiming to govern vital processes: these are the lines of flight on which Foucault's works on sexuality will subsequently be oriented.

*

I would like to offer my sincere thanks to all the members of the editorial committee of Michel Foucault's courses, as well as to Mariana Broglia de Moura and Alexandre Tanase, for their suggestions and careful readings.

C.-O. D.

*

1. The course and the manuscript on philosophical discourse are preserved in the BNF archives, Box 58.

2. On the genesis and history of this center, see, for example, Charles Soulié, ed., *Un mythe à detruire? Origens et destins du Centre universitaire expérimental de Vincennes*, preface by S. Charle (Saint-Denis, France: Presses universitaires de Vincennes, 2012). For details on Foucault's courses at Vincennes, see Didier Eribon, *Michel Foucault*, 3rd ed. (Paris: Flammarion, 2011 [1989]), 201–11.

3. For a history of the *Cahiers pour l'analyse (CPA)*, particularly useful for understanding the immediate context of Foucault's course, we refer to the remarkable work of Peter Hallward and Knox Peden, *Concept and Form*,

vol. 2 (London: Verso Books, 2012), and to the website, where one can find the whole of the *CPA* and various interviews with witnesses: http://cahiers .kingston.ac.uk (accessed August 8, 2018).

4. The BNF archives do not appear to have the set of manuscript notes for the 1970 course, but we can get an idea of it both through Foucault's *Notebooks* 8 and 9, which contain a number of very rich reflections on the epistemology of the sciences of life as well as, on October 14, a sort of course plan (see above, Vincennes course, lecture 6, note 1, pp. 237–238); and from documents preserved in Box 70, in particular dossier 5, which seems to bring together two sets of material from this course, one on "error in the realm of the sciences" and the other on scientific problems.

5. "Candidacy Presentation: Collège de France, 1969," *EW*, 1, 8.

6. *Notebook* 4, red, July 15 and 20, 1969, immediately following the draft of lecture 7, "The Discourse of Sexuality" (June 7, 1969).

7. See *Lectures on the Will to Know*, ed. Daniel Defert, trans. Graham Burchell (Basingstoke, UK: Palgrave Macmillan, 2013), which flow directly from these reflections initiated in the summer of 1969. The presentation of his first three courses at the Collège de France, given in Rio de Janeiro in May 1973 ("Truth and Juridical Forms," *EW*, 3), is still marked by this questioning. From this point of view, the Vincennes period plays a pivotal role.

8. "Michel Foucault explique son dernier livre" [1969], *DÉ*, I, 800; "The Archaeology of Knowledge [1969]," trans. John Johnston, in *Foucault Live (Interviews, 1966–1984)*, ed. Sylvère Lotringer (New York: Semiotext(e), 1989), 45–46.

9. BNF, Box 58.

10. See in particular "On the Ways of Writing History" [1967], *EW*, 1, 289–90, and especially "Réponse à une question" [1968], *DÉ*, I, 58, and "On the Archaeology of the Sciences," *EW*, 1.

11. See above, Vincennes course, lecture 1, p. 146, and note 3, p. 151–152.

12. "On the Ways of Writing History," 289.

13. See below, pp. 345–346.

14. To use the distinction Foucault establishes in his "Foreword to the English Edition" of *The Order of Things* (London: Tavistock, 1970), xi–xiv.

15. See "(Discussion)," *DÉ*, I, and "Cuvier's Situation in the History of Biology" followed by "Discussion," trans Lynne Huffer, *Foucault Studies* 22 (January 2017).

16. See "(Discussion)," 897. "In the substance of scientific discourse, what is a matter of true or false scientific assertion must be distinguished from what concerns epistemological transformation. That some epistemological transformations take place through . . . a set of false scientific propositions seems to me to be a historically possible and necessary observation."

17. *Notebook 8*, October 24, 1969. We can see that the problem of the "*archai*" has not disappeared but has been shifted to two levels: toward the problem of the fundamental postulates orienting a field of knowledge and defining particular forms of will-knowledge—what Foucault will describe, in *Penal Theories and Institutions*, trans. Graham Burchell, ed. Bernard Harcourt with Elisabetta Basso, Claude-Olivier Doron, and Daniel Defert (London: Palgrave Macmillan, 2019), as "epistemological matrices," themselves articulated on "juridical-political matrices" (the measure, the test, the inquiry, the examination) (214–15); and, in addition, toward the constitutive division to which Foucault will return in *Lectures on the Will to Know*: the division of truth and error that subordinates knowledge-*savoir* to the problem of knowledge-*connaissance*. These two shifts make it possible to pass to the level of power-knowledge, or what Foucault will call the dynastic of knowledge, and more profoundly, to the problem of the historical constitution of the subject of truth.

18. BNF, Box 70, dossier 5, "Problems."

19. *Notebook 4*, July 15, 1969.

20. François Jacob, *The Logic of Living Systems: A History of Heredity*, trans. Betty E. Spillman (London: Allen Lane, 1974 [1970]).

21. *Notebook 9*, October 27, 1969.

22. See above, Vincennes course, lectures 2–4.

23. "Politics and the Study of Discourse" [1968], trans. Colin Gordon, in *The Foucault Effect: Studies in Governmentality*, ed. Graham Burchell, Colin Gordon, and Peter Miller (Hemel Hempstead, UK: Harvester Wheatsheaf, 1991), 64.

24. See above, Vincennes course, lecture 4, pp. 000–000, and note 21, p. 000.

25. *Annales ESC* 24, no. 6 (1969).

26. See above, Vincennes course, lecture 2, note 2, p. 000.

27. *The History of Sexuality: Volume 1. An Introduction*, trans. R. Hurley (New York: Pantheon, 1978), 141–42. However, here Foucault does not

abandon the class reading when he analyzes the history of "the "apparatus (*dispositif*) of sexuality." He refines it and above all opposes it to a repressive reading in which the popular classes were the first targets of this apparatus. For Foucault, "sexuality is originally, historically bourgeois, and . . ., in its successive shifts and transpositions, it induces specific class effects" (127, and more generally, 119–31).

28. "Entretien avec Michel Foucault" [1971], *DÉ*, I, no. 85, 1029. This interview, which actually took place in 1970, clearly echoes Foucault's reflections in lecture 3 of the Vincennes course (see above, p. 000 et seq.). For Foucault, the question is how to characterize the relationships between discursive formations and social and economic formations—"how to adjust in the most exact way the analysis of discursive practices and extra-discursive practices"—the connection having to be, according to him, sought at the level of the "rules defining the possible objects, the subject positions in relation to the objects": what, in the course, he characterizes as "the hold of ideology on the field of knowledge."

29. It is at the heart of *Lectures on the Will to Know*; clearly expressed in *Penal Theories and Institutions*, 197–227, and in "Truth and Juridical Forms," 1–16.

30. See, for example, Althusser's two contributions to Louis Althusser, Étienne Balibar, Jacques Rancière, Pierre Macherey, and Roger Establet, *Reading Capital: The Complete Edition*, trans. Ben Brewster and David Fernbach (London: Verso, 2015), parts one and four, or all of Althusser's philosophy course for scientists, given by Althusser and his students in 1967–1968, in Louis Althusser, *Philosophy and the Spontaneous Philosophy of the Scientists*, trans. Ben Brewster and others (London: Verso 1990).

31. "On the Archaeology of the Sciences." The article first appeared in issue 9 of the *CPA* (Summer 1968), significantly with the title "Genealogy of the Sciences."

32. *The Archaeology of Knowledge*, trans. A. M. Sheridan Smith (London: Tavistock, 1972), 184–86.

33. Michel Pêcheux, "Remarques pour une théorie générale des idéologies," *CPA*, no. 9 (1968).

34. *The Archaeology of Knowledge*, 186.

35. We should note the extent to which, prior to this, the analysis was bound up with the definition of cultural formations seen precisely as

heterogeneous systems articulating institutions, discourses, concepts, and silent practices—with the difference here that it is a matter of analyzing the operations of class coding that make these heterogeneous elements function, rather than the divisions that constitute them. Subsequently, the analysis comes closer to the definition Foucault will give of the "*dispositif*" as a "resolutely heterogeneous ensemble comprising discourses, institutions [etc.]: the said and the not-said," of which "the nature of the bond" that unites them needs to be analyzed. However, if a *dispositif* has a "dominant strategic function," this cannot be reduced to a thought-out, homogeneous, and coherent strategy with a class as its authorizing subject (see "Le jeu de Michel Foucault" [1977], *DÉ*, II, no. 206, 306–8).

36. See, for example, *Lectures on the Will to Know*, 151–65, on the "effect of incomprehension" of the *nomos* as caesura that masks the relations of the political and the economic; or *Penal Theories and Institutions* (198), for the notion of ideological operation. The analysis of these games of coding, disguise, and masking are at the heart of what, from 1971, Foucault will call the "dynastic."

37. See above, Vincennes course, lecture 3, p. 179–180, and note 9, pp. 185–186.

38. Louis Althusser, "Philosophy and the Spontaneous Philosophy of the Scientists (1967)," trans. Warren Montag, in *Philosophy and the Spontaneous Philosophy of the Scientists*, ed. Gregory Elliot, trans. Ben Brewster and others (London: Verso, 1990), 83.

39. Louis Althusser, "Ideology and Ideological State Apparatuses (Notes Towards an Investigation)," trans. Ben Brewster, in *Lenin and Philosophy and Other Essays* (New York: Monthly Review Press, 1971).

40. See above, Vincennes course, lecture 3, p. 179.

41. Louis Althusser, "Freud and Lacan," trans. Ben Brewster, in *Lenin and Philosophy and Other Essays*.

42. See, for example, Jacques-Alain Miller, "Suture (Elements of the Logic of the Signifier)," in *Concept and Form: Volume 1. Selections from the Cahiers Pour L'Analyse*, by Peter Hallward and Knox Peden (London: Verso, 2012); François Regnault, *Cours de philosophie pour scientifiques*, no. 11 (February 28, 1968): 9–10.

43. Pascale Gillot, *Althusser et la Psychanalyse* (Paris: PUF, 2009), 120–21.

44. See above, Vincennes course, lecture 3, p. 000.

45. "Truth and Juridical Forms," 2.

46. According to the expression taken from a very important passage Foucault devotes to this question in his *Notebook* 9, November 1, 1969. It is clear that Foucault devotes his first course at the Collège de France to the Greeks (*Lectures on the Will to Know*) in order to reconsider this problem at the root.

47. *Notebook* 6, "Notes sur *Lire Le Capital*."

48. Louis Althusser, *Philosophy and the Spontaneous Philosophy of the Scientists and Other Essays* (Lecture I, November 20, 1967, Thesis 9), 79.

49. *Notebook* 8, October 2, 1969. See above, Vincennes course, lecture 6, p. 226, and note 22, pp. 243–244.

50. See *Lectures on the Will to Know*, 1–30, and *Penal Theories and Institutions*, 204–27. As Foucault notes in *Notebook* 8: "We won't get anywhere so long as we superimpose the science/ideology problem and the truth/error problem. We need to get rid of Spinoza." This will be the meaning of the first lectures at the Collège de France: "Spinoza is the condition of Kant. One can avoid Kant only after having freed oneself from Spinoza. . . . Naivety of those who thought they could escape the idealism of philosophical discourse by resorting to Spinoza" (*Lectures on the Will to Know*, 28).

51. *Notebook* 9, November 1, 1969.

52. Above, Vincennes course, lecture 3, p. 180.

53. See Althusser, *Reading Capital*, 58–62.

54. Michel Pêcheux, "Réflexions sur la situation théorique des sciences sociales et, spécialement, de la psychologie sociale," *CPA* 2 (1966): 142.

55. The *CML* clearly attest to this initial primacy of the theoretical and of science, the first number, "Sciences et idéologies," opening with an article by J.-A. Miller, "Fonction de formation théorique," which makes theoretical work an essential condition of the political struggle, aiming to "convert perception, reform discourse" against illusion and ideology. The quotation from Lenin adopted as leitmotif—"Marxist theory is all-powerful because it is true"—is another example of this. On the *CML* and their development, see Frédéric Chateigner, "From Althusser to Mao: Les *Cahiers Marxistes-Léninistes*," trans. Patrick King, *Décalages* 1, no. 4 (2014): 1–15, https://scholar.oxy.edu/handle/20.500.12711/12928.

56. Jacques Rancière, "On the Theory of Ideology—Althusser's Politics," in *Ideology*, ed. Terry Eagleton (London: Routledge, 2013). The echoes between this article and the reflections developed by Foucault at this time should be emphasized.

57. *Notebook* 9, November 1, 1969.

58. "Il y aura scandale, mais . . ." [1970], 943.

59. "Cuvier's Situation in the History of Biology," 236.

60. "Croître et multiplier" [1970], *DÉ*, I, no. 81, 967.

61. "Croître et multiplier," 968.

62. *Notebook* 9, October 29, 1969.

63. "Entretien avec Madeleine Chapsal" [1966], *DÉ*, I, no. 37, 544–46. See also "L'homme est-il mort?" [1966], *DÉ*, I, no. 39, 568–72, and "Qui êtes-vous, professeur Foucault?" [1967], *DÉ*, I, no. 50, 629–48, especially pp. 643–647.

64. "Entretien avec Madeleine Chapsal," 544, and "Qui êtes-vous, professeur Foucault?," 644.

65. "Interview avec Michel Foucault" [1968], *DÉ*, I, no. 54, 679–90, and "Human Nature: Justice vs. Power: A Debate Between Noam Chomsky and Michel Foucault," in *The Chomsky-Foucault Debate: On Human Nature*, by Noam Chomsky and Michel Foucault (New York: New Press, 2006).

66. Daniel Defert, "Chronology," in *A Companion to Foucault*, ed. Christopher Falzon, Timothy O'Leary, and Jana Sawicki (Oxford: Blackwell, 2013).

67. See above, lecture 7, note 1, p. 270.

68. We should also stress that in this period Foucault frequently notes the political importance of sexuality; see, for example, "Qui êtes-vous, professeur Foucault?," 644.

69. On the reception of Marcuse in France up to 1968, see M. Quinon, *La Réception en France d'Herbert Marcuse*, ed. J.-M. Berthelot, University of Paris IV–Sorbonee, 2003.

70. See above, lecture 7, note 21, pp. 275–276.

71. Jacques Julliard, "Questions sur la politique," *Esprit* 378, no. 2 (1969): 337.

72. Julliard, "Questions sur la politique," emphasis in the original.

73. Herbert Marcuse, "The End of Utopia," in *Five Lectures: Psychoanalysis, Politics, and Utopia*, trans. Jeremy J. Shapiro and Shierry M. Weber (London: Allen Lane, 1970), 63. See above, Vincennes course, lecture 7, p. 263, and note 35, p. 280–281.

74. See below, pp. 345–349.

75. See above, Vincennes course, lecture 7, pp. 268–269.

76. Tunis course, folio 175.

77. "An Historian of Culture" [1972], trans. Jared Becker and James Cascaito, in *Foucault Live (Interviews 1966–1984)*, 84 [translation slightly modified —G.B.].

78. We should also note that the dialogue with Giulio Preti already attests to Foucault's distancing himself from Sade ("An Historian of Culture," 81–83), which subsequently becomes much more pronounced.

79. Tunis course, folios 195–99.

80. *The History of Sexuality: Volume 1. An Introduction*, 18.

81. *The History of Sexuality: Volume 1. An Introduction*, 33, italics in the original. Foucault thus distinguishes the Christian pastorate, transgressive literature, the political-economic discourse on population, the crusade against infantile masturbation, etc.

82. In particular, "Body/Power" [1975], trans. Colin Gordon, in *Power/ Knowledge: Selected Interviews and Other Writings 1972–1977*, ed. Colin Gordon (Brighton, UK: Harvester, 1980); "Asiles. Sexualité. Prisons" [1975], *DÉ*, I, no. 160, 1639–50; and "Sade, Sergeant of Sex" [1975], *EW*, 2.

83. *The History of Sexuality: Volume 1. An Introduction*, 11. Foucault adds two other levels here: the techniques of power and the "will" or "strategic intention" that sustains them (8–12).

84. See "Entretien avec Michel Foucault" [1971], 1029–31. Foucault announces here that he is going to study the connections between the discursive and the extra-discursive on the basis of criminology and penal practices—that is, the area of work opened by *Penal Theories and Institutions* and closed with *Discipline and Punish*.

85. On the dynastic, see *Penal Theories and Institutions*, note 16, 51–53.

86. See *The Punitive Society*, trans. Graham Burchell, ed. Bernard E. Harcourt (London: Palgrave Macmillan, 2015), 170–224 (on the worker's body, desire, and debauchery as targets of power); "Truth and Juridical Forms," 81–82; *Psychiatric Power*, ed. Jacques Lagrange, trans. Graham Burchell (London: Palgrave Macmillan, 2008), 297–333 (on the "sexual body" of hysterics).

87. See "Body/Power," 56–57.

88. *The History of Sexuality: Volume 1. An Introduction*, 11–12.

89. After 1969, the theme of sexual repression and liberation only gets stronger. We recall among other things the French translation of Jos Van Ussel's book, *Histoire de la répression sexuelle*, trans. C. Chevalot (Paris:

Robert Lafont, 1972), and the publication of the second issue of *Partisans* *(Sexualité et Répression II)*, no. 66–67 (July 1967).

90. "Michel Foucault: Les réponses du philosophe" [1975], *DÉ*, I, no. 163, 1681. Whether psychoanalysis is necessarily a work of liberation or has a function of normalization and offers "many examples of the extension of relations of power" is discussed in "La vérité et les formes juridiques" [1974], *DÉ*, I, no. 139, 1491–1514. [The roundtable discussion following Foucault's São Paulo lectures, to which this refers, is omitted from the English translation, "Truth and Juridical Forms" —G.B.]

91. "Michel Foucault: Les réponses du philosophe," 1682.

DETAILED CONTENTS

Sexuality
Lectures at the University of Clermont-Ferrand (1964)

Lecture 1. Introduction

Questioning the relationships between sexuality and our culture. The opposition between the biology of sexuality and culture is typical of Western civilization. Definition of what is to be understood by "Western culture". A. Synchronically: monogamy and patriarchy. Imbalance of men-women relationships and compensatory mechanisms. Entails a structure and problems which are found whatever the political regime. B. Diachronically: transformations marking our contemporary culture since the nineteenth century. 1. Evolution of compensatory mechanisms for imbalances between men and women:

tendency towards a progressive equalization and logic of men-women complementarity. 2. Transformation of the relations between law and sexuality: sexuality ceases to play a central role in marriage as a legal institution. 3. Appearance of a "problematic consciousness of sexuality": sexuality as anthropological theme; sexuality as privileged site of subjective values; sexuality as space of challenge and radical transgression: tragic experience of modern man. Sade, on the threshold of modernity.

Lecture 2. The scientific knowledge of sexuality

Modern European specificity of a science of sexuality. Its central place in the human sciences: privileged site of intrication of the psychological and the physiological as well as of the individual and the social. Sexuality occupies the place of the contract and imagination in the classical age, and of religion and sensation in the nineteenth century. This explains why psychoanalysis is the key to the human sciences. Three domains of the human sciences of sexuality: a. psychophysiology; b. psychopathology; c. psychosociology. Sexuality is a negative object here, apprehended in its deviations, except in psychophysiology. 1. The psychophysiology of sexuality: A. Brief history of the biology of sexuality. B. The different modes of sexuality: sexuality is one mode of reproduction among others; the distinction of the sexes is itself complex, variable, and exists at multiple levels in nature. C. The determinants of sexuality: 1. Hormones: history of their discovery and characterization. 2. Genetic sex: theories of the genetic determination of the sexes. The notion of "sex" refers to two distinct notions (genetic and genital) and brings into play a complex interplay of determinations and differentiations.

Lecture 3. Sexual behavior

Psychology knows sexual behavior only through deviations. Poverty of knowledge about "normal" sexuality and confusion around "sexual

is given first of all only through negativities. A. History of knowledge about sexual perversions: until the eighteenth century, included in the world of unreason and confinement; at the end of the eighteenth century: confinement becomes differentiated: patient or criminal. What status is to be given to sexual quasi-madness or quasi-delinquency? The case of Sade at Charenton. Sexual transgression has a floating status. It is related to illness without being confused with it. The example of Krafft-Ebing: classification and origin of perversions. B. At the end of the nineteenth century: intersexual states and Marañón's theory. C. The Freudian analysis of perversions. Its importance and originality. 1. A formal analysis of perversions according the object and aim: perversion is not the symptom of something else; it is, like sexuality, a process with an object and an aim; 2. An analysis of their content; 3. An analysis of the relations between perversion, illness, and normal life: elements of perversion are always present in normal life; relations of signification and evasion between neuroses and perversions. Congenital perversion as common base of neuroses, perversions, and normal sexuality: infantile sexuality.

Lecture 5. Infantile sexuality

I. Long disregard and resistance to the direct study of infantile sexuality. 1. Cultural reasons: history of childhood (eighteenth–nineteenth century). Postulate of the child's purity in the nineteenth century. War and the economic crisis at the beginning of the twentieth century raise the question of pedagogy in a new way. 2. Psychological reasons: amnesia and neurotic relationships to childhood: childhood is always viewed indirectly by adults. 3. Psychoanalytic technique: difficulties raised by the psychoanalysis of children. II. Analysis of infantile sexuality. A. Elements: a nongenital sexuality, focusing on one's own body, linked to different erogenous zones, and made up from

Appendix to Lecture 3

Lecture 4. Legal forms of marriage up to the Civil Code

Sexuality and marriage exist within a set of regularities. Weak matrimonial rules in Indo-European societies. But, from the Middle Ages, tendency to make marriage more complicated (notably legal constraints); this is coupled with an ideological criticism of marriage and desire for sexual liberation. I. Christian marriage: late, it superimposes the marriage sacrament on Roman marriage; initially, easy marriage without social coercion. II. Increase in the social cost of marriage: Council of Trent: hardening of social controls and constraints; increasing weight of the family. Example of marriage in peasant smallholders (Bourdieu). III. Marriage in bourgeois society: 1. The Revolution: ideological themes and legal measures: the marriage contract and divorce. 2. The Civil Code: marriage is not assimilable to a contract; authorization of divorce is not the result of the contract but of human weakness. Marriage, natural and structuring element of society; sexuality as disturbing threat that has to be framed by marriage and socially excluded.

Lecture 5. Epistemologization of sexuality

Studying how sexuality was able to become the object of discursive practices. What relations with madness? 1. Some common characteristics: between the organic and the social; objects of different discourses; first person but excluded discourses; development of scientific practices aiming to free them from ideology. The recent theme of a kinship between madness and sexuality derives from these analogies. 2. But also some major differences: a. madness is always excluded; there is a division between tolerated and excluded sexuality; b. synchronic homogeneity of different discourses about madness; synchronic diversity of the rules of formation of discourses about sexuality; c. change of referents of discourses about madness in different periods; the referent of sexuality remains generally the same. Hence different approaches to their archaeology. Place of psychoanalysis in this framework: it claims to give a single referent to madness and to give a discursive homogeneity to sexuality. What must an archaeology of sexuality be?

Lecture 6. The biology of sexuality

Existence of a non-epistemologized knowledge of sexuality linked to multiple practices (human sexuality, agronomy, medicine, religion); verbalized in different forms (ad hoc justification, theories); impossible to oppose true practice and false ideology; the science of sexuality does not emerge as a rational take-up of these practices but has certain relations with them. Maintaining the autonomy of the science of sexuality while locating it within a given social formation. The sexuality of plants as guideline. I. Miscomprehension of the sexuality of plants up to the seventeenth century even though there are practices involving it, the sex of plants is accepted, etc. This miscomprehension is not linked to analogies-obstacles or to a lack of concepts: it is explained by the rules of the discursive practice of naturalists. II. Characteristics of this discursive practice: 1. continuity of the phenomena of individual growth and reproduction: no specificity of sexual function; 2. status granted to the individual: between individuals there are only resemblances and differences: no meta-individual biological reality dictating its law to individuals; 3. the limits between individuals are insurmountable: no meta-individual or individual-milieu continuum. Consequence: impossibility of thinking a specific sexual function. More broadly: a discourse is a rule-governed practice and its resistances are linked to the rules that organize it as practice (versus ideology as representation). III. Transformations: 1. dissociation of male/female characters and individuals; 2. fertilization is not a stimulation but a transfer of elements: importance of the milieu; 3. reversal of the relation between sexuality and individuals: sexuality is a meta-individual strain that determines the law governing individuals. Conclusion: death, sexuality, and history as constituents of the biological. Discontinuity and limit, fundamental concepts of biology, against the continuum of natural history. Humanist philosophy is a reaction to the epistemological structure of biology in order to give meaning to death, sexuality, and history.

Lecture 7. Sexual utopia

1. Distinguishing utopias and heterotopias. Sexual heterotopias: heterogeneity of sexual norms in different places in society. Primitive societies and ours: some institutions are alternators of sexuality. Sometimes linked to utopian themes: the witches' Sabbath as mixture of utopia and heterotopia. 2. Summary of introduction: relations between utopias and heterotopias. Homotopic and heterotopic utopias. Sexual utopias: importance of the sexual theme in utopias (Sade, Campanella); either integrative utopia: return to a normal sexuality prevented by society; or transgressive utopia: a radically de-normalized sexuality (Sade, The Story of O.*). Presence of these utopian elements in Marcuse and Reich. III. Comparative analysis of transgressive and integrative utopias: 1. desire-difference-subject: sovereignty of desire instituting an absolute difference (Sade,* The Story of O*) versus harmonious distribution of differences suppressing desire (Comte, Fourier, Rétif de La Bretonne); 2. law and disorder: asocial and unnatural, asymmetrical, and disordered law in the transgressive utopia* versus *restitution to sexuality of its natural law in which conduct sticks to the rule in the integrative utopia. IV. The problem of sexual revolution: Marcuse or the double utopia. Liberating normal sexuality alienated by society. Criticism of different postulates of Marcuse: how they diverge from Freudian analysis.*

INDEX OF NOTIONS

INDEX OF NAMES